THE ORIGINS OF THE UNITED ARAB EMIRATES

By the same author

Qatar: Past and Present (forthcoming)

THE ORIGINS OF THE UNITED ARAB EMIRATES

A Political and Social History of the Trucial States

Rosemarie Said Zahlan

ST. MARTIN'S PRESS NEW YORK

Library of Congress Cataloging in Publication Data

Zahlan, Rosemarie Said.
    The origins of the United Arab Emirates.

    Bibliography: p.
    Includes index.
    1. United Arab Emirates—History. I. Title.
DS247.T88Z34   953'.5   78-6964
ISBN 0-312-58882-8

To Tony

Contents

The Consequences of the Decline of a Ruler's
Authority 67

5 Saudi Arabia and Iran: Outside Pressures 72
The Back Door: Wahhabi Influence in 1925 81
The Sea Front: Iran in 1928 88

6 Establishment of the Air-Route: Test of
Imperial Policy 92

7 The Preliminary Oil Concessions: Triumphant
Enterprise 107
Petroleum Concessions Ltd 110
Implementation of 1922 Agreements: Ultimatum of
1937 117
Capitulation of Abu Dhabi 120

8 Territorial Claims: Saudi Arabia and Iran 125

9 Boundary Disputes: Chaos in Order 141

10 The Reform Movement of Dubai: The Beginnings of
Democracy 150

11 The Exercise of Power: British Representatives 162
K. B. 'Isa bin 'Abd al-Latif OBE, Residency Agent
1919–35 167
Lieutenant-Colonel Sir T. C. W. Fowle KCIE, CBE,
Political Resident 1932–9 173

12 The Trucial States in 1939: The Dawn of a New Age 180

13 Epilogue: The Emergence of the United Arab Emirates 190

Notes 199
Appendix 1: Genealogy of the Ruling Families of the
Trucial States 236
Appendix 2: British representatives 243
Bibliography 251
Index 271

List of Illustrations

Acknowledgements

Unpublished Crown Copyright material in the India Office Library and Records, and in the Public Record Office transcribed here appear by permission of the Controller of Her Majesty's Stationery Office. My article, 'The Preliminary Oil Concessions in Trucial Oman, 1922–1939', that appeared in *International Interactions*, vol. 3, no. 2, 1977, is based on Chapter 7 of this book.

While it would be impossible to thank everyone who helped me in the preparation of this study, I would like to single out a few persons to whom I am particularly grateful. The staff of the India Office Library and Records, especially Martin Moir and Penelope Tuson, have provided me with generous assistance in my efforts to locate and understand the wide variety of records available on the Gulf. I also wish to thank Lady Honor Fowle for providing me with an apt description of her life in Bushire when her late husband was Political Resident. Khaldun S. Husry, Joseph J. Malone and George Rentz have read and made useful comments on the manuscript. I owe much to my family, my mother and brother, Edward W. Said, in particular, for all their help. Above all, however, I wish to thank my husband, A. B. Zahlan, to whom this book is dedicated: his valuable insights, together with his patience and encouragement, greatly facilitated the completion of this book.

It goes without saying that I alone am responsible for all errors and shortcomings.

Introduction

The creation of the United Arab Emirates in December 1971 ended a century and a half of the existence of the Trucial States in special treaty relations with Britain. When they first signed the General Treaty of Peace in 1820, the tribal chiefs in the southern part of the Arabian Gulf could hardly have been described as rulers even in the loosest sense of the word, for their respective positions were governed by the vicissitudes of tribal loyalties, which caused an amorphous and fluctuating political structure. As time went by, and the same chiefs, and later their descendants, were drawn into further treaties with Britain, they began to acquire a certain amount of stability and authority as rulers: the responsibility of each new ruler for fulfilling his treaty obligations towards Britain made for continuity and a gradual stratification of certain political and social elements in the land he controlled, so adding a new dimension to his sovereignty. The tribal chiefs gradually evolved into rulers and the areas over which they exercised a certain amount of jurisdiction into shaykhdoms. Although both elements were upheld by commitments to Britain, it would be wrong to disregard the British role in the development of the tiny states, and it would be equally wrong to maintain that the only relevance of these states was in their relation to the power that dominated them for 151 years.

The treaty of 1820 was imposed on the chiefs by the British government of Bombay, which wanted to keep the Gulf route to India safe and open. Although the most important clause of the agreement was the cessation of plundering and piracy on land and sea, other terms, such as the commitment to desist from the slave trade, were to become central to the internal and external evolution of the states. The 1820 agreement protected British vessels from attack but it did not prevent warfare at sea between the tribes of the coast; so in 1835 the chiefs of Abu Dhabi, Dubai, Sharjah and Ajman signed a one-year truce in which they undertook to report any aggression to the British authorities rather than take it upon themselves to retaliate. The truce was renewed the next year and at various intervals until 1853, when the Perpetual Maritime Truce was signed and the chiefs undertook to call a complete halt to all hostilities at sea. Other treaties with Britain included the undertaking by the chiefs to stop the importation of slaves into their respective territories (never actually committing themselves to the total suppression of the slave trade), and the 1902 agreement whereby they promised to prohibit the importation and exportation of arms for sale in their lands. The climax was reached in 1892, when the Exclusive Agreement was signed; in it, the rulers, for by now their relations with Britain had added an impressive dimension of stability to their respective positions, undertook not to enter into any agreement or correspondence with any power other than Britain, and not to cede, sell or mortgage any part of their territory.

Although the binding influence of the treaties with Britain consolidated the positions of the chiefs, the clauses of the treaties reflected Britain's overwhelming concern for the safety of the route to India. The treaties affected the social and economic conditions of the area that were of concern to British interests—the curbing of Qasimi sea power, the slave trade, the arms trade, and the cessation of all foreign relations and communications—but did not attempt to intervene in tribal relationships. One feature of these relationships was the rivalry between the Hinawi and Ghafiri factions into which the entire area, from the Trucial Coast to the inner reaches of Oman, was divided. This factionalism was exacerbated in the early eighteenth century when a civil war broke out between tribal chiefs and 'ulema' (religious leaders) over the disputed succession to the imamate of Oman. The war soon engulfed the whole of Oman, including the Trucial Coast, dividing it into the two factions, those who followed the Bani Hina and those who followed the Bani Ghafir. The alignment of the tribes into Hinawi and Ghafiri factions continued long after the war was over, and survived well into the twentieth century.

On the Trucial Coast, the opposition between the Ghafiriyyah and the Hinawiyyah was manifested in the enmity that existed between the two main tribes, the Bani Yas and Qawasim (plural of Qasimi). The nineteenth century was chequered with the immense struggles between them, the Bani Yas being Hinawi, the Qawasim Ghafiri. The Qawasim, with headquarters in Sharjah and Ras al-

Khaimah as well as an outlet on the Gulf of Oman in the Shimay-liyyah, were basically a seafaring people who achieved fame as able sailors and notoriety as pirates; indeed it was they who were responsible for the appellation 'Pirate Coast' for the Trucial Coast. As the potency of the Qawasim became curtailed by the successive treaties with Britain that bound them to refrain from any form of sea warfare, that of the Bani Yas, a land power, began to grow correspondingly. It reached its peak during the rule of Zayid bin Khalifah (1855—1909) of Abu Dhabi. He consolidated the power of the Bani Yas and extended his influence and authority over the neighbouring tribes of the Manasir, the Na'im and the Dawahir (plural of Dahiri), thus becoming a potent force in the Dafrah and Buraimi areas, well beyond the confines of Abu Dhabi town. By the turn of the century, Zayid had achieved for Abu Dhabi a position of unquestioned importance on the Trucial Coast; it could command respect not only in the coastal regions but in the hinterland as well. Almost concurrently with the rise of Abu Dhabi, another Bani Yas shaykhdom, Dubai, began to challenge the importance of Sharjah as a seafaring centre; the growth of Dubai as the major entrepot of the Trucial Coast led to its development as the focal point of the trade in the region, the position held by Sharjah being supplanted once again.

The ascendancy of the Bani Yas in the twentieth century can thus be regarded both as a result of the treaty relations with Britain that curbed the sea power of the Qawasim, their main rivals, and as the natural outcome of the evolution of Abu Dhabi and Dubai, coupled with the decline of Sharjah and Ras al-Khaimah. On the one hand, therefore, Britain maintained a loose form of protectorate over the shaykhdoms, and this provided for their stratification as such; on the other, their own development was relatively unhampered by the confines of overlordship, for British policy was officially against interference in internal affairs. The local history of the shaykhdoms developed at most times as an independent process, for they were governed in the traditional style of bedouin society, the ruler having absolute power and governing in a manner that had to be accepted as fair to all. No administrative policies or constitutions were superimposed by Britain. No attempt was made by the British authorities to introduce even the slightest change in the existing political framework. In fact, until the twentieth century, the only outward signs of the Raj were official visits by British naval and political authorities, and the special privileges accorded to the Indian traders resident in the area.

The purpose of this study is to examine, for the seven shaykhdoms known as the Trucial States, their internal development during a vital and neglected period of their history. The local history of the Arabs of the Trucial Coast has always been seen as an almost extraneous detail in the development of the Gulf as a major arena of conflict between the great powers before World War I, and later as an important strategic and economic focal point for Britain. With the emergence of the United Arab Emirates in 1971, a spate of literature on the member states of the new federation suddenly appeared, in numerous languages; articles and books discussed the area from every conceivable point of view—economic, political, financial, technological, agricultural, social, and so on—for the relatively brusque birth of the UAE, eager to take its place amongst the sovereign independent nations of the world, was accompanied by an awareness of its long isolation and a desire to end it. One factor is common to all the varied works on the UAE: a silence on anything pertaining to the internal history of the former Trucial States, apart from a few anecdotal episodes. This is especially true for the period following the detailed historical narrative drawn up in J. G. Lorimer, *Gazetteer of the Persian Gulf, Oman and Central Arabia* (Calcutta, 1908–1915). The *Gazetteer*, which is still the greatest reference work on the Gulf and Oman, was compiled in 1908 by an officer of the Indian Political Service, and has only recently been generally available. It provides a vast amount of knowledge on the internal history of the Gulf states, particularly during the nineteenth century, but its narrative concludes just before the outbreak of World War I. A vacuum did not exist from that time to the present, although the existing literature on the development of the Trucial States would lead one to believe so. This work attempts to bridge part of the gap.

In the aftermath of World War I, as the old order in Europe and Asia collapsed, the Trucial States at first seemed untouched by the turbulence of outside events. Their people continued in their occupations and preoccupations at the same unhurried pace as before, and seemed likely to do so for a long time to come. But, despite their remoteness, the shaykhdoms were drawn, almost reluctantly, into the foreground of events during the early years of the twentieth century, for the creation of Saudi Arabia and the rise of nationalism in Iran directly affected the relations of the shaykhdoms with each other and with their neighbours. Furthermore, the area could not escape the ramifications of the new technological age. While 'Abd al-'Aziz ibn 'Abd al-Rahman Al-Sa'ud (usually referred to as Ibn Sa'ud) and Riza Shah were asserting themselves as the new forces in the Gulf, the Trucial Coast became involved in the development of the British air-route to India for civil and military aircraft. It was because of the air-route that a new shaykhdom, Kalba, was created in 1936; and it remained in existence until 1952, when it disappeared almost as suddenly as it had come into being. Also, and here the repercussions are only too obvious today, the Arabian peninsula began to be marked as a great potential oilfield, thus making the shaykhdoms especially vulnerable to the machinations of governments and big business. In this book, the first contact of the Trucial Coast with these new forces is examined in detail, together with the parallel internal evolution of each shaykhdom. The latter has been disregarded all too often, in the face of the vast incongruity of the implications of British imperial history and the limitations of local Arab history. Another reason has undoubtedly been the paucity of local Arab historical materials, which appear particularly few and barren when compared with the remarkably detailed annals that have been preserved in Britain and India, through the smoothly operating machinery of officialdom. This study has taken advantage of the new regulations regarding access to the official records of British administrators in the Gulf, which are kept on file in London. Of these, the most valuable for present purposes are the recently declassified Persian Gulf Territories Residency Records in the India Office Records. In the absence of Arab records, they provide the best source material for any aspect of the local history of the Arab shores of the Gulf. They include the Bushire Residency Records, and the Bahrain, Muscat, Kuwait and Sharjah Agency Records, all of which contain a wealth of information on local events—events that were often considered irrelevant to imperial considerations and so not notified to London or Delhi. Many of these records are in Arabic.[1] They include reports on day-to-day events compiled by the Residency Agent (an Arab stationed at Sharjah, until 1939 the only British representative on the Coast), whose intimate knowledge of the area and its people, assiduously cultivated and maintained, was owing not only to his official position, but also to his wide financial interests in the shaykhdoms themselves; correspondence addressed to the Political Residents and Agents by the rulers and leading men of the shaykhdoms, and copies of the answers; petitions to the British authorities about outstanding debts and the manumission of slaves; and regular series of reports, compiled in the form of intelligence summaries and diaries, on all movements, tribal and otherwise, within the coastal and inland regions of the shaykhdoms.

No comprehensive conclusion on the history of the area can be reached without a detailed knowledge of the internal and external factors that shaped its affairs. The interaction and synthesis of these factors are particularly relevant to the first half of the twentieth century, for it was this period that provided the vital link between the nineteenth century, when the Raj was at its zenith, and the middle of the twentieth century, when the British government of

India was dissolved, the first and most conclusive feature of the dismemberment of the British Empire. It was this period also that lay the foundations for the modern development and transformation of the Gulf. It is therefore important to examine the internal and external features of the shaykhdoms of the Trucial Coast in the light of contemporary Anglo-Arab relations during the inter-war period, the period referred to by one writer as 'The Years of Good Management'.[2]

> And yet, in spite of these vicissitudes [basically, the turbulence in 1929 in Palestine], Britain remained paramount in the Middle East, unchallenged by any power of equal magnitude, and able to maintain order thanks to its serenity, and aura of empire, and its ability to summon reinforcements from Malta or India in case of need. British paramountcy endured until the end of the Second World War, and for longer in Middle Eastern imaginations; the shadow of power is long, and remains after the substance has gone.[3]

The 'substance' in the Arab countries was totally different in form and texture from that in the Gulf region as a whole. In Egypt, where British interest had been kindled by the 'overland route' to India, a project that culminated in the building of the Suez Canal, Britain had reigned supreme since the occupation of 1882. Yet nationalist movements and popular uprisings did much to curb its influence, and the Anglo-Egyptian Treaty of 1936 officially terminated the British occupation. Although Britain still controlled Egypt, and this is best illustrated by the forcible intervention by the British ambassador in 1942 that resulted in Mustafa Nahas becoming the Prime Minister, the parliamentary monarchy had a fair amount of self-determination. In Iraq, where the British presence was established when British forces captured Baghdad from the Ottomans in 1917 and then proceeded to set up an internal government administration, the Hashimi Amir Faysal ibn Husayn became king in 1921. The next year an Anglo-Iraqi Treaty was drawn up (ratified in 1924) that gave Britain the instrument by which to exercise the mandate in Iraq; this was followed in 1930 by another treaty, which gave Iraq considerably more independence, allowing it to become a member of the League of Nations in 1932. As in the case of Egypt, the British presence continued to be a potent force, and in 1941 the British again took control there, because of the pro-German sympathies of the Rashid Ali Gaylani movement. Transjordan was an emirate created in 1921 and allotted to the Hashimi Amir 'Abdallah ibn Husayn by Britain. In 1923, 1928 and 1934, successive treaties gave Transjordan a greater measure of independence, but it was not until 1946 that it became an independent kingdom. Palestine was administered as a British mandate, and never allowed to achieve even a minimal degree of self-determination, because of the promises made in 1917 by Balfour regarding the establishment of a national home for the Jewish people; the Palestinians, although deprived of their civil rights, reacted violently to the British administration, the best examples of this being the outbreaks of civil disturbance in 1922, 1929 and 1936.

With the well-known exception of Palestine, all these states gradually achieved, in varying degrees and with varied success, the semblance of independence. With the advice and help of the British authorities, government administrations were set up, to see to the establishment and operation of the requisite machinery of modern states; a national press was formed; armies were built; and passports were issued. Relationships with other Arab countries began to develop, culminating in the formation of the Arab League in 1945.

The Gulf states lived in a world apart. The binding clauses of the 1892 agreements meant that the shaykhdoms lived in almost complete isolation. As time passed, they became more introverted and effectively more remote, having little interest in the events of the outside world. The British authorities guarded the area with a jealous eye, and during the inter-war period no foreigner was granted a visa to visit the Coast; the isolation of the area can best be seen from the striking dearth, in the mass media, of news items on the Gulf (with the exception of Bahrain, and this only because of the intricacies of British policy in the islands). According to an India Office memorandum, British policy in the Gulf had been to

discourage any attempt by other Powers to compete with ourselves for their [the local rulers'] favours. The motive has not been a selfish one but is based on the knowledge gained from long experience that in dealing with Eastern Rulers it is essential to avoid placing in their hands the opportunity to play off one country against another.[4]

Bahrain and Kuwait were relatively less restricted than their southern neighbours, and it might be noted here that Woodrow Wilson's famous reference to the doctrine of self-determination had filtered through to the ruling family of Bahrain, although Political Agents there were not wont to take it seriously.

The long isolation of the Coast has been lifted completely today.

The United Arab Emirates, greatly helped by the income derived from oil, has shown its determination to adapt as quickly as possible to contemporary conditions. Desalination plants have brought water into areas that have been parched since time immemorial; vast agricultural projects have resulted in the export, albeit on a small scale and only as an experiment, of fruit and vegetables; four-lane highways have opened up hitherto intractable desert areas; modern luxury hotels dot the coast and inland regions, in glaring contrast to the old *barasti* huts; a new satellite earth station gives all the territories of the UAE a link with the international satellite system; the largest dry-dock of its kind in the world is being built in Dubai; jumbo jets roar in and out of UAE airports at regular intervals; the UAE's businessmen play an important role in international markets; its leading statesmen are listened to with respect; and, finally, a modern defence system is being formed that will serve to strengthen the political unity of the states of the federation by the establishment of a common defence force.

Even with the most sophisticated infrastructure, however, it is impossible completely to shake off the centuries in just a few years. Occasionally there occurs an incident in which the essential characteristics of the land and its people, as determined by geography and long historical experience, break through the surface modernity and stand fully revealed. One such incident deserves mention. In August 1973, the son of the ruler of Dubai, Muhammad bin Rashid, also the Minister of Defence of the UAE, became involved in an armed clash over a timeless Gulf issue: rights to a water well. The well in question, on the ill-defined border between Sharjah and Dubai, had been dug by Dubai, and, when the inhabitants of Sharjah drew water from it, despite warnings to desist, Muhammad bin Rashid shot at them from a helicopter; undaunted, the people of Sharjah returned fire, and the helicopter was brought down.[5]

In this way the old pattern of life showed through again. Despite desalination plants and despite a written constitution that strongly emphasises the unity of the member states of the UAE, the old rivalry between Sharjah and Dubai erupted into violence. Instead of old and rusty rifles, a helicopter and modern machine-guns were used; otherwise, the incident could well have taken place in 1933, 1893 or even 1853. It is when time seems to stand still, as in this case, that we can see the past most clearly in perspective.

NOTE ON TRANSLITERATION

The transliteration of Arabic words in this study originally followed the system adopted in the second edition of the ENCYCLOPAEDIA OF ISLAM (except in the case of place names that have a generally accepted form in English), with the following alterations:

ح is transliterated thus: j
ق is transliterated thus: q
ظ is transliterated thus: z

For the sake of simplicity, however, I have dropped the diacritical marks, apart from the 'ayn (') and the hamzah ('), in all but Appendix 1 and the bibliography.

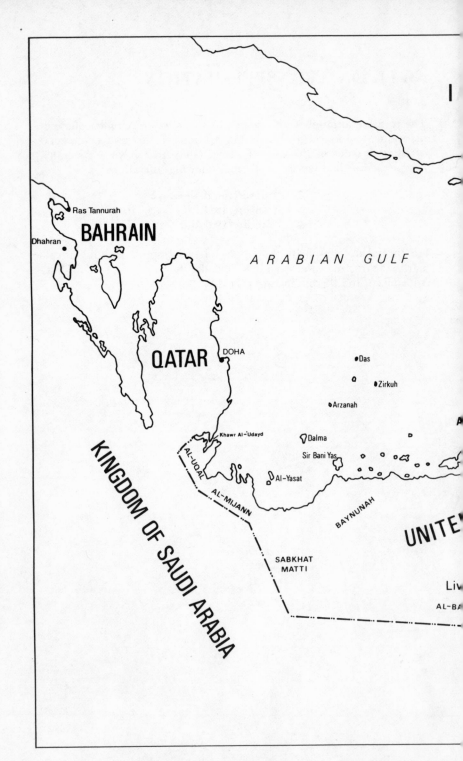

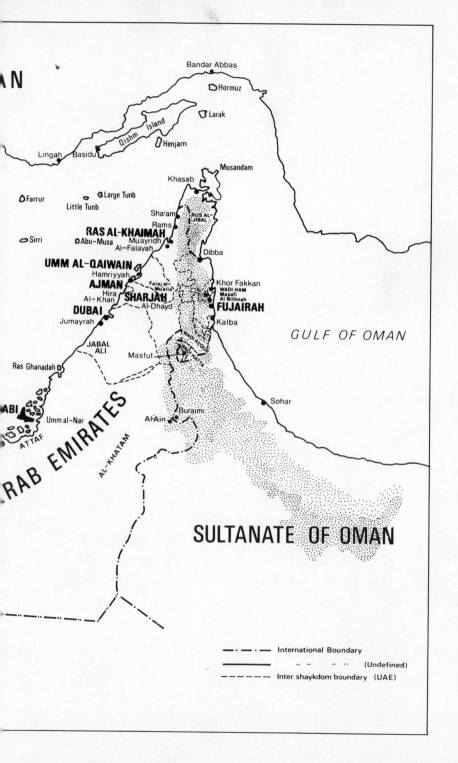

1 The Trucial States in 1919: Rule by Tradition

The United Arab Emirates occupies the southern shores of the Gulf, an area that has long been known either as the Trucial Coast, because of the treaties under which the tiny shaykhdoms scattered along the coast concluded a maritime truce with Britain; or as Trucial Oman, since it was from Oman, the territory occupying the south-eastern portion of the Arabian peninsula, that these treaties separated it. Its eastern extremity, a narrow strip of mountainous land known as the Shimayliyyah, cuts off from the rest of the present state of Oman (formerly known as the Sultanate of Muscat and Oman) its northernmost part, the Musandam peninsula. The UAE is thus bordered on the west by Qatar, on the south-west by the Hasa province of Saudi Arabia, on the south by the great sands of the Rub' al-Khali, on the north by the Arabian Gulf and Oman, and on the east by Oman and the Gulf of Oman.

The UAE has an area of about 30,000 square miles, which may be divided into three geographical sections. First, there is the land lying along the coast of the Arabian Gulf. The coast itself is characterised by numerous islands, reefs and shoals, making navigation hazardous; and the land along it is for the most part low-lying, barren and monotonous, especially in the south, around Abu Dhabi. Further north, however, around Ras al-Khaimah, it does support a degree of cultivation. Second, there are the inland plains, which are made up almost entirely of sandy desert. These run into the Rub' al-Khali on the south, and into a hilly area on the north, near Ras al-Khaimah. Third, there are the mountains in the east. These run north from Oman, through the UAE for about fifty miles, to the Musandam peninsula. The UAE section of the mountains is about twenty miles across, and on the east borders the Gulf of Oman. In consequence, this coast is far more dramatic than the Arabian Gulf coast of the UAE. The bulk of the UAE's inhabitants live along its coasts, and, though there is a lack of sweet water there, certain inland oases, such as Buraimi, Liwa and Dhayd, have adequate supplies and therefore are important agricultural centres.

The harshness of the UAE's geography is matched by the severity of its summers, which are long, oppressively hot and excessively humid; temperatures during the season can reach 120°F (49°C), and the combination of heat and humidity produces conditions not dissimilar from those of a steam-bath. The winter months, by contrast, are mild, with pleasant temperatures and a minimal rainfall. The UAE's geographical position makes it subject to frequent dust-storms, which usually are accompanied by a strong north-west wind, the *shamal*. This adds greatly to the dangers of coastal navigation.

The area's inhospitable geography and climate contributed substantially to its long isolation. This became more complete after the treaties with Britain, which curbed the seafaring activities of the people of the Trucial Coast and so restricted their main channel of communication with the outside world; they did not, however, discontinue fishing and pearling, and so remained expert sailors. Inevitably, though, the attention of the Coast's inhabitants was largely turned inland; and the 1892 treaty called a final halt to any foreign contacts by them, except with Britain. The result of all this was a gradual withdrawal from all but the most essential form of social and economic intercourse with other peoples, and a preoccupation with local events that was lacking in any kind of awareness of their wider implications, either for the region or in the context of the British Empire. The remoteness of the people of the Coast caused them to live in a world where time was an unimportant factor. For their part, the British were not dissatisfied with their condition, but regarded them as savage and backward.

The most illuminating example of this occurred in December 1910. when a party of men from HMS *Hyacinth*, acting on suspicion of a traffic in arms, landed at Dubai to make a search. The townspeople were alarmed at the entry of the armed men, and strongly resented and resisted their presence. In the ensuing hostilities, four men of the search party were killed and nine were wounded. Immediate reprisals followed. A command issued jointly by the Political Resident in Bushire and the Naval Commander-in-Chief of the East Indies Division ordered the ruler, Shaykh Butti bin

Suhayl, to pay a fine and deliver up certain arms within forty-eight hours; he was told that he would have to accept a British agent in Dubai and that a proper post office might be installed there as well. Although Butti paid the fine and surrendered the arms, he showed a marked fear at the possibility of a resident British agent: he knew that his people would be violently opposed to any such intrusion, and that it would in turn jeopardise his own position. The British authorities understood the realities of Butti's predicament, and concluded that the Coast was too 'wild' a place for an agent to be accepted without a strong show of force; it was finally decided to defer the matter until a more propitious time.[1] In the inter-war discussions of British policy, this incident was used as a touchstone of the attitude on the Coast towards foreigners. It strengthened belief in the backwardness of the people there, though no questions were asked about why they were so insular as to refuse to have a British agent among them.

The history of the shaykhdoms before World War I was remarkably unaffected by developments elsewhere. Although, in the two decades preceding the war, the Gulf area became the arena of major competition between France, Britain, Russia, Germany and the Ottoman Empire,[2] the Trucial Coast felt little of this. The treaty of 1892, which had followed from the possibility that the French would try to extend their interests in the area, had effectively cut it off from the stream of events. It continued to be governed by political officers of the British government of India, and, instead of being a part of the Arab world, was more an extension of the Indian sub-continent. For example, since there was no local currency, the Indian rupee had become the accepted form of payment, except in the hinterland, where Maria Theresa dollars circulated. Furthermore, the largest foreign community in the region was made up of Indian merchants. The effect of all this was that India had the major share of the Coast's foreign trade.

The conditions on the Coast were reflected in the population itself. In 1908, this was estimated at 80,000,[3] and in 1939, just over thirty years later, it was estimated at the same figure.[4] The restrictions of day-to-day living, the illiteracy of the people because of the general absence of educational facilities, and their ignorance of even the most rudimentary forms of public health all contributed to a high rate of infant mortality and a short life expectancy, which in turn resulted in zero population growth.

Although the population was static, a comparison of the population figures for the principal towns in the same two years (see Table 1) reveals that the people responded positively to the various economic and political challenges facing them. There was a great deal of internal migration, which demonstrates the dynamic nature of the society. When conditions in Sharjah stopped being conducive to socio-economic growth, Dubai and, to a lesser extent, Abu Dhabi became the new centres of the Trucial Coast. The people acted within the confines of the existing situation and responded to the economic changes by migrating to nearby towns. Thus, despite their long isolation and the poverty in which they lived, it is inaccurate to say that the people of the Coast had become atrophied. On the contrary, they had an innate sense of survival that defied the harshness of the conditions of life on the Coast.

Socially, they were divided into the bedouin (*badu*) and the settled people (*hadar*), the organisation of both being based on the tribe. The bedouin made up only 10 per cent of the total population, but the role they played far outweighed their actual numbers. They roamed the inland regions, with their camels, sheep and goats, in search of grazing land, moving about among the numerous wells that existed there. Their migratory habits were determined by the aridity of the land and the harshness of the

TABLE I

Population of Principal Towns

	1908	*1939*
Sharjah town	15,000	5,000
Abu Dhabi town	6,000	10,000
Dubai town	10,000	20,000

climate, yet their mode of life provided ideal conditions for the strengthening of their tribal ties. As a rule, each bedouin tribe had its *dirah*, the land it habitually roamed, and the tribe roamed as a group. The leader of the tribe, the shaykh, was responsible for the welfare of his people in peace and wartime, and, depending on the size and strength of his following, was regarded as an independent leader, answerable to no one else; indeed, his friendship was usually sought by the rulers on the coast, for his control over a section of the hinterland and its people placed him in a position of great strength.

The *hadar* lived in rural areas and towns. In the rural settlements in the inland oases, such as Dhayd and Buraimi, in the coastal region around Ras al-Khaimah, and in the Shimayliyyah on the Gulf of Oman, the cultivation of date and other fruit trees, some barley and vegetables were the main occupations. In the coastal towns, by contrast, the economy was centred on fishing and pearl-diving. The towns resembled each other, and generally were formed on the same pattern: a square stone fort with towers around it was the symbol of the ruler's power; the houses of the ruler and leading men were made of stone, and the rest were of mats made with date-leaf stalks.

The system of government on the Coast was paternalistic. The ruler governed with absolute authority, but often consulted with his *majlis* (assembly of notables) on matters of outstanding importance. The position of the ruler was not always an easy one. The rule of primogeniture did not apply, and accession to power was often accompanied by ruthless family competition, with murder and bloodshed; fratricide and patricide were almost regular features of the pattern. Once in power, a ruler had to placate above all the members of his family, for the fact of their birth gave them the right to occupy the seat of power, and any weakness of or injustice by the ruler could unleash the enmity of his ambitious relatives. He therefore not only included them in his *majlis* and consulted them before taking any major decision, but also paid them a regular salary out of his income as ruler; not to do so would inevitably be to incur their wrath and would be very likely to bring about his downfall.

The ruler had to remain accessible to all his people and hear their petitions and complaints. He also had to prove his authority by extending his rule over the inland tribes, and often paid them large sums to ensure their loyalty. No government services or departments existed, no armies or police force, and communications were at the most primitive level. The ruler also had to contend with the terms of his shaykhdom's various treaties with Britain, which he had to sign at his accession to confirm their validity. He also had to abide by all the formalities regarding the British authorities; for example, when the Political Resident sailed to a shaykhdom and had his standard raised, the ruler had to go on board to pay his respects. Furthermore, the resident Indian traders were regarded as British subjects and had to be treated with due care and deference, although no extra-territorial jurisdiction existed for them until 1946.[5]

Throughout the nineteenth century, and because of the successive treaties, Britain reinforced the separate identity of the shaykhdoms and helped the chiefs to establish themselves more securely. At the same time the focus of the area's internal affairs shifted from the interior to the coast. This had much to do with the fact that Britain was primarily interested in the security of the route to India, and therefore recognised the authority of only those leaders who had jurisdiction over the coast. There therefore developed a marked difference between the settled society of the coastal area and the more turbulent society of the nomadic peoples of the interior. The emphasis on the coast became an established feature of Trucial politics in the twentieth century, and was not challenged until the 1930s, when exploration for oil began; the divergence between the coast and the interior then became glaringly obvious, especially when local tribal opposition prevented geologists from entering certain inland regions that the coastal *de jure* ruler of the territory had given them permission to enter.

Thus, despite the power and prominence of the coastal area, the role played by the hinterland cannot be overlooked. The foremost measure of a coastal ruler's strength and prestige was his ability to command the tribes of the interior; his rise or decline in coastal politics could usually be measured by his ability to enforce his authority over the tribal chieftains in the area he claimed as his territory. Conversely, the extent of a ruler's territory was governed by the extent to which the tribes roaming the area would support him in time of need.

There was thus an important interaction between the coast and the interior, and this directly affected the political structure of the area. One example is the persistence in the coastal districts of the bedouin custom of exacting *diyah*, or blood-money, that was the accepted form of compensation for the murder of a man where the ties of blood relationship were connected with the substitute of blood revenge. Another is the attempts that have been made during the present century, mostly without success, at exactly defining the boundaries of the shaykhdoms and their frontiers with neighbouring states.

Until it became known that oil might be found in the eastern part of Arabia, little attention had been paid to the delineation of boundaries in the Western sense. The desert law that governed societies throughout most of the Arabian peninsula did not concern itself with fixed boundaries: 'The Arabian desert has sometimes been compared to the high seas. Caravans come and go like ships and nomads roam at will in search of grazing ....'[6] One of the few accepted tests of the extent of a ruler's territory was his ability to enforce the payment of *zakat* (a tax in return for the payment of which he promised his protection)[7] on the tribes whose *dirah* was adjacent to his territory. Another was his capacity to protect these same tribes, and avenge any raids against them occurring within his precincts. Boundaries, therefore, fluctuated according to pastoral and political conditions, and could never achieve any degree of permanence—a consideration that is central to any understanding of the Arabian peninsula in the twentieth century.

Until the 1930s, when they began to receive regular payments resulting from oil and air agreements, the rulers' revenues were restricted to customs duties (which in places like Dubai and Sharjah were substantial, and in Umm al-Qaiwain, by contrast, minimal) and the tax levied on every pearl boat of the shaykhdom. This latter tax was fairly large in all places, for, until the early 1930s, when the industry began to decline, owing to the world depression and the introduction of the Japanese cultured pearl, the pearling industry was the pivot of the economic and social structure of the Trucial Coast. The industry was well organised and functioned according to a regular and reliable pattern. The season lasted from May to September, when the sea was calm and the water a reasonable temperature, During this time, the fleets remained at the pearling banks, rarely returning to shore until the diving was over. Since pearling was such a vital source of income to the Coast, the fleets were large, and the majority of the able-bodied men in the towns were away from home working at the pearl beds for the entire four-month period.

The division of labour aboard the pearling boats was clear-cut and rigidly adhered to: captains, divers, haulers, cooks and apprentices all worked according to a well-defined plan that had evolved over centuries of practice. The divers had a hard and dangerous task: with wooden pegs closing their nostrils, to help them hold their breath, and with the aid of a rope anchored to the sea-bed, they dived into the sea and searched about for oysters. When they had found them, it was a race against time to remove them, and there were the added hazards of sharks and jelly-fish. If the diger tugged at the rope, the hauler had to pull him up instantly, or his life might be in danger. The entire crew later assisted in opening the oysters; the pearls were extracted, and the rest was put aside for mother-of-pearl. Merchants then carried the pearls, among the most perfect and beautiful in the world, to the rich luxury markets of Europe and India.[8]

The pearl trade brought many Indian and Persian merchants to live in the towns of the Trucial Coast, the majority settling in Dubai, the rest in Abu Dhabi and Sharjah.[9] These merchants usually lent money to the owners of the pearling boats before the pearling season started; the owners were then expected to repay the amount at *qaffal*, the end of the season. The arrangements were often complicated by the fact that the money had to be returned in instalments, and in this regard many disagreements arose. The situation had been regulated in 1879, when the rulers of the Trucial shaykhdoms signed a mutual agreement under British auspices to provide for the return of debtors or be held responsible for their debts by payment of a fine. The agreement called for the establishment of a council of arbitration presided over by the Residency Agent for cases ending in dispute; the decisions of the council would be binding when confirmed by the Political Resident, who would then enforce them.[10] The enforcement of the payment of debts was thus a major feature of the pearl trade, and the Indian traders were supported by the 1879 agreement.

The gruelling work that the diver had to perform and the terrible hazards to which it subjected him made his occupation singularly unpleasant. Owing to their extreme poverty, many divers were forced into service so as to pay off their debts to the handful of rich merchants who reaped the benefits of the pearl trade. Many of the divers were also slaves, for slave-trading existed on the Trucial Coast well into the twentieth century. The treaties with Britain bound the rulers of the Coast (as well as those of Bahrain, Muscat and Qatar) to suppress and abstain from the trade in their territories, agreeing to the right of the British Government to search their vessels not only on the high seas, but also in the Arabian Gulf and the Gulf of Oman. Yet, though the treaties helped to curtail the slave trade substantially, they did not suppress it entirely. The British authorities were aware that they could do no more, and reiterated time and again that slavery was recognised in the Quran.[11] They did, however, reserve the right to issue manumission certificates at any of their Political Agencies, to slaves who wished to be freed, and the validity of these certificates was upheld at all times by the British Government. Even so, slavery persisted. One way in which it did so was through the owners' retention of the children of their domestic slaves. Another factor was the extreme poverty of the area, particularly after the economic depression of 1929 had drastically reduced the profits of the pearl trade: rather than seek their freedom and so expose themselves to the worst, most slaves were content to remain assured of food and shelter by remaining in bondage. With all this, the slave trade continued to operate, principally from Nejd, in central Arabia, and from Persian Baluchistan, and the British authorities could do no more about it than occasionally to make an effort at enforcing the ban on the importation of slaves into the area.

ABU DHABI

Just before World War I, by far the most important and influential of the shaykhdoms of the Trucial Coast was Abu Dhabi, which had known a period of unprecedented power and prestige during the long reign (fifty-five years) of Shaykh Zayid bin Khalifah. Besides consolidating his own position and strengthening the internal security of Abu Dhabi, Zayid extended his authority over a number of inland tribes that had hitherto been loyal to his rivals, the Qawasim; this extension of authority was naturally followed by a parallel expansion of *de facto* rule in a desert society where boundaries were flexible and depended on political conditions for their verification. By the latter part of the nineteenth century, Shaykh Zayid was unquestionably the most powerful of the rulers on the Trucial Coast, thus supplanting the hegemony held by the Qawasim for close on a hundred years. But, as one Political Resident remarked, the relative positions of the shaykhdoms on the Coast depended largely on the personalities of their rulers,[12] and with the death of Shaykh Zayid in 1909 the succession became the subject of ruthless competition among his sons, whose unremitting power struggles plunged Abu Dhabi back into the chaos that it had experienced before Zayid's succession. For a decade, fratricide decided the claims of Zayid's sons, and gradually much of what he had strived to build in Abu Dhabi was destroyed. It was not until the accession, in 1928, of Zayid's grandson, Shakhbut bin Sultan, who went on to reign for almost forty years, that it became possible to restore the political structure on which the Trucial shaykhdoms hinged.

The ruling family of Abu Dhabi belongs to the Al-bu-Falah or Al-Nuhayyan[13] section of the Bani Yas, a loose tribal grouping—made up largely of settled elements but also including a small bedouin population—that is distributed throughout the coastal and inland areas of Oman, and makes up about half the population of Abu Dhabi. Although the Al-bu-Falah is one of its smallest sections, the leading role it has played within the Bani Yas has been out of all proportion to its size, for the various sections of the Bani Yas have always looked to the ruler of Abu Dhabi as paramount shaykh; likewise, the Bani Yas form the basis of the power of the ruler of Abu Dhabi. Other sections of the Bani Yas include the Al-bu-Falasah, who in 1833 broke away from Abu Dhabi and founded the shaykhdom of Dubai; the Qubaysat, who live along the coast and in Liwa, and who in the nineteenth century made a series of unsuccessful attempts to secede from the authority of the Al-bu-Falah in order to establish themselves in Khawr al-'Udayd at the foot of the Qatar peninsula; the Mazari',[14] who are principally bedouin and who roam from Liwa in Dafrah east to Abu Dhabi, where some live in Dalmah island; and the Al-bu-Hamir, another bedouin section, who live around Abu Dhabi town. Of the other sections, the Hawamil and the Maharibah live in Abu Dhabi town and Liwa; the Al-Sultan, the Qasal, the Bani Shikr and the Qanaysat live principally in Liwa; and the Qumzan and the Rumaythat are inhabitants of Abu Dhabi town.[15]

The other principal tribe of Abu Dhabi is the Manasir, who are bedouin with headquarters in Dafrah. Their range extends from Qatar to Buraimi, including Liwa. A few Manasir are also settled at Khan and Jumayrah in Dubai. The main sections of the Manasir are the Al-bu-Mundhir, the Al-bu-Rahmah and the Al-bu-Sha'r. For some time in the nineteenth century, the Manasir paid *zakat* to the Wahhabis, but by the time Lorimer compiled his *Gazetteer* they were 'independent of all control but maintain some degree of intercourse with the town of Abu Dhabi'.[16]

During Shaykh Zayid's rule, because of his strength and the unusual length of his tenure, a certain stability in those areas under his *de facto* control was noticeable. His influence extended along the coast for about 200 miles, roughly from Khawr al-'Udayd to the boundary with Dubai, at a point near Khawr Ghanadah.[17] Inland, the shaykhdom reached the Buraimi oasis, 'but without taking it in'.[18] At the beginning of the twentieth century, the Buraimi oasis consisted of

> ten separate villages situated roughly in a circle about 6 miles in diameter. Baraimi village, being the original settlement, has given its name to the whole. ... The water supply is from more numerous *fuluj* or underground aqueducts coming in from the hills to the east. ... Light though it is the soil is evidently most prolific, and it was calculated that the oasis supported not less than 60,000 date palms besides all the fruits and vegetables to be found in that region, e.g., grapes, melons, limes, figs, pomegranates, a few mangoes, and in the way of crops, wheat, barley and jowari and quantities of lucerne.[19]

To the west, Abu Dhabi extended to the margin of the Rub' al-Khali and included Al-'Uqal, a small littoral district on the eastern part of the base of the Qatar peninsula; Mijan, a coastal desert tract between Sabkhat Matti and Al-'Uqal; Sabkhat Matti, a saline marsh usually considered to be the natural boundary between Hasa (the eastern section of present-day Saudi Arabia) and geographical Oman;[20] and Dafrah, which lies between the coastal area and the Rub' al-Khali. Dafrah is made up of a number of tracts: Baynunah, Taff, al-Qufa and Liwa. The last, the ancestral home of the Al-bu-Falah,

> consists mainly of white undulating sand dunes, altogether without vegetation; but it contains a score of small depressions. ... These depressions are divided from one another by sandy wastes; but at the bottom of each depression there is fertile soil, supporting the cultivation of a village which generally stands upon a sandy eminence near by.[21]

In the middle of the twentieth century, Liwa had about fifty-two settlements, inhabited by the Bani Yas and the Manasir.[22] Another area that Lorimer believed came within the shaykhdom of Abu Dhabi was al-Khatam, a sandy tract that divided Dafrah on the west from north-eastern Oman and whose principal inhabitants were the Bani Yas, the Manasir and the Na'im.[23] Abu Dhabi town, the capital of the shaykhdom, lies on an island; until the discovery of oil, the inhabitants lived almost entirely by diving for pearls and by fishing. Date cultivation was limited, because of the aridity of the area, but grazing for animals was plentiful. The shaykhdom also contains countless small islands that lie off the coast between Sabkhat Matti and Abu Dhabi town; these include Arzanah, Dalma, Das, Qarnayn, Sa'diyyat, Sir Bani Yas, Umm al-Nar, al-Fayya and al-Yasat.

Although Abu Dhabi was the largest in area of all the Trucial shaykhdoms, it ranked third in terms of population. In 1908, towards the end of Zayid's rule, it had around 11,000 inhabitants, most of whom belonged to the Bani Yas. The foreigners settled there, mostly Persians, numbered about 500. By 1939, largely because of the instability of the ruling family and the economic depression, which greatly hampered the pearl trade, the population had fallen to only 10,500. It was not until the early 1960s that there occurred the large-scale migration that gave Abu Dhabi its present population of around 250,000.

DUBAI

The geographical location and physical characteristics of Dubai, coupled with the initiative of its various rulers, have contributed greatly to its rise as a thriving centre of trade, as a result of which it is today the principal entrepot of the UAE. Its history during the first half of the twentieth century is essentially that of a vigorous merchant community.

In 1939 Dubai had a population of about 20,000, making it the most populous of the Trucial shaykhdoms, and also giving it the highest density of population. At least one-quarter of its inhabitants were foreign: there were around 2000 Persians, 1000 Baluchis and a large number of Indians; the rest were from Hasa, Bahrain and Kuwait. Almost the whole of the shaykhdom's settled population lived in Dubai town.

The people of Dubai were in the vanguard of the economic and social transformation of the Gulf, for it was there, beginning early in the twentieth century, that a new merchant class, who did not rely entirely on the pearl trade, began to be formed.

These merchants engaged in many forms of trade, both within the Gulf region itself and as far away as East Africa and India. Thus, when the pearl economy declined in the 1930s, Dubai alone had other means of survival.

Dubai lies on the coast between Abu Dhabi and Sharjah, only seven miles from the latter. It stands astride a creek, which provides good anchorage and separates the two main quarters of the town: Dayrah, the business section, and Dubai proper.

Little is known of the early history of Dubai, which at one time came under Abu Dhabi. In 1833, two members of the Al-bu-Fa-lasah section of the Bani Yas, 'Udayd bin Sa'id and Maktum bin Butti, along with about 800 followers, seceded from Abu Dhabi authority and settled in Dubai. Before long, Dubai attained the status of an independent shaykhdom; much of this was owing to the personal courage and ambition of Maktum bin Butti, who ruled Dubai until 1852. The changeover from one ruler to the next was always peaceful, although there was invariably some dis-agreement about who should succeed. In 1886, for example, Hashar bin Maktum, who had ruled since 1859, died; the succession of his brother Rashid was contested by Maktum bin Hashar, the son of the former ruler. When Rashid died in 1894, Maktum became ruler, and the sons of Rashid, Mani' and Hashar, immediately formed a conspiracy against him. However, Maktum discovered their plan in good time and arrested and imprisoned them; they were later released and went to live in Sharjah. Thirty years later, they severely challenged the authority of Maktum's son Sa'id.

It was during Maktum's rule, from 1894 to 1906, that Dubai began to grow as a commercial centre. Maktum himself was liberal and enlightened, and was quick to seize the opportunity that the decline of the port of Lingah in Persia offered for Dubai to develop. Lingah had been governed by the Qawasim, who administered it as an independent Arab principality until 1887, when the Persian Government replaced them with Persian officials. Lingah was then subjected to the reformed customs administration of Persia, which in 1902 had been handed over to Belgian control. The new customs regulations put an end to the port's free trade, and gradually much of the commercial activity carried on there was transferred across the Gulf to Dubai. Before 1902, only four or five steamers called at Dubai annually; in that year, however, twenty-one steam-ships, primarily of the Bombay and Persia Steam Navigation Com-pany, made Dubai a port of call. Soon after, in 1904, the British India Steam Navigation Company began calling at Dubai once a fortnight.[24]

The merchants who had previously lived in Lingah began to settle in Dubai, and others arrived in search of prosperity and

free trade. Dubai became the main port for the entire Trucial
Coast, and the chief distribution centre for foreign goods destined
for the interior, especially the Buraimi oasis. The foreign population
grew, with Indians, Persians, Baluchis and others making Dubai
their home. Its character as the centre of a bustling and flourishing
trade community began to develop, and in 1954 the city-state
was aptly described as follows:

> its *suqs* or markets on either side of its broad creek are the
> most picturesque I have ever seen in the Middle East and take
> one back to the time of the Arabian Nights. In the narrow
> lanes roofed with matting, where the gloom is flecked by spots
> of sunlight, Arabs, Persians and Baluchis display their multifarious
> and many-coloured wares. Wild-eyed tribesmen with their camel-
> canes and daggers haggle with the shopkeepers and the wealthier
> Persian merchants with their long flowing robes and gold-brocaded
> headdresses pass to and fro, intent upon their business. Graceful
> dhows glide into the creek, lower their sails and cast anchor
> while the whole day long small craft are busy ferrying shoppers
> from one bank to the other. The rectangular houses of the Shaikhs
> and merchants with their tall wind-towers cast white reflections
> on the water. Conditions are no doubt primitive, but there is
> an air of bustle and prosperity about the place that gives it
> a peculiar charm.[25]

SHARJAH

The decline in the power and prestige of Sharjah that had set
in towards the end of the nineteenth century continued well into
the twentieth. Whereas its rulers had previously commanded events in
the Trucial Coast—indeed, in the whole of the Gulf region—Sharjah
now became insignificant in the power structure of the area, and
the men who ruled over it were barely able to maintain their
positions. The pattern of decline that had started during the two
decades preceding World War I continued without respite into
and beyond World War II: the bedouin upon whom the ruler
had traditionally relied for support openly flaunted their defiance
of his authority, and those parts of the shaykhdom that had previously
attempted secession now obtained official British recognition of their
independence.

In order to understand this diminution in the status of Sharjah,
it is necessary to glance back to the middle of the eighteenth
century, when its ruling family, the Qawasim, achieved fame and
notoriety as a great seafaring power in the Gulf. Their fleet was

renowned for its strength, and, although they engaged in a fair amount of trade, it was their piratical activities—owing to which Europeans came to know the Coast as the Pirate Coast[26]—that made them the terror of the rich merchant ships that sailed the Gulf waters. The ships of the East India Company were not spared, any more than any others, and in the first two decades of the nineteenth century the attacks grew in frequency. Thus it was that in 1819 the Government of Bombay dispatched a punitive expedition to put an end to the insecurity of Gulf waters. The force mercilessly bombed the principal towns from which the Qawasim ordinarily sailed, and before long the leading men of the Coast tendered their submission and offered their friendship to the British naval force. The next year, the first in a series of treaties between the Government of Bombay (and later, the Government of India) and the principal chiefs of the Coast was signed; known as the General Treaty of Peace, it bound the signatories not to engage in piracy or pillage, either on land or at sea.[27] In 1835 the chiefs bound themselves to a maritime truce, and in 1853 this was extended into a Perpetual Maritime Truce, whereby the rulers agreed to a complete end to hostilities at sea. The effect of these treaties was disadvantageous to the development of the Qawasim, who were predominantly a maritime power. In order to maintain their supremacy on the Coast they had to contend with the rivalry of the Bani Yas, a land power, whose position was strengthened by the maritime truce. On land, the Qawasim relied on the force of their allies, the Bani Qitab bedouin, and from 1820 until 1866, when he died, Sultan bin Saqr, the paramount shaykh of the Qawasim, ably made use of their strength and consolidated the internal position of Sharjah; in 1850, for example, he extended his rule to the Shimayliyyah tract on the Gulf of Oman, by wresting control of the towns of Kalba, Dibba, Fujairah and Khawr Fakkan from the sultan of Muscat.

After Sultan's death, however, his brothers and sons were involved in endless intrigues to seize control of the shaykhdom, or of parts of it. In 1883, Saqr bin Khalid, a grandson of Sultan bin Saqr, overthrew his uncle Salim bin Sultan; he went on to rule over Sharjah until his death in 1914. It was during his reign that the prestige of the Qawasim suffered its greatest decline. Much of this was owing to Saqr's weak personality and his marked inability to command the loyalty of the Bani Qitab. Concurrently with the weakening of the Qawasim, the Bani Yas were gaining in strength, and Abu Dhabi and Dubai began to exercise a strong presence in Trucial affairs.

In 1914, when Saqr bin Khalid died, Sharjah was still a large shaykhdom, with a population of around 45,000, and outlets on the Arabian Gulf and the Gulf of Oman. Its western section, on the Arabian Gulf, consisted of Sharjah town, the fishing villages of Hirah and Hamriyyah, the inland oasis of Dhayd, Ras al-Khaimah, Jazirat al-Hamra (an island not far offshore from Ras al-Khaimah), Rams and Sha'am; the eastern section, on the Gulf of Oman, included Dibba, Khawr Fakkan, Fujairah, Kalba and Khawr Kalba. Thus, the northern boundary extended from Sha'am on the Arabian Gulf to the southern extremity of the Jirri plain, and east to Dibba on the Gulf of Oman; the southern boundary cut across from the town of Sharjah to Khawr Kalba on the Gulf of Oman. Sharjah town, built on a creek, was the second most important trading centre on the Coast, although by 1939 its population was only one quarter that of Dubai. Pearl diving and fishing were the main occupations, and they attracted a number of Indian and Persian residents to the town. The Arab residents belonged principally to the 'Abadilah, Na'im, Shawamis, Al-Sudan and Al-'Ali tribes. Ras al-Khaimah was likewise situated on a creek; and the inhabitants, equal in number to those of Sharjah, were primarily pearl divers, with a few engaged in the cultivation of dates. Sharjah was large and varied enough for the population not to be wholly dependent on the pearl trade. In Dhayd, for example, there was sufficient water available for the cultivation of sizable quantities of dates, oranges and mangoes; in Khawr Fakkan, the cultivation of wheat and dates was equal in importance to the pearl industry; Fujairah and Kalba also had an economy based on both agriculture and trade. In addition, Sharjah owned the islands of Abu Musa and Sir Abu Nu'ayr, both of which contained rich deposits of red oxide, and Tunb and Little Tunb.

AJMAN AND UMM AL-QAIWAIN

The remaining Trucial shaykhdoms before World War I were Ajman and Umm al-Qaiwain, tiny states of no more than 100 and 300 square miles, respectively. The population of both was made up largely of pearl divers and fishermen, a fact reflected in their political life. Ajman forms an enclave in Sharjah, and consists basically of the town of Ajman, which lies about five miles north-east of Sharjah town. Its population in 1908 was only 750, but by 1939 this had grown to 2000. The ruling family belongs to the Al-bu-Khurayban branch of the Na'im, a large and important tribe including both settled and nomadic people and scattered over a large area, including Sharjah, Buraimi and the Batinah coast of Oman.

Umm al-Qaiwain is situated around twenty-seven miles south-west of Ras al-Khaimah town. It extends northwards to Jazirat al-Hamra and southwards part of the way to Hamriyyah. About sixteen miles south-east of the town of Umm al-Qaiwain is the oasis of Falaj-al-'Ali, where rich date gardens have always existed. The ruling family and most of the people are of the Al-'Ali. The shaykhdom is small: its population during the first half of this century never exceeded 5000 people, and its importance in the political life of the coast during the same period was slight. There were violent struggles over the succession in the 1920s.

2 The Aftermath of War: Perpetuation of Control

RECONSIDERATION OF POLICY

During the period preceding the outbreak of World War I, British policy in the Gulf had primarily been concerned with asserting Britain's omnipotence and exclusive rights in the area. Following a series of elaborate agreements and conventions, assisted by the strong personalities of Lord Curzon as Viceroy of India and Sir Percy Cox[1] as Political Resident in Bushire, the British position was defined and confirmed. The possibility of the extension of French interests to the Trucial Coast had been sharply terminated in 1892 by the Exclusive Agreement with the rulers, and French competition for control of the sultanate of Muscat and Oman was virtually ended in 1904 with the Anglo-French Entente.[2] The Anglo-Russian Convention of 1907 had the effect of removing Russian opposition to the British presence in the Gulf. The other two powers that Britain regarded as a direct threat in the field were Germany and the Ottoman Empire, and during the period from 1908 to 1914 much effort was made to diminish their respective positions. The gravest menace came from the German policy of *Drang nach Osten*, which culminated in the project of the Baghdad Railway with a terminus in Kuwait; although British negotiations in the years immediately preceding the war had been successful, and conventions had been drawn up and initialled, the outbreak of hostilities in 1914 prevented ratification. The conventions in question were the Anglo-Turkish Convention of 1913, in which Kuwait was recognised as an autonomous *qada'*[3] of the Ottoman Empire, its boundaries were defined, and Ottoman interference was excluded; the Anglo-German Convention of 1913, which was concerned primarily with containing the Baghdad Railway; and the Anglo-Turkish Convention of 1914, in which the southern boundary of Turkish Arabia from the Red Sea was defined. Other agreements with Germany confirmed British rights of navigation on the Tigris and Euphrates, as well as demarcating the Turco-Persian frontier from the Gulf to Mount Ararat.

In November 1903, Curzon paid a visit to the Gulf, the first by any Viceroy of India, in order to ensure international recognition of Britain's special position; the visit was concerned to display evidence of British naval supremacy and was accompanied by much pomp and ceremony. On 21 November the Viceroy held a durbar off Sharjah for the rulers of the Trucial Coast. His address on that day confirmed Britain's special rights and outlined the main points of British policy, a policy that he had been instrumental in formulating:

> We were here before any other Power, in modern times, had shown its face in these waters. We found strife and we have created order. It was our commerce as well as your security that was threatened and called for protection. At every port along these coasts the subjects of the King of England still reside and trade. ... We saved you from extinction at the hands of your neighbours. We opened these seas to the ships of all nations, and enabled their flags to fly in peace. We have not seized or held your territory. We have not destroyed your independence but have preserved it. ... The peace of these waters must still be maintained; your independence will continue to be upheld; and the influence of the British Government must remain supreme. ...
>
> The British Government have no desire to interfere, and have never interfered, in your internal affairs, provided that the Chiefs govern their territories with justice, and respect the rights of the foreign traders residing therein.[4]

The British Government added its voice to this statement. In an address to the House of Lords on 5 May 1903, the Foreign Secretary, Lord Landsdowne, declared,

> It seems to me that our policy should be directed in the first place to protect and promote British trade in those waters. In the next place I do not think ... that those efforts should

be directed towards the exclusion of the legitimate trade of other Powers. In the third place—I say this without hesitation—we should regard the establishment of a naval base, or of a fortified fort, in the Persian Gulf by any other Power as a very grave menace to British interests, and we should certainly resist it with all the means at our disposal.[5]

Although the position and importance of the Gulf changed considerably during the next four decades, Curzon's address and Lansdowne's declaration remained the main guides to policy. Despite the endless correspondence on the advisability of altering that policy, in view of the new situations that arose, the outline remained the same, and constant references to the statements of 1903 affirm this. In September 1933 a durbar was held for the rulers of the Trucial Coast; the Officiating Political Resident repeated Curzon's address with few alterations, thus reiterating the policy laid down thirty years before. The only differences were in the way the established courses of action were interpreted, which usually depended on the individuals most closely concerned with Gulf affairs.

Despite the end of the pre-war rivalry with the Ottoman Empire, Russia and Germany, and with it the resultant entanglements of European diplomacy, British involvement in Gulf affairs was increased after the victory of 1918. Britain had occupied Iraq during the war, and was about to secure a mandate there; and Ibn Sa'ud, who had shown himself friendly to Britain, had dislodged the Ottomans from Hasa in 1913, thus extending his territory to the shores of the Gulf. On the face of it, therefore, British interests could be expected to meet with few of the challenges that had faced them in earlier days; but the great increase in those interests meant that even greater official involvement was called for. In 1914, after the discovery of oil in commercial quantities in southern Persia, the British Government took a controlling interest in the Anglo-Persian Oil Company; and later there were strategic plans to develop an air route from England to India that would pass through the Gulf. The area was thus no longer the primary concern of India alone; its destiny held implications that were far-reaching and that extended to Britain and its empire as a whole.

In 1919 the Gulf emerged an undisputedly British lake, but shortly afterwards two new countries entered the field of Gulf politics and began to give the British cause for concern: the Iran of Riza Shah and the Saudi Arabia of Ibn Sa'ud. Both countries gradually succeeded in unsettling the British position. Iran did so by directing its militant nationalism against British domination, and constantly attempting to assert its claims to sovereignty over the islands of the Gulf; and Saudi Arabia did so by dint of its spectacular growth, culminating in its domination of most of the Arabian peninsula from the Red Sea to the Gulf.

Britain had previously been able to command the Gulf area from the Residency at Bushire in southern Persia thanks to the special privileges it held there; but, after the rise to power of Riza Shah, in 1921, the maintenance of the *status quo* became impossible. One of the first acts of the new government was to denounce the Anglo-Persian Agreement of 1919 which had placed Britain in control of the Persian army and finances; in the following years it became only too clear that Iran was not willing to accept foreign domination in any form. British concessions gradually began to diminish, and with them the former prestige and control. In 1936 it was finally decided to remove that bastion of authority, the Residency, from Bushire to Bahrain. Although for various reasons the removal did not actually take place until 1946, there were in the meantime other manifestations of the reduction of British influence in Iran. One such was the evacuation, in 1935, of the naval bases at Henjam and Basidu to Bahrain and Khawr Kuwai, indicating the new and added importance of the Arab coast.

The centre of gravity of British interests in the Gulf was thus deliberately moved from the Persian to the Arab side of the Gulf. The new emphasis was seen as requiring special measures to secure British supremacy on the Arab side, and as a result efforts were made to take a tighter hold on the Arab shaykhdoms, especially Bahrain. In 1923, direct interference in the internal affairs of Bahrain was considered necessary, following an uprising there; the ruler, Shaykh 'Isa, was deposed in favour of his son, Shaykh Hamad, and a series of reforms was imposed. A proper police force was organised, under the guidance of a British commandant; the Customs Department was rearranged, with a British director in charge; and a Briton was appointed adviser to the ruler.[6] Before long, Bahrain was, to all intents and purposes, a British province.

The shaykhdoms of the Trucial Coast were never subjected to such close control, but they gradually began to lose their former remoteness and were brought more firmly within the British orbit. Two basic questions dominated the formulation of policy towards them during the 1920s and 1930s: whether direct interference in local affairs, a deviation from the accepted procedure, was advisable, and whether the stationing of a British agent on the Coast was necessary.

Generally speaking, it was the successive Political Residents in the Gulf who advocated a policy of greater involvement, in order both to seal the Trucial Coast off from Ibn Sa'ud, and to ensure the peaceful establishment of the air-route. But, despite much discus-

sion, neither London nor Delhi was eager to take on new commitments that could only entangle them in the region's internal disputes.[7]
This viewpoint was expressed with great cynicism in 1924, when,
with a war about to break out between Ajman and Sharjah, the
Resident warned the Political Agent at Bahrain,

> we do not want to become involved in their internal quarrels.
> In fact it is probably fortunate that behind these ports there
> lies a convenient hinterland, where they can work off their superflu-
> ous energies in the immemorial Arab custom of raid and counter-
> raid without affecting us.[8]

The maintenance of the *status quo* on the Arab side of the Gulf
was the only officially accepted policy. This was confirmed in 1928,
when there was a possibility of declaring protectorates in the Arab
states from Muscat to Kuwait in order to strengthen the British
position in light of the changed relations between Britain and Iran.
This was not the first time that the establishment of formal protectorates had been considered. The subject had been debated in 1902,
but it had then been decided not to alter the existing situation.
The conclusions reached in 1928 were similar. In the case of Muscat,
a protectorate was regarded as unnecessary: 'Happily our actual
hold on Muskat is well nigh complete.'[9] The possibility of making
Bahrain a protectorate was considered, since a permanent foothold
was needed on the Arab side of the Gulf;[10] but it was felt that,
if Bahrain were to become a protectorate, Kuwait should become
one as well.[11] As for the shaykhdoms on the Trucial Coast, the
arguments in favour of making them protectorates were based on
a 'humanitarian impulse to put down savagery' and the desire
to present 'a definite hands-off to Bin Saud';[12] the arguments
against were the tremendous problems that would be raised by
the need to provide for the shaykhdoms' defence and administration,
and the possibility that certain commitments might extend to Ibn
Sa'ud. The overall conclusion of the debate was that, although
it was of great importance for Britain to retain its special position
in the Gulf region, the *status quo* was sufficient to protect British
interests there.[13]

The question of establishing protectorates was not brought up
again, but a number of Residents suggested the appointment of
a full-time Political Agent on the Trucial Coast. The suggestion
was prompted by the knowledge that there was 'a complete absence
of real political touch' with the Coast, since the Resident visited
it only once, or at most twice, a year, and all political duties
had to be carried out by the Residency Agent.[14] But, once again,

neither London nor Delhi considered the appointment necessary, and the matter was left in abeyance.

It was not until 1930 that the decision to include the Trucial Coast in the air-route to India was reached. The rulers' reluctance to grant the required facilities then became a reality that had to be dealt with immediately, and all the previous discussions of policy seemed academic by contrast. Ways and means to enforce British priorities began to be evolved to suit the problems as they arose; and the granting to Britain of oil concessions for which it had been pressing intensified the process. Although non-interference in internal affairs, as stated by Curzon in his Sharjah address of 1903, remained the official policy, the fact belied the theory.

It is difficult to give a precise definition of the form that the modified policy took in the 1930s: each case was dealt with separately, always accompanied by claims of 'non-interference'. The situation was best described by Hugh Weightman, the Political Agent in Bahrain in 1939, who voiced his unease at this discrepancy:

> let us be strictly fair and remember, as the Coast remembers, how often we have had to resort to 'power politics', how often a deal has been clinched or an argument ended by the appearance of a warship, or a threat, expressed or implied, at direct action. At intervals over the century the ships have fired their guns. . . .[15]

This is probably the most realistic of the contemporary definitions of policy. Despite the fact that any assertions of British interference in the Coast's affairs were being shrugged off, Weightman realised that such interference existed and to a considerable extent. Little had changed from the prewar days:

> The forms of control were as varied as the challenges. As a general policy Britain disdained direct protectorates or control of internal affairs of the littoral states; as an equally general exception to that policy, the same internal affairs received close British attention whenever deemed necessary.[16]

REORGANISATION OF ADMINISTRATION

The active reorganisation by Britain of the administration of its interests in the Middle East was the natural outcome of post-war events, and had a direct bearing on the Arab shaykhdoms in the Gulf. The question of political control in the Gulf now came under close scrutiny; it had, in fact, been sporadically discussed before 1914, but had been left in abeyance until 1921, when definite conclusions were reached. The pre-war situation in the Gulf can be traced back to 1763, when the Residency at Bushire was first established. Primary responsibility for political control in the Gulf passed from the East India Company to the Government of Bombay and later to the Government of India. From 1824, the control was concentrated in the hands of a political officer known as the Political Resident; from 1878, the Political Resident also became the Consul-General for Fars, Khuzistan, Luristan, and for the coasts and islands of the Gulf within the dominions of Persia. The Political Resident, therefore, had dual responsibilities: to the Government of India as Political Resident, and to the Foreign Office, through the jurisdiction of the British Minister to Persia, as Consul-General. Naturally enough, the cost of the Residency at Bushire was divided between Britain and India. Subordinate to the Political Resident were the Political Agents (officers of the Indian Political Service) in Muscat,[17] Bahrain[18] and Kuwait,[19] the Political Agent in Muscat also being British Consul there. At Sharjah was stationed the Residency Agent for the Trucial Coast, an Arab who came under the direct supervision of the Political Resident.

Until 1921, the Political Resident as such was responsible to the Government of India only. In 1920, however, the British Cabinet discussed changing this, as part of the general post-war reorganisation of the administration of British interests in the Middle East; the mandates in Iraq and Palestine, the 1915 treaty with Ibn Sa'ud, the relationship with the Sharifian dynasty of the Hijaz all needed urgent departmental regulation. The Masterton-Smith (Sir John Masterton-Smith, Under-Secretary, Ministry of Labour) Committee[20] was set up, and recommended the creation within the Colonial Office of a Middle East Department with responsibility for all Middle Eastern Arab areas, with special provisions for the Hijaz. With reference to the Gulf, the Committee recommended that the control of policy be transferred to London and exercised through the Middle East Department, but that the Government of India should continue to administer British interests in the Gulf, seeking the permission of the Colonial Office for any measures of political significance. It was further suggested that the Political Resident remain the channel of control in all cases, and that, as before, he should be recruited from the service of the Government of India.

Although the Government of India did not formally assent to the Committee's recommendations, of which the India Office never approved, the Cabinet accepted them in February 1921.[21] Thus the Colonial Office took control of policy in the Gulf, with the Government of India remaining responsible for everyday administration. Although the arrangements reached did not specifically refer

to the Trucial Coast, it was generally accepted that they would
follow the same lines as those for Bahrain: that the India Office
would instruct policy, and would act together with the Colonial
Office on matters involving relations with Ibn Sa'ud.

But the *raison d'être* of the Middle East Department was diminished
by the steadily rising power of Ibn Sa'ud, and, in Iraq, the increasing
demands for complete independence. In 1928, a closer examination
of the machinery of control in the Gulf was decided on by the
Committee of Imperial Defence (CID),[22] following a proposal by
the Government of India, agreed by the India Office, that it have
restored to it the degree of control removed in 1921. In March
1929, the Persian Gulf Sub-Committee of the Committee of Imperial
Defence set up an *ad hoc* sub-committee under the chairmanship
of Sir Warren Fisher, Secretary to the Treasury, 'To make recommendations as to the methods by which the existing machinery for
political control in Arabia can be simplified and speeded up.'[23]
The report, which was delivered in December, recommended the
setting up of two standing co-ordinating sub-committees of the CID—
one ministerial, the other official—to deal with Middle Eastern
questions concerning two or more Departments. It was recommended
that the Ministerial Sub-Committee should include the Secretaries
of State of the Foreign Office, the Colonial Office, the India Office,
the War Office, the Air Ministry and the Admiralty, and that
the Official Sub-Committee should include representatives from the
same Departments and have a chairman nominated by the Colonial
Office. When the Official Sub-Committee could not reach a decision,
the Ministerial Sub-Committee should be convened; the latter should
also meet if a Minister were unable to approve a recommendation
of the Official Sub-Committee.

Since the most important new development at this time, in terms
of strategic interests, was the development of the air-route to India
via the Gulf, the Warren Fisher Committee strongly recommended
that the authorities be given the greatest possible latitude concerning
the establishment and maintenance of the route. It was stated
that the Air Ministry should be brought into policy-making decisions,
and that the Air Officer Commanding in Iraq and the Political
Resident in Bushire should co-operate closely. Furthermore, the
Committee recommended that, in view of the worsening of Britain's
relations with Iran, the Political Resident should move from Bushire
to the Arab side of the Gulf, which henceforth would necessarily
be the centre of British influence in the area.[24] The actual position
of the Political Resident was recognised as being of great importance,
and it was recommended that the post should carry greater prestige
and better remuneration, and that the British Government should
have a say in the appointment.[25]

The Warren Fisher Report, which was approved by the Cabinet, did a great deal to clarify questions of administrative policy. The establishment of the co-ordinating committees, obviously necessary because of the wider range that Gulf affairs had assumed within the new Near Eastern political framework, broadened the scope of control. Important changes occurred shortly after that brought with them further administrative reorganisation: under the 1927 Treaty of Jeddah, Ibn Sa'ud was acknowledged as an independent ruler who thus had to deal directly with the Foreign Office rather than with the Colonial Office; and in 1932 Iraq became independent. After that the Colonial Office no longer had a major role to play in Near Eastern affairs, and, a few weeks after Iraq's admission to the League of Nations, it recommended that its role in this area be handed over to the Foreign Office. The India Office protested, and the matter was put before the Cabinet.

The case of the Foreign Office was based on the fear that, with the increase in the number of Indians in the Government of India, the Gulf would become Indianised, and on the belief that many of Britain's concerns in the Gulf—Iranian claims to sovereignty, relations with Saudi Arabia, oil, and the air-route to India—were also naturally Foreign Office concerns. The India Office, on the other hand, insisted that there was no question of one Department controlling the area, especially in view of the interdepartmental committees that had been set up; but argued that continuity of policy (the Political Resident had often been hard pressed to differentiate between internal and external matters) and the fact that it had executed most of the work allocated to the Colonial Office, made it the latter's logical successor.

In July 1933 the Cabinet decided in favour of the India Office, which, after 1 August 1933, assumed the functions previously performed by the Colonial Office.[26] The main advantage of the new situation was that it saved the Political Resident from making arbitrary decisions on the distinction between internal matters and affairs of political importance.

TREATIES WITH ARAB RULERS

In the quarter-century before the outbreak of the First World War, Britain, in accordance with its policy of maintaining its supremacy in the Gulf, had concluded a number of treaties with the rulers of the shaykhdoms. In 1892, as a result of the fear that Ottoman influence might be extended from Hasa, exclusive agreements with the rulers of the five Trucial states[27] and Bahrain[28] were signed. In them, the rulers undertook not to enter into any agreement or correspondence with other countries except through the British Government, and not to permit the residence of any foreign agent except with British consent; they also undertook not to cede, sell or mortgage any part of their respective territories except to the British Government. These agreements had the effect of limiting the authority of the rulers in any of their internal affairs that might impinge on foreign relations. In 1899, following fears of an Ottoman advance, coupled with rumours of a Russian claim to an outlet for a Mediterranean-to-Kuwait railway,[29] an agreement was signed with Kuwait.[30] In it, the ruler, Mubarak bin Sabah Al-Sabah, undertook not to permit entry to the representatives of any foreign powers and not to cede, sell, lease, mortgage or give for occupation any part of his land to a foreign power without the previous sanction of the British Government. In 1900 he agreed to suppress the arms trade,[31] and in 1904 to accept the establishment of a British post office in Kuwait.[32] In 1914, Kuwait was recognised as 'an independent Government under British protection'.[33]

Thus, by the outbreak of the war, Kuwait, Bahrain and the Trucial States were all firmly within the British sphere of influence. The only shaykhdom on the Arab coast that was not was Qatar, which had come under Ottoman domination in 1872 with the occupation of Hasa. The Ottoman position was constantly regarded as a threat to British interests in the Gulf, especially as Muhammad bin Thani of Qatar had signed an agreement with Britain in 1868 in which he had undertaken not to commit any breach of the maritime truce. Early in the twentieth century, the British authorities discussed the possibility of concluding a regular treaty with Qatar, but it was not until November 1916 that it was signed. Shaykh 'Abdallah bin Qasim Al-Thani then undertook to guard Qatar against slavery, piracy, the arms trade and concessions to foreigners, in return for which Britain assured him of protection against all aggression by sea, of Britain's 'good offices' in case of an attack by land.[34] Apart from this latter undertaking, which was unique to Qatar, the agreement was worded much the same as the agreements with the Trucial shaykhdoms.

Other agreements included those of 1902 with the Trucial shaykhdoms, whereby their rulers undertook to prohibit the import and export of arms;[35] and those of 1911 with the Trucial States, Bahrain and Kuwait, whereby their rulers promised not to grant pearling or sponging concessions without the prior consent of the British Government.[36] The most important new agreements, however, and those that were radically to affect policy during the inter-war period, were those that promised that no concessions for oil would be granted except to a person appointed by the British Government.

Kuwait signed in 1913,[37] Bahrain in 1914[38] and the shaykhdoms of the Trucial Coast in 1922.[39]

THE OFFICERS OF GOVERNMENT: TITLE AND FUNCTION

The Political Resident in Bushire

Curzon referred to the Political Resident as the uncrowned king of the Gulf. Certainly by 1900 the position had become one of paramount importance and influence, and during Percy Cox's tenure (from 1904 to 1920) it gained much in power, dignity and authority.[40] Much of this was owing to Cox himself, who gradually broke down the suspicion with which the Resident had been regarded, especially on the Trucial Coast; and he enjoyed great personal popularity among the rulers and their people. His successors did not, however, maintain the direct influence that he had cultivated, and the Residency became increasingly remote to the Coast and its inhabitants, particularly after World War I. This became so acute that in 1929 a Resident who had just made a tour of the Coast was startled to realise that not one of Cox's successors was known by name there.[41]

Strictly speaking, the decline can be seen to have set in during the latter part of Cox's tenure, and to have stemmed directly from the *Hyacinth* incident of 1910, which did much to destroy the position he had built, ruining the personal touch of the Resident and alienating the position at the same time. The following years did little to improve the situation. At the outbreak of the war, the Resident became preoccupied with other matters and increasingly lost touch with the Coast. After 1918, his despatch vessel was withdrawn and his visits to the Coast became infrequent, usually numbering only one or two a year, and lacking in the dignity that had attended previous visits. The Resident was reduced to travelling on a steamer of the British India Steam Navigation Company, which did little to enhance his prestige.[42] The situation was improved from 1930, when a yacht, the *Patrick Stewart*, was placed at the disposal of the Resident for a large part of the year;[43] this greatly eased the problems of mobility, which were eased still further by the introduction of air travel.

But other problems existed. There were no direct telegraphic communications between Bushire and the Trucial Coast; urgent messages had to be sent to Henjam on the Persian coast and then forwarded by means of special sailing arrangements. Other correspondence was carried by the mail steamer, which until 1932 called only at Dubai, and then only once a fortnight. However, the strongest reason for the deterioration in the standing of the Resident was undoubtedly the shortness of tenure of many incumbents of the office. From 1920 to 1932 there were no fewer than seven Residents, whose respective roles were hampered by the fact that the retiring age in the Political Department was fifty-five; given the seniority of the post,[44] many Residents were not far from retirement when they arrived in Bushire. They had little or no time to familiarise themselves with the political situation, especially on the Trucial Coast; even less to formulate a feasible policy of their own.

The situation changed in July 1932, when Lieutenant-Colonel T. C. W. Fowle was appointed to Bushire. He was already familiar with the Gulf, having served as Secretary to the Resident in 1929, and as Political Agent at Muscat from 1930 to 1932, during which time he had officiated as Political Resident. Since he remained in office until September 1939, his tenure, in marked contrast to that of many of his predecessors, was long enough for him to gain great personal knowledge of the area. This and his experience made him eminently well suited to the office, and he soon came to be seen as a dominating figure of British authority.

The Residency Agent in Sharjah

The Residency Agent was an Arab based in Sharjah who moved up and down the Coast as required. He was directly responsible to the Resident in Bushire, and, as Britain's only representative on the Trucial Coast, wielded considerable power and authority. The role played by 'Isa bin 'Abd al-Latif, Residency Agent from 1919 to 1935, is an outstanding example of this, and was central to the political structure of the area. No British officer replaced him, despite occasional inquiries into the advantage of extending British representation.

Many arguments were put forward in favour of a new appointment, but the outcome was a decision to maintain the *status quo*. Changes were acceded to slowly and with reluctance, and it took a long time before Dubai was accepted as a better headquarters than Sharjah. The suggestion of appointing a British officer as agent was first made in 1908. With the transfer to Dubai of the trade formerly conducted at Lingah, the Board of Trade suggested to the Foreign Office that a British representative be stationed at Dubai to protect and advance British interests.[45] Cox, who was Political Resident at the time, did not feel that the time was ripe to establish a British officer on the Trucial Coast.

The Sheikhs require cautious handling, and there is some fear that the permanent presence of a British office might have the effect of provoking issues in connection with the status of the Sheikhs and the pearling industry which are quiescent at present . . . .[46]

He agreed that Dubai was a rising trade centre and should ultimately replace Sharjah as the headquarters of the Residency Agent, but suggested that a British officer should be appointed to Lingah instead: it was close to Dubai, and the two towns could be connected by wireless. The first of these suggestions was put into effect in 1910 with the establishment of a vice-consulate at Lingah. But the *Hyacinth* incident that same year, and the consequent resistance to any extension of British interests, caused the Government of India to reject the idea of erecting a wireless station at Dubai.

Nineteen years later, the question of British representation on the Coast was raised by F. W. Johnston, the Political Resident; he had been particularly struck by the 'complete absence of real political touch' with the Coast, and was clearly appalled at the inadequacies of the Residency Agent, who was liable to intrigue and bias.[47] He suggested the establishment of a Political Agency at Dubai.

Johnston's successor, C. C. J. Barrett, did not agree completely. While he admitted that the Residency Agent was capable of interference in local affairs, he regarded him a better judge than any Englishman of the intrigues of the Coast, and recommended continued use of his influence. Another reason for Barrett's opposition was the great local hostility to foreigners and the determination to resist any intrusion; the example of Bahrain, regarded as a British possession, was viewed with great alarm on the Coast. The Resident did not feel the time was ripe for any extension of influence, but recommended instead that the Political Agent in Bahrain supervise the work of the Residency Agent.[48]

The next Resident, Hugh Biscoe, was concerned with the remoteness of the Coast, and considered the inefficient means of communication between Bushire and the Agency at Sharjah as central to the problem. He strongly urged the erection of a wireless station, and saw Dubai, undoubtedly the most important of the shaykhdoms, as the best place for this.[49] Nothing came of the idea. Lingeh and Bahrain continued to be the closest towns with telegraphic communications, but an administrative reorganisation occurred in 1932 that brought the Coast under somewhat closer British control.

A few months after he had become Resident, in 1932, T. C. Fowle sought a more practical means of communication with the

Coast. An airfield had been constructed at Sharjah, and, owing to the ease with which the Political Agent in Bahrain could visit the Trucial Coast by air, he placed that area semi-officially under the Agency in Bahrain. Fowle informed the Residency Agent of this in December 1932 and instructed him to report to Bahrain rather than Bushire in the future.[50] Although this did not necessarily limit the power of the Residency Agent, it did mean that Bushire could have a closer knowledge of the events on the Coast; it also proved useful during the period when negotiations for oil concessions were in progress, since the Agent in Bahrain and the Resident in Bushire were between them able to maintain a comprehensive survey of the various developments.

One of the main questions that troubled the Government of India with regard to policy decisions, and thus with regard to increasing the number of officers in the Gulf, was that of expenditure. It was financially responsible for all the Agencies on the Arab side of the Gulf,[51] and in view of the British Government's added interest in the area, wished to share the cost with London. Although this was discussed, no decision was reached, and India continued to pay for the establishments. In 1939, with the outbreak of war in Europe imminent, the Government of India realised the need to create an office to protect British interests on the Coast, and in August sanctioned the appointment, should war follow, of a Political Officer based in the Trucial States and directly responsible to the Resident at Bushire. The first appointment was made in October 1939; after World War II, the Political Officer became Political Agent in Dubai.

The Political Agent in Bahrain

After 1932, the Political Agent in Bahrain became responsible for the Trucial Coast and communicated with the rulers on all matters of importance. Since Qatar too was under his charge (it had been since April 1928), and since he acquired still further commitments as a result of the establishment of the Bahrain Petroleum Company, and the discovery of oil in Bahrain in 1932, his responsibilities were very wide indeed. Fowle therefore urged the Government of India in 1933 to provide the Agent with an assistant, to relieve him of all the routine work of the Agency and so release him to negotiate air agreements with the rulers of the Trucial Coast.[52] The post of Assistant Political Agent had existed from 1900 to 1905, and had been revived for six months in 1924. In March 1934 Delhi said that it would appoint a temporary assistant, to serve for six months; but this was later extended to a year.

The Medical Officer on the Trucial Coast

The appointment of a Medical Officer on the Trucial Coast in 1938 was the direct outcome of a search for means to combat the influence of American missionary doctors at a time when there were fears that American oil interests might try to gain a foothold on the Coast. The appointment had originally been suggested in 1935 by Colonel Loch, Political Agent in Bahrain, who had been startled by the American missionaries' renewed interest in Qatar and the Trucial Coast.

The missionaries were attached to the Arabian Mission, which had been founded in 1889 in the United States. Although the Mission was an independent project, it had ties with the Reformed Church, which later took it under its wing. Much of the work done was medical, and, although the missionaries did not establish any hospital on the Trucial Coast, there was one at Matrah in Muscat and another in Bahrain to which patients from the Coast went.[53] The work of the missionaries was humane and of great value, especially as the British authorities had made no attempt to establish any form of medical service; the only hospitals in the Gulf area were those of the missionaries.[54] Their personal influence was consequently so great that they won respect, if not proselytes, up and down the Arab coast of the Gulf. 'Thus before the oil men came, Americans had won regard in Arab eyes, for there is no doubt that something was added to the repute of the West on these coasts by the devotion of American doctors in Arabia.'[55]

Until the advent of oil, the American missionaries were respected and admired by the British authorities as well, and cordial relations existed. The attitude changed after 1933, when the Standard Oil Company of California (Socal) obtained an oil concession from King Ibn Sa'ud of Saudi Arabia. No longer regarded as apolitical, the missionaries began to be viewed with suspicion by the Resident and his Agents, who feared that the influence of these Americans might be deployed in the subtle intrigues that were widespread in the battle for oil concessions. When, in 1935, Doctor Storm of the American Mission applied for permission to visit Sharjah, Loch at once suspected the motives of the visit. He reported that Storm and Doctor Dame, also of the Mission, had recently spent some time in Qatar; and, although he admitted lack of proof, he connected their presence there with the interest shown in that shaykhdom by Socal, and suggested that they might have tried to persuade the ruler to give his oil rights to that company.

In order to contain any possible American intrigue, Loch argued, a British medical officer would have to be provided for the Coast, and he urged Fowle to petition for it.[56] The Government of India, however, was not willing to bear all the cost of the new appointment. In 1938 Fowle managed to convince the Foreign Office of the importance of dividing the expenses with India, and the appointment was sanctioned. That same year a dispensary was opened in Dubai, and an Indian doctor was placed in charge.[57]

The Political Agent in Muscat

The Political Agent in Muscat, like the Political Resident in Bushire, had two functions: he was Political Agent and British Consul. As Political Agent, he was directly responsible to the Resident in Bushire, and was concerned with Oman, not *de facto* under the jurisdiction of the Sultan, and those areas of the Trucial Coast that were on the Gulf of Oman (i.e. Kalba and Fujairah). His title of British Consul was in deference to the fact that technically Muscat was independent.

The Senior Naval Officer, Persian Gulf Division

In the early years of the twentieth century, Europeans (i.e. mainly the British) were generally distrusted and disliked on the Trucial Coast, and the *Hyacinth* incident of 1910 exacerbated this animosity. In subsequent years, however, there occurred a marked improvement in the attitude towards the British, and this was largely owing to the naval officers who visited the Coast—until the 1930s, when the visits of the Political Resident became more frequent—almost the only Europeans to call there.

The Senior Naval Officer performed the practical duties of a Political Agent until 1932, when the Agent in Bahrain assumed charge of the Coast, and he was well acquainted with the rulers and problems of the area. His effectiveness, however, was limited by the size of the area he had to cover, from Ras al-Hadd in Muscat to Basrah, which made it difficult for him to concentrate his abilities on one particular area. His efficiency was further curtailed by the shortness of his term of office—just two years—which made the acquisition of any extensive knowledge of the language and customs virtually impossible.

The role of the Senior Naval Officer was of great importance, for he represented the instrument of British power that controlled the Gulf, and had to oversee the policing of its waters.[58] He kept in close touch with the Resident and Agents in the Gulf, and was largely responsible for the constant interchange of intelligence that resulted. He also had to co-ordinate policy with the Admiralty, the Government of India and the India Office. One Senior Naval

Officer outlined as follows the complex duties attendant on that office:

> a ceaseless vigil, visiting ports, investigating rumours of gun-running and slave trading ... complaints of British subjects residing on the Arab littoral, keeping the peace amongst the pearl banks, settling disputes between Arab Sheikhs ... and obtaining redress for insults to the British Government or its representatives.[59]

3 The Challenge to Power: Brother, Nephew and Son

One of the most distinctive features of the history of the Trucial shaykhdoms is the frequency with which their rulers have been challenged by ambitious members of their own families in unmasked struggles for power. The result has been that all but one of the shaykhdoms have witnessed devastating internecine quarrels in their ruling families. Much of this turmoil has been owing to the absence of the law of primogeniture, and of any other fixed procedure for the peaceful succession of rulers. The struggle for power has thus been almost a natural adjunct to the death, natural or otherwise, of a ruler, and successors have had to make sure of wresting complete control of the shaykhdom from their relatives before beginning to exercise absolute power. To survive, rulers have had to display a remarkable combination of fearlessness, fairness, honesty, intelligence and generosity, and to make sure that none of their relatives become disaffected in any way. Not to do so has often proved itself fatal. Only in Dubai, where all the rulers in the last century and a half have died a natural death, have more sophisticated methods prevailed.

Although the absence of fixed and peaceful procedures may at first seem to have produced a generally chaotic system of succession, a closer look at the list of the rulers of the Coast during the past 150 years reveals a fairly distinctive pattern, in which some order can be discerned. (See Tables 2–6.)

The pattern is as follows: most of the rulers of Abu Dhabi and Sharjah have been deposed or murdered; in Ajman and Umm al-Qaiwain just a few have; and in Dubai not one ruler has been formally deposed. The pairing of Abu Dhabi and Sharjah, and

Table 2
Rulers of Abu Dhabi

Ruler	Dates of rule	Length of rule (years)	Relationship to predecessor	Termination of rule
Tahnun bin Shakhbut	1818–1833	15		killed
Khalifah bin Shakhbut	1833–1845	12	brother	killed *
Sa'id bin Tahnun	1845–1855	10	nephew	deposed
Zayid bin Khalifah	1855–1909	46	cousin	natural death
Tahnun bin Zayid	1909–1912	3	son	natural death
Hamdan bin Zayid	1912–1922	10	brother	killed
Sultan bin Zayid	1922–1926	4	brother	killed
Saqr bin Zayid	1926–1928	2	brother	killed
Shakhbut bin Sultan	1928–1966	38	nephew	deposed
Zayid bin Sultan	1966–		brother	

* Not killed by his successor

of Ajman and Umm al-Qaiwain is not entirely coincidental; and in this explanations for the pattern can be sought.

In the course of their history Abu Dhabi and Sharjah have had much in common. For a long time they were rivals for the leading position on the Coast, and as such they needed forces to control their extensive territories. During the nineteenth century their rivalry often erupted into violence. Both shaykhdoms accepted force as a way of life: as the only means for ensuring their survival, in face of their enemies; and as the arbiter of the shaykhdom's

Table 3
Rulers of Sharjah

Ruler	Dates of rule	Length of rule (years)	Relationship to predecessor	Termination of rule
Sultan bin Saqr	1803–1866	63		natural death
Khalid bin Sultan	1866–1868	2	son	killed in battle
Salim bin Sultan	1868–1883	15	brother	deposed
Saqr bin Khalid	1883–1914	31	nephew	natural death
Khalid bin Ahmad	1914–1924	10	cousin	deposed
Sultan bin Saqr	1924–1951	27	nephew	natural death
Saqr bin Sultan	1951–1965	14	son	deposed
Khalid bin Muhammad	1965–1971	6	cousin	killed
Sultan bin Muhammad	1971–		brother	

TABLE 4
Rulers of Dubai

Ruler	Dates of rule	Length of rule (years)	Relationship to predecessor	Termination of rule
Maktum bin Butti	1833–1852	19		natural death
Sa'id bin Butti	1852–1859	7	brother	natural death
Hashar bin Maktum	1859–1886	27	nephew	natural death
Rashid bin Maktum	1886–1894	8	brother	natural death
Maktum bin Hashar	1894–1906	12	cousin	natural death
Butti bin Suhayl	1906–1912	6	cousin	natural death
Sa'id bin Maktum	1912–1958	46	cousin	natural death
Rashid bin Sa'id	1958–		son	

internal affairs. After 1835, when the first maritime truce was concluded, armed conflicts could take place only on land. The Bani Yas, as noted already, consequently became stronger than the seafaring Qawasim; and their mastery over the inland tribes, who by tradition were fierce and loyal warriors, formed the basis of their strength.

Furthermore, in both Sharjah and Abu Dhabi, the ruling family was very small: Lorimer estimated in 1908 that the Al-bu-Falah of the Bani Yas had only fifteen houses,[1] and that the Qawasim included no more than eighteen adult males.[2] The existence of such a small, tightly-knit elitist group in each shaykhdom naturally gave rise to competitive power struggles. In Dubai, by contrast, the ruling family, the Al-bu-Falasah branch of the Bani Yas, had 400 houses in Dubai town alone in 1908.[3] This large number obviously acted as a deterrent to the expulsion of the ruler; any

TABLE 5
RULERS OF UMM AL-QAIWAIN

Ruler	Dates of rule	Length of rule (years)	Relationship to predecessor	Termination of rule
'Abdallah bin Rashid	pre-1820–1853	c. 23		natural death
'Ali bin 'Abdallah	1853–c. 1873	c. 20	son	natural death
Ahmad bin 'Abdallah	c. 1873–1904	c. 31	brother	natural death
Rashid bin Ahmad	1904–1922	18	son	natural death
'Abdallah bin Rashid	1922–1923	1	son	killed
Hamad bin Ibrahim	1923–1929	6	cousin	killed
Ahmad bin Rashid	1929–		cousin	

TABLE 6
Rulers of Ajman

Ruler	Dates of rule	Length of rule (years)	Relationship to predecessor	Termination of rule
Rashid bin Humayd	pre-1820– 1838	c. 18		natural death
Humayd bin Rashid	1838–1841	3	son	deposed
'Abd al-'Aziz bin Rashid	1841–1848	7	brother	killed in battle
Humayd bin Rashid	1848–1873	25	brother	natural death
Rashid bin Humayd	1873–1891	18	son	natural death
Humayd bin Rashid	1891–1900	9	son	killed
'Abd al-'Aziz bin Humayd	1900–1910	10	uncle	killed
Humayd bin 'Abd al 'Aziz	1910–1928	18	son	natural death
Rashid bin Humayd	1928–		son	

factionalism within the family group would have had serious consequences in terms of the size of the opposition, which could be
expected to amount to well over 100 people. Factionalism of such
a kind would clearly be disastrous for a commercial community
like that of Dubai.

Ajman and Umm al-Qaiwain also had much in common. Both
were small and relatively unimportant in the power hierarchy of
the Coast. There are no available estimates as to the respective
sizes of their ruling families early in the present century, but it
is clear that both were quite small, as in the case of Sharjah
and Abu Dhabi. Since they were both less important and less
powerful than the latter two shaykhdoms, however, there were
fewer rulers deposed or murdered.

The period of instability following the death of a ruler was
usually greatest where he had held power for a long time. Two
reasons for this seem clear. The first is that, with the passing
of the years, the number of contenders for the leadership—brothers,
nephews, cousins and sons—would naturally increase. Secondly, the
length of his reign would give the ruler time to consolidate his
position and that of the shaykhdom, leaving the rest of the ruling
family more to fight over.

We have already seen how the death of Sultan bin Saqr of
Sharjah, who ruled for over sixty years, brought on great internal
instability. As it was, his rule was punctuated by much turbulence
within the Qasimi family, particularly over the administration of

the different towns in Sharjah. Although Sultan was able to hold
his own, his long reign was followed by a marked weakness in
the position of the ruler. Likewise, the death of Zayid bin Khalifah,
who ruled for forty-six years, brought a series of upheavals in
Abu Dhabi. The case of Umm al-Qaiwain is also comparable.
From 1820 to 1904, it was ruled by only three people, 'Abdallah
bin Rashid and his sons 'Ali bin 'Abdallah and Ahmad bin 'Abdallah,
all of whom succeeded by peaceful means. The unusual stability
of the position of the ruler during the nineteenth century enabled
him to amass a large fortune for himself, a fortune that made
the position even more attractive to his successors.

The struggles for power in the shaykhdoms will be described
here in some detail, in order to emphasise the social, economic
and political implications of the absence of the law of primogeniture.
Although the succession is restricted to members of the ruling family,
others in the shaykhdom, from slaves to tribal leaders, may become
involved in the struggle for power, which in the conditions of
a small society is not unlike civil war, with new and intense hostilities
being created. Because of this, it is essential for the new ruler
to normalise conditions as quickly as possible.

The worst power struggles lasted for several years (in Umm
al-Qaiwain for seven and in Abu Dhabi for sixteen) and had
severe economic consequences. Pearling, fishing, trade and grazing
were interrupted for various lengths of time. The disruption of
economic activity added to the hardships of the people and consequently to the difficulties facing a new ruler. It was probably
at such times that substantial migration occurred, leading to a
redistribution of population (see above, Ch. 1).

Power struggles sometimes produced alliances between neighbour-
ing shaykhs and contenders, leading to serious political complications.
This invariably led to British intervention, through the Political
Resident and the Residency Agent.

The last wave of violence within the ruling families occurred
in the 1920s, after which the growing importance of the Coast
meant that the British kept it under closer scrutiny and tried
to ensure greater political stability in the area. The violence in
question occurred in Abu Dhabi and Umm al-Qaiwain. In both
cases, a cycle of killings culminated in the rise to power of two
men, Shakhbut bin Sultan of Abu Dhabi and Ahmad bin Rashid
of Umm al-Qaiwain, who were strong enough to bring the bloodshed
to a decisive end; the best proof of this lies in the fact that
Shakhbut ruled Abu Dhabi until 1966 and that Ahmad remains
ruler of Umm al-Qaiwain today. The main difference between
the two cases is that Abu Dhabi is much larger and more important
than Umm al-Qaiwain; the repercussions of its instability were

more far-reaching, and, as in the case of Umm al-Qaiwain, were not confined to the capital.

In August 1922, Rashid bin Ahmad, who had ruled Umm al-Qaiwain since 1904, died peacefully of pneumonia. After his death, the shaykhdom was contested and fought over for seven years. (See Table 5 and Figure 1.) When Rashid died, his closest male relatives did not happen to be in Umm al-Qaiwain town, and only his mother and slaves were with him. Consequently, the slaves took matters into their own hands and occupied the house of the ruler, at the same time sending word to Rashid's son 'Abdallah, who was at Falaj-al-'Ali, to come home. When 'Abdallah returned, he quickly took possession of the ruler's house and the shaykhdom. Afraid of the possibility that his uncles, Rashid's brothers Ibrahim

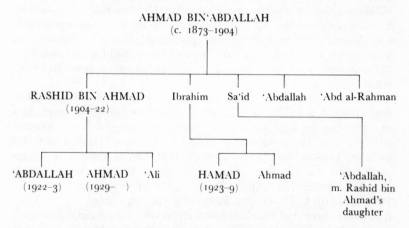

FIGURE 1   Umm al-Qaiwain, ruling family: members involved in dynastic struggles following the death of Ahmad bin Rashid

and Sa'id, would try to wrest control from him, 'Abdallah bin Rashid sent for Muhammad bin 'Ali bin Huwayydin, the headman of the Bani Qitab tribe,[4] who were traditionally loyal to the Al-'Ali. Muhammad bin 'Ali himself arrived, bringing with him 100 men to guard the forts of Umm al-Qaiwain. The presence of the Bani Qitab removed any opposition to 'Abdallah bin Rashid that might have existed in Umm al-Qaiwain, and acted as a temporary restraint on his uncles; Ibrahim bin Ahmad decided to remain at Falaj-al-'Ali, where he had been when his brother died, and Sa'id bin Ahmad went to Ras al-Khaimah. Another possible claimant to 'Abdallah's position, 'Abdallah bin Sa'id, who was married to Rashid bin Ahmad's daughter, discovered that by remaining at Umm al-Qaiwain his wings were clipped: he was disarmed and placed under house arrest.[5] Although the people of Umm al-Qaiwain had shown no signs of disloyalty, 'Abdallah bin Rashid could never trust his uncles; he refused, for example, to allow Sa'id bin Ahmad to return home, despite many assurances of goodwill and friendship. Exasperated, Sa'id complained to the Residency Agent, 'Isa bin 'Abd al-Latif, who went to Umm al-Qaiwain early in October 1922 in order to mediate between the ruler and his uncles.

He found that 'Abdallah was far from being convinced of the need for mediation, and at first ignored his pleas for reconciliation; later, he promised 'Isa that he would reconsider the matter and then transmit his decision to the Agency in Sharjah. During the time he spent in Umm al-Qaiwain, the Residency Agent discovered that the young ruler (about twenty years old) had managed to alienate most of his family, including his paternal grandmother and his cousins, the sons of Ibrahim bin Ahmad; and that Sa'id bin Ahmad had given up hope and had moved to Ajman. 'Isa also heard that many people from Umm al-Qaiwain who were disenchanted with the ruler were making secret visits to Sa'id bin Ahmad in Ajman.[6]

Sa'id was not silent about his predicament, and complained to the Political Resident about his nephew, blaming, in particular, the Bani Qitab bedouin for the continued animosity to which he and his relatives were being exposed at home. He warned that his son and nephews, the sons of Ibrahim, were still at Umm al-Qaiwain and loyal to him, and added that he was sure the Resident would not object if they all united against 'Abdallah.[7] In March 1923 Trevor, the Political Resident, visited Ras al-Khaimah, and there met Sa'id. He was impressed with Sa'id's grievances against 'Abdallah, especially when he discovered that the ruler had dispossessed Sa'id. Anxious to avert an outbreak of violence within the ruling family, Trevor wrote to 'Abdallah advising him to make peace with the dissident members of his family. He gave the letter to the Residency Agent to deliver, and instructed him to try to establish peace so that 'Abdallah could be recognised by the British Government.[8]

'Isa went to Umm al-Qaiwain late in September and found 'Abdallah firmly established as ruler. He proceeded to give him all the requisite papers regarding treaty relations with Britain, and 'Abdallah gave him written acknowledgement and promised to abide by the treaties.[9] 'Isa then pleaded with the ruler to go with his uncle to Dubai to settle the outstanding inheritance claims with the rest of his family and so avoid bloodshed. But 'Abdallah refused, and before long his cousin Hamad bin Ibrahim devised a successful plot to remove him from power: a slave who lived in Hamad's

house murdered 'Abdallah in October 1923. Hamad then skilfully
out-manoeuvred 'Abdallah's younger brother, Ahmad, and his guards
by occupying the government house immediately after 'Abdallah
had been buried. But the hatred within the Al-'Ali was not yet
at an end. Hamad now had to defend himself against the enmity
of Ahmad bin Rashid and his brothers, and also his own uncles,
who had previously acted against 'Abdallah. Hamad's father advised
him to leave Umm al-Qaiwain to avoid being killed, but this
he refused.[10] In a short time he succeeded in making peace with
his cousin Ahmad bin Rashid, after which the people of Umm
al-Qaiwain accepted him as ruler.[11] When the Political Resident
visited Umm al-Qaiwain in March 1924, he noted that Hamad
was still friendly with the various members of his family, and
he observed of him, 'He is not a very imposing or prepossessing
person, but the Agent reports he is doing well. . . .'[12]

The goodwill within the ruling family did not last, however,
for on 9 February 1929 Hamad was shot and killed by a slave
at the instigation of his blind uncle 'Abd al-Rahman bin Ahmad,
who lived in the same house. 'Abd al-Rahman had plotted the
murder with Ahmad bin Rashid and certain notables of Umm
al-Qaiwain, and, according to the Residency Agent, had also solicited
the secret collaboration of Shaykh Sultan bin Saqr of Sharjah.[13]
'Isa substantiated the latter claim by reporting that when Sultan
had heard of the death of Hamad he had sailed to Umm al-Qaiwain—
ostensibly to offer his condolences, but really to congratulate Ahmad
bin Rashid on his succession, and to urge him to expel the former
ruler of Sharjah, Khalid bin Ahmad, who was living there.[14]

The day after Hamad's death, the fort of Umm al-Qaiwain
was attacked by the people of the town, who set fire to it; during
the ensuing chaos both 'Abd al-Rahman bin Ahmad and the slave
who had murdered Hamad were killed. Johnston, the Political
Resident, was inclined to accept the Residency Agent's theory that
the death of these two men had not been accidental and that
the fire was a convenient way of burying all evidence of the plot
that had brought Ahmad to power. The Resident was also deeply
suspicious of the role played in the affair by Sultan bin Saqr
of Sharjah, and was afraid that he would begin to exercise some
form of control over the young ruler.[15] Ahmad, however, managed
to keep his alienated family at bay and then gradually made his
peace with them; he also showed little sign of being influenced
by Sharjah. A while later, he was duly recognised by the British
Government, and he has kept his position till the present day.[16]
When he first assumed power, he did not seem to impress the
British authorities who met him. In 1929 Johnston said of him,
'The new Shaikh is a heavy irresolute looking individual . . .',[17]

and in 1935 the Senior Naval Officer remarked, 'Gross in person
and apparently lacking in intelligence, the Shaikh has certainly
the least attractive personality on the Coast . . . .'[18] Despite these
unflattering remarks, Ahmad managed to maintain a secure and
peaceful hold on his shaykhdom.

Ahmad remained a strong and able ruler, always enjoying the
popularity of his people. He consulted a *majlis* before making any
major decisions, especially when they concerned foreign affairs; the
leading members of the *majlis* were his brothers-in-law 'Abdallah
bin Sa'id and 'Abdallah bin Nasir, his brother 'Ali bin Rashid,
and Ahmad bin Ibrahim, brother of his predecessor. He was extremely
wealthy, and as such showed himself primarily concerned with

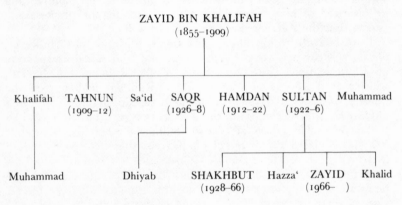

FIGURE 2   Abu Dhabi, ruling family: members involved in dynastic
struggles following the death of Zayid bin Khalifah

his investments in the pearl trade; but he was also by nature
a nervous man, and rarely ventured outside the shelter of his
fort. 'The history of his family is sufficient to make a bolder
man than he nervous.'[19]

The same statement may be applied to the rulers of Abu Dhabi
in the 1920s. Within a period of sixteen years, four rulers came
to power as a result of murder. (See Table 2 and Figure 2.)
The death of Zayid bin Khalifah was the starting point. The
old ruler had seven sons, the eldest of whom, Khalifah, did not
wish to succeed, being content with the role of kingmaker; so
Tahnun, the second son, ruled for three years until he died peacefully.
The next ruler, Hamdan, Zayid's fifth son, was the first in a
number whose tenure of power was put to an end violently by
a rival member of the family. The apparent reason for his murder
by his brother Sultan in August 1922 was his oppressiveness; he

was responsible for obstructing trade and had discontinued the subsidies usually paid to the members of the ruling family.[20] His brothers were divided in their attitude towards the murder: Saqr, the fourth of Zayid's sons, approved, but Khalifah and Muhammad, the youngest, disagreed and became estranged. As a result of this dissension, the town of Abu Dhabi became restless and disorderly, but Sultan was quick to realise the danger of the situation and was successful in re-establishing a friendly relationship with his brothers; he then took positive steps to restore normal life in Abu Dhabi and encouraged the resumption of the pearl trade, which had been temporarily disrupted. As a final confirmation of his stability, he emulated his predecessor by sending his son Hazza' to Riyadh to tell Ibn Sa'ud of his succession.[21]

But the same grievances as he had brought against his predecessor were levelled against him four years later. His discontinuation of the allowances paid to his brothers and sisters left them in straitened circumstances, and in their anger they decided to depose him. On 12 July 1926, Sultan sent his family, including his sons Shakhbut and Hazza', to the Buraimi oasis. On the evening of 4 August, when at Sultan's invitation his brother Saqr was present for dinner, Saqr fired on the ruler, killing him instantly. Khalid, another son of Sultan, was at the scene; although he fled, he was caught and wounded, but he managed to reach his maternal uncles, who were of the Qubaysat. Saqr then proclaimed himself ruler and was accepted by the people of Abu Dhabi.

During his short reign of just over a year, Saqr was haunted by the possibility of vengeance by his nephews Shakhbut and Hazza'. Immediately after his accession, he sent his son Dhiyab to Buraimi with a forged letter, purportedly written by Sultan, asking Shakhbut and Hazza' to return home on urgent business; in actual fact, Dhiyab was instructed to have the boys killed as soon as they were clear of Buraimi. Shakhbut and Hazza', however, had already learned of the death of their father, and they took refuge in the town of Jimi with the powerful shaykh of the Dawahir, Ahmad bin Hilal.[22] The Dawahir, a tribe with headquarters in Buraimi, had become loyal to the ruler of Abu Dhabi during the days of Zayid bin Khalifah, and Ahmad bin Hilal was at the time Abu Dhabi's *wali* (governor) in the oasis. He was a much-respected man who often acted as arbitrator in disputes, his decisions almost always being accepted as final.

Saqr at first tried to win the boys back to Abu Dhabi, sending them gifts and promises of friendship and safety. They were aware of their uncle's motives and left Buraimi on a series of journeys in quest of safety. Early in November 1922 they went to Dubai; unable to see the ruler, who was away at the time, they proceeded to Sharjah.[23] There they prepared to go by way of Qatar to Dalma, an island off the coast of Abu Dhabi that was inhabited largely by the Qubaysat, whose headman, Humayd bin Butti, was their maternal uncle. The ruler of Qatar, Shaykh 'Abdallah bin Qasim Al-Thani, wrote to Saqr bin Zayid, promising no help to the fugitives,[24] but Lionel Haworth, the Political Resident, reported later that 'there is little doubt that they [Shakhbut and Hazza'] also had the moral support of the Shaikh of Qatar from whose territories they sailed'.[25]

The two boys went first to Hasa to ask the governor, 'Abdallah ibn Jaluwi, to intercede with Saqr to allow them to stay in Dalma. The governor wrote to Saqr, who, afraid of showing any signs of defiance, gave his permission.[26] Reassured, the sons of Sultan proceeded to Wakrah in Qatar, where they were joined by armed men of the Qubaysat and sailed for Dalma. On learning that his nephews had reached the island, Saqr prepared a fleet to pursue them[27] and put his son Dhiyab in command. The force made for Sir Bani Yas, an island twenty miles away, in order to gain access to Dalma; but the night before Dhiyab reached Sir Bani Yas, Shakhbut and Hazza', on the advice of the residents of the island,[28] who were not prepared to become involved in the family feud, went back to Qatar. At a loss to do any more, they then travelled on to Riyadh, to meet with Ibn Sa'ud.[29]

In the meantime, Saqr was facing dissension from his family at home, and tried to keep control by means of murder. His animosity was directed principally at his brothers Khalifah and Muhammad, who had the support of the Al-bu-Sha'r section of the Manasir, who had wanted Khalifah to be ruler.[30] When Khalifah realised the extent of Saqr's enmity, he skilfully manoeuvred his demise. Since he had no intention of gaining the shaykhdom for himself, he sent word to his exiled nephews to go to Sharjah and to send him a Baluchi slave. When the slave arrived, Khalifah hid him in his house, and invited a number of men of the Al-bu-Sha'r to be his guests. On 1 January 1928, the Baluchi, supported by the Manasir, attacked and killed Saqr.

When Shakhbut and Hazza' arrived in Abu Dhabi shortly after, Khalifah handed the ruler's fort over to them[31] and then ordered Saqr's sons out of Abu Dhabi. They first went to Dubai, where they remained until August. After that, they sailed to Bahrain, where on arrival they sent word to 'Abdallah al-Qusaybi, the Wahhabi agent there, who sent a motor-launch to disembark them and take them to 'Uqayr.[32] After a visit to Hasa to see Ibn Jaluwi, they gave up hope of regaining Abu Dhabi, and, once Shakhbut had been recognised as ruler there, settled in Dubai.

The violence within the ruling family was at an end. Shakhbut remained in charge of Abu Dhabi for almost forty years, contrary to the expectations of the Political Resident at the time, who, because of the adverse conditions that marked the beginning of Shakhbut's reign, expected it to be short. The opposition of the sons of Saqr, the dangers posed by the 'stronger and more brutal character' of Hazza', and the displeasure of the Bani Yas, who resented the role played by the Manasir in the last stage of the struggle for power all seemed to bode ill for Shakhbut. But he was able to eliminate all of these dangers. Almost immediately after he became ruler, his mother, Shaykhah Salamah bint Butti, made her sons swear never to resort to fratricide; this enabled Shakhbut to attain a degree of internal security in Abu Dhabi that his father and uncles had never known. When, for example, his exiled cousins in Dubai tried to wrest control of the shaykhdom from him in 1930, he was in a sufficiently strong position to foil their plans without endangering his hold on Abu Dhabi in any way.[34] Likewise, his authority began to extend itself to the tribes whose loyalty to Zayid bin Khalifah had been unquestioned, and before long the Bani Yas found little to complain about.

The resurgence of the Bani Yas following the accession of Shakhbut in Abu Dhabi was in strong contrast to the continued decline of the Qawasim in Sharjah. After Saqr bin Khalid had deposed his uncle Salim bin Sultan, in 1883, he governed the shaykhdom weakly, and by the time of his death, in 1914, the prestige of the Qawasim had reached a very low ebb indeed. Just before his death, he had named his first cousin Khalid bin Ahmad (the fathers of Saqr and Khalid had been brothers—see Figure 3) as his successor, since all of his own sons were infants. Khalid, who ruled for ten years, was unpopular with the people of Sharjah, and did little to strengthen the shaykhdom internally, though in later years he was to show considerably more skill when, as regent of Kalba, he extended his authority over a large segment of Qasimi territory. The period from 1914 to 1924, however, was marked by a number of challenges, internal and external, that he was clearly unable to withstand, and his failure in this weakened not only his personal prestige but that of Sharjah as well. The most striking of these challenges was that posed by British recognition (granted in 1921) of Ras al-Khaimah as an independent shaykhdom, although it had enjoyed *de facto* independence for some years; Khalid's failure to protest at British recognition of the secession strongly underlined his weakness. His impotence regarding Ras al-Khaimah was in large part owing to mismanagement by his predecessors, but in the course of his own reign he had done little to put matters right.

At the time when the British recognised the secession, however,

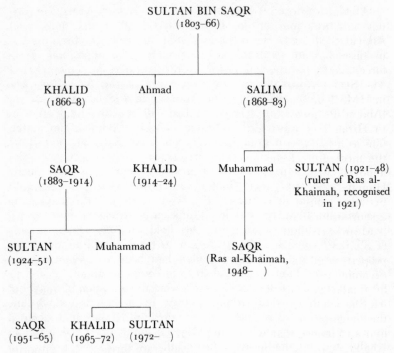

FIGURE 3   Sharjah and Ras al-Khaimah, ruling family

Khalid was confronted by a much more direct threat to his authority, one that caused him considerable anxiety and finally helped to bring about his downfall: the rise to prominence of 'Abd al-Rahman bin Muhammad of the Al-bu-Shamis, headman of Hirah, a fishing village in Sharjah close to Ajman. The Al-bu-Shamis had originally been a section of the Na'im tribe, but by the beginning of the twentieth century they had acquired a separate identity. In mid June 1920, 'Abd al-Rahman bin Muhammad laid claim to the shaykhdom of Ajman, which was ruled by Humayd bin 'Abd al-'Aziz of the Na'im tribe, and seized the fort of Ajman.[35] Humayd did not have a force strong enough to dislodge 'Abd al-Rahman, and appealed to the Residency Agent for help. 'Isa bin 'Abd al-Latif mediated between the two parties and succeeded in persuading 'Abd al-Rahman to leave Ajman, promising him that his home and property in Hirah would not be seized. Like most townsmen in the area, 'Abd al-Rahman made his living from the pearl trade, but that year his debts to the Indian merchants had reached the overwhelming figure of 20,000 rupees. In an attempt to obtain money, he went from Ajman to Dubai and Bahrain, but eventually returned to Hirah as headman of the village.

'Abd al-Rahman's presence in Hirah was regarded as a threat not only by Humayd bin 'Abd al-'Aziz but also by Khalid bin Ahmad, who could not tolerate such a potentially dangerous man in his shaykhdom. Together the two rulers prepared an armed force, and in January 1921 they attacked 'Abd al-Rahman in Hirah. The Senior Naval Officer, Captain Pearson, was cruising close by in HMS *Triad*, so he intervened and arranged a settlement between 'Abd al-Rahman and Khalid whereby the former would go back to Hirah and cause no more trouble and Khalid would protect him as his subject.[36] Humayd of Ajman, however, refused to accept the mediation of the Senior Naval Officer,[37] and was particularly annoyed with Khalid bin Ahmad for having done so. Despite Humayd's attitude, the agreement was implemented and trouble between Khalid and 'Abd al-Rahman was averted, but only for a short while.

Meanwhile, Sultan bin Saqr, eldest son of the previous ruler of Sharjah, had been petitioning for restitution of the money and property rightfully belonging to him that Khalid had seized on becoming ruler. His petitions to Khalid were in vain, and in 1921 he finally gave up trying, bitter about his impecunious state. He left Sharjah and settled in Dubai, where, in March 1923, he married the daughter of 'Abd al-Rahman bin Muhammad, thus entering into an alliance that was radically to alter the course of his career. Khalid regarded the marriage as a deliberate threat to his authority, and began making preparations to attack 'Abd al-Rahman once again. He won the Baluchi guards of the Hirah fort over to his side, and then tried to persuade the residents of Sharjah to attack Hirah, but they refused, afraid of harming relatives. At this juncture, Khalid approached the Residency Agent and asked him to intervene. In the course of his inquiries, 'Isa questioned both parties, and the ensuing correspondence in the Agency records leaves it in no doubt that Khalid and his brother 'Abdallah were the initial aggressors. Furthermore, 'Abd al-Rahman complained bitterly of Khalid's oppressiveness: the people of Hirah were being taxed very heavily on their income from pearls and dates; some were being illegally deprived of their property; and 'Abd al-Rahman himself had barely managed to escape an attempt on his life by Khalid.[38]

The Residency Agent devised a scheme for the reconciliation of the opposing parties; this included the restoration by Khalid to the people of Hirah of all that had been taken from them illegally, and the stationing of two of the Agent's men to guard the fort at Hirah until Khalid and 'Abd al-Rahman could reach an amicable settlement. The terms of 'Isa's plans were accepted, written down, and signed by the two antagonists in the presence of the Senior Naval Officer.[39] But a lasting peace was still not in sight. A few months later, trouble erupted when Khalid appointed a *wali* at Hirah whom 'Abd al-Rahman then arrested and deposed. By January 1924, preparations were under way for another combined attack on Hirah by Khalid and Humayd bin 'Abd al-'Aziz. Before long, Khalid's guns were turned on Hirah, and his forces had surrounded the village, waiting for the signal to attack. 'Abd al-Rahman barricaded the town so well that it became impregnable. The people of Sharjah town, however, were worried about and disapproving of the possibility of an armed conflict, and general unrest and fear prevailed in the area. In the meantime, the Residency Agent had written to Humayd of Ajman[40] and to Sa'id bin Maktum of Dubai,[41] warning the former not to interfere, and asking the latter not to allow Sultan bin Saqr to join in the impending battle. Aware of the deadlock he faced, and afraid of the consequences, Khalid asked 'Isa to intervene for peace. The Residency Agent complied, peace was established, and 'Abd al-Rahman was forced to leave Hirah; this time he went to Dubai, where he joined his son-in-law, Sultan bin Saqr.[42]

By then, Khalid's unpopularity in Sharjah was complete. The people regarded him as oppressive, especially in view of the high customs duties he levied, and his prestige had waned enormously. Khalid was also resented for his mistreatment of Saqr's sons, exiled in Dubai and deprived of their inheritance, so it was the inhabitants of Sharjah who, on 1 November 1924, brought Sultan bin Saqr and his brothers back to Sharjah. It did not take Sultan long to seize power from Khalid. With the help of his father-in-law, and ably assisted by a force he brought with him,[43] he managed to break the ruler's resistance in only eleven days. On 12 November Khalid admitted defeat and agreed to step down in favour of Sultan bin Saqr; both men signed covenants[44] that Shaykh Sultan bin Salim of Ras al-Khaimah, in Sharjah for the purpose, helped to draw up, and that 'Abd al-Rahman bin Sayf of Hamriyyah, 'Abdallah bin 'Ali bin Huwayydin of the Bani Qitab, and the Residency Agent and his uncle Haj Yusuf bin 'Abdallah also signed.

Khalid first went to live in Dubai, but then settled in Umm al-Qaiwain. He could not, for a year at least, be reconciled to his deposal, and repeatedly petitioned the British authorities to help him reclaim the shaykhdom. By 1925 he seemed to have given up hope, and to be resigned to remaining at Umm al-Qaiwain; but two years later he was roused to anger by Sultan bin Saqr, who, contrary to the terms of the 1924 agreement, had confiscated Khalid's property in Sharjah. Khalid gathered strength to attack his nephew for this breach of promise, and in May 1927 he and his brother 'Abdallah went to Sharjah and there barricaded themselves in the house of a notable, Ahmad bin Darwish. Sultan and his brother Muhammad collected some bedouin of the Manasir and attacked the house, but neither side emerged truly victorious from the fierce fighting that followed, and many on either side were killed or wounded. Shortly afterwards, however, Khalid and his brother agreed to leave Sharjah. Sultan then seized some of the men they left behind and tortured them cruelly in a futile attempt to extract from them a confession that the Baluchis who worked in the Agency at Sharjah had helped Khalid.[45]

Although that was Khalid's final attempt to regain control of Sharjah from Sultan, the relationship between the two men never achieved any degree of cordiality. Sultan continued to refuse to abide by the terms of the 1924 agreement, and Khalid continued to press him to do so; it was only after 1937, when Khalid had strengthened his power immeasurably as regent of Kalba, that he was able to force Sultan to give him his due. Sultan died in 1951 and was succeeded by his son Saqr, who was deposed in 1965 by his cousin Khalid bin Muhammad, son of Sultan's brother Muhammad. Saqr went to Egypt and plotted the overthrow of Khalid. In January 1972 he murdered him, but the United Arab Emirates had by then been formed; it refused to allow Saqr to succeed by bloodshed, and banished him once again, at the same time placing Khalid's brother Sultan in the seat of power.

In Ras al-Khaimah before 1921,[46] power struggles were invariably over attempts to secede from the authority of the Qawasim of Sharjah. The present shaykhdom of Ras al-Khaimah can be traced back to the days of Sultan bin Saqr al-Qasimi, who, after 1820, when Ras al-Khaimah was restored to him after a period of six years,[47] was 'indifferently described as "Shaikh of Sharjah" and "Shaikh of Ras al-Khaimah"'.[48] During his long reign Sultan designated his brothers and sons as his representatives in charge of the towns of Sharjah and Ras al-Khaimah. Sultan's representatives tried to throw off his authority and declare themselves independent; in 1840, for example, one of his sons tried to establish himself as independent ruler of Sharjah. In this he was unsuccessful, but he retained the post of *wali* of Sharjah until his death in 1846. The unquestionable power of Sultan bin Saqr kept the Qasimi territories united despite occasional secessionary movements encouraged by the Bani Yas, his principal enemies. When Sultan died, in 1866, his son Ibrahim, who had been governing Ras al-Khaimah, immediately declared his independence. His brother Khalid, Sultan's successor as shaykh of the Qawasim, refused to accept the situation, and in May 1867 he attacked Ras al-Khaimah town, expelled Ibrahim, and brought the region firmly under his own control. In 1868 Khalid was killed in a battle with the ruler of Abu Dhabi, and his brother Salim then assumed the role of ruler of Sharjah. Salim's nephew Humayd bin 'Abdallah became responsible for the administration of Ras al-Khaimah and in 1869 was able to achieve the status of an independent ruler. Humayd's position was strengthened when a combined attack on him by Salim bin Sultan and Ibrahim bin Sultan caused the Political Resident to intervene, because of a breach of the maritime peace. The Resident, Colonel Lewis Pelly, ordered Sultan and Ibrahim to withdraw their force from Ras al-Khaimah, and subsequently Sharjah acknowledged Humayd's independence.[49]

Humayd proved to be a strong and able ruler. During the thirty-one years of his reign, he consolidated the internal position of Ras al-Khaimah, acting swiftly when any district showed signs of insubordination, and was acknowledged and respected by his fellow rulers on the Coast, not least by those of Sharjah. In 1900 he suffered a stroke, and died shortly after. He apparently had not designated any successor, so a month later Saqr bin Khalid of Sharjah peacefully annexed Ras al-Khaimah and reincorporated it in the shaykhdom of Sharjah. At first Saqr sent his cousin Hamad bin Majid to govern Ras al-Khaimah, but, being displeased with his administration, he recalled Hamad and appointed his own son Khalid instead. Khalid died in 1908, after which Salim bin Sultan, who had been ruler of Sharjah from 1868 to 1883, when Saqr had seized power from him, became the next governor of Ras al-Khaimah. As Saqr's hold on Sharjah gradually became weaker, Salim was able to increase his own power in Ras al-Khaimah. Saqr realised that he was powerless either to recall or to depose his uncle, and until he could muster the strength for this was forced to accept Salim's *de facto* independence in Ras al-Khaimah.

Although the British authorities were aware of the situation, they withheld any official recognition of Salim's status, particularly as Saqr made it clear that he had not given up hope of ousting his uncle. The British refusal to grant Ras al-Khaimah separate status was also prompted by fear that the Germans might seize the opportunity to petition Salim, as an independent Qasimi ruler, to restore to them the red-oxide concessions that Saqr, at British prompting, had cancelled in 1907.[50] These had been held by the German firm of Wönckhaus and had related to the island of Abu Musa.

In December 1907 Salim became paralysed, but he continued nominally in power, with his eldest son Muhammad as the effective leader of Ras al-Khaimah. In July 1919 Muhammad renounced his position in favour of his brother Sultan,[51] who became ruler of Ras al-Khaimah when his father died, in August 1919. Although German interests in the Abu Musa oxide concessions had been removed automatically as a result of the German defeat in the

World War, British recognition of Ras al-Khaimah was not immediately forthcoming. In December 1919, Trevor, the Political Resident, visited Ras al-Khaimah and decided that Sultan bin Salim was a young and ignorant man whose position, owing to a strong internal faction favouring Muhammad, was insecure. Trevor did not think it wise, therefore, to recommend any form of recognition, but, when he revisited Ras al-Khaimah the next year, he acknowledged that Sultan had proved his ability to govern: he had consolidated his power, although he was still 'rather headstrong and inclined to have disputes with the Shaikh of Umm al-Qawain',[52] and he had removed all traces of opposition to his rule, a fact attested by Muhammad's disinterest in politics and total involvement in his career as a pearl merchant. Before Trevor could recommend recognition, he wanted to make sure that Sharjah had no serious claims on Ras al-Khaimah. Khalid bin Ahmad, who had become ruler of Sharjah in 1914, had been in close touch with his cousin in Ras al-Khaimah, but did not 'appear to claim any authority over him'.[53] Once he was satisfied that all the previous objections no longer existed, Trevor recommended that the Government of India recognise Ras al-Khaimah as an independent shaykhdom.[54] The Government of India accepted the recommendation, and Trevor officially conveyed the news to Sultan bin Salim on 7 June 1921, thus making Sultan the sixth Trucial shaykh.[55]

The new shaykhdom was the northernmost of the Trucial States, extending along the Arabian Gulf coast for about forty miles, and bordering Muscat territory (the Musandam peninsula) on the north. Within the shaykhdom lay Sha'am, a village about seventeen miles north of Ras al-Khaimah town; Rams, a large village built on a creek, about eight miles north of Ras al-Khaimah town; and Jazirat al-Hamra, an island lying parallel to the coast and about twelve miles south of Ras al-Khaimah town. Ras al-Khaimah town, the capital, lies nearly fifty miles north of Sharjah town and was described by Sir Percy Cox as 'built on a large narrow spit of sand running parallel to the coast and enclosing between it and the mainland a wide lagoon which provides a very convenient and sheltered anchorage'.[56] The inland boundary of the shaykhdom ran, approximately, from Jazirat al-Hamra to the southern extremity of the Jirri plain and then to Wadi al-Qawr (about 100 miles south of Ras al-Khaimah town), where it pierced Sharjah territory. The main occupations in the coastal villages were fishing and pearling, and the hilly and mountainous inland areas of the shaykhdom practised agriculture. Furthermore, Ras al-Khaimah claimed the islands of Tunb and Little Tunb as dependencies some time after 1921.

Sultan bin Salim's long rule of Ras al-Khaimah (until 1948, when he was deposed by Saqr, the third son of his brother Muhammad) was stormy and far from peaceful. In 1927 he had a major clash with one of his younger cousins, as a result of his discontinuation of his relatives' allowances. Sultan was angry when one of his younger cousins pressed him for money, so he attempted to have him murdered. The Bani Qitab bedouin together with the notables of the shaykhdom managed to save the young man's life, but were unable to prevail on Sultan to pay him a salary. The ruler was firm in his refusal, and agreed to spare his cousin only if he left the shaykhdom.[57]

Having established his right to disregard the members of his family, and not to share his income with them, Sultan embarked on a course that was ultimately to weaken his position. The fact that his income was not very great (especially during the world depression) helped to protect him, but in 1945, when he granted an oil concession to Petroleum Development Ltd, he became exposed to the dangers of a *coup d'état*. This occurred in 1948, when he was overthrown by Saqr bin Muhammad, his nephew, with the concurrence of others of his relatives who had received no share in the concession income.

The one Trucial shaykhdom that has not experienced the violent overthrow of its ruler is, as noted earlier, Dubai, one of the most distinctive features of which is the existence of a loyal opposition within its ruling family. Indeed, before Sa'id bin Maktum succeeded Butti bin Suhayl in 1912, Dubai had never even experienced a serious movement to depose its ruler. (See Table 4 and Figure 4.) Sa'id's long rule of forty-six years was characterised by his reputation along the Coast as an excellent arbitrator in disputes that without his help would have erupted into full-scale wars (and that he no doubt recognised might have had a detrimental effect on the pearl trade), but also by his marked inability to command the members of his family, the Al-bu-Falasah, in Dubai affairs. He was an affable man whose hospitality made him popular with the bedouin of the Manasir and the Bani Yas; and as a peacemaker his wisdom and patience were usually rewarded with success, and he was always treated with respect. His relations with the British authorities were generally cordial, and in 1937 the Political Agent in Bahrain remarked that he was 'one of the pleasantest persons on the Coast with whom to have dealings as he always behaves as a gentleman'.[58]

Yet, though Sa'id's abilities were constantly acknowledged abroad, at home his authority was periodically threatened. He was dominated by a clever and forceful wife, Hussah bint Murr (Umm Rashid), whose talents as a business-woman were uncontested. She owned land in Dubai, was engaged in trade, and also took an active interest in the affairs of the shaykhdom. In a society where the position of the woman was unspeakably inferior, and where a woman was obliged not only to cover her face but also to live in almost total seclusion, Hussah bint Murr was clearly outstanding, and her name continues to be remembered on the Coast today. She defied convention by entering public affairs, and she even held

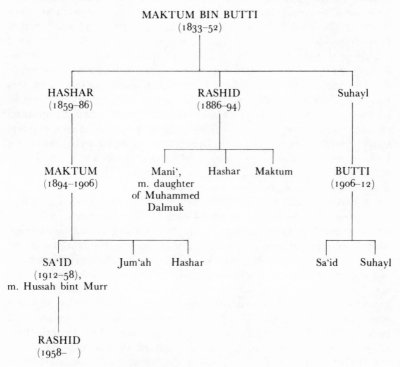

FIGURE 4   Dubai, ruling family

her own *majlis*—for men, rather than for women—in competition with her husband's.[59] She did not, however, act against her husband's best interests, but tended rather to bolster his weakening financial and political position whenever necessary. This was not the case with his relatives, who often challenged his authority and position. The movement against Sa'id was led by his cousins Mani' and Hashar bin Rashid, who had returned to Dubai after a period of exile in Sharjah, and also by the sons of Sa'id's predecessor Suhayl and Sa'id bin Butti.

The first major uprising occurred in 1929. Sa'id usually consulted his large and influential *majlis* before taking any major decisions, and was usually able to obtain the support of its members, but in 1929 he found it difficult to convince them of the validity of his method of governing. That year, the *majlis* was annoyed at Sa'id's general acquiescence to the British Government, particularly in view of the firmness with which he enforced the payment of debts: the members of the *majlis* were principally pearl merchants and were resentful that the ruler obliged them to honour their debts to the Indians of Dubai, especially as the pearl market had been flagging and this had had a severe effect on their financial positions. Furthermore, Sa'id had not proved strong enough to protect the people of Dubai from the ravages of marauding bedouin, notably the 'Awamir, in the outlying districts of Dubai, and this had greatly diminished his prestige. Above all, however, he was taken to task for the Iranian authorities' seizure of a Dubai vessel in 1928, and reminded that British help had not been immediately forthcoming.[60] On a visit to the hinterland in April 1929, therefore, Sa'id wrote to the *majlis* and offered to resign if the members would not help him to honour his duties.[61] The tribal elders at first viewed the letter with some suspicion and refused to accept the resignation. On 15 April, however, they met under the leadership of Muhammad bin Ahmad bin Dalmuk, an influential merchant who was also the father-in-law of Mani' bin Rashid, and proclaimed Mani' ruler of Dubai; they gave as their justification Sa'id's letter.

Mani' then notified the Residency Agent that Sa'id had resigned and that he had replaced him. But the British Government was not prepared to recognise a new ruler who had come forward in such 'unsatisfactory circumstances'. Therefore the Residency Agent was instructed by the Resident, Lionel Haworth, to inform the *majlis* that only a change that could be properly established as having been brought about by the will of the people would be acceptable.[62] Haworth's decision was based on the assumption that Sa'id commanded the loyalty of the majority of the people of Dubai as well as that of the bedouin, and he hoped that his message would bolster the ruler's weakened position. It had the desired effect, for on 17 April 400 men of the *majlis* met to discuss the Resident's message. The next day they decided that Shaykh Sa'id was to remain in power,[63] although his strength was by no means established; and for the next decade he continued to be beleaguered by his family. By 1938 the opposition had grown so strong that Sa'id was forced to accept the terms laid down by the Al-bu-Falasah.

4 Maintenance of Power: Political and Social Fabric

The often violent and disruptive process by which one ruler succeeded another in the Trucial shaykhdoms had a considerable impact on the fragile economy and power structure of the entire region. The ruler of a shaykhdom operated in an environment where tribal loyalties, political and economic considerations were deeply entangled. In this chapter, a number of major events will be reviewed in order to illustrate the complexity of the ruler's task and the precariousness of his position.

A ruler's principal concern was to survive, both politically and economically. In view of this, one of his first tasks upon assuming power was to find suitable positions for members of his immediate family and to make them allowances, in order to safeguard against conspiracies. The ruler had to rely entirely on himself, since by and large his relatives were not to be trusted. Despite enormous efforts in this direction, individuals such as 'Abd al-Rahman bin Muhammad of the Al-bu-Shamis remained an indefatigable source of unrest in the region. Furthermore, the weakening power of the Qawasim resulted in the emergence of two power centres, Kalba and Fujairah, that throughout the 1920s and 1930s struggled for recognition as independent shaykhdoms. The inordinately long gestation period preceding their birth was dominated by conflicts between them that frequently involved other shaykhdoms, the Shihuh tribe and Muscat.

Because the pearl industry was the mainstay of the region's economy, and in view of the fact that this activity involved almost the entire male labour force, any conflict during the pearling season had very serious economic and social repercussions, since it necessarily withdrew the pearling manpower for military purposes.

During the inter-war period there occurred a number of external events that hastened major changes in the position and functions of the ruler. The growth of British interests in the area progressively led to direct British intervention in the internal affairs of the shaykh-doms. The conclusion of oil agreements, beginning in the 1930s, made it necessary for boundaries to be defined and increased the importance of the hinterland. One of the casualties of the world depression of 1929 was the vital pearling industry. With the advent of new sources of revenue, the growth of trade centres (Bahrain, Kuwait, Dubai) and the sudden demise of well-established economic activities, the entire political economy of the region underwent a major transformation.

THE RULER'S ECONOMIC BASE

The economic activities of a shaykhdom naturally provided the ruler and his dependents with their main source of income, the size of which depended on the size and wealth of the shaykhdom. The ruler's income was also, of course, related to his power and standing, which affected the rhythm of economic activity and deter-mined whether his *wali*s paid their taxes—indeed, whether taxes could be imposed. In general, the largest tax was on the pearling industry: the ruler would usually collect duty on every pearl boat in operation, and sometimes a commission on the sale of pearls. Customs duties and taxes on certain forms of agricultural produce were also usual. Having acquired a reasonable income from these dues, the ruler would then himself be able to become a pearl merchant of some standing or a dealer in rice or other agricultural products.

In 1908, Lorimer estimated that Zayid bin Khalifah derived an annual income of as much as $MT 75,000 (Maria Theresa dollars) or around £6711[1] from various sources, the most outstanding of which (82 per cent) was the pearl trade. The rest came from agricultural taxes collected from the Liwa oasis; a tax on the dates produced in the Buraimi oasis; a tax on the horses maintained by Zayid in Buraimi; and a subsidy paid him by the sultan of Muscat in return for preventing the tribes of Buraimi and the Dahirah from raiding his territory.[2] The income of the shaykh of Sharjah was considerably less: 33,400 rupees, or around £2227. This was because many of his governors kept for themselves much of the tax they levied. The ruler of Dubai had an income of

$MT 51,400, or around £4569, and the shaykh of Umm al-Qaiwain, which had fewer boats and fishermen engaged in pearling than the larger shaykhdoms had,[3] received only 19,269 rupees, or around £1285, from pearling taxes, but, by obliging the owners of the boats to buy all their provisions from him, accumulated 80,000 rupees, or around £5333, in the one year.[4]

Not every man in the shaykhdom had to pay taxes. Exceptions were usually made for members of the ruling family, and friends and servants of the ruler. Lorimer listed the exemptions for 1907, and the figures give a strong indication of the status of the ruler himself. Abu Dhabi, whose ruling family was small and whose ruler was strong and secure, made exemptions for only twenty-one boats, worth 2004 rupees in dues foregone. Sharjah had approximately the same size ruling family, but, because the ruler himself was much weaker, exemptions were made for ninety-one boats, to a total value of 12,062 rupees. Dubai's ruling family was very large and exemptions were made for 210 boats, to a total value of 20,528 rupees.[5]

After ensuring his family's livelihood, the ruler had minimal expenses to bear. The only other major claim on his income was the salaries of his guard in the main towns of the shaykhdom. The amount differed from place to place, and in Dubai the ruler paid his guard simply by exempting them from taxes on their pearl boats.

ADMINISTRATIVE FUNCTIONS

The shaykhdom's administrative infrastructure was so rudimentary as almost to be non-existent. The ruler had no civil service; no judges or law courts, except for the *mahkamah*; no army, apart from his personal guards; and no police force. He could rarely, if ever, delegate authority to an appointed person or group of persons without risking his position. Thus, when in 1919 a Somali sailor was murdered at Ras al-Khaimah by men who then escaped to Umm al-Qaiwain, Sultan bin Salim of Ras al-Khaimah was obliged to swallow his pride and accept the situation as it was, despite the anger of the friends of the murdered sailor, who obviously considered Sultan irresponsible.[6]

There were no formal extradition treaties between the shaykhdoms, and a shaykhdom to which a person wanted in another shaykhdom escaped would usually grant him refuge rather than return him to justice. Thus the relationship between the two states (usually neighbours) would suffer. In the case of the murder of the Somali sailor, Sultan was clearly loath to start hostilities against Umm al-Qaiwain. Instead he sent bedouin to keep watch on his borders with Umm al-Qaiwain in case the murderers should be sighted. In retaliation, Rashid bin Ahmad sent the murderers to raid Jazirat al-Hamra, where they burned huts and were generally destructive. Although Sultan complained to Rashid, he received no answer to his letter. In despair, he appealed to Khalid bin Ahmad of Sharjah, still technically the ruler of Ras al-Khaimah, who sent back an evasive reply. Sultan then had no alternative but to begin an attack on Umm al-Qaiwain. Rashid bin Ahmad immediately complained to Khalid bin Ahmad of Sharjah, who sent his brother 'Abdallah to intervene. Although 'Abdallah realised the extent of Rashid's guilt, he seized the opportunity to weaken Sultan's position by collaborating with Umm al-Qaiwain. Feeling outnumbered, Sultan appealed to the rulers of Ajman and Dubai. They both promised to come to his aid if Khalid bin Ahmad allowed his brother to join forces with Umm al-Qaiwain.[7]

Worried that a full-scale war was about to break out, the Political Resident wrote to Rashid bin Ahmad, warning him against starting hostilities and urging him to accept mediation.[8] Apparently convinced of the danger involved, Rashid allowed Khalid of Sharjah to mediate, and peace was restored. But Sultan bin Salim was still left with responsibility for the murder of the Somali sailor. Despite strict injunctions from Knox, the Political Resident, to pay *diyah* to the family of the sailor, and despite the threat that not to do so would 'bring on you the displeasure of the Great Government',[9] Sultan refused to accept the situation. When the Resident finally threatened to send a warship against Sultan,[10] the ruler capitulated and paid the *diyah*. Thus the Political Resident intervened to prevent the reluctant Sultan from settling the matter by force, yet used the threat of force to induce Sultan to pay *diyah*.

Relations between Umm al-Qaiwain and Ras al-Khaimah had never been very cordial, their proximity being an important reason for the perennial friction. Neighbouring shaykhdoms were often cool or hostile towards each other, the lack of clearly defined, mutually agreed boundaries doing much to encourage squabbling and distrust. Yet, as noted earlier, it was not until the advent of oil companies seeking concessions that the question of defining boundaries came to be regarded seriously. How it was then tackled is discussed in later chapters.

MAINTENANCE OF THE RULER'S AUTHORITY

As may be observed from the Somali murder case, the ruler was personally responsible for defending the legitimate rights of all people in his shaykhdom. Yet the means available to him for protecting those rights were often blunted by British intervention. Since the ruler had to rely almost entirely on himself, he had all the time to be conscious of the need to win and maintain the respect of his people. He had to prove the extent of his authority over the entire shaykhdom, both the settled people and the bedouin.

Sultan bin Salim was the ruler of Ras al-Khaimah when it was re-established as an independent shaykhdom early this century. Thus, over and above the normal problems of ruling, he had to cope with the problems of consolidating his authority over his shaykhdom. His career was marked by an unusually fiery attitude towards both his fellow rulers and the British authorities, prompted largely by his desire to establish himself firmly in his new role.

One threat to his authority and to his people's respect for him was the alliance that the headman of Rams, a village in Ras al-Khaimah, concluded with the Shihuh, the hereditary enemies of the Qawasim. The Shihuh lived in the region between Ru'us al Jibal and the Musandam peninsula, north of a line between Sha'am in the west and Dibba in the east; this was *de jure* under the rule of Muscat, but the Shihuh in most cases refused to accept any authority other than their own. Shihhi territory was separated from Muscat by Qasimi land, the Shimayliyyah tract. The proximity of Ras al-Khaimah to Ru'us al Jibal was the main source of the continual hostility between the Qawasim and the Shihuh, whose lands were so interlocked that it was virtually impossible for relations between the two to remain calm. Dibba, for example, was divided into two sections: the northern part of the town was ruled by the Shihuh, the southern by the Qawasim. Throughout the inter-war period, and as a result of the decline of Sharjah, Sultan bin Salim regarded Dibba (south) as being part of Ras al-Khaimah.[11]

The Shihuh remain even today the least known and most remote people of Oman—living, as they do, in a mountainous region that provides them with a natural asylum.[12] 'They are by far the most primitive tribe in Oman, the most superstitious, and, as regards the mountain folk, the most difficult to cultivate friendly relations with.'[13] The tribe is composite, and its ethnic origins have long puzzled historians and anthropologists. One branch, the Kumazara, were described by Bertram Thomas as being

physically peculiar in their lack of Semitic features characteristic in some degree of their fellow-tribesmen. It is they ... who speak the strange tongue which has baffled and confused strangers. ... It is a compound of Arabic and Persian but it is distinct from them both, and is intelligible neither to the Arab nor to the Persian nor yet to the bilinguist of both.[14]

The Shihuh were primarily hill shepherds, but along the coast there were a number engaged in fishing, boat-building and cultivating dates.

With the permission of Sultan bin Salim, the Shihuh used the village of Rams as the main port of entry for their imports from Dubai. The inhabitants of Rams belonged to the Tanayj tribe,[15] whose headman, 'Abd al-Rahman bin Salih, sometime in 1920 reached a secret agreement of friendship with the Shihuh. This treaty was a direct threat to Sultan's sovereignty, especially as the Shihuh began to interfere in the local affairs of Rams. Sultan first tried to solve the matter peacefully, and complained to the Political Resident about the new alliance. The Resident seems to have done little, however, for the hostility between Sultan and 'Abd al-Rahman bin Salih, the latter obviously strengthened by the Shihuh, grew steadily and culminated in an armed clash in June 1921. Soon after, Sa'id bin Maktum of Dubai went to Ras al-Khaimah in order to mediate, but met with little success. His chief motivation for going was that the fighting was disrupting the pearling season, Sultan bin Salim having recruited all the available divers into his forces.[16] Sa'id bin Maktum was not the only person who stood to lose by the situation. The interests of the Indian merchants were also at stake, since, if pearling did not proceed as usual, they ran the risk of not having their debts honoured. Because of the financial danger to the Indian community, the Senior Naval Officer, Commander Brandon, sailed to Ras al-Khaimah to seek a suitable settlement.

He arrived in HMS *Cyclamen* in late July, and found that the Residency Agent had already arranged for a truce of four months, but that in the meantime, on 16 July, 'Abd al-Rahman bin Salih had been murdered by his cousin 'Abd al-Rahman bin Muhammad.[17] Brandon knew that the situation was still far from being normal, and began lengthy negotiations with all concerned until an agreement was finally reached. This was written down, and was signed by Sultan bin Salim and Muhammad bin Salih, the new *wali* of Rams, brother of 'Abd al-Rahman bin Salih. Under the terms of the agreement, Sultan promised to recognise Muhammad bin Salih as the *wali* of Rams, and to arrest the murderer of 'Abd al-Rahman; Muhammad bin Salih in turn undertook to obey the ruler of Ras al-Khaimah and to get clear of all obligations that 'Abd al-Rahman might have had with the Shihuh.[18] Three days after the conclusion of the agreement, however, Muhammad and his brother Salim refused to abide by its terms, saying that it was not acceptable to either them or the Shihuh.

The Senior Naval Officer tried to find an alternative solution to the dispute by sailing to Khasab, where he met with the President of the Muscat Council, who was there on a visit to the Shihuh. The President of the Council sent his private secretary and two Shihhi leaders with Brandon to Rams, on board the *Cyclamen*. After lengthy negotiations with all parties, a settlement was reached whereby both sides agreed to a six-months truce, and Sultan bin Salim promised to allow the Shihuh free use of the port of Rams.[19] In order to ensure the effectiveness of the treaty this time, Brandon deported Muhammad and Salim to Sharjah, where Khalid bin Ahmad promised to keep them in custody and out of mischief. But four months later, in December, the brothers escaped from Sharjah after obtaining the support of the Shihhi Salih bin Muhammad of Dibba, and went to Rams with a number of men from the Shihuh. Sultan bin Salim could not accept the situation, and before long fighting broke out yet again.

Brandon then assembled all the disputants on board the *Cyclamen*, and a lasting settlement was finally attained; this was written down by each side and signed on 27 February 1922 in the presence of Brandon.[20] Muhammad bin Salih swore allegiance to Sultan bin Salim, promised to sever his connections with the Shihuh, and agreed to pay Sultan 1000 rupees a year; Sultan, on the other hand, recognised Muhammad as *wali* of Rams. It was also agreed that all prisoners taken during the fighting would be returned to their homes, and that, if either side did not abide by the terms, the Residency Agent would be called on to mediate.[21]

Another example of the manner in which a ruler acted when his authority and position were undermined is provided by the way in which Humayd bin 'Abd al-'Aziz of Ajman responded to the threat posed by 'Abd al-Rahman of the Al-bu-Shamis. We have already seen how, after having made public his claim to the shaykhdom of Ajman, 'Abd al-Rahman settled in the town of Hirah in Sharjah, following which the rulers of Ajman and Sharjah joined forces to launch an attack on him. When the Senior Naval Officer tried to restore the peace, Humayd categorically refused to see him.[22] He obviously considered any acceptance of British mediation as a weakness on his part and he had to prove that he could hold his own against any usurper. His obduracy in ignoring the British officer was to cost him a great deal, however. He had already been in trouble with the British authorities for refusing to communicate with Trevor, the Political Resident, late in December 1920, when Trevor had sailed to Ajman to inquire into a report that Humayd had torn up a manumission certificate. When he arrived off Ajman, Trevor hoisted the Resident's flag, indicating his desire to meet the ruler, but Humayd ignored it. In May 1921, after the second insult, Trevor felt provoked to pay another visit to Ajman, and this time Humayd saw him.

'He assumed a most truculent and defiant attitude, in fact during my 17 years experience of these parts I have not yet come across a Shaikh or Khan who adopted so insolent a demeanour.'[23] Although Humayd denied having torn up the manumission certificate, Trevor found sufficient proof to substantiate the claim. 'Apart from this the Shaikh told so many lies in rapid succession about the matter that I came to the conclusion that no reliance whatever can be placed on his statements.'[24] Determined to punish him, Trevor imposed a fine of 1000 rupees. Humayd 'was most defiant, practically asking what would happen if he did not pay'.[25] The Resident threatened bombardment of the Ajman fort (HMS *Crocus* and *Cyclamen* were present), to which Humayd defiantly replied that it would 'be the worse' for the British if they destroyed his towers. Since he refused to pay the guns began to fire: one tower was totally demolished and another partially. Soon after, Humayd acceded defeat, and hurriedly sent the money to Trevor.

For the remainder of his life, Humayd took care not to involve himself in any more disputes with the British authorities, and, although he never softened his hatred for 'Abd al-Rahman of the Al-bu-Shamis, he managed to keep his feelings under control. The animosity he felt for the Al-bu-Shamis only grew after the accession to power of Sultan bin Saqr of Sharjah, for 'Abd al-Rahman's position as father-in-law of the ruler added to his prestige and authority. Hirah gradually became a place of refuge for people trying to escape punishment in Ajman—'Abd al-Rahman willingly granting them entry, in order to spite his old enemy. The people of Ajman also found this a convenient way to escape the payment of their debts, so leaving Humayd with responsibility for the situation so far as the Indian traders and the British authorities were concerned.

The ruler of Ajman was only too pleased when, in 1926, the Political Resident banished 'Abd al-Rahman to Aden for four years because of his suspected role in the murder of the cousin of 'Isa bin 'Abd al-Latif, the Residency Agent, in October 1925. The murder had occurred in the course of an affray that had been instigated with the murder of 'Isa himself in mind. 'Isa immediately reported the murder to the Political Resident, saying that the precipitating factor had been his attempt to raise the British flag over the Agency at Sharjah.[26] Later, he reported the rumour prevalent in Sharjah that 'Abd al-Rahman, 'one of the stormy petrels of the Trucial Coast',[27] a man feared by everyone in and around Sharjah, including 'Isa, had been responsible.

In order thoroughly to investigate the death, Stuart Horner, secretary to the Political Resident, went to the Agency at Sharjah with Yusuf Kanu of Bahrain.[28] Although it was obvious from Horner's findings that 'Abd al-Rahman had hated the Residency Agent, no conclusive proof of his guilt was available. Thinking it highly probable that 'Abd al-Rahman was the culprit, Horner decreed that, pending a final verdict, 'Abd al-Rahman should be deported to Ras al-Khaimah and placed in the custody of Shaykh Sultan bin Salim.

In the meantime, Sa'id bin Maktum of Dubai had arrived at Sharjah, in an effort to mediate, for the affair had aroused wide consternation; together with Sultan bin Salim, Sultan bin Saqr and some notables of Sharjah, Sa'id wrote to the Political Resident and asked that 'Abd al-Rahman remain at Ras al-Khaimah until further information on the murder was available, and that, in any case, 'Abd al-Rahman should not be allowed to return to Hirah or Sharjah for at least one year.[29] But adequate proof of the identity of the murderer was not forthcoming.

In March 1926 the Residency Agent received letters from Rashid bin Ahmad and Muhammad bin Rahmah of the Al-bu-Shamis. They were angry at the continued detention in Ras al-Khaimah of 'Abd al-Rahman, especially as no proof of his guilt had been established. In his letter, Muhammad bin Rahmah stated that he had been to 'Abdallah ibn Jaluwi, who had ordered him to explain to 'Isa bin 'Abd al-Latif that 'Abd al-Rahman was Muhammad bin Rahmah's responsibility as a member of the Al-bu-Shamis.[30] A while earlier, Prideaux, the Political Resident, had reported that the governor of Hasa had asserted his presence in the Trucial Coast by sending a 'posse of police' to Sharjah, Ajman and Ras al-Khaimah in order to pursue a man wanted for murder in Nejd.[31] In view of the increasing tension over 'Abd al-Rahman, the threat of Wahhabi encroachment, and the loss of British prestige because of the attack on 'Isa's cousin, the British authorities decided that 'Abd al-Rahman had to be exiled to Aden for a period of four years.

On 11 June 1926 Captain Parry went to Ras al-Khaimah with the decision, and asked Sultan bin Salim to take 'Abd al-Rahman on board HMS *Triad* for his voyage to Aden. The next day the Senior Naval Officer reported that Sultan, afraid of the consequences, refused to surrender 'Abd al-Rahman, but later claimed that he was willing to give him up for trial provided it were before a *mahkamah*.[32] Prideaux refused to accept any compromise, so he discussed with the Senior Naval Officer various measures to enforce the surrender of 'Abd al-Rahman. These included returning him to Sharjah and then bombarding the towers of Sharjah and Hirah, thus laying Sharjah open to attack from Ajman; issuing an ultimatum to Sultan bin Salim, to be backed up, if needs be, by the bombardment of his town and the destruction of his pearling fleet; deposing Sultan bin Saqr, reinstating Khalid bin Ahmad and destroying

Hirah; and sending a British political officer with an infantry guard to live for a while at Sharjah.[33] News of these discussions was leaked out, subduing all opposition to the sentence; and on 16 June 'Abd al-Rahman was surrendered to Captain Parry and sent to Aden.

The exile produced so many protests that it did not last the prescribed four years. The Al-bu-Shamis continued to express their anger, and continually harrassed the Residency Agent; 'Abd al-Rahman's family, together with the ruler of Sharjah, made continuous pleas for the return of the prisoner; and the British authorities eventually decided that the banishment should be terminated. 'Abd al-Rahman's return to Sharjah occurred a year after the death, in 1928, of Humayd of Ajman, who was succeeded by his son Rashid. The new ruler perpetuated his father's feud with Sharjah, especially after 'Abd al-Rahman's return, which led to sporadic hostilities between Sharjah and Ajman. Rashid continued to fight the Al-bu-Shamis bedouin as when, in August 1929, he sent some 'Awamir bedouin to raid them. On their way there, the 'Awamir came across a messenger carrying letters from Sultan bin Saqr to the Al-bu-Shamis. The 'Awamir suspected a Sharjah–Shamis alliance against them and shot the messenger; they carried him to Ajman, where they discovered that the letters contained no evidence of intrigue.[34] The Al-bu-Shamis bedouin could not overlook Rashid's aggressiveness, and in February 1931 made an unsuccessful attempt on his life.[35]

Undaunted, Rashid twice tried to have 'Abd al-Rahman killed, once in 1931 and again in 1932, but on both occasions the intended victim succeeded in escaping in time.[36] Matters reached a head in 1933, when a further attempt on 'Abd al-Rahman's life was made. Three residents of Ajman who were being entertained at 'Abd al-Rahman's house shot at their host, just missing him.[37] Rashid admitted to the Senior Naval Officer that he had sent the men on their mission, and said that he intended to kill 'Abd al-Rahman even if it meant declaring war on Sharjah.[38] The Senior Naval Officer recognised the danger of this threat and became involved in a lengthy process of mediation that culminated in an armistice that was to last for four months from August 1933. When the truce ended, late in December, fighting broke out again; this time hostilities were brought to an end, a month later, through the mediation of Sa'id bin Maktum of Dubai.[39]

It is clear from the behaviour of both Humayd and then Rashid, as rulers of Ajman, that they realised how closely their internal and external affairs were linked. The presence of 'Abd al-Rahman in Hirah, although outside Ajman, had a direct bearing on the security of its ruler, both as regards his relationship with his people, on whose respect he depended on for the maintenance of his power, and as regards his relationship with the British government and their representatives in the Gulf. It obviously was difficult for the ruler of a shaykhdom to know when the issues at stake and the attendant circumstances were such that he should act on a situation and when they were such that he should ignore it.

Of all the rulers on the Trucial Coast, Sa'id bin Maktum was by far the best judge in this respect. A master of the art of compromise, he spent a large slice of his time in trying to patch up all the foreign and domestic problems of his fellow rulers. The difference between him and them in the way they conducted their respective affairs was striking. He represented a society that was quickly adapting itself to a new way of life where tribal alliances, tribal disputes, *zakat*, all were becoming self-defeating. When he felt that he had lost the confidence and support of his *majlis*, in 1929, he decided that, rather than fight, as his fellow rulers would surely have done, he should resign. He obviously did not think that the total disruption of the economy was a fair price to pay merely to save his position. Trade and a vital economy, no matter how restricted they were in the 1920s and 1930s, were clearly the new norms of Gulf society. Kuwait and Bahrain were also in the process of transformation, but they had become more open to outside influences: young Kuwaitis were being educated in Iraq; and Bahrain, particularly after oil was struck there in 1932, began to sent its youth abroad for higher education. Dubai had not yet advanced so far, but its people followed much the same trends as the Bahrainis and Kuwaitis.

RELATIONS WITH BRITAIN

Generally Sa'id also knew how to balance the situation with the British authorities. He was unique among the rulers on the Coast in having never had a clash with a British representative, and the British generally liked and respected him: they often called on him for help in solving local problems. The fact, however, that the British, in order to protect their interests in the Gulf, were prepared to go beyond the terms of their treaties with the shaykhdoms in intervening in local affairs meant that Sa'id's fellow rulers, who were not as careful as he was, often found themselves at odds with the British in some way or other.

One of the first concerns of a ruler after he had assumed power was to obtain recognition of his status from the British Government. Without it he could not survive for very long, for it was his relationship with Britain that allowed him to continue in power.

We have already seen how for some time Britain held off recognising Sultan bin Salim as an independent ruler; it was not until 1921, when this recognition was finally accorded, that Sultan's status was fully accepted in Ras al-Khaimah and on the rest of the Coast. Of course, in this case the delay in British recognition was owing to the secession of Ras al-Khaimah from Sharjah, but British opposition to a new ruler in an established shaykhdom did occasionally occur, thereby preventing that person from attaining power. This happened in 1929, when the British refused to accept the proclamation by the Dubai *majlis* that sought to make Mani' bin Rashid ruler in place of Sa'id bin Maktum. Although the British were acting against their policy of non-interference, their move strengthened the position of Sa'id and for the moment eliminated moves to depose him.

One of the adjuncts to recognition by the British Government was the commitment to abide by the terms of all the treaties with Britain approved by previous rulers. To show his willingness to do so, the new ruler had to sign each of those treaties, thereby promising to desist from the slave trade, the arms trade and maritime warfare, and agreeing not to have any relations with other countries except through the British Government. His power, therefore, was remarkably limited in scope.

Because British policy was so uncertain and idiosyncratic, not always conforming to the treaties (which were always binding on the rulers), the management of relations with Britain was far from easy. The ruler could not safely predict how the British would react to a given question, basically because it often was difficult for the British representatives themselves to know how London or Delhi would choose to interpret policy. Moreover, British policy in the Gulf was in a state of transition: what new courses of action the increased importance of the Coast demanded had not yet been fully decided.

In 1926, for example, when Saqr bin Zayid of Abu Dhabi was obsessed by the fact that his dead brother's sons would try to avenge their father's death, he appealed to the British authorities to give him personal protection. The Political Resident, Sir Lionel Haworth, to whom the appeal was made, was in favour of responding to it and thereby deviating from the policy of non-interference. Since Britain guaranteed to protect the shaykhdoms only from attack by sea, this would be a radically new departure, as Haworth realised; but he firmly believed that the British policy of abstention from all but naval commitments should not be replaced by one of responsibility for ensuring the orderly succession of rulers, their maintenance in power, and the protection of shaykhdoms from attack by land.

This system of policing the sea and leaving the land to look after itself has been carried on successfully during the last half century. If a Shaikh murdered his brother it affected us not at all. As long as he held his power, we recognised him and shook him by the hand. When he in turn was murdered by another brother, we greeted the new power with equal readiness. It was none of our business and the Shaikhs were as anxious to keep us out of their lands as we were anxious to avoid being drawn into their quarrels on shore.[40]

The Resident noted that times had changed, and that another power could easily be drawn into the internal politics of the Trucial Coast. The power to which he explicitly referred was Saudi Arabia, which he thought could take advantage of the turmoil in Abu Dhabi to encroach on its territory inland. He urged the Government of India to concern itself with suppressing such violent dynastic struggles, which exposed the entire Coast to great insecurity.

But the Government of India opposed Haworth's proposals, and Saqr was left to fend for himself. Three years later, the policy of non-interference was overlooked, and the Political Resident refused to sanction the appointment of Mani' bin Rashid as ruler of Dubai, even though the *majlis* had elected him. At the same time, in 1926, the British had interfered so far in the Coast's internal affairs as to exile 'Abd al-Rahman of Hirah. It was thus extremely difficult for a ruler to maintain a stable relationship with the British authorities; he had to rely on his wits and political intuition.

THE CONSEQUENCES OF THE DECLINE OF A RULER'S AUTHORITY

The continued decline of the ruler of Sharjah led to secessionary movements within the territory over which he claimed authority. After the independence of Ras al-Khaimah, the towns of Kalba and Fujairah also began to press for independence. In this section, the complex processes that preceded the secession of these two towns will be described, together with the roles played by the sultan of Muscat, the British authorities and some of the leading figures of the Trucial Coast. The conflicts that occurred can be viewed as power struggles between a ruler and his subordinates, and formed part of the last wave of armed conflicts to take place on the Coast, in the 1920s. After that the region came under closer control from outside, owing to its oil potential and its location on the imperial air-route to India.

We have already noted the existence of a bitter enmity between the Qawasim and the Shihuh. This feud was used by the headman of Fujairah, in the Shimayliyyah, in order to promote his own independence. The Shimaylliyyah is a tract of land bordering the Gulf of Oman and extending roughly from Dibba in the north to Khawr Kalba in the south. Its main towns are Dibba, Khawr Fakkan, Fujairah, Kalba and Khawr Kalba. The Qawasim first gained control of the area in the latter part of the eighteenth century, but the sultan of Muscat contested their claim for a long time. Control began to alternate between the Qawasim and the sultan, until in 1850 Sultan bin Saqr of Sharjah successfully annexed the area. Even after that, however, the Qawasim were unable to keep a peaceful hold on it and constantly had to put down attempts at secession—principally by the headmen of the town of Fujairah. This town, situated between Khawr Fakkan (on the north) and Kalba (on the south), a few miles inland from Gharayfah, which serves as its port, was inhabited almost exclusively by members of the Sharqiyy tribe, whose main sources of income had always been agriculture and fishing. Fujairah's long history of unsuccessful attempts at secession from Sharjah began in 1866, when the headman of the town refused to pay tribute. He was finally forced to submit to Qasimi control, but in 1884 Shaykh Hamad bin 'Abdallah, the Sharqiyy leader of Fujairah, expressed his independent spirit by seizing Gharayfah and also the town of Bithnah, in the Jirri Ham, a valley that starts near the village of Adhan in the Jirri plain and reaches the Gulf of Oman a few miles south of Fujairah, providing the only direct route between the Shimayliyyah and the rest of the Trucial Coast. Hamad then appealed for protection to the ruler of Ras al-Khaimah, which at that time was independent of Sharjah. In view of this, Saqr bin Khalid of Sharjah had to accept the situation, but when, in 1900, Ras al-Khaimah was reabsorbed into Sharjah, Hamad refused to accept Saqr's overlordship, and in 1901 he openly defied his orders. In 1902, when Saqr was about to launch an attack on Fujairah, in order to force Hamad to submit, the British authorities decided to intervene, especially when it became clear that the rulers of Dubai and Ajman were willing to enter the conflict on Hamad's side. Although hostilities were temporarily averted, little was accomplished by the British intervention, for Hamad absolutely refused to recognise the ruler of Sharjah as his overlord. In 1903 Saqr made a successful attack on Fujairah. This time Hamad admitted defeat and acknowledged Sharjah's authority over him, so conforming with the decision of the British Government and the Government of India, when earlier that year they had considered British policy in the area, that the Shimayliyyah should be regarded as part of Sharjah.[41] This policy was echoed by Curzon, who, during his speech at the Sharjah durbar, in November 1903, referred to the authority of the 'Chief of the Jowasims' in Shimayliyyah.[42]

Hamad, however, continued to act independently, and became a source of terror to the people of Kalba and Khawr Fakkan, who were governed by Sa'id bin Hamad. He was a Qasimi who was a cousin of Shaykh Sultan bin Saqr of Sharjah and father-in-law of Khalid bin Ahmad, Sultan's predecessor. The main trouble between Fujairah and Kalba was territorial, for the Fujairah constantly encroached on Kalba territory. Hamad and Sa'id were bitterly antagonistic towards each other, and the situation improved only slightly when Hamad married Sa'id's daughter.

The ancient enmity between the Sharqiyyin and the Qawasim was too strong to lay dormant for long, and in 1926 relations between the two became so strained that fighting broke out. The direct causes of the hostilities, which persisted for three years, were simple enough and followed a familiar pattern. A man who had enjoyed good standing at Kalba, but who was discontented with his treatment by Sa'id bin Hamad, decided to leave and settle in Fujairah. Hamad, seizing his opportunity, openly favoured the new resident, who continued to visit Kalba and, because of the protection of the headman of Fujairah, felt brave enough to vilify Sa'id. To begin with, Sa'id bore these taunts, but finally he felt compelled to forbid the man to return to Kalba. This in turn brought on the anger of Hamad, who interpreted the action as an insult to himself. The old enmity arose to the surface. Both headmen declared boycotts of the other's territory, as a result of which fishing and diving became restricted. In the meantime, Sa'id built a warehouse in a garden on the road from Kalba to Fujairah, and Hamad, deciding that it was camouflage for a fort, destroyed it, claiming that Sa'id had no right to erect a building outside the town limits. The destruction of the warehouse marked the outbreak of hostilities, and by March 1926 there was open fighting between the two towns.

Sa'id bin Hamad soon realised that he was weaker than his adversary, and secretly solicited the help of Hamad bin Faysal, *wali* of Sohar in the sultanate of Muscat and Oman. The *wali* sent an emissary to the scene of the fighting and was able to arrange a limited truce. A few days before the truce was due to expire, Sultan Sa'id bin Taymur of Muscat arrived at Sohar, on the first leg of a tour that had been arranged two months earlier. His presence prompted the belligerents to sue for peace. Bertram Thomas, who was accompanying the sultan, primarily to collect *zakat* and to establish a customs post in Shimayliyyah (he was the sultan's financial adviser), took no part in the negotiations for peace, but described the events that preceded the settlement:

> On 1st May the Shaikh of Kalba took the initial step. He with 32 followers came down to Sahar to request the Sultan's adjudication in the dispute with Fujaira. H. H. [His Highness the Sultan] pointed out that his, i.e. H. H.'s mediation had small chance of success unless a similar invitation came from the other side. Three days later this other invitation arrived. It was brought by hand of the Shihuh Shaikh of Dibba, Salih bin Muhammad, an ally of Fujaira's, though subordinate to the Sultan of Muscat.
>
> The non arrival of the Shaikh of Fujaira in person was regarded as an indication of Fujaira's doubtful desire for a genuine settlement. The Shaikh of Kalba and the Fujaira emissary having said their say, departed from Sahar for their rival camps. The Sultan at this stage despaired of peace, but his attitude was one of unconcern. .... On 19th May our party moved up to Abu Baqra according to programme. Here events were to prove more propitious. We were met by the Shaikh of Fujaira—his first visit to Muscat territory for ten years—drawn thither no doubt for fear of Kalba having got in first and won a powerful ally by advocacy of one side of the case. The Shaikh of Fujaira cordially invited us to visit Fujaira and be his guests. That same evening the Shaikh of Kalba arrived and pressed a similar invitation upon us to visit Kalba. H. H. replied that so long as discord divided them he would decline their hospitality. Both Shaikhs then invited him to make a settlement, and the evening of the 19th and the morning of 20th were spent in conversation. Agreement was reached on 20th and signed by all parties.[43]

The basis of settlement was that both sides accepted to drop claims, and that no inquiry into or reparations for the recent fighting would be necessary. After the agreement had been signed, the sultan and Thomas visited Kalba and then Fujairah. When they reached Fujairah, they were surprised to find that on the same day Sultan bin Salim of Ras al-Khaimah, Hamad bin Ibrahim of Umm al-Qaiwain, 'Abd al-Rahman bin Sayf of Hamriyyah and 'Abdallah bin Ahmad (brother of Khalid bin Ahmad, ex-ruler of Sharjah) had all arrived to mediate. The sultan confided to Thomas that he found their related interest in the dispute curious; he suspected that Hamad of Fujairah had appealed to them, in order to counteract Sa'id's request for help from the sultan. The visitors, however, expressed their satisfaction with the settlement and left the same day. The agreement remained the basis for settling later outbreaks of hostility between Kalba and Fujairah, the outcome of which greatly weakened Kalba.

A few months later there was another clash, resulting in the escape to Sharjah of Sa'id bin Hamad.[44] Fujairah's position had been greatly strengthened by the conclusion of an alliance with the Shihuh, and this had in turn prompted the ruler of Sharjah to solicit the help of the Na'im of Buraimi; soon it became clear that a full-scale tribal war was imminent. The Political Resident was so exasperated by the situation that he telegraphed the Political Agent in Muscat,

> As Shaikh of Fujayrah is friendly with Shihuh tribe who are subjects of Muscat, it occurs to me that extinction of trouble might be effected by exchange of territory between Sultan and Trucial Shaikhs. Kalba to be given to the Shihuh of west coast and latter removed from Rams Tibat and perhaps Bakha, which would be added to Ras al Khaima state.[45]

The Resident sought Bertram Thomas's advice. Thomas thought that partition was not feasible, principally because the sultan of Muscat would not feel himself capable of keeping Shaykh Hamad in order. By December 1926 the round of hostilities between Kalba and Fujairah had been brought to an end through the mediation of Shaykh Salih bin Muhammad of Dibba, whose settlement was based on the agreement signed in May.[46]

But, before long, the fighting had started once more. In January and again in September 1927, minor troubles between Kalba and Fujairah, fomented in both cases by the latter, erupted into violence. The situation threatened to deteriorate further when the rulers of Ras al-Khaimah and Sharjah expressed an interest in actively supporting their Qasimi relative. This time the Senior Naval Officer went to Kalba and negotiated a new settlement.[47] It achieved a temporary peace, which broke down almost regularly, but there was little doubt that Shaykh Hamad had emerged victorious. He gradually became powerful enough to claim most of the land over which Shaykh Sa'id ruled. The balance of power was much in Hamad's favour; but in 1936 other considerations took precedence over this fact, and the British Government granted Kalba independent status, which did much to strengthen Sa'id against his great enemy.

5 Saudi Arabia and Iran: Outside Pressures

During the first decade after World War I, while Britain adjusted its perception of its interests on the Trucial Coast, the pressures being created by its policy in the area were far from obvious. It was not until the air-route to India was actually being established and oil concessions were being obtained that a major clash over it occurred. Prior to that, there occasionally were minor collisions between the British authorities and the local rulers, but these usually concerned local matters and were of little significance in imperial terms. Added to this, the area's internal affairs were still not regarded very seriously by policy-makers in London and Delhi.

Other powers, however, were beginning to have a significant influence on the internal development of the shaykhdoms. No longer remote from the daily life of the Coast, Saudi Arabia and Iran were gradually taking their place as important components of the political structure of the area and showing themselves serious threats and possible rivals to British supremacy in the Gulf region. They were alike in the way in which they came to prominence: during the 1920s they were consolidating themselves, and did not hesitate to use force as a means of self-assertion; but during the 1930s they mellowed their respective strategies, finding diplomacy their most effective weapon. Three striking differences between them must be pointed out, though. First, although both countries laid claim to part of the Arab side of the Gulf, it was not until it became known that oil might be discovered there that Saudi Arabia clearly voiced its claim; Iran, by contrast, upheld its own claim unremittingly (recently, though, it relinquished part of its claim, at almost the same time as it occupied the remainder). Second, Saudi Arabia's interest in the Gulf shaykhdoms was with their inland regions; Iran's with their littoral. Third, and most important, Saudi Arabia is an Arab country, with close links with the Gulf shaykhdoms; and Iran, though a Muslim country is non-Arab. This last fact is essential to any understanding of Gulf politics, particularly where they concern territorial disputes.

Iran's and Saudi Arabia's efforts to extend their respective spheres of influence to the Trucial Coast, as well as to other Arab shaykhdoms in the Gulf region, were made relatively easy by the fact that all the rulers were bound by treaty to defer from dealing directly with any government other than Britain. The result was that the shaykhdoms, apart from being woefully inadequate at resisting any form of onslaught, had to rely on British mediation for the solution of their problems with their neighbours. Technically, therefore, no relations between the Trucial States and Iran or Saudi Arabia existed; Anglo-Iranian and Anglo-Saudi diplomacy had to serve instead. This placed the rulers of the Coast on a particularly weak footing, since any appeal they made to Britain had to be subjected to various interdepartmental meetings and discussions in London before agreement could be reached on what action should be taken; as often as not, the policy of non-interference would be invoked. In consequence of this, many a ruler found that, rather than wait for help to reach him from Bushire, it was more expedient to bypass his treaty obligations and enter secretly into independent agreements with Iran or Saudi Arabia. This chapter seeks to analyse the various relationships between the Trucial shaykhdoms and these two powerful neighbours of theirs, but first it is necessary briefly to consider internal developments in Iran and Saudi Arabia during the period of their consolidation as modern states.

The renaissance of the Wahhabi movement, which had lain dormant since the Ottoman occupation of Hasa in 1871, began in 1902, when Ibn Sa'ud captured Riyadh.[1] As, in an impressive show of singlemindedness, he began to build his forces, organise his strategy, and form the *Ikhwan*, (a paramilitary Wahhabi bedouin movement), other events in the Arabian peninsula, particularly the Arab Revolt and the rise of the Sharifian dynasty, were of greater concern to Great Britain.[2] In 1913, however, Ibn Sa'ud captured Hasa, the fertile area stretching between Kuwait and Qatar, on the western coast of the Gulf, and appointed his cousin 'Abdallah ibn Jaluwi governor of the province; in this way Wahhabi authority was extended to the eastern coast of Arabia and became a force to be reckoned with by the British in the management of their interests in the Gulf region. Thus began a relationship that, although never outwardly hostile, was of a strangely nebulous quality. Based at first on an assumption of the superiority of Great Britain, it

eventually grew into a relationship between equal powers, and
yet uneasiness and strain persisted between the two. Formal Anglo-
Saudi relations commenced in 1915, when Ibn Sa'ud and Percy
Cox met at Qatif and on 26 December signed a treaty; in it,
Ibn Sa'ud undertook to abstain from aggression against or interference
with the Arab shaykhdoms of the Gulf, in exchange for which
his independence was recognised and guaranteed against foreign
aggression.[3]

Over the next decade, Ibn Sa'ud's forward policy began to reap
him great territorial rewards. In 1920 he established his power
and authority over the borderlands of the Hijaz, and later that
year he annexed Abha, the inland portion of 'Asir. In 1921, his
campaign in Jabal Shammar led to a great victory over his enemy
Ibn Rashid, whose territory he annexed. The next year the Wahhabi
forces pushed northwards, where the boundaries were undefined,
and captured Jawf. His power consolidated, Ibn Sa'ud assumed
the title of Sultan of Nejd and its Dependencies, thus giving his
newly-acquired territory an international, and temporal, status. The
final expansion came in 1924, when his armies entered the Hijaz;
and on 13 October 1924 Mecca surrendered to the Wahhabis.
The abdication of Sharif Husayn in favour of his son 'Ali was
followed by the total collapse of the Hashemite dynasty in the
peninsula. This came in December 1925, when Medina and Jeddah
fell to the Wahhabi forces, leaving Ibn Sa'ud master of an area
that extended from the Gulf to the Red Sea, and from Yemen,
'Asir and the Rub' al-Khali (in the south) to Kuwait, Transjordan
and Iraq (in the north). In January 1926 he was proclaimed
King of the Hijaz, and in 1932 he became King of Saudi Arabia.

Much had changed since the treaty of 1915. Ibn Sa'ud was
now a monarch with complete sovereignty and independence, and
he ruled over an area larger than that of the British Isles, France,
Benelux, West Germany and Spain combined. Anglo-Saudi relations
were no longer on the same footing as before, and on 20 May
1927 a new treaty, known as the Treaty of Jeddah, was signed,
annulling the earlier treaty. Although the Government of India
wished it to include an undertaking similar to that that the 1915
treaty had contained regarding the Trucial Coast and Qatar,[4] Ibn
Sa'ud refused to concede more than an assurance to 'maintain
friendly and peaceful relations with . . . the Sheikhs of Katr and
the Oman Coast who are in special treaty relations with His Majesty's
Government'.[5]

Throughout the period of his expansion, and following the establishment of his kingdom, Ibn Sa'ud had little direct contact with
the Trucial Coast—particularly in view of his great territorial ad-
vancement elsewhere in the peninsula. From the beginning of his

career, he recognised the value of an alliance with Britain and showed a marked interest in maintaining its friendship. This was based on pragmatic considerations, for one of his greatest assets was his ability to perceive the limitations of his own power, especially in the face of British opposition. It was not accidental that Yemen, the only neighbouring state not under some form of British protection, was also the only neighbouring state with which the Wahhabi forces clashed. Furthermore, it was after 1928, when the *Ikhwan* began attacks on Iraq and Kuwait, thus jeopardising his relations with Britain, that he decided to suppress them.[6] Consequently, the British authorities had remarkably little to complain of as regards Saudi encroachments on their sphere of influence in the Gulf region.

The presence of Ibn Sa'ud, however, remained powerful throughout the period under study, and it would be wrong to assume that, despite the very few official complaints to the king, the British authorities in the Gulf were unaware of his influence, direct and indirect, on the shaykhdoms of the Trucial Coast. This awareness prompted an aloofness in the British attitude towards him, and one that he was unable to comprehend. As Philby says, 'He could not understand that his own insistence on the incontestable fact of his absolute independence, both in the domestic and in the foreign fields, constituted a barrier which British sympathy could not surmount.'[7] The fact of his great power in the peninsula, and his determination to uphold his rights as an independent ruler, made his status problematic in terms of imperial concerns; it also created certain apprehensions regarding the ability to check or control any advances he might make. The fear of his penetration into British spheres of influence was based on historical precedent and shared alike by the British authorities and by the various rulers of the Gulf states, for whom Ibn Sa'ud's existing power was a constant reminder that the Wahhabis had once before been able to seize and control part of the Trucial Coast. There was too a recognition, reiterated many times in official British correspondence, that Ibn Sa'ud was the natural successor to Britain on the Arab side of the Gulf; the fact that the shaykhdoms had the same language, religion and social order as Saudi Arabia strengthened the likelihood that, were it not for the British presence, Wahhabi rule would have embraced them as well. Although a full-scale invasion was never actually feared, the presence of Ibn Sa'ud was constantly felt: in all major discussions of policy regarding the Gulf region in general and the Trucial Coast in particular, great emphasis was placed on how the king could be expected to be affected by any decision taken.

It was not only the historic precedent that prompted the British authorities to fear Wahhabi encroachment on the Trucial Coast.

The role played by Ibn Sa'ud in the more developed shaykhdoms of Kuwait and Bahrain, where British influence was strong, brought on many crises and many interdepartmental meetings in London. The Wahhabi interest in Bahrain began during World War I, when a commercial forwarding station was established there with the Qusaybi family as agents. This was made necessary by the fact that, although Ibn Sa'ud had annexed Hasa, bordering the Gulf, he possessed no port of any value and so was dependent on Bahrain and Kuwait for an outlet on the sea. A dispute arose between him and Shaykh 'Isa of Bahrain when the latter imposed customs duties on goods passing through Bahrain to Hasa or Nejd; this was eventually resolved, after much trouble, in 1920, when Bahrain agreed to levy only a 2 per cent transit duty on goods to Hasa. Ibn Sa'ud continued to show an interest in the affairs of Bahrain. During the year of troubles preceding Shaykh 'Isa's renunciation of the shaykhdom in 1923, the Wahhabis played a prominent role in events, with serious repercussions. In 1922, Shaykh Hamad bin 'Isa, who was to assume the leadership of Bahrain from his father, planned to reform the tax system by extending it to the entire population—hitherto, the Shi'ah alone were liable to taxation. This reform had been urged by the Political Agent, the Government of India and the Foreign Office, who wished to diminish any cause for Iranian charges of anti-Shi'ah discrimination in Bahrain. But the Dawasir, a powerful Sunni tribe, had no desire to start paying taxes; their leaders therefore went to Ibn Sa'ud, who promised to support their resistance to Sunni taxation. This caused the Political Agent to cool noticeably in his enthusiasm for tax reforms. Another instance of Wahhabi interference occurred in April 1923: 'Abd al-'Aziz al-Qusaybi was the chief instigator of the great trouble that broke out between the Nejdis and Persians residing in Manamah.

In Wahhabi relations with Kuwait, the main causes of friction were boundary disputes and customs duties. The 1915 treaty with Britain mentioned the need to determine the boundaries of Kuwait with Nejd when the war was over. In the meantime, the border was in constant turmoil, with raid and counter-raid occurring regularly. In April 1920 Kuwait suffered greatly from an attack by the *Ikhwan*, repeated six months later. Although attempts were made by Cox, Shaykh Khaz'al of Muhammarah and others to solve the dispute, it was not until November 1922, at the Conference of 'Uqayr,[8] that the territory of Kuwait was finally defined. This considerably reduced its size, because of its diminished desert power in the face of the growing Wahhabi strength. Using one of the few weapons he had available, the shaykh of Kuwait retaliated by levying a 4 per cent customs duty on goods in transit to

Hasa, and that in turn provoked Ibn Sa'ud to issue an embargo on trade with Kuwait. This led to great commercial stagnation in Kuwait, which Ibn Sa'ud suggested should be solved by the establishment of a Nejdi customs house there; afraid of the stranglehold of the Wahhabis if he accepted, the shaykh of Kuwait refused to acquiesce, and a deadlock ensued.

In Qatar and on the Trucial Coast, by contrast, Wahhabi pressure was more subtle. Ibn Sa'ud knew exactly how to gauge the dissensions existing between the Ghafiriyyah and Hinawiyyah, the bedouin and the settled people, the Bani Yas and the Qawasim, and how to exploit them. He confidently assured the Lebanese writer Ameen Rihani that he did not need to reach out to the Coast; the Coast instead would reach out to him.[9] Although his power in the area grew perceptibly during the 1920s and 1930s, there were few incidents that could be pointed to by the anxious British authorities as positive encroachments on their sphere of influence. After a visit to inland Oman in 1927, Bertram Thomas concluded, 'The prestige of Ibn Saud in Peninsular Oman is in direct proportion to his strength and ability to harm it.'[10] The king was a strong force in the background, a father-figure who could be turned to for help against enemies. He knew how to use the available sources of power, and how to use them effectively. It consequently is extremely difficult to analyse the extent of his influence accurately, especially as regards his personal knowledge of the activities of 'Abdallah ibn Jaluwi, his governor in Hasa.

Since Ibn Jaluwi was the Wahhabi official nearest the Trucial Coast, the fear and terror he inspired there were often mistakenly attributed to Ibn Sa'ud, who remained distant and slightly aloof, a man of great legend. Ibn Jaluwi's effectiveness was known and tested; it was very often he who instigated Wahhabi pressure on the tribes and rulers of the Coast, even interfering in the manner in which they conducted their affairs. The stories of his power and determination to enforce the law were so full of rumours that it was difficult to separate fact from fiction. One such tale that reached the Coast runs as follows. A bag of coffee, a stimulant forbidden by Wahhabi doctrine, was found by a woman, who took it to Ibn Jaluwi. On being asked how she knew what the bag contained, the unfortunate woman said she had tested the contents with her finger. The Governor ordered her finger to be cut off, since it had been in direct contact with the forbidden stuff.[11]

The first formal intimation of possible Wahhabi influence in the Gulf shaykhdoms occurred in May 1921, when 'Abdallah bin Qasim Al-Thani of Qatar appealed to the Political Resident for help.[12] He expressed alarm at the growing strength of the *Ikhwan* in Qatar, afraid that his people would join ranks with them in order to endanger his own position, and asked the Resident if he would help him if he were attacked or if an uprising occurred. Colonel Trevor, the Resident, made it very clear that the 1916 treaty bound Britain to protect the shaykh from attack by sea only, and that, if hostilities between him and Ibn Sa'ud did occur, the only form of help he could rely on would be in the diplomatic sphere. This answer was in keeping with the British policy of non-interference in the internal affairs of the shaykhdoms, but did not take into account the difficulties facing the ruler of Qatar. The disaffected members of his family, led by his older brother Shaykh Khalifah, were in constant communication with Ibn Sa'ud, who gave them moral, as well as financial, support. Sure of Wahhabi backing, they openly defied 'Abdallah; the result was a state of growing lawlessness in Qatar and a great decline in the ruler's authority. The only source of power to which 'Abdallah could turn would assure him of nothing but diplomatic assistance. This left him almost entirely to his own devices to combat the subtle attacks of the Wahhabis. He realised that Ibn Sa'ud would not risk an open attack on Qatar, but he also knew that the king could make his role as shaykh of Qatar so impossible that sooner or later he would have to place himself under the protection of the Wahhabis.[13]

It was not until the latter part of 1922 that any official British statement was made regarding Wahhabi encroachments on Qatar. During the conference at 'Uqayr, a conversation took place between Cox, Ibn Sa'ud and Frank Holmes regarding an oil concession in Hasa. Cox was startled when he realised that Ibn Sa'ud considered all of Qatar as part of Hasa, and sharply told the Wahhabi ruler that Qatar was outside his jurisdiction. Although Ibn Sa'ud did not argue the point,[14] he also did not accept it; and in the next decade the issue of his boundaries with Qatar and with Abu Dhabi was of major importance. Ibn Sa'ud continued to seize every possible opportunity to undermine the authority of Shaykh 'Abdallah until the latter finally realised that it was time for him to work out a new policy. Since he could not rely on British protection, his only hope was to come to an agreement with the king. In 1930 he admitted to the Political Agent in Bahrain that he paid the Wahhabi ruler a secret subsidy of 1 *lakh* of rupees (i.e. 100,000) a year.[15] Thus, by employing subtle forms of pressure, Ibn Sa'ud was able to gain control of Qatar; he received a secret subsidy from Shaykh 'Abdallah, and his representatives in Hasa were strong enough to control events in the shaykhdom without incurring British wrath by open aggressiveness.

Whereas Saudi Arabia was a young country whose king well

knew how ineffective he would be in any direct confrontation with Britain, Iran had known a long period of domination by Britain and Russia in the nineteenth century, and, after the accession to power of Riza Shah, in 1921, became openly assertive of its rights and integrity, on both the national and the international level. The period ░░░░░░░░░░░░░░░░░░ Instead of being allowed to partici░░░░░░░░░░░░░rence, the Persian Government was ░░░░░░░░░░░░ of Czarist Russia had only served ░░░░░░░░░ on Persia. This realisation became░░░░░░░░ the Anglo-Persian Treaty of August░░░░░░░░ greatest possible influence, short o░░░░░░░ the country; for example, the Britis░░░░░░░le for the reorganisation of not only ░░░░░░░ry, administration of the country. Th░░░░░░░ e natural outcome of the restrictive cl░░░░░░ aim on assuming control was to co░░░░░░ government: first, by centralising its ░░░░░░░he state's external independence. During the 1920s and 1930s, therefore, it was these concerns that, as the British Government was fully aware, governed Anglo-Iranian relations.

Following the basic principles of his internal policy, Riza Shah first concentrated on systematically destroying the semi-autonomy of the provinces of Iran: in 1921, Khurasan and Gilan were subdued; in 1922, after the Government had quelled a rising in Tabriz, the Kurds submitted; and in 1924 a revolt by the tribes of Luristan was suppressed. Riza took a particularly close interest in establishing and organising an efficient Iranian armed force. The first step was to dismiss the foreign—mostly British and Swedish—officers of the existing military. In 1924 his forces were strong enough to tackle the province of Arabistan (present-day Khuzistan), which was governed by Shaykh Khaz'al of Muhammarah, in whose territory the oilfields of the Anglo-Persian Oil Company lay, and who consequently had special assurances of protection from Britain. When Shaykh Khaz'al publicly denounced Riza, the latter swiftly threatened military operations against him; unable to resist, the Khaz'al bowed to the pressure and in November 1924 tendered his submission. The next month a military government was established in Khuzistan, and in April 1925 Khaz'al was arrested and sent to Tehran, where he lived under house arrest until his death.

Riza's treatment of Khaz'al necessarily brought on the possibility of a confrontation with the British Government, which had given the shaykh a good deal of support. But, although the British made official protests regarding his submission and exile, little else was done. The resurgence of nationalism in Iran had caused widespread resentment of the privileged position that Britain had held in the south of the country; one of the first acts of the new government, which rejected the Anglo-Persian Treaty of 1919, was to expel British advisers and deliberately to court American companies with offers of oil concessions. The Foreign Office in London was generally not averse to the existence of a strong Iranian government, but the Government of India refused to accept the situation, arguing that the new government was not stable.[16] This conflict was manifested in the Gulf region between the wars: the Government of India regarded any Iranian claim as an infringement of the rights of the Arabs and, consequently, of the integrity and power of the Government of India, while the Foreign Office tended to consider the matter with less firmness and more flexibility, depending on the issue at stake.

During this period, the Iranian Government, in continuation of its policy on the mainland, was much preoccupied with claiming sovereignty over the islands in the Gulf. The British Government was strongly opposed to any extension of Iranian power in a British sphere of influence, especially as the Arab side of the Gulf was becoming increasingly important; it consistently sought, therefore, to uphold Arab ownership of the islands of the Tunbs,[17] Abu Musa,[18] Sirri[19] and Bahrain.[20] With the exception of Bahrain, these islands shared a common history and status. They were claimed by the Qasimi rulers of Sharjah, a branch of which had established itself at Lingah on the Persian coast in the middle of the eighteenth century; they were also claimed by Persia, on the basis that the Qawasim had governed Lingah as Persian officials. The Arab claim was upheld by the British Government in the face of Persia's many attempts to assert its sovereignty over the islands. In 1887 the Persian flag was hoisted on Sirri. Although the British Government objected to the occupation of the island, it decided to acquiesce quietly and uphold the Arab claim to Abu Musa and the Tunbs, despite the fact that the Qawasim never dropped their claim to Sirri. In 1904, Persian customs officials forcibly removed the Arab flags from Abu Musa and the Tunbs, hoisted the Persian flag, and placed guards on the islands. The ruler of Sharjah appealed for help to the British Government, which in turn contemplated despatching a gunboat to deal with the situation if warnings to Persia went unheeded. A few weeks later, the Persian Government ordered the removal of the flags and guards from the islands, but made it clear that it still laid claim to them.[21] In 1913 the Government of India had a lighthouse erected on Tunb. After 1921, when Ras al-Khaimah became independent of Sharjah, Sultan bin Salim claimed the Tunb islands. The exact date on which the ownership of them changed hands is not clear, but in 1929

Sultan hoisted his flag on Tunb, and the ruler of Sharjah made no protest. The Persian claim was revived in 1923, when the Iranian Foreign Ministry sent the British Minister in Tehran a note reasserting Iranian rights to Abu Musa and Tunb.[22] This followed a rumour in Tehran that the Iranian Government had been pressured by an Iranian red-oxide concessionaire to press claims at the League of Nations for Bahrain and Abu Musa.[23] Abu Musa had a large deposit of red oxide, and in 1925 the Iranian customs authorities inspected the island and removed a bag of the oxide. Following warnings from the British Minister, the Iranian Government ordered its customs officials not to interfere in Abu Musa until the status of the island had been determined.[24]

In order to strengthen its position in the Gulf, the Iranian Government needed to organise the building of a navy. Overtures for help were made to the British Government, but finally it was from Italy that gunboats and patrol vessels, serviced by Italian officers, were purchased. The navy provided Iran with an instrument to challenge British authority in Gulf waters, and this was manifested largely by the seizure of Arab dhows in an attempt to control the smuggling carried on by the Arabs to the southern coast of Iran. During the 1920s and 1930s there was a spate of such incidents, following the Iranian Government's imposition, in 1925, of a tax on all consignments of tea and sugar imported into Iran.[25] A thriving contraband traffic in these commodities was carried on from the Arab coast, principally from Kuwait, Bahrain and Dubai, and the Iranian Government found it difficult to control. An official appeal to the British Minister in Tehran for aid in quelling the traffic was refused, and the Government of India made it clear that 'it is not our business to control harmless exports like sugar from our Arab Protectorates, and Persia's apparent expectation to the contrary ... has, as far as we know, no basis in international usage'.[26] The Iranian Government, therefore, took the matter into its own hands, and, with the purchase in 1931 of patrol vessels from Italy, was able to stop and search Arab dhows in Gulf waters.

THE BACK DOOR: WAHHABI INFLUENCE IN 1925

In 1930, Biscoe, the Political Resident, accurately defined the inadequacies of the British position on the Coast in the face of the power of Ibn Sa'ud: 'We hold the front door to these principalities on the littoral, but we do not hold the back door.'[27] It was precisely through this back door that Ibn Sa'ud was able to increase his influence on the Coast, for it was in the inland areas that the extent of jurisdiction of the rulers on the Coast was determined, and it was there, away from direct British influence, that Wahhabi power was most acutely felt. The technique used to control the tribes, the enforcement of the payment of *zakat*, in turn raised the vital issues of Saudi Arabia's boundaries with the shaykhdoms, and the extent of its future active interference in their internal affairs.

The Wahhabis' most direct attempt to gain some form of control in the Trucial States occurred in 1925. The turmoil of events and also the movements and customs of the tribes involved make it difficult to discern the extent of Wahhabi aggression, but there can be little doubt that the forces of Ibn Sa'ud, particularly those controlled by Ibn Jaluwi in Hasa, increased to an unprecedented level and seriously threatened the internal security of the Trucial Coast, besides providing the motivation for the campaign of the Ibadi[28] imam of Oman. The methods used were subtle and potent: support of one tribe against its traditional enemies, thus isolating the latter; enforcement of the collection of *zakat* on certain tribes, to bring them under Wahhabi protection; and muted interference in the internal affairs of the shaykhdoms. Throughout his career, Ibn Sa'ud displayed a marked ability to recognise an opportunity and use it to his greatest advantage. This was manifested in 1925, when he seized on the weakness of the tribal situation in Oman and turned it into the chance to bring pressure to bear on the Trucial Coast and the sultanate of Muscat and Oman; in this case, he took advantage of the chaos in Abu Dhabi, the hostility felt towards the imam of Oman, and the weakness of the sultan of Muscat.

The major upheavals that Abu Dhabi had undergone because of the dissension within its ruling family after the death of Shaykh Zayid had unsettled the whole of the shaykhdom. By 1925 the Dafrah region, which includes the Liwa oasis and lies between the western coast of Abu Dhabi and the Rub' al-Khali, had become the arena of prolonged tribal hostilities, which had lasted, on and off, for at least five years. The situation could be traced back to the rule of Shaykh Hamdan bin Zayid (1909–12), when fighting between the Manasir and the Bani Yas of Dafrah, on the one hand, and the southern bedouin of the 'Awamir,[29] Duru',[30] and the Al-bu-Shamis,[31] on the other, broke out as a result of looting and murder. In an attempt to gain the upper hand, the chiefs of the Manasir and the Mazari' section of the Bani Yas went to Hasa and obtained the protection of Ibn Jaluwi;[32] the rest, including the remaining Bani Yas, left their camels in the Buraimi area and migrated to Abu Dhabi and the islands around it. Shaykh Hamdan then went to Buraimi and was instrumental in bringing about a truce, after which the Bani Yas and the rest of the Mazari returned to Dafrah.

In 1922, after the accession of Sultan bin Zayid, fighting broke out again. Sultan, at a disadvantage because his murdered predecessor had been an ally of the Wahhabis, reportedly having helped *zakat* collectors, became involved. This time the Manasir were fighting the Duru', the Bani Qitab and the 'Awamir in Buraimi, and Sultan was expected to protect the Manasir from their enemies in exchange for protection of Abu Dhabi town by them.[33] He found that his authority in Buraimi was at a low ebb. In December 1923 he sent his brother Saqr, together with his own sons Shakhbut and Hazza', at the head of a mixed Abu Dhabi and Manasir force to al-Mu'tarid, a village in Buraimi populated largely by the Dawahir and under the authority of the ruler of Abu Dhabi; there the forces of the interior were to assemble, and, when all was ready, Sultan would join them. News of the expedition reached the Duru' of Tun'um, the Bani Qitab of al-Falayah (a village in the plain of Sir, a few miles south of Ras al-Khaimah town), and the 'Awamir bedouin, whose range was coextensive with the Duru' lands; they in turn raised a force of 200 men and marched to meet Saqr's party. They came across twenty men who were on their way to join the Abu Dhabi force, and killed seven of them, including Sa'id bin Butti of the Qubaysat, a relative of Sultan; the rest of the twenty surrendered, were disarmed and dispossessed.

When Sultan reached al-Mu'tarid, he gathered 500 men under the joint leadership of his brother Saqr and Rashid bin Mani', shaykh of the Al-bu-Mundhir section of the Manasir. This force attacked al-Falayah.[34] In retaliation, Sultan's villages in Buraimi were attacked; and, in response to this, Sultan's force raided Duru' land and captured fifty she-camels. The Duru' understood that men from Dubai had participated in this last move, so breaching a covenant whereby Dubai and the Duru' each agreed to remain neutral where the other was fighting a third party. The Duru' therefore stole twelve she-camels from the outskirts of Dubai.

These endless skirmishes exposed the entire Coast to danger, and placed the pearl trade in serious jeopardy. In order to guard it from any further disruption, a band of conciliators comprising Shaykh Salim bin Duyayn[35] of the Bani Ka'b, Hamad bin Ahmad al-Yahyayyi of the Al-bu-Shamis and chief of Dhank, and Sultan bin Rashid,[36] shaykh of 'Ibri, intervened, and peace was declared. The peace did not last long, however, for late in February 1925 the Manasir and the Bani Yas, much to the chagrin of Sultan, raided the homes of some of the 'Awamir living near the *dirah* of the Bani Qitab, in the desert, killing a man and making off to Liwa with a slave and three camels.

This time the renewal of hostilities prompted representatives of the 'Awamir, the Duru and the Al-bu-Shamis to seek the protection of Ibn Jaluwi, exactly as their enemies had done a few years earlier. The paramount shaykh of the Bani Qitab,[37] anxious to avoid more trouble, went to his ally, Hamad bin Ibrahim of Umm al-Qaiwain, and asked him to press the Manasir and Bani Yas for blood-money. Meanwhile, Saqr bin Zayid and Rashid bin Mani' of the Manasir had gone on a series of visits to Dubai, Sharjah and Umm al-Qaiwain, in order to strengthen their unity, afraid of the recent appeal to Hasa and the risk that it would cause the entire area to be brought under Wahhabi influence. In order to placate the Bani Qitab, whose friendship would be essential in the event of any Wahhabi encroachment, Saqr and Rashid agreed on the compromise suggested by Hamad bin Ibrahim: no blood-money would be sought, but all captured slaves and camels would be returned to their owners. Realising the obvious weakness of Sultan bin Zayid and taking advantage of it, the Bani Qitab and the 'Awamir joined forces shortly after and raided al-Sumayh, the place near Abu Dhabi town where Sultan and his brother kept their camels; the raiders came away with forty-seven camels after having killed two men. Powerless to do more, Sultan sent Ahmad bin Hilal al-Dahiri first to Dubai and then to Umm al-Qaiwain to complain. The ruler of Umm al-Qaiwain prevailed upon the Bani Qitab to return stolen property, but the 'Awamir would not. Since Ramadan, which that year was to begin on 26 March, was approaching, an armistice was declared; after Ramadan, Ahmad bin Hilal and the rulers of Umm al-Qaiwain and Dubai would reconsider what should be done.[38]

But much more important than the continued plundering was the protection given by Ibn Jaluwi to the 'Awamir, Duru' and Al-bu-Shamis tribes. In order to manifest his guardianship, Ibn Jaluwi first sent a strong force of the Al-Murrah tribe[39] to raid the Bani Yas and Manasir shortly after Ramadan, and then dispatched an agent, Su'ayyid,[40] to Buraimi to collect zakat.[41] Su'ayyid was the guest of Ahmad bin Hilal in Jimi (a town in Buraimi), and then went to Hamasah, sending his officials to collect the zakat from the Duru', Al-bu-Shamis and 'Awamir, at the rate of 1 riyal per camel and 40 riyals per goat.[42] Collectors also went to Baynunah, and forced the Manasir and Mazari' to pay zakat. Sultan bin Zayid was totally powerless to prevent this, and this caused his influence with the Manasir to diminish considerably. Su'ayyid then informed the rulers of Abu Dhabi and Dubai that the 'Awamir and the Duru' were now officially under the protection of Ibn Jaluwi.[43]

The tribes that paid zakat to the Wahhabi agent did so to

protect themselves from their more powerful neighbouring tribes rather than because they were afraid of a Wahhabi invasion, as in the nineteenth century. The methods of Ibn Sa'ud and Ibn Jaluwi were radically different from those of their forebears:

> Today it is the power of letting loose a strong tribe to raid a weaker Dhahirah one and carry off its camels without hope of redress or retaliation that is Ibn Saud's strength. Thus immediately before the arrival of Ibn Saud's zakat collector, one of the Bani Yas tribes was raided by the al-Murra and lost a hundred and fifty camels. Payment of zakat to Ibn Saud is therefore a kind of insurance against the raider. It is the wisdom and economy of the present Abdul Aziz to bring his insiduous pressure to bear on a wavering tribe through a strong and loyal neighbour whose interest it is to be ensured the fruits of victory. . . . In reality it is not Ibn Saud himself whom they desire to propitiate, but his viceroy, Ibn Jaluwi. . . .[44]

The dispatch of the *zakat* collector had immediate repercussions. The forces of the Ibadi imam of Oman, led by 'Isa bin Salih, began to mobilise for a march on Dahirat al-Sir, the southern half of the Dahirah plain, which lies between the mountains of northern Oman and the desert in the west, in order to resist any form of Wahhabi aggression in Oman. The Hinawi elements in the Trucial Coast rallied around 'Isa bin Salih and quietly declared their support for him. Late in July 1925, Shaykh Sa'id bin Maktum of Dubai secretly sent his cousins Sa'id bin Butti and Suhayl bin Butti to 'Isa, to assure him of his backing and that of Sultan bin Zayid of Abu Dhabi in the event of Wahhabi encroachment. Rumours of an invasion had been strengthened by a statement, attributed to Su'ayyid, that Ibn Sa'ud intended to send an army to Buraimi,[45] and wild stories were circulating that the fort at Buraimi village, originally built by the Wahhabis in the nineteenth century, was being restored for use by Ibn Sa'ud.[46] Other supporters included the chiefs of the Na'im, Bani Ka'b and Bani Qitab tribes, who negotiated with Shaykh Sultan bin Saqr of Sharjah for mutual assistance in case of Wahhabi encroachments; and the ruler of Umm al-Qaiwain.

Sa'id bin Maktum denied that his cousins had gone to Oman to see 'Isa bin Salih,[47] as for obvious reasons he was anxious to hide the facts of his new alliance from the Wahhabis. The details were disclosed in the Cairo newspaper *Al-Shura*[48] on 29 October 1925 in an item contributed by Shaykh Sulayman al-Baruni al-Nafusi,[49] which claimed that Sa'id's cousins had carried to 'Isa bin Salih a letter, signed by the rulers of Dubai and Abu Dhabi, in which they strengthened their ties with the Ibadi leader and promised help against the Wahhabis.[50] Ibn Jaluwi was greatly angered by this move on the part of the two Bani Yas rulers, and blamed Sultan bin Zayid for having influenced Sa'id bin Maktum. He wrote to Sa'id saying, 'Our brother Sultan is mad; he does not know that we are stronger than he. ... However, sooner or later our power shall prevail upon him and others.'[51]

In December 1925 the forces of 'Isa bin Salih invaded the southern half of the Dahirah. At first the expedition was accepted on the basis of its declared intention to resist any Wahhabi encroachments in Oman; later, however, the general fear pervaded that the move was actually a means to subordinate the predominantly Ghafiri area to Hinawi control. The inevitable confusion that ensued from misinterpretation of motives caused the expedition to disintegrate: Sulayman bin Himyar, the powerful Ghafiri shaykh of Jabal Akhdar, who at first had lent 'Isa his support, withdrew it when he realised the motives of the expedition; the remaining Ghafiri tribesmen in the Dahirah decided to follow suit and resist any advances made by 'Isa, who was soon unable to cope with the situation; he succumbed to a severe illness, and before long his army was disbanded.[52]

This left the field open to the Wahhabis.[53] During the next four years, they collected *zakat*, on and off, from the various tribes of the Dahirah.

> Its design seems to be to bring the Baduin camel tribes of the Dhahirah ... to acknowledge a nominal degree of subordination and pay zakat without trouble or expense, or military measures calculated to rouse their antagonism. Clearly the tribes in close proximity to Hasa, e.g. Minasir and Mizariya' are unable to resist, those further removed, the Bani Yas Badu ... the Na'im, Dhuwahir and Duru are in a stronger position, while the Bani Ka'ab and Bani Qitab are sufficiently remote to say 'No'. It is the wisdom of Ibn Saud to demand from the first, request from the second, and leave it to the volition of the third.[54]

By thus extending a degree of control over the tribes of Oman, Ibn Sa'ud or Ibn Jaluwi—or both—could command certain events on the Coast. The rulers of the shaykhdoms had a constant, almost nagging, fear of the Wahhabi influence on the inland tribes and knew the bearing it had on their own security. It also served to deter the expression of any overtly anti-Wahhabi sentiments, for the rulers were anxious to avoid giving Ibn Sa'ud or his cousin any pretext for anger.

Besides using the inland tribes as leverage against the rulers of the Coast, Ibn Jaluwi made his presence felt there in other ways. In February 1926, for example, showing no respect whatever for the sovereignty of Shaykh Sultan bin Saqr, he sent a police force to Sharjah in pursuit of an escaped criminal from Nejd. He demanded the extradition of the criminal, although, of course, no extradition treaty with Sharjah existed. When the hunted man was not found, the police force continued the search in Ajman and Ras al-Khaimah.[55] The same year, Ibn Jaluwi censured the *qadi* of Sharjah and Shaykh Sa'id of Dubai for not having satisfied Nejdi complainants in judicial cases. It was not accidental that, with the exception of Abu Dhabi and Dubai, all the men who performed the duties of *qadi* on the Coast had strong Nejdi connections. Wahhabi influence in these places was so strong that the Political Resident reported with alarm a rumour that Shaykh Sultan of Sharjah had sent his *qadi* to Hasa and Mecca to ask for a Wahhabi Resident at Sharjah.[56]

Although Abu Dhabi was vehemently anti-Wahhabi, its rulers recognised the importance of courting the favour of their powerful neighbour. When Shaykh Hamdan came to power in 1912, he sent a mission to Ibn Sa'ud to announce his succession. Ten years later, Shaykh Sultan sent his son Hazza', bearing gifts, to Riyadh, to do the same thing.[57] When Sultan was in turn murdered by his brother, his sons appealed to Ibn Jaluwi for protection against their uncle and for permission to live in Dalma island. Their uncle, Saqr, ruled for about a year, and during his tenure courted Ibn Jaluwi by sending presents and by helping *zakat* collectors in their task, in the hope that the governor of Hasa would strengthen his (Saqr's) position against the recalcitrant members of his family. Ibn Jaluwi, however, did not force his authority. In 1930 the Bani Yas complained to Shaykh Shakhbut about the *zakat* collectors; Shakhbut complained to Ibn Jaluwi, who withdrew the collectors without further ado.[58] The ruler of Dubai was also vehemently anti-Wahhabi, but was not as deferential as the rulers of Abu Dhabi; he did not hesitate, however, to rid Dubai of any elements that were anti-Wahhabi, as he was always nervous of retaliation.

The remaining shaykhdoms maintained a more friendly rapport with the Wahhabis, and in 1927 the Political Resident claimed that they were all in private communication with Ibn Sa'ud.[59] They knew the effect this had on the British authorities, and often used a call to Ibn Sa'ud as a weapon against British pressure. In 1930, for example, when Shaykh Sultan of Ras al-Khaimah was being pressured into accepting a Royal Air Force fuel barge, he desperately warned the Residency Agent that, if the pressure persisted, he would place himself under the protection of Ibn Sa'ud.

THE SEA FRONT: IRAN IN 1928

Three years after the Wahhabi expedition to Buraimi that caused such turmoil in the inland areas of the Trucial Coast, Iran diverted attention to the coastal regions, where it precipitated two major, direct clashes. The Iranian Government was acting in accordance with its policy of strengthening its position in the Gulf, and the Arabs were powerless to resist, not only because of their non-existent military strength, but also because of their treaty relations with Britain, which forbade them to undertake direct dealings with foreign governments. In both instances the Arabs had to depend on the British Government for support; and in both instances minimal support was forthcoming.

The first of the clashes occurred in May 1928, when Iran expelled the shaykh of Henjam. Henjam is an island off the southern coast of Qishm; and its inhabitants, mostly living in Henjam village, were Arabs of the Bani Yas whose main occupation was pearl-fishing. With the permission of the Sultan of Muscat, who held a land-lease from the sultan of Bandar Abbas, the Bani Yas had settled on the island early in the nineteenth century. The sultan of Bandar Abbas, however, argued that Henjam was not mentioned in the lease and therefore not covered by it. The Persian Government never acknowledged the Muscati rule, and reiterated its claim to sovereignty over the island; in 1868 and in 1904, both the Government of India and the British Government recognised the Persian claim, thus setting a precedent for the attitude they adopted in 1928.

The Iranian Government of Riza Shah reasserted the old Persian claims to Henjam by establishing a customs agent and a post office there, so bringing the island under closer control. Relations between the Arab inhabitants and the Iranians grew from bad to worse, and in 1927 the shaykh of Henjam complained that the stationing of Iranian customs officials was in violation of his rights.[60] The shaykh, Ahmad bin 'Ubayd bin Jum'ah, was the father-in-law of Shaykh Sa'id of Dubai, and his people enjoyed cordial relations with the Trucial Coast, with which they had very close ties. Ahmad's resentment of Iranian authority reached a climax in April 1927, when one of his dhows was seized by Iranian customs officials. He was outraged; in retaliation his followers attacked the customs post, and, in the fighting that ensued, the Iranian Director of Customs was killed.[61] Punitive action against Shaykh Ahmad followed in May, 1928, when Iranian armed force expelled him from Henjam. He fled to the Trucial Coast, where great sympathy for his plight was shown. The feeling grew as anti-Iranian sentiments ran high, and the inhabitants hopefully to Britain for support.

The Political Resident recommended some form of help, arguing that British relations with the Coast would deteriorate if the British Government showed an attitude of detachment.[62] Both the Foreign Office and the Government of India, however, were against any form of direct intervention on behalf of Ahmad; they decided that unobtrusive pressure on Iran, applied locally, would be the only solution. The solution proved useful, for in September 1928 an Iranian envoy from Henjam invited Ahmad and his followers on the Coast to return, an offer the shaykh accepted.[63]

The second major incident also occurred in 1928, and brought Iranian–Arab relations to breaking-point. It had much more serious repercussions than the expulsion of the shaykh of Henjam, since it directly affected the safety and property of many people living in the shaykhdoms. The central issue was the ownership of Tunb and the methods used by the Iranian Government to stake its claim. In July 1928 a *jalbut* (a small passenger vessel) carrying travellers, including women and children, was seized on the southern side of Tunb by a motor vessel that the Iranian customs had been operating from Tunb for two months. The *jalbut* belonged to Badr bin Muhammad of Dubai and had called at Tunb on its route from Dubai to Khasab. The passengers and the *jalbut* were taken to Lingah, where the women were stripped of their jewellery, and money and other possessions were confiscated.[64]

This had immediate repercussions along the Coast, particularly in Dubai, where the outrage felt was channelled into plans for an armed naval force to release the women and avenge the injustice. The Residency Agent managed to dissuade the people from going against their treaty relations by taking any such retaliatory measures; they decided instead to rely on the force of the British assistance promised in the treaties of 1820 and 1892, and in the assurances given by Curzon in his durbar address of 1903.[65] The Political Resident urged action supporting the Trucial rulers, saying of them, 'we punish them quickly when they are in the wrong, and they demand equally quick protection when they are attacked'.[66] The reaction of the Government of India was also strong. 'It is in itself offence against humanity, and in case of Moslem(s) an almost unbearable outrage, specially for Arabs who despise the Persians.'[67]

A few days after the *jalbut* had been seized, HMS *Lupin* went to Dubai and arrived just in time to prevent an outbreak of rioting, for the rulers of the shaykhdoms had been finding it particularly difficult to restrain the husbands of the detained women, and the people had reached the end of their tether. While the Admiralty and the India Office were discussing the possibility of sending a gunboat to Lingah, Parr, the British Chargé d'Affaires in Tehran, made urgent representations to the Chief of Customs, who claimed that the *jalbut* had been seized because it carried 400 pounds of sugar and two tons of rice.[68] This was contested by the Political Resident, who said that only two bags of sugar were on board the vessel, enough for the use of the passengers. Finally, diplomatic pressure won through, and the boat and the passengers were released early in August, although some money and goods were detained; furthermore, the representative of the Qawasim on Tunb, Mahmud Salman, who had been a passenger, died soon after he had been released.[69]

Once the *jalbut* had been released, there remained two matters to be dealt with by the British authorities. The first was the question of the release of the confiscated goods, and of general compensation for the retention of the vessel; and the second was the more vital issue of the Iranian claim to Tunb, for the incident had from the beginning been regarded by the Iranian authorities as a flagrant smuggling offence on an Iranian island. Two definite stands were now taken. The Foreign Office wanted the Political Resident to settle the affair locally, especially as the customs service had indicated that the incident had occurred without the knowledge of the government in Tehran. The India office, the Admiralty and the Government of India, on the other hand, wanted to put political and diplomatic pressure on the Iranian Government. They were worried about their responsibility to the Arabs of the Trucial Coast, whose condition was deteriorating because of their inability to avenge themselves. The Senior Naval Officer reported the agitation on the Coast, particularly in Dubai, where the ruler was under great strain and barely able to contain the anger of his people, who held him responsible for the obvious lack of British support.[70] Sir Arthur Hirtzel of the India Office noted of the report that, 'It . . . ought to make even the F. O. blush.'[71]

Finally, a compromise was reached. Both the Government of India and the British Government decided that, owing to the long delay that could be expected before the Iranians paid the compensation claimed,[72] they should themselves pay out the compensation fee of 5000 rupees, in the hope that it would have a settling effect on the Arabs. The Treasury, however, refused to sanction the payment, rejecting the decision that the Arabs of the Coast had a right to expect it as a result of their relationship with Britain.[73] Since Anglo-Iranian negotiations that the British Government hoped would result in a new treaty were about to start, no further action was taken regarding compensation; since in May 1928 the two governments had reached a verbal agreement whereby Tunb and Abu Musa were recognised as Arab possessions, and the British Government did not want to do anything that might prevent the Iranians from recognising the same in a formal treaty.[74]

A few weeks later, the family of Shaykh Sa'id of Dubai made their first attempt to remove him from power. The Senior Naval Officer named as one of the reasons for this the ruler's failure to obtain any compensation from Britain for the victims of the captured *jalbut*. He urged that some way to appease the Arabs be found, and admitted that he could not understand 'why compensation to Arabs [of] Dubai molested on high seas should be further delayed owing to possibility of settlement with Persia concerning an island belonging to Ras al-Khaimah'.[75] The Foreign Office, on the other hand, refused to press the Treasury for payment:

> From the purely financial point of view ... the proposal that the British tax-payer should be asked to pay for the misdemeanours of the Persian Customs Service is quite indefensible; and the only question at issue therefore is whether such payment could be justified on the grounds of overwhelming political necessity. ... We have reluctantly come to the conclusion that the relationship of these Arabs towards us is not such as to justify them in expecting compensation from us. ...[76]

While these discussions were taking place in London, Shaykh Sa'id's position was becoming increasingly difficult. His people relied on him for protection against Iranian attacks, and he in turn was bound by his treaty relations to rely on the British Government for the same protection. No such protection appeared, and Sa'id obviously regarded the British preoccupation with hopes of concluding an Anglo-Persian treaty as irrelevant to his predicament, especially as he had already that year faced an attempt to dislodge him because of his acquiescence to British treatment. The Government of India alone was conscious of the situation, and in November 1929 it decided that it would itself pay out, in full, the 5000 rupees compensation.[77] This was eventually done in the presence of Shaykh Sa'id early in 1930.

6 Establishment of the Air-Route: Test of Imperial Policy

Almost immediately after World War I, the British Government recognised the need for an organised civil and military air-route linking Egypt, Iraq and India. As the air-route began to take shape, the Arabian shores of the Gulf – Bahrain, the Trucial Coast and Muscat, in particular – assumed a new and fundamental importance as the essential link for British air communications. We have already noted the many discussions in London and Delhi on the possibility of extending British rule in the Gulf in order to establish the air-route and safeguard its security; we have also noted the repeated decisions that the maintenance of the *status quo* was sufficient. In the case of the Trucial Coast, the British presence was remarkably limited, and yet within a short period of time the region was drawn into a series of agreements that provided the British Government with all it wanted for the new route to India. Although the role played by certain individuals, such as the Political Residents and the Residency Agent in Sharjah, was central to the fulfilment of imperial interests, the individuals themselves ultimately relied on British political supremacy in the Gulf. This was constantly reinforced by the British making it impossible for any other power to establish itself in the area, and by the control that Indian merchants exercised over trade, shipping and ports. In the final analysis, it was British sea power that held the Gulf at its mercy, and nowhere was this better understood than on the Trucial Coast, whose people were essentially seafarers and well knew the meaning of naval force.

The first Royal Air Force flight between Iraq and India took place in December 1918; it went along the Persian shore of the Gulf at a time when the Persian Government had little control over its coastline and no permission to fly there was necessary. But conditions in the country changed radically after Riza Shah assumed power, and the RAF had to consider an alternative route. The Arab coast had two distinct advantages over the Persian. First, it was topographically superior, since it possessed many inlets and large stretches of water sheltered by reefs and shoals and these could provide good bases and refuges for flying-boats.[1] The second and more important advantage was political; for on the Arab coast there was no danger of sudden expulsion orders from the ruler, and there were no problems of neutrality (which would exclude a strategic air-route). In order to set up the route, the RAF needed refuelling grounds at intervals of about 200 miles and emergency landing grounds at intervals of about forty miles. The RAF chose Bahrain as the main centre for the Arab route: its location, Shaykh Hamad's willingness to accord facilities, and its topography all combined to give it a key position. Accordingly, the RAF secretly purchased the old quarantine station from Shaykh Hamad for use as a rest-house, and later a suitable landing ground was acquired in the same way. The next step was to find a landing ground near Muscat, to acquire a house in Muscat town to serve as an RAF wireless and telegraph station, and to arrange for refuelling and mooring facilities in Muscat Cove. All this was achieved with little difficulty, and by 1930 the RAF was making regular visits to Bahrain and Muscat.

But on the Trucial Coast, where the acquisition of facilities did not progress so smoothly, a more forward policy, albeit one nominally within the bounds set by the rule of maintaining the *status quo*, was implemented. The first step was to find a suitable place for the storage of oil and petrol. The RAF chose Ras al-Khaimah town, which possessed a fine creek with flat land immediately behind that made it eminently suitable for the landing of aircraft. Previous consultation with the ruler having been overlooked or considered unnecessary, the Anglo-Persian Oil Company was directed to send oil and petrol stores to Ras al-Khaimah. When Barrett, the Political Resident, realised that no warning had been given, and that even the Residency Agent had not been advised, he made arrangements in May 1929 for the stores to be temporarily based at Sharjah. He then sent word to Sultan bin Salim of Ras al-Khaimah that he would be going to visit him. He arrived at Ras al-Khaimah on 15 May 1929, and, together with the Air Commodore in Iraq and officers of the RAF, waited for one and a half hours for Sultan to appear. The ruler was polite, but wanted to know why Ras al-Khaimah, and not Sharjah or Dubai, had been chosen for storing the petrol. Although he did not actually object, he emphasised that he would not be responsible for the safety of the tank. After this first meeting, the Resident was to return Sultan's call at his brother Muhammad's house; but the ruler never appeared, much to the anger of the Resident, who was kept waiting in vain for thirty minutes. Matters were made worse when Barrett, on leaving the house, 'saw Shaikh Sultan arriving accompanied by the young Shaikh of Umm al-Qawain, both walking very slowly, followed by their guard.'.[2]

Barrett later wrote to Sultan demanding an apology for his rudeness and showing his own anger by forcing the ruler to accept the petrol barge anyway. Sultan duly sent his regrets, but refused to accept the oil stores, which despite his protests arrived in a dhow, which anchored in the creek of Ras al-Khaimah. Although Sultan allowed the boat to remain there, he at first refused permission for the petrol in it to be unloaded;[3] later he relented on condition that the supply would not be replenished. One of the reasons he gave for his refusal to grant air facilities was that he had been deprived of Tunb island lighthouse[4] dues and could not therefore trust Britain to pay him for the fuel depot. This reason was totally disregarded by Barrett, who viewed it as an attempt 'to draw a red herring across the path'.

The RAF next wanted to substitute a petrol barge for the dhow, so Barrett sent the Residency Agent to Ras al-Khaimah with a friendly letter. Sultan was not at Ras al-Khaimah at the time, but 'Isa discussed the question with Sultan's brother Muhammad and the notables of the shaykhdom. He found them ready to accept the fuel barge, but unwilling to accede to anything more. When Sultan returned, 'Isa gave him the Resident's letter, and with the help of 'Abd al-Rahman bin Sayf of Hamriyyah, who was visiting Ras al-Khaimah, tried to persuade him to accept to grant air facilities. Sultan refused; he claimed that it would place him in a difficult position with those of his people who opposed the idea. The Residency Agent regarded this reason as a mere excuse, and claimed that the only opposition came from Sultan himself.[5] 'Isa also reported that Sultan had threatened to leave Ras al-Khaimah if his wishes were put aside.

It was Hugh Biscoe, Political Resident from November 1929, who decided that it was time to push through a new, firm policy if the air-route were to be effective. 'I cannot help feeling that it was perhaps a mistake to adopt towards these petty Shaikhs so suppliant an attitude in the first instance.'[6] He was convinced that the moderation shown by the British authorities had been mistaken for weakness; that the general feeling on the Coast that Britain had become less powerful had been strengthened by the assumption that the League of Nations was a new super-government that could check Britain. Furthermore, events on the Iranian coast, such as the failure of Britain to help her protégé the shaykh of Muhammarah, the refusal of Iran to recognise British passports issued to people of Bahrain, and other assertions of Iranian independence, seemed to have been regarded on the Trucial Coast as indications of the general decline of Britain.[7] As further proof of diminishing prestige, Biscoe cited the many acts of discourtesy to which British officers had in recent years been subjected by the rulers of the Coast, and complained of the inadequacy of the British position: 'our policy in the Gulf seems to be to grovel on the one side and to bully on the other'.[8]

The stronger line that he suggested, and put into operation, was to inform the rulers that aircraft would land in their various territories, and that any hostile act against them 'would meet with the gravest displeasure'.[9] Accordingly, he sent the petrol barge to Ras al-Khaimah on 21 May 1930. At its arrival, Sultan's frustrated anger and sense of humiliation was redoubled. He protested about the barge and ordered its removal, threatening all kinds of trouble. Although the notables of Ras al-Khaimah informed the Residency Agent that they were opposed to their ruler's attitude, armed men were posted alongside the creek, obstructing the progress of the barge, which had to be anchored a mile outside the town. Sultan remained firm in his opposition to the barge, even though it was outside the town, and warned that he would not be responsible for the safety of the Residency Agent if it remained where it was. An attempt to dissuade him from his stand was made without success by the rulers of Dubai and Umm al-Qaiwain, and the headman of Hamriyyah, all of whom went specially to Ras al-Khaimah; so Biscoe decided to go there himself.[10] He arrived on 1 June 1930, and promptly sent for Sultan.

Although at first the ruler announced that he would visit the Resident, he finally sent his brother in his place. Once again, the Resident asked to see Sultan, and he stated a deadline by which he had to appear. Sultan ignored this, and soon both men began to assume entrenched positions. Sultan cut off the water supply to the Residency Agent's house at Ras al-Khaimah, obliging 'Isa to live, temporarily, on board HMS *Triad*. Next, the rulers of Dubai and Umm al-Qaiwain and the headman of Hamriyyah declared a boycott of Ras al-Khaimah until Sultan showed some courtesy.[11] Although the British authorities regarded the matter as a test case for the successful establishment of the air-route, and consequently decided to deal severely with Sultan for his obdurate behaviour, an official of the India Office remarked, 'one cannot help feeling some sympathy with the Trucial Sheikhs who are required to afford facilities for an air route which they readily recognise must end in their coming to a larger degree under British control'.[12]

The use of force finally made Sultan accept the barge, for on 6 June the HMS *Cyclamen* arrested eight pearling dhows belonging to Ras al-Khaimah.[13] By what Biscoe regarded as a fortuitous coincidence, Shaykh Salih of Dibba also sent word to Sultan that he would attack him if he did not come to terms with the British.[14] At first, Sultan remained firm. He continued to refuse to visit the Resident and sent messages that he was unwilling to modify his earlier stand. This so infuriated the Resident that he asked for permission, firmly refused by the Government of India and the India Office, to issue an ultimatum to the ruler that his towers and fort would be bombarded if he did not sign an agreement. Finally, however, Sultan succumbed to all the pressures, and, after long sessions with Sultan of Sharjah, who acted as mediator,[15] signed a document, on 15 June, that allowed the barge to remain at Ras al-Khaimah for one year. He also gave permission for the petrol store to be replenished, and promised to appoint a guard to protect the barge.[16] Furthermore, he accepted responsibility for the safety of the Residency Agent and his dependents, his brother Muhammad undertaking to compensate 'Isa for the damage caused by the cutting off of his water supply.[17]

This incident proved to be the first in a long series of power struggles, for the attitude of the Iranian Government made the Trucial Coast essential to the establishment of a civil air-route in the region. In 1925, Imperial Airways Ltd[18] announced that it wished to operate a regular civil air-service between Cairo and Karachi, and sought permission to fly along the Iranian shore of the Gulf. Although at first it seemed likely that the service would be allowed, in December 1926 the Iranian Government gave definite orders that all plans for the projected route must cease. The British Minister in Tehran participated in a number of discussions and conferences in an attempt to obtain permission, but a deadlock ensued until the initialling, in May 1928, of a draft Anglo-Persian treaty, in which the Iranian Government undertook to reopen negotiations for the air-route. Later that year, the Iranians agreed to allow Imperial Airways to operate a service for three years from January 1929, with Bushire and Jask as airports and Lingah as an emergency landing ground, but permission was not to be renewed after that. These restrictions obliged the Air Ministry and Imperial Airways urgently to consider the Arab coast as an alternative, while negotiations for the renewal of permission by Iran continued. When hopes for the further use of the Iranian route began to wane, the Cabinet officially contemplated preparing for the establishment of an Arab route in July 1931.[19] In September 1931 the India Office decided to start negotiating for concessions, and consulted the Air Ministry on possible landing places. With the aim of keeping the route approximately parallel with the Bushire–Lingah–Jask line, it was decided that it should run by way of Kuwait, Bahrain and a place on the Trucial Coast. The RAF had already established a landing ground in Kuwait, and a landing area in Bahrain was also available, but there remained the most important question of where on the Trucial Coast an airport could be established and a rest-house built for the overnight accommodation of passengers. The arrangements for the night-stop, which the plans envisaged as being on the Trucial Coast, thus became imperative for the continuation of the civil air-route; in view of the deadline on use of the Iranian route, there was little time to spare, and the political and RAF authorities worked closely together to find a suitable location and then reach an agreement with the ruler concerned.

In December 1931, after the RAF had eliminated Umm al-Qaiwain as a possibility, Ras al-Khaimah and Dubai were examined and both considered suitable. In both places, however, Biscoe encountered great opposition and was unable to reach the point where even a preliminary agreement could be drawn up. In the case of Ras al-Khaimah, it was not so much the ruler, who had already experienced the penalties of resistance, as the notables and, more ominously, the Shihuh tribe, who opposed the granting of further facilities.[20] Biscoe realised the intensity of the opposition, and, deciding not to aggravate it, turned instead to Dubai. He visited the shaykhdom in the latter part of December 1931, but was unable to see the ruler, who was severely ill at the time. The Resident waited for Shaykh Sa'id to recover, and during his stay a wave of agitation against Sa'id began, strengthened by rumours that he was about to enter into secret engagements with the British. Aware of its commercial potential, Sa'id was genuinely interested in the establishment of an airport, but he realised that the opposition, led by his cousin Mani' bin Rashid, was too powerful to ignore. He asked Biscoe for time to consider the matter, and in February 1932 he was forced to admit that he had been unable to obtain the necessary agreement from his family. For a while Biscoe was at a loss; in view of the determined local opposition, and the risk this posed for the security of an airport at Ras al-Khaimah or Dubai, he was reluctant to force an agreement on either Sultan or Sa'id.

The turning-point came in March 1932, when Shaykh Sultan bin Saqr of Sharjah, who had closely followed the events in Dubai and Ras al-Khaimah wrote to the Residency Agent and said that he would be willing to grant the facilities for an airport in Sharjah.[21] Sultan was in straitened financial circumstances and welcomed the opportunity to earn an extra income; he also realised that an air-service would bring more trade and commercial activity to his shaykhdom. After the RAF had approved of Sharjah, which had a stretch of sand that was flat and hard enough to accommodate the land craft that Imperial Airways planned to use instead of flying-boats, Biscoe went there in April to start negotiations. The visit bore little fruit, for bad weather obliged him to leave soon after his arrival, and the shaykh was not willing to commit himself to anything without consulting his brothers. The Residency Agent, 'Isa bin 'Abd al-Latif, was instructed to act as deputy for Biscoe, but he found himself unable to make much progress with Sultan, who finally admitted that he had changed his mind and was unwilling to grant any concessions.

Meanwhile the Iranian Government extended its agreement with Imperial Airways until 31 May, and the Foreign Office, particularly anxious that the new air-service begin before that date, asked that Biscoe be made aware of the urgency of the situation. After consultation with 'Isa, who suggested that Sultan of Sharjah might become more willing to enter discussions if a warship were to appear, Biscoe sent HMS *Triad*, commanded by Captain L. E. Crabbe, the Senior Naval Officer. The *Triad* arrived at Sharjah on 1 May, and Crabbe found widespread opposition to the air-route, led by the shaykh's brothers. His report was not optimistic. 'Apparently great play has been made by the anti-air agitators who presented lurid pictures of what might happen to the women and children while their husbands were absent on the pearling banks.'[22] Crabbe assured Sultan that there would be no interference in Sharjah affairs as a result of the airport, but the ruler remained firmly opposed to it, despite his strong wish to have a secure form of income. The ensuing deadlock brought Biscoe, accompanied by an officer of the RAF, to Sharjah on 3 May, and, after two futile days of attempting to persuade Sultan, the Political Resident decided to issue an ultimatum: the airport would be built in Sharjah, with or without the ruler's permission; if Sultan refused to give his formal agreement, no allowance of any kind would be paid him.[23] Biscoe had previously warned Sultan that he was bound by his original offer to grant the air facilities, and he knew the effectiveness of pressuring the ruler with *force majeure*. The Resident then left Sharjah.

Faced with this dilemma, Sultan became greatly introspective: 'he had shut himself up in his fort, had, as it were, clothed himself in sackcloth, covered himself with ashes and refused to eat. His meditations in retreat evidently did him good. . . .'[24] He

Lt.-Col. Sir Trenchard Fowle KCIE, CBE, Political Resident in the Persian Gulf, 1932-9. (Courtesy Mrs D. Hall)

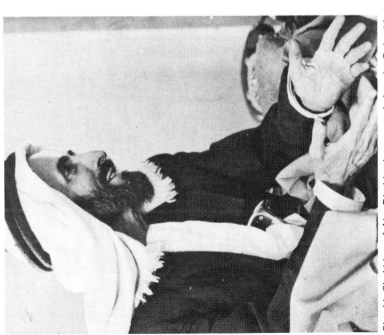

Shaykh Shakhbut of Abu Dhabi, who succeeded to the Rulership in 1928. (Paul Popper Ltd)

Ras al Khaimah. (G. M. Lees: Courtesy of the Royal Geographical Society)

The Fort at Fujairah. (Lt.-Col. Sir R. Hay: Courtesy of the Royal Geographical Society)

Petition from rulers and notables concerning 'Abd al-Rahman of Hirah (see p. 63) (Courtesy of the India Office Records R/15/1/279)

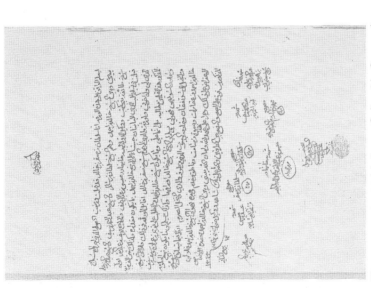

The peace agreement between Sultan bin Saqr and Khalid bin Ahmad of Sharjah, 1924 (see p. 48) (Courtesy of the India Office Records R/15/1/276)

A humorous approach to the difficult task of delineating boundaries in desert areas. (Initialled by J G L, probably J. G. Laithwaite, Principal at the India Office, 1935, during the Anglo-Saudi negotiations) From the Public Record Office, F0371/18906, E2724, 30 April 1935

Dubai (Lt.-Col. Sir R. Hay : Courtesy of the Royal Geographical Society)

Frank Holmes

The Creek at Dubai. (Lt.-Col. Sir R. Hay : Courtesy of the Royal Geographical Society)

The Ruler of Umm al-Qaiwain. (Lt.-Col. Sir R. Hay: Courtesy of the Royal Geographical Society)

The Fort of the Shaykh of Abu Dhabi. (H. Burchardt: Courtesy of the Royal Geographical Society)

The Ruler of Ajman and his camel. (Lt.-Col. Sir R. Hay: Courtesy of the Royal Geographical Society)

Shaykh Shakhbut of Abu Dhabi coming off to call upon the Political Resident. (Lt.-Col. Sir R. Hay: Courtesy of the Royal Geographical Society)

Triad 1916 (Crown Copyright. Courtesy of The Ministry of Defence)

Crocus September 1942 (Crown Copyright. Courtesy of The Ministry of Defence)

Fowey June 1942 (Crown Copyright. Courtesy of The Ministry of Defence)

sent for the only source of help available to him, his support
in earlier days—his father-in-law, 'Abd al-Rahman of Hirah. 'Abd
al-Rahman 'proceeded most resolutely to overcome the objections
of the common people, the notables and Mohamed. He posed
as a man of experience, told them of British power and experience,
called them children etc.'[25] and obviously made progress. 'Abd
al-Rahman's entry into the dispute put an end to the opposition
by Sultan's family and people to the civil air agreement.

Taking advantage of the temporary lull, and in view of renewed
threats from Sultan bin Salim of Ras al-Khaimah, Sultan bin Saqr
signed a secret agreement around 20 May that was based on a
draft that Biscoe had left behind. He then asked 'Isa for the
personal support of the Political Resident; Biscoe, however, sent
word that he would not be able to visit the Trucial Coast before
mid June. In the meantime, further opposition to the establishment
of an airport at Sharjah arose; led by the rulers of Ajman and
Ras al-Khaimah, it accused Sultan bin Saqr of selling Sharjah
to the British.[26] In order to avert an outbreak of trouble, the
Senior Naval Officer sent the HMS *Bideford* to Ajman and Ras
al-Khaimah with a warning from Biscoe to their rulers that they
must not interfere in Sharjah affairs.

Sultan bin Saqr was keen to sign an official agreement, but
was clearly afraid of his family's opposition. He told no one of
his secret agreement, and played for time, hoping to resolve the
predicament in which he found himself. When Biscoe returned
to Sharjah as scheduled, he was unable to accomplish much. The
opposition of Sultan's family was strengthened by that of the people
of Dubai, who were afraid that the mail steamer that called at
Dubai once a fortnight would be diverted to Sharjah, for it was
known that Sultan had made it a precondition for the granting
of air facilities that the mail steamer should call at Sharjah. Biscoe
tried to alleviate Dubai hostility by asking that the mail steamer
make an extra call at Sharjah while continuing to go to Dubai,
and then proceeded to assure Sultan that his independence would
in no way be endangered by the signing of an air agreement.
After issuing a draft letter to that effect, Biscoe, unable to do
more, decided to leave Sharjah and await results. He thought
that, if the opposition of Sultan's brothers continued, particularly
that of Muhammad, there would be nothing for it but to resort
to drastic measures. 'We cannot allow one man to obstruct the
air route . . . and should he [Muhammad] persist in this attitude
I think it will be necessary to deport him or order him to reside
outside Shargah.'[27] Biscoe had been particularly impatient with
Sultan's fears that his independence would be curtailed by the
establishment of an airport, and he remarked with exasperation,

'The Shaikhly families of the Trucial Coast are ... quite the stupidest people with whom it has ever been my misfortune to deal—a country yokel from a remote village in England or Scotland is a highly intelligent individual compared with a Trucial Shaikh. ...'[28] Biscoe was weary, and had little sympathy with Sultan's suspicions. It is ironic to note that all the promises he gave the ruler, impatiently, as if they were unnecessary, were in very little time to amount to nothing.

After receiving approval from London on the draft agreements he had drawn up, Biscoe planned to return to Sharjah in July, this time to obtain Sultan's signature to the final agreement. The Iranian Government had once again renewed its agreement with Imperial Airways, this time until the end of October, so Biscoe was able to plan carefully for his visit. He decided to ask H. R. P. Dickson, the Political Agent in Kuwait, to accompany him and help in the negotiations, for Dickson had spent most of his life in the Arab world, and knew well the language, customs and people.[29] The two men boarded HMS *Bideford*, where, a few hours later, Biscoe suffered a severe heart attack and died shortly after. The Political Resident was buried at sea with full naval honours.[30]

After he had recovered from the shock of Biscoe's death, Dickson decided the only course open to him was to proceed to Sharjah and continue as originally planned. When he arrived there on 20 July, he found the atmosphere conducive to discussion, the news of Biscoe's death having subdued the opposition. On 22 July the agreement was signed by Dickson and Sultan; on the same day, Dickson signed a supplementary letter to Sultan in which he guaranteed the continued independence of Sharjah.[31] Under the agreement, which was to last for eleven years, Sultan promised to accept an airport at Sharjah and to build a rest-house there under the supervision of a British engineer; he also undertook responsibility for the safety of the passengers and the staff of Imperial Airways and to supply thirty-seven guards for that purpose. In return, he would receive payment for the guards, as well as a monthly rental fee (of 800 and 300 rupees, respectively) for the airport and rest-house. The British Government would advance Sultan the money for the rest-house, which he would repay, and the Government would provide doors, windows, steel joints and corrugated iron *gratis*, leaving Sultan to supply the stone (from the islands off the coast), plus transportation and labour. Furthermore, Sultan was to receive a personal subsidy of 500 rupees per month, and a 5 rupees landing fee for every aeroplane, excepting those of the RAF. It was also agreed that Imperial Airways and their employees would not deal directly with Shaykh Sultan, but through the Residency Agent and Political Resident.

This was a major breakthrough in the establishment of the new air-route, which began to function on 1 October 1932. One of its most significant aspects was the shape assumed by the Imperial Airways rest-house: this, the first permanent British establishment on the Coast, was a fort-like building, so providing a perpetual reminder of the true source of authority in the shaykhdom.

After the success of his visit to Sharjah, Dickson was reassured by certain facts. First, he was convinced that Sultan's suspicions of the air-route were really based on a fear that closer British control of Sharjah would reveal the continued existence of the slave trade, which, according to Dickson, supplied 85 per cent of pearl divers; this fear also prompted the neighbouring shaykhdoms to oppose any extension of British interests. Dickson had not been impressed by the people of the Coast, and remarked that 'it would be hard to find anywhere in Arabia a more uncouth suspicious and backward lot of Arabs'.[32] Second, he came to the conclusion that there was no menace to the airport from the bedouin of the hinterland; the only possible danger there was that the ruler of a neighbouring shaykhdom might order his bedouin to fire a shot or two at the station merely to weaken Sultan's position. 'Such child's game is not new to us ... and if ever such a thing happened, it would not be difficult to trace the guiding hand and inflict the necessary chastisement.'[33]

With Dickson's assurances that the security of the airport was in little danger, the Air Ministry and the India Office could confidently proceed to authorise the next step in the establishment of the civil route. An emergency landing ground was needed, and Kalba, situated on the Gulf of Oman, was chosen as the most suitable site. The headman of Kalba, Sa'id bin Hamad al-Qasimi, was not as amenable as Sultan bin Saqr had been, and it took four years for him to give the required permission. During that time, the classic methods of persuasion employed by the British authorities in the Gulf were put to the test: two different forms of threatened pressure were applied, and, when they failed to frighten Sa'id into accepting an agreement, Dickson's written promise to Sultan bin Saqr was totally disregarded and the shaykh of Kalba was officially declared independent of Sharjah.

The first approach to Sa'id took place in September 1932, when the Political Agent in Muscat was authorised to sound him out on the subject of the landing ground. He found Sa'id unwilling to discuss the matter before consulting with his fellow Qawasim, Sultan bin Saqr of Sharjah and Sultan bin Salim of Ras al-Khaimah, so the Agent left Kalba. A second mission to Kalba in January 1933 also met with little success, so T. C. W. Fowle, who had succeeded Biscoe as Political Resident in 1932, devised a plan for action. Although he suspected Sultan bin Salim of having influenced Sa'id against the signing of an agreement, he wrote to the shaykh of Kalba in firm tones: if an aeroplane was forced to land at Kalba and received help, the shaykh would be well rewarded; if, on the other hand, he proved to be obstructive, he would be called to task and considered personally responsible.[34] This ultimatum was issued only after another, more devious, plan by Fowle to enforce the submission of Sa'id had failed. In view of the great enmity between Kalba and Fujairah, and the fact that the shaykh of Fujairah claimed all the territory around Kalba, including the site proposed for the landing ground, the Resident had sent the HMS *Bideford* to visit Fujairah in November 1932. From Fujairah, the sloop could easily be seen in Kalba, and this was intended to frighten Sa'id into action, especially as Fowle sent him a message that his rival was being approached instead.[35]

But all these plans failed to have the desired impact on Sa'id, who held out with great persistence. Fowle was unable to find a means to subdue him, especially since both the Foreign Office and the Air Ministry had urged that no force be used to obtain the concession. The matter was therefore left in abeyance for three years. In May 1936 the subject was taken up again with Sa'id by Tom Hickinbotham, Officiating Political Agent in Bahrain, on a visit to Kalba. This time Sa'id stated his terms: he would sign an agreement provided Kalba were declared independent of Sharjah, the ruler declared entitled to a gun salute, and assistance provided in the event of a serious attack.[36]

Fowle seized the opportunity to push through acceptance of the landing ground, and suggested that Sa'id's terms be met. He saw no reason why Kalba should not be recognised as independent, especially since the ruler of Sharjah had had little control over it for many years.[37] The India Office hesitated to break the promise officially given by Dickson to Sultan bin Saqr in July 1932, which explicitly stated, 'the British Government will respect you and your successors' independence, complete freedom and authority over your subjects and properties and will do nothing to take away your lands from you'.[38] Any deviation from this promise would be nothing short of a bare-faced breach of it. But the advantages of proceeding with the establishment of the air-route far outweighed any moral considerations, and the India Office began to realise the advantages of granting independence to Kalba; gradually, the arguments against it were put aside. The principal reason for the reluctance of the India Office to grant Sa'id's wish for independence was the precedent set in 1903 when the Government of India recognised Kalba as a part of Sharjah.[39] But the air-route was essential to imperial communications, and even precedents, which were always so central to British policy decisions, could be disregarded. To begin with, the Resident Clerk at the India Office argued that 'it is not clear whether this ruling [of 1903] was ever communicated to the Shaykh of Sharjah'.[40] Furthermore, the granting of the independence of Ras al-Khaimah from Sharjah in 1921 could be cited and used as an alternative precedent. 'If it is advantageous to us to recognise the independence of Kalba I doubt whether we need be deterred by the rather shadowy vestiges of Sharjah sovereignty.'[41] One last point had to be cleared before independence could be sanctioned, and Fowle was asked whether Sultan bin Saqr would 'take umbrage', and whether there was a chance that the promises given by Dickson would be regarded as broken.[42] Fowle's answer was swift and forceful: 'I do not think it matters even if Shaykh of Sharjah takes umbrage.'[43] The Resident argued that if a ruler ceased to control an area under the *de facto* rule of another shaykh, the former had to lose his claim; also, that Kalba, situated on the Gulf of Oman, was not even contiguous with Sharjah. Sultan's claim, therefore, had to be regarded as extinct. 'This being so, promise contained in Dickson's letter . . . does not apply.'[44]

Fowle thus swept aside any hesitation that might have been felt regarding the promises to Sultan. An interdepartmental meeting was held in July at which the India Office, Foreign Office, Air Ministry and Admiralty were represented; the conclusions reached were in keeping with Fowle's line of thought, for the Departments decided to sanction the independence of Kalba. Accordingly, Sa'id bin Hamad agreed to grant Imperial Airways an emergency landing ground in Kalba and signed an agreement to that effect on 28 August 1936.[45] On the same day letters were exchanged between Hickinbotham and Sa'id bin Hamad regarding the new, independent status of Kalba,[46] which then became the seventh Trucial state and so remained until 1952, when it was reincorporated into Sharjah.

Other concessions required by the establishment of the air-route involved less complicated and dramatic decisions, but were not necessarily without problems. When, in 1930, Shaykh Shakhbut of Abu Dhabi refused to allow the RAF to keep at Sir Bani Yas island a petrol tank that it had installed there without his permission, little attention was paid to his refusal, because of the general resistance on the Coast to the air-route; four years later, he was induced to accept the petrol tank, in exchange for the granting of his request to have geologists search for artesian wells in Abu Dhabi.[47] Geologists would be sent to Abu Dhabi, but only if the necessary facilities—an emergency landing ground, a flying-boat anchorage, and storage tanks—were accorded to the RAF, along with any other air facilities that might be needed.[48]

The Political Agent and Sa'id bin Maktum of Dubai were able to convince Shakhbut of the merits, mostly financial, of granting the required permission; and on 13 February 1935 he signed and sealed an agreement for the petrol tank at Sir Bani Yas, and for the establishment of a landing ground there and near Abu Dhabi.[49] He was also given a lump sum of 5000 rupees instead of the arrears he had asked for from the date when the petrol tank was first installed at Sir Bani Yas.

But when the HMS *Fowey* went to Abu Dhabi to mark the landing grounds and to build a petrol store for the RAF, Shakhbut reacted strongly. He did not call on the captain of the *Fowey* as required, and went on board only when he was sent for. He refused to allow the construction of the petrol store, saying that there was no specific mention of this in the February agreement. Shakhbut also wrote to the Political Agent in Bahrain, offending him by claiming that Sir Bani Yas had been ruined.[50] Shakhbut knew the terms of the air agreement well, and was not prepared to allow for any extra concessions such as the building of a petrol store. The Political Agent was instructed to inform him that the store was 'one of the natural adjuncts' of a landing ground, and therefore implicitly understood in the February agreement.[51]

But Shakhbut was adamant and determined not to back down, despite his awareness of the double insult to the Political Resident: he had refused to go on board the *Fowey* until specifically called, and he had opposed the erection of the petrol store. Fowle was not willing to show acquiescence, and immediately issued an ultimatum: the pearling fleet of Abu Dhabi would be prevented from proceeding to the banks if Shakhbut persisted in his refusal to allow the petrol store to be erected.[52] The message was delivered by Captain G. A. Cole, officiating as Political Agent in Bahrain, who was also instructed to tell Shakhbut to apologise for his behaviour to the captain of the *Fowey*.[53] On receipt of the message, Shakhbut lost his temper and refused to apologise. But he was frightened by the prospect of the immobility of his pearling fleet, and agreed to the construction of the store.[54] Furthermore, when the Political Agent in Bahrain visited Abu Dhabi a week later, Shakhbut went on board his ship immediately. He was visibly shaken, and, almost incoherently, expressed sincere apologies for the previous insults to the British Government.[55] There was consequently no trouble when, in 1936, Shakhbut gave permission for the erection of a beacon on Halul island, especially as he realised that it was self-working and needed no attendants.[56]

In 1937, Imperial Airways started a flying-boat service on its route to India. The stops *en route* included Alexandria, Lake Galilee, Baghdad, Basrah, Bahrain and Gwadur. Basrah was one of the places for a night-stop, and Imperial Airways considered Umm al-Qaiwain and Dubai as possibilities for another night-stop. The former was considered first, and Shaykh Ahmad bin Rashid was approached for permission to survey his territory. After a good deal of persuasion, he agreed, but stipulated that the surveying party remain at Umm al-Qaiwain for no longer than fifteen days. Fowle retorted that, if the party found it so necessary, it would stay longer than fifteen days, and that Ahmad and his people would be held responsible if anything untoward occurred; the Resident refused to allow any shaykh to dictate his terms, always afraid of the deterimental effect it would have on British prestige. He planned, if Ahmad bin Rashid remained obstructive, and if the surveying party were obliged to remain at Umm al-Qaiwain for longer than fifteen days, to inform the ruler that 'certain local pressure would be brought to bear against him and his people';[57] if this warning proved insufficient, he would send a sloop to capture the pearling fleet of Umm al-Qaiwain. A few weeks later the Political Agent in Bahrain warned Ahmad of the 'local pressures', and hinted at the possibility of the seizure of the pearling fleet. It had the desired effect, for Ahmad gave his permission;[58] the surveyors, however, found Umm al-Qaiwain unsuitable for a landing place, and an alternative had to be found.

Dubai was finally chosen: its natural facilities, combined with its proximity to the existing airport and rest-house at Sharjah were the determining features. At first there was little opposition, for on 22 July 1937 Shaykh Sa'id bin Maktum signed an agreement for one year in which he undertook to provide the required facilities for a charge of 440 rupees per month on the understanding that any buildings to be used would be paid for separately.[59] Thus the passengers of the flying-boats which started to arrive at Dubai in August 1937 were taken to the rest-house at Sharjah, where they spent the night, and whence they returned the next day to proceed with their journey. In order to ensure the safety of the passage from Dubai to Sharjah and back, Shaykh Sa'id and Shaykh Sultan each signed an agreement (on 17 and 18 September 1937, respectively) in which they promised to be responsible for the safe conduct of the passengers.

The renewal of the agreement with Dubai did, however, present a few problems, for in February 1938 Shaykh Sa'id made it clear that, instead of 440 rupees, he wanted 1000 rupees a month. In March, after the forcible eviction by Fowle of two gun-runners from Dubai,[60] Sa'id was angry and said he would not be prepared to renew the agreement. Despite Fowle's suggestion that Ras al-Khaimah be considered as an alternative, the Air Ministry wished to continue the night-stop in Dubai. Accordingly, Weightman, the

Political Agent in Bahrain, went to Dubai in June to negotiate a five-year agreement. He discovered that Sa'id was under considerable pressure, particularly from his wife, to press for more than 1000 rupees a month. After lengthy discussions and strong persuasion by Weightman, on 6 June Sa'id signed an agreement under which he was to be paid 940 rupees a month, plus 500 rupees a month as a personal subsidy, and a landing charge of 5 rupees for every aeroplane.[61]

This was the last of the air agreements. Within the space of a few years, and using all the resources available to them, the Political Resident and his subsidiaries, plus naval and RAF officers, had ensured that the Coast would be a regular halting place on the route to and from India, for both military and civil aircraft. Besides providing petrol stores and a seaplane-alighting area for the RAF, the Coast provided bases for Imperial Airways, at Sharjah for land aircraft and at Dubai for flying-boats. The services included: at Sharjah, an airport one and a half miles from the town, with a fully marked landing ground, accommodation for passengers, a petrol and oil store, and a barbed-wire enclosure housing an RAF bomb store; in Kalba, an emergency landing ground for Imperial Airways; in Abu Dhabi, an RAF petrol store and a landing ground; in Dubai, an alighting area for flying-boats; in Ras al-Khaimah, an RAF seaplane-alighting area, an RAF fuel barge moored in the creek, and an emergency landing ground just outside the town. The efficient and orderly manner by which provision of the facilities required on the Coast for the operation of the air-route was ensured was probably the best argument that could be supplied for the official British policy of maintaining the *status quo*. 'There is only one test of a policy and that is its success or failure. Judged by this test our policy on the Trucial Coast ... however hand-to-mouth and peculiar it may appear ... emerges with flying colours.'[62]

7 The Preliminary Oil Concessions: Triumphant Enterprise[1]

Almost concurrently with the establishment of the air-route, preliminary oil concessions were being signed on the Trucial Coast. While the air-route was vital to British imperial communications, a more far-reaching achievement was the channelling of the Coast's oil into a British-controlled company, thereby laying the foundations for the economic and political future of the shaykhdoms. Owing to the interest in oil, two of the main concerns of British policy on the Coast during the inter-war period were: first, application of the 1922 agreements by which the rulers were bound to submit for British approval any commercial agreement regarding oil; and, second, precise definition of the shaykhdoms' boundaries. The 1922 agreements and the question of boundaries are central to the history of the exploration of oil on the Coast—a history that is little known but highly relevant today.

Taken on its own, the quest for oil agreements can be seen as a microcosm of the inter-war history of the Trucial Coast. Two of its most basic features were pitted against the other. The first was the British policy to keep the Gulf a British lake, and the second was the general and overriding weakness of the Trucial shaykhdoms themselves. The confrontation between the rulers, who wanted the freedom to choose to which company to grant a concession, and the British authorities, who were determined to enforce their own choice, resulted in the defeat of the rulers.

It is clear, however, that despite instances of British intervention during the period of the preliminary oil concessions, British policy on oil was slow in being developed. It evolved at an unhurried pace; the problems were discussed as they appeared, little thought being given to them beforehand. One senses from the available correspondence that there was little understanding of what the probability of the existence of oil in commercial quantities might mean. Despite the discovery of oil in Bahrain in 1932, it seems that no serious consideration was given to the possibility that a corresponding discovery might be made on the Trucial Coast. Viewed from this perspective, the official British attitude primarily reflects a concern to exclude foreign interests from the Coast, and shows little interest in purely financial gain.

Any study of oil on the Coast, and, indeed, in Arabia as a whole, must start from May 1932, when oil was struck in Bahrain. Not only did this event quicken oil companies' interest in Arabia, leading to the granting of a concession to the Standard Oil Company of California by Saudi Arabia in 1933,[2] but, in addition, it also revived the flagging economy of Bahrain, bringing with it undreamed-of prosperity to what had previously been a wretchedly poor area. The renaissance of Bahrain, which was transformed into a bustling shaykhdom and the economic centre of Arabia, reaping unparalleled social and financial advantages, was viewed with admiration by its neighbours, who were eager to stumble on the same riches themselves. They had first to overcome their instinctive suspicion of the machinations of the oil companies, but in a short while their fears were allayed. Shaykh Shakhbut of Abu Dhabi was the first of the Trucial shaykhs to approach an oil company, and in 1934 he suggested that geologists of the Anglo-Persian Oil Company search for artesian wells in his shaykhdom. Shakhbut's greatest interest was in the possibility of the existence of oil, but he did not want to acknowledge this openly; besides, water was a more immediate necessity, and both Ibn Sa'ud and Shaykh Hamad of Bahrain had evinced to the petroleum geologists the same desire for the discovery of artesian wells. The rulers of Dubai, Sharjah, Ajman and Umm al-Qaiwain followed with similar requests, but no water was discovered, although the geologists found Abu Dhabi particularly promising for oil.

In 1935, Shaykh Sultan bin Salim of Ras al-Khaimah became the first Trucial Coast shaykh officially to ask for geologists to explore for oil. Predictably, he took advantage of a visit of the French destroyer *Bougainville* in February to ask its commander for surveyors, rather than ask the British authorities first.[3] The French admiral told Shaykh Sultan that he would try to arrange to send a geologist; Sultan then reported the details of his conversation to Fowle, whose first thought was to exclude French and all other foreign geologists from the area. Acting on this principle, and convinced that, if there were any signs of oil, negotiations should be opened immediately, with a view to securing the rights to survey the shaykhdom, Fowle approached the Anglo-Persian Oil Company (APOC). He wished this company, in which the British Government had held the controlling interest since 1914, to enter the field before any other concern. As a result, on 1 August 1935 Sultan granted the D'Arcy Exploration Company, a subsidiary of the APOC, a two-year option to explore for oil; the object of the option was to secure the right to negotiate for an oil concession within that period of time.[4] Following this, the D'Arcy Exploration Company opened negotiations for similar options elsewhere on the Trucial Coast.

Hajji Abdallah Williamson, who led the negotiations, was to be a leading figure in the development of oil on the Trucial Coast until 1937, and was at first regarded warmly by the rulers and the British authorities alike. A great adventurer whose life story was as remarkable as it was varied, Williamson was an Englishman who became converted to Islam towards the end of the nineteenth century; after living as a bedouin in areas within what are now Iraq and Saudi Arabia, during World War I he re-established his ties with Britain, and in 1924 joined the APOC.[5] His great knowledge of Arabia made him ideally suited to the job of securing options, and before long he was able to obtain the signatures of the shaykhs of Sharjah and Dubai to agreements similar to the one signed by Shaykh Sultan of Ras al-Khaimah.[6]

The Anglo-Iranian Oil Company (AIOC), as it became known after 1935, thus became the first company to enter the Trucial Coast through the options granted to its subsidiary. When the APOC first showed an interest in the Trucial Coast, it was clear to the India Office that any form of activity relative to oil should be limited to British subjects. In 1935 a representative of the company asked for permission to allow an American geologist of the Iraq Petroleum Company (IPC)[7] to go to Abu Dhabi for exploration work. The India Office confirmed that it was 'very anxious to facilitate the task of the British element in the Iraq Petroleum Company of establishing themselves in these areas', but would not 'welcome the despatch to the Trucial Coast of an American, or of any foreigner'.[8] Although all foreigners were included in the general policy of excluding non-British interests, the principal fear underlying the policy was that of infiltration by American interests. American oil companies established themselves swiftly and efficiently in Arabia, beginning in 1928, when the Standard Oil Company of California (Socal) won the Bahraini concession from the shaykh of Bahrain after the Iraq Petroleum Company, which, under the Red Line Agreement of 1928,[9] had priority rights there, had made it clear that it was not interested. The discovery of oil in Bahrain was followed in 1933 by Socal's success in competing with IPC for oil rights in Saudi Arabia.[10] Early in 1934, following diplomatic negotiations between the United States and British Governments regarding a concession in Kuwait,[11] a compromise was reached through the formation of the Kuwait Oil Company, whose interests were shared equally by APOC and the American-owned Gulf Oil Corporation. A strong determination to seal off the rest of eastern Arabia from American companies led to the granting of a concession to the APOC by Shaykh 'Abdallah of Qatar in May 1935; the conclusion of the agreement was largely owing to Fowle's efforts to divert the great interest that Socal displayed in the shaykhdom's potential.

Although the APOC had gained a footing in the Trucial Coast through the options of D'Arcy Exploration, another company tried to enter the area. Frank Holmes,[12] whose oil career in Arabia began when he obtained a concession from Ibn Sa'ud in 1923 for Eastern and General Syndicate, and whose enterprising spirit refused to accept defeat, was regarded with considerable suspicion by the British authorities, and it is to Fowle's credit that he listened seriously to the proposition put forward by Holmes in May 1935. Holmes told the Resident that he thought he could get together a British company with a view to exploring Abu Dhabi and Dubai; the company would be 80–100 per cent British-owned, and based on the Anglo-American Corporation of South Africa Limited.[13] Fowle was not averse to the entry of a totally British company, provided it were reasonably well qualified—especially as the IPC, into whose area the Trucial Coast fell, had a strong foreign element. Although the India Office thought it would be more practical to leave the Trucial Coast in the charge of the APOC, particularly as the company operated in Qatar, it agreed to consider the propositions put forward by Holmes. The new company came to nothing, however, and in October 1935 Holmes communicated this to the India Office.[14] He had not, however, been inactive during the period from May to October; he had written to both Shaykh Sa'id of Dubai and Shaykh Shakhbut of Abu Dhabi, requesting permission to search for oil. Shaykh Sa'id, acting on the advice of the Residency Agent, ignored the letter; Shaykh Shakhbut, on the other hand, encouraged Holmes and embarked on a long period of confrontation with Fowle and his representatives.

PETROLEUM CONCESSIONS LTD

In the meantime, in October 1935, Petroleum Concessions Ltd was formed and registered. All its shares were held by the same interests, in the same proportion, as in the IPC, the only exception being that there was no representative of the Iraqi Government on the board of directors; this latter fact was the *raison d'être* of the new company, which could then create affiliates in the different countries where it developed concessions. Under the Red Line Agreement, the APOC could not operate concessions in Qatar and the Trucial Coast except in conjunction with its partners in the IPC; therefore, after the formation of the new subsidiary, the APOC transferred to Petroleum Concessions its rights in the options obtained by D'Arcy. For a while, then, the situation was confused: the options of Ras al-Khaimah, Sharjah and Dubai were transferred to Petroleum Concessions, with whose representative the respective rulers had to deal, while D'Arcy's representative was on the Trucial Coast trying to obtain exploratory options from Abu Dhabi, Ajman and Umm al-Qaiwain. Matters were further complicated by the decision of Petroleum Concessions to appoint Frank Holmes as its Trucial Coast representative. Holmes had a strong personal antipathy towards Hajji Williamson, the D'Arcy representative. Both men were very individualistic and forceful, and their mutual jealousy and dislike was exacerbated by the friction between their respective positions and by their rivalry to win the confidence and friendship of the rulers.

Generally speaking, the rulers were eager for the exploitation of oil. They were stimulated by the example of Bahrain, whose rise from bankruptcy to affluence was striking. They also saw the financial advantage of a concession alone—as in Qatar, where the annual income from it greatly relieved the economic depression from which the entire Gulf region had suffered as a result of the decline of the pearling industry. Of the six rulers, Shaykh Shakhbut was probably the most eager for the exploration of his shaykhdom. He was almost convinced of the existence there of oil; he reported that bubbles of oil had been seen in the water around some of the islands of Abu Dhabi and that a tarry deposit had been washed up on the shores.[15] Furthermore, Holmes had already impressed him with the possibility of its existence. But Shakhbut had a keen business sense, and was unwilling to negotiate even an exploratory option without showing resistance and bargaining for a better deal. He held off negotiations with Williamson, and in November 1935 refused to deal with him unless he received 20 lakhs of rupees (i.e. two million) as a monthly payment.[16] This made Fowle suspicious that Shakhbut was in secret negotiation with Holmes, who was in turn acting on behalf of a company other than Petroleum Concessions. But the delay proved rewarding to Shakhbut. When he finally, in January 1936, granted D'Arcy a three-year option, he was given 3000 rupees a month, as opposed to the 1000 rupees paid to the ruler of Dubai, and the 750 paid to the ruler of Ras al-Khaimah. The ruler of Ajman followed suit a few weeks later with a two-year option and 500 rupees a month. Umm al-Qaiwain was temporarily ignored, in view of the ruler's refusal to discuss terms for an option on the basis of a private agreement he had with Shaykh Sultan of Ras al-Khaimah; the shaykhdom was small and unimportant, and little attention was paid to it. Thus, by February 1936, Petroleum Concessions was responsible for negotiating concessions, within the period stated in the various D'Arcy options, with five of the Trucial Coast shaykhs.

In October 1935, after consultation with the Foreign Office, the Admiralty, Petroleum Department and the Air Ministry, and on the basis of suggestions put forward by Fowle, who was then in London,[17] the India Office officially approved the transfer of the D'Arcy options to Petroleum Concessions. Although French, Dutch and American interests in the company were strong, it was the most British company available, and as such was authorised to obtain concessions. The India Office made certain stipulations about the conduct of the negotiations, and explained them to J. S. Skliros, Managing Director of IPC from 1934 to 1949: any geologist or employee who visited the Coast had to be British; any surveying party had to have the guidance of the Political Resident; the ruler in whose shaykhdom a surveying party wished to explore had to give a written guarantee promising responsibility for the safety of the party; permission from the British Government was necessary before the opening of negotiations with a ruler; and the concession would be subject to the approval of the British Government.[18]

Having established a preliminary working basis with Petroleum Concessions, the India Office next—before negotiations for concessions could reach an advanced stage—turned its attention to the question of the shaykhdoms' boundaries. An interdepartmental meeting was held in February 1936 during which the extent of the problems of defining boundaries was fully realised. Not only were the shaykhdoms' boundaries with each other disputed, but, in addition, their boundaries with the neighbouring states, Saudi Arabia and Muscat, were extremely vague, especially in desert areas. Much depended on tribal loyalties and on the extent of each tribe's grazing lands—an uncertain yardstick in bedouin society.[19] The meeting did little to solve the predicament, which was temporarily shelved with the conclusion that, for the purposes of the concessions, 'it would be sufficient to define the areas in question as "the territories of the Sheikh"'.[20] The Foreign Office alone wanted to tackle the intricacies of the situation as soon as possible; since 1934, it had become involved in a dispute with the Saudi Government over boundaries with Muscat, Abu Dhabi and Qatar, and it knew only too well the dangers of ignoring such a crucial issue in the face of the great potential wealth of every square inch of land. George Rendel of the Foreign Office,[21] himself responsible for the negotiations with Saudi Arabia, urged that the problem of the shaykhdoms' boundaries be confronted; in the existing negotiations, the only Trucial state concerned was Abu Dhabi. Fowle's recommendations were sought. He obviously disagreed with the Foreign Office, and did not wish to attempt any immediate solution. 'This cannot be done without, *inter alia*, enquiry from the Shaikhs, and will be, I imagine, a thorny question which may upset them. I think it would be better to wait until Petroleum Concessions Limited have obtained their concessions before taking this matter up.''[22]

The question of boundaries was not regarded as an issue of immediate relevance, so, with relief, the more practical details of obtaining concessions were turned to. Holmes proposed to establish headquarters in Bahrain and 'request the Rulers of the Trucial Coast to call one at a time, discuss terms, sign and take away their bags of rupees'.[23] First, however, the India Office instructed Fowle to obtain from the rulers assurances of safety for surveying parties. The Resident told the rulers that the British Government approved of the D'Arcy options provided that they, the rulers, accepted responsibility for the safety of the company's surveyors; if the surveyors were attacked, the rulers would be held responsible for punishing the culprits and would also have to pay such compensation as the British Government thought appropriate. A few weeks later, the Resident addressed the rulers again. This time they were informed that the British Government had given its approval for Petroleum Concessions to negotiate for concessions, and that Frank Holmes was the company's representative. The Resident also told the rulers that all concessions were subject to the approval of the British Government, and that Petroleum Concessions was required to conclude a separate political agreement with the British Government. Fowle reiterated the importance of guarantees of safety.[25]

Almost immediately, the rulers of Dubai and Abu Dhabi gave the required undertaking, but the others were slow to follow. The shaykh of Sharjah wanted more specific information on the amount of compensation he would have to pay, Shaykh Sultan of Ras al-Khaimah flatly refused to guarantee the safety of surveyors, and Shaykh Rashid of Ajman simply ignored Fowle's letters. Stephen Longrigg, who had become General Manager of Petroleum Concessions in 1936, suggested to the India Office that the rulers of Sharjah and Ras al-Khaimah both needed reassurance about the security clause. Holmes had telegraphed Longrigg that the two men disliked 'indeterminate nature as to what mulet would be imposed therefore their objections to signing protection agreement until maximum of their liability is agreed'.[26] When Shaykh Sultan of Sharjah asked that the compensation be paid in terms of *diyah*, the India Office decided to agree.[27] There seemed no point in bargaining on an obscure detail of payment; the most important point was to impress the rulers with the seriousness of the situation. Furthermore, fear of intrigues by Socal on the Trucial Coast urged that negotiations get under way soon. By December 1936 Sharjah and Ras al-Khaimah had accepted the security clause,[28] and in February 1937 Shaykh Rashid of Ajman followed suit.[29]

Having agreed to compromise on the question of compensation, Fowle and the India Office were not prepared to go further, and wished to encourage the completion of concessions as soon as possible. Although Shaykh Sa'id of Dubai entered negotiations soon after signing the security clause, there was little sign that the others would to the same. By November 1936 it had become clear to Fowle and the Political Agent in Bahrain that, aware of possibly greater reward from Socal, the rulers were unwilling to commit themselves to Petroleum Concessions. Suspicion of the machinations of Socal continued despite the visit to the India Office in October 1936 of Ballantyne (a representative of the Bahrain Petroleum Company) on behalf of the California company. Ballantyne officially expressed Socal's interest in the Trucial Coast. Although its representatives had been approached by the various rulers there, Socal wanted first to inform the British Government of its intentions.[30] The India Office made it clear to Ballantyne that Petroleum Concessions had the priority on the coast, because of the D'Arcy options, and that the British Government could not approve of any approach to the rulers by a competitor.[31]

The reasoning for this was clear. Although Petroleum Concessions was not owned exclusively by British interests, it operated as a British company in that its personnel, finances and outlook were British. In the absence of a fully British company, it served to exclude a completely foreign company. Socal was regarded with the greatest fear. Its concession in Saudi Arabia was assigned to the California Arabian Standard Oil Company (Casoc), which in 1936 brought in the Texas Company (now Texaco) on an equal basis.[32] Casoc's concession in eastern Saudi Arabia raised the problem of the Saudi boundary with Qatar and Abu Dhabi. It was known that Casoc was seeking from Ibn Sa'ud an extension of its concession so that it would cover the whole area that the king claimed in eastern Arabia; if this were granted before Petroleum Concessions established itself in Abu Dhabi, the *fait accompli* would ruin all hopes of negotiations over the boundary. Thus it was crucial that Petroleum Concessions should quickly negotiate concessions of its own—especially in view of news that the American company was resorting to subterfuge.

One form of subterfuge adopted by the Americans particularly annoyed Fowle. In December 1936 he reported that an Indian (Afghani) employee of Casoc, Ajab Khan, had paid a visit to the Trucial Coast from Hasa via Bahrain late in November. He had delivered letters to the rulers from William Lenahan (the American representative of Casoc in Jeddah), and asked them to show him their files of correspondence relating to oil matters. He had also asked the rulers to give him letters of invitation to Lenahan for a visit to the Coast, and went through other preparations for a forthcoming tour of the Coast by Lenahan.[33] The rulers rebuffed Khan's overtures, saying that they were already committed to Petroleum Concessions.[34] A further report from Fowle indicated that Khan had told the ruler of Umm al-Qaiwain that, if he doubted the sincerity of Lenahan, Ibn Sa'ud would give him a reference.[35] Khan was put out of the Coast when it was discovered that he had travelled on a Saudi passport. His British passport was impounded, and it was seen that no British official would grant him a visa for the Trucial Coast or Bahrain.[36]

Despite the failure of Khan's mission, Fowle was worried that the rulers did not completely believe his warnings about negotiating with the California company, for there was little progress in the talks with Petroleum Concessions. The only serious negotiations were with Shaykh Sa'id of Dubai, and there much confusion prevailed. Shaykh Sa'id was not on good terms with Frank Holmes and asked for the participation of Hajji Williamson. The two men, with headquarters in Bahrain, were able to make little headway in the early part of 1937, and Loch, the Political Agent in Bahrain, reported the chaotic situation with amusement:

Poor old Hajji Williamson, who is himself apt to be tiresome at times, complained about the geologists' hurry—they complained of the length of his prayers—the geologists complained of Holmes— Holmes complained of Hajji poking his nose into affairs that had nothing to do with him and of the geologists' lack of tact (and incidentally misusing his furniture in his Bahrain house!)—all united in complaining vaguely of their Company sending them out into the blue without adequate instructions!! The Airways Station was beset with sinister and furtive looking people. Money chinked and the verandah was blocked by a toy motor car (at which Hajji sniffed audibly) for the favourite Dubai baby![37]

The negotiations with Shaykh Sa'id continued slowly and were impeded by the personality clash between Holmes and Williamson. Furthermore, the realisation that the final agreement was about to be signed brought a wave of reaction. The rulers of Sharjah and Ras al-Khaimah, aware that oil was less likely to be struck in their shaykhdoms than in Abu Dhabi or Dubai, tried to press Shaykh Saʿid to hold out for better terms, thus ensuring the same for his fellow rulers. Shakhbut of Abu Dhabi, on the other hand, was concerned about his boundaries with Dubai, and urged that they be defined before the final signature.[38] Although Saʿid resisted the efforts of the rulers of Ras al-Khaimah and Sharjah, he did agree to negotiate a settlement on the border issue with Abu Dhabi. Finally, on 22 May 1937, he signed an agreement granting Petroleum Concessions Ltd a concession, which was then transferred to Petroleum Development (Trucial Coast) Ltd for development.

The procedure for the oil agreements was as follows: first, a commercial agreement between the company and the ruler was signed; then, a political agreement between the British Government and the company was signed; and, finally, an exchange of letters took place whereby the ruler endorsed the political agreement. The last of these steps was to safeguard the terms of the political agreement, which would prevail in any conflict with the commercial agreement; and to provide a lever to ensure that the company would abide by the provisions of that agreement. The political agreement safeguarded the position of the British political authorities, along with British strategic and other interests; it enabled the production and resources of the company to be placed at the disposal of the British Government in case of emergency or war. Furthermore, the company undertook to remain British by registration, with at least one director a British subject.

Fowle had hoped that the completion of negotiations for the Dubai concession would help speed negotiations elsewhere on the Coast, but he was to be disappointed. Holmes reported that the ruler of Sharjah wanted better financial terms than Shaykh Saʿid, and that Shaykh Sultan of Ras al-Khaimah was stubbornly refusing to negotiate. Fowle saw two reasons for the lack of progress: continued intrigues by Socal, and lack of initiative by Petroleum Concessions. The rulers were procrastinating while waiting for the D'Arcy options to expire, which would then leave them free to negotiate with the Americans. Furthermore, reports reaching Fowle about the activities of Hajji Williamson led the Resident to believe that Williamson was working for Casoc.[39] He had apparently written three times to Shakhbut of Abu Dhabi and Sultan of Ras al-Khaimah: in the first letter, he had offered each of them a motor-car; in the second, he had invited both men to visit him in Basrah; and finally he said that he had asked the AIOC to send him to the Trucial Coast to negotiate for a concession, and that if the company refused he would resign and negotiate on his own account.[40] Even his former champion Shaykh Sa'id of Dubai, reported the existence of intrigues by and involving Williamson.[41] These reports made Williamson *persona non grata* on the Coast: after that, he retired from the service of the AIOC and reverted to his life as a bedouin.

Fowle would have approved of the theory that the conditioning of policies with regard to oil was based on a fundamental difference between American and British companies: that, whereas the Americans solve their own problems, the British rely on government support to liquidate theirs.[42] The Resident was impatient of the excuses made by the company for its lack of progress, and was generally suspicious of Holmes's motives for not doing his utmost to speed the negotiations.[43] He dismissed as 'rubbish' Holmes's theory that the rulers were playing for time because they were afraid of the implications of the political agreement,[44] and concluded that Petroleum Concessions was not seriously aiming for concessions, but merely trying to extend the options.[45] Fowle's irritation with the company persisted after Holmes's dismissal from it in the latter part of 1937, when he was replaced by Basil Lermitte, and after the company had been granted concessions by most of the rulers. In 1939, Fowle reported that there was an impression in Bahrain, shared by the Political Agent there, that the company, having obtained the concessions, was not out to work them. He compared the activities of Petroleum Concessions with those of its more active American competitors. 'Invidious comparisons are drawn between what they do or rather not do, and what the Americans actually carry out.'[46] He admitted the unfairness of comparison with the American company, but felt that Petroleum Concessions should be 'kept up to the mark', especially since its concessions on the Trucial Coast had been obtained with the help of the British Government.

IMPLEMENTATION OF 1922 AGREEMENTS: ULTIMATUM OF 1937

Seeing that Petroleum Concessions was unable to obtain any more concessions after Dubai, Fowle took matters into his own hands and formulated a successful plan. He proposed to tell all the rulers that, with reference to the 1922 agreements, His Majesty's Government approved of Petroleum Concessions and would not approve of any other company; this had been decided when Dubai had granted its concession, thereby setting a standard that was fair to all.[47] The proposal was approved by the India Office, which suggested that Fowle make it clear that the Government wanted only one company, Petroleum Concessions Ltd, on the Trucial Coast. 'In these circumstances His Majesty's Government are prepared to approve agreements with Petroleum Concessions Limited but they are not prepared to consider permitting negotiations with any other company.'[48]

It was this statement, issued by Fowle in the form of an ultimatum in July 1937, that finally brought the company further concessions; but first reactions to the statement were angry. Shaykh Sultan of Ras al-Khaimah defiantly claimed that he would turn to any company he pleased,[49] and Shaykh Shakhbut shrugged it off as *hawa*.[50] Fowle was unperturbed. The rulers were now bound to Petroleum Concessions and had to accept the terms it offered. Reports reached the Resident that Shaykh Shakhbut refused to consider anything less than the same terms as Kuwait had secured, and that the ruler of Ras al-Khaimah had made demands that could only be those of a 'demented creature'.[51] Fowle was uninterested in the details; he urged all concerned to leave the rulers alone for a while, to give them time to comprehend the implications of his ultimatum.

The next person to sign a concession with Petroleum Concessions was Sultan bin Saqr of Sharjah. Holmes led the negotiations on the understanding that the Dubai concession was to be the standard. The date set for signature was 6 July 1937,[52] but at the eleventh hour Sultan refused to sign, declaring his unwillingness to exchange the letters that took cognisance of the political agreement. The text of the ultimatum, that the rulers had to accept Petroleum Concessions or nothing, was delivered to Sultan, who was then left alone to decide for himself.[53] In September he declared his willingness to accept the exchange of letters; on 17 September he signed the concession, but refused to write the required letters. Fowle informed him that he had consequently 'lost the good offices of His Majesty's Government', and his travel papers, together with all those of Sharjah people, were withdrawn. Fowle knew that this measure would 'produce the correct letter within a reasonable time';[54] and by the end of March 1938 Sultan had capitulated, after which the travel papers were restored.[55]

In March 1938, Shaykh Sultan of Ras al-Khaimah was reported ready to sign an agreement granting a concession. At the last minute he refused and asked for the same terms as Qatar. He also wanted to discuss the political agreement with the Political Resident before signing the concession. Sultan, who at the time was deprived of his travel papers, because of discourtesy to the Senior Naval Officer, was anxious to have his passport returned so that he could travel to Kuwait, presumably to visit Holmes, who was there, and then maybe to see Williamson, who was at

Basrah.[56] Longrigg saw no alternative but to instruct his representative to withdraw from negotiations with Shaykh Sultan, and hoped that 'the passage of time (with continued absence of competitors) and/or the intervention of His Majesty's Government' would solve the difficulties.[57]

At an informal meeting at the India Office on 12 April, while Fowle was in London, a representative of Petroleum Concessions suggested that Sultan's last-minute refusal to sign might have been connected with the requirements of the political agreement. Although the India Office thought that the procedure accepted by the rulers of Sharjah and Dubai had set a precedent, the question was examined. After his return to Bushire, and when he had had time to look into the matter, Fowle admitted that the political agreement was viewed with suspicion by the rulers, but that it was also an excuse for not coming to terms with Petroleum Concessions. The Resident likewise thought that the company used the political agreement as an excuse for not having obtained concessions. 'If the political agreement were out of the way neither Company nor Shaikhs would have this excuse.' He recommended that the political agreement remain, but not the requirement of its cognisance by the rulers. After much interdepartmental correspondence in London, this was agreed.

But it did little to remove the opposition of Sultan bin Salim. In December 1938 Longrigg visited Ras al-Khaimah in an attempt to persuade him to grant a concession. Although Sultan gave a number of reasons for refusing (such as that Petroleum Concessions was planning to negotiate directly with the Bani Qitab tribe for a visit to Jabal Fa'iyah in Sharjah territory),[59] the Political Agent in Bahrain said that what lay behind such objections was Sultan's wish 'to avoid what is to him the repulsive prospect of having to make up his mind finally'.[60] Longrigg was, however, able to procure an agreement (signed on 7 December 1938) granting Petroleum Concessions exclusive exploration rights over Ras al-Khaimah; this was to last for two and a half years, with the option of renewal for a further year.[61] But it was not until 21 June 1945 that an agreement granting the company a concession in Ras al-Khaimah was at last signed.[62]

When Petroleum Concessions first became interested in the Trucial Coast, it provisionally decided not to approach Kalba, then in the process of establishing itself as an independent shaykhdom. In 1937 its ruler died, and, although he was nominally succeeded by his seven-year-old son, the effective power in Kalba was wielded by the regent, Khalid bin Ahmad, a former ruler of Sharjah. The strength of Khalid's personality impressed the company, which turned with renewed interest to the shaykhdom—not, basically, because of any prospect of oil there, but because Khalid had extended his influence throughout the Shimayliyyah and would thus be a useful contact for future negotiations concerning the hinterland. The India Office informed Longrigg, however, that Khalid had to be approached as regent of Kalba, and that any concession he granted could cover only recognised Kalba territory, and not all of the Shimayliyyah;[63] but the main object of Petroleum Concessions in concluding an agreement with Khalid was to secure his friendship. The terms of the agreement concluded between the parties, on 20 December 1938, gave the company a seventy-five years concession and promised it the regent's help in its relations with other rulers and with neighbouring tribes.

CAPITULATION OF ABU DHABI

Shaykh Shakhbut was the sole remaining ruler whose territory Petroleum Concessions was keen to explore and secure rights for. His determination to resist Fowle's ultimatum of Petroleum Concessions or nothing was outstanding, especially as he was the only shaykh on the Coast who did not capitulate soon after it was issued. He was clearly anxious to negotiate with the more generous American company (with which he on more than one occasion expressed his willingness to come to an agreement[64]) and claimed that it was the political agreement that had been detrimental to his negotiations with Petroleum Concessions. When the requirements regarding the political agreement were waived, and no excuse for Shakhbut's unwillingness could be found, Fowle found other means to bring the ruler to the discussion table.

From the beginning, the Resident had tried to impress on Petroleum Concessions that the only way to deal with Shakhbut was with firmness. In February 1938, for example, Longrigg had called at the India Office to express his concern at his company's failure to 'clinch matters' on the Coast, especially with Shakhbut, who had made known his refusal to accept any terms that were not equal to those granted to Ibn Sa'ud. Longrigg declared himself willing to go to the area himself if there were any prospect of a settlement with Shakhbut,[65] but Fowle, convinced that Shakhbut, if left alone to consult with his fellow rulers, would come around in time, recommended that the company do nothing to change its terms and said that he saw no reason for Longrigg to go to the Coast.[66]

Fowle confirmed this viewpoint shortly afterwards when he went to Abu Dhabi, where Shakhbut visited him on board HMS *Bideford*. The Resident purposely did not mention the oil concession, but did ask for the ruler's permission, firmly refused, for an exploration party from Petroleum Concessions to visit Buraimi. 'He could give no adequate reason for his refusal, but persisted in it, and relapsed into a sulky silence which continued until the end of his visit.'[67]

The opportunity for finding a crack in Shakhbut's armour was presented when Basil Lermitte[68] reported that a certain amount of trading in slaves was taking place in Abu Dhabi; he related a specific case of a slave who, about to be sold, tried to seek refuge with him. Fowle was prepared to accept Lermitte's statement that the case was not an isolated one. He argued that Lermitte knew Arabic and could not have been mistaken; furthermore, the Resident admitted that Abu Dhabi was far from Bahrain, where the Political Agent could not possibly know everything that transpired on the Coast. On the rather flimsy evidence of Lermitte's information, together with a report from Weightman, who claimed evidence from secret sources, Fowle decided to reveal the possibilities of British power to the defenceless Shakhbut. Without consulting either the India Office or the Government of India, and acting through a third person, he instructed Weightman to instruct the Residency Agent, then K. S. 'Abd al-Razzaq,[69] to tell Shakhbut that he had lost the 'good offices' of His Majesty's Government—i.e. his travelling papers and those of his people were cancelled until further notice.[70] This was done on 11 March 1938, and Shakhbut's reaction seems to have amazed the Political Agent in Bahrain: 'The Shaikh of Abu Dhabi has had the impertinence to enquire why he has been deprived of the good offices of His Majesty's Government, and to enquire also what reasons we have for stating that slave trading goes on through his territories.'[71] When, however, Weightman visited Abu Dhabi in June of last year, he reported that the ruler's 'bearing towards me [was] unexpectedly pleasant and cordial, and he professed to be eager to please His Majesty's Government.'[72] He tried to impress the Agent with his innocence regarding the slave trade, but Weightman bluntly told him that 'protestations of loyalty and so forth are better supported by deeds than by words'.[73] Shakhbut told the Agent that he had already started inquiries regarding the slave trade, at the same time challenging him to point out a definite case, so he could prove his loyalty and punish the culprit.[74]

Alarmed that, so soon after the British Legation in Jeddah had renounced its right of manumission,[75] slaves from Abu Dhabi might be being imported into Saudi Arabia, the Foreign Office asked the India Office for a report on the consequences of punishing Shakhbut and for any other information relevant to the slave trade. The India Office accordingly asked Fowle for a further report on slave-trading on the Trucial Coast, and requested that he start an inquiry into the possibility that the traffic was being directed into Saudi Arabia.[76] Instead of proceeding according to the instructions given by the India Office, Fowle, obviously considering the stoppage of travel papers inadequate, suggested strong measures to stop the slave trade. He admitted his inability to produce substantial proof of the existence of the trade, but dismissed this on the basis that Britain did not administer Abu Dhabi and therefore could not have a strong hold on it. He wanted to deal with the shaykhdom swiftly and firmly, especially as he had recently heard of a general revival of the slave trade on the Trucial Coast. He argued that, if Shakhbut were faced with a devastating show of strength, he would take active steps to halt the illicit trade, and this would be noted throughout the area and would serve as an example. He wanted to inform Shakhbut that the trade in slaves was being carried out contrary to treaty regulations, and to tell him that, as a security against its continuance, he would have to pay a fine of 8000 rupees, which would be returned in annual instalments of 2000 rupees if the Resident were satisfied that the trade had been discontinued. If the sum were not paid within fourteen days, a sloop would seize the pearling vessels of Abu Dhabi, tow them to within a few miles of the town, remove the rudders and sails, and then let the crews tow the vessels ashore with rowing boats.[77] Fowle regarded this as the most effective way to reassert British authority and subdue Shakhbut, who would face great insecurity at home if the pearling fleet of Abu Dhabi, upon which the entire shaykhdom depended for its livelihood, were destroyed. That no proof of the existence of the slave trade had been established did not bother Fowle unduly, and he was unperturbed when Weightman reported that it was generally believed on the coast that the reason why Shakhbut's travel papers had been withdrawn was that he had refused to grant a concession for oil. To this Fowle answered that he had no interest in local opinion on the matter, and that the only problem he was willing to discuss was the practical aspect of the destruction of the pearling fleet. After consultation with the Senior Naval Officer, who informed him that the entire Persian Gulf Division would need to be employed for the operation, Fowle agreed to an alternative suggestion: Shakhbut's fort would be destroyed by shell-fire in a manner that would not unduly endanger lives or property, since the ruler's house was well away from the town.[78]

The officials at the India Office, annoyed that Fowle had withdrawn Shakhbut's travel papers without consulting them and that he had failed to answer their specific questions regarding the slave trade, discussed the Resident's proposals. J. P. Gibson, Principal of the Political Department, admitted he would be 'delighted to

see Abu Dhabi getting a good knock on the head'.[79] Although
he conceded that the evidence against Shakhbut was 'a little lacking
in precision', R. T. Peel, Assistant Secretary of the Political Department, thought that security considerations made a strong case for
taking a tough line.[80] So Fowle's suggestions were circulated to
the Admiralty, the Foreign Office and the Government of India,
all of which agreed to them.

In the meantime Fowle went on leave to London, where he
discussed the whole problem of Abu Dhabi with the India Office.
Weightman, who officiated as Resident during his absence, reported
that Ahmad bin Khalaf bin 'Utaybah, one of the most influential
men of Abu Dhabi and related by marriage to Khalifah bin Zayid,
Shakhbut's venerable old uncle, had told the Residency Agent that
he could negotiate the concession in ten days. Weightman did
not trust Ahmad bin Khalaf, but he did not discount the possibility
that Ahmad's claim signified that Shakhbut had had a change
of heart.[81] After his meeting at the India Office, Fowle was inclined
to agree that it would be foolish to enrage Shakhbut by inflicting
any form of punishment on him; he felt that the wisest course
would be to stay action until Petroleum Concessions had made
a fresh approach to the shaykh.

The policy proved successful, for in the first few days of 1939,
and in face of the British stand on slave-trading, Shakhbut's
resistance crumbled. He agreed to negotiate with Petroleum Concessions, and Longrigg went to Abu Dhabi to conclude an agreement.
He took with him a letter from the Political Agent in Bahrain
that reaffirmed Fowle's ultimatum of Petroleum Concessions or nothing, should Shakhbut need a reminder.[82] After an especially difficult
time, during which his entire family helped to convince him, Shakhbut signed, on 11 January 1939, a commercial agreement for seventy-five years.[83] Longrigg reported that one of the main reasons
why the ruler of Abu Dhabi had finally consented to commit
himself to Petroleum Concessions was his 'hope that an agreement
would be gratifying to the Political authorities, whose better opinion
he would gladly have.'[84] Fowle was delighted. He regarded the
letter that Longrigg took with him as the best proof of his own
policy. 'I have always held the view ... that once the shaikhs
were convinced that His Majesty's Government were in earnest
as to their "ultimatum" they would come to terms.'[85] Apparently,
however, Longrigg kept the letter in his pocket and did not show
it to Shakhbut.[86]

The two remaining shaykhdoms, Ajman and Umm al-Qaiwain,
had no territory of possible interest to Petroleum Concessions, which
consequently did not approach their rulers. Fowle contested the
wisdom of this, afraid that Socal would try to seize the opportunity

to enter the field. Longrigg, on the other hand, convinced the India Office that there was no possibility that a rival company would seek a concession in the two shaykhdoms, and the matter was not referred to again. On 23 March 1939, however, Petroleum Concessions obtained from Ajman an exploration permit similar to that granted by Ras al-Khaimah, and on 20 March 1945 Umm al-Qaiwain entered into a commercial agreement with the company.

Within six years, then, the rulers of all the Trucial states had committed themselves to the company that the British Government had selected to explore for and exploit oil on the Coast. Although Longrigg, in his authoritative study on oil in the Middle East, says that no preliminary agreement was forced on the rulers against their will,[87] it is clear from the above account that the British political authorities did use a variety of subtle forms of pressure in order to secure a firm footing for British interests and to exclude possible American competition. No gunboat diplomacy was used; not a shot was fired; and no extra expenses were incurred for the Treasury to bear. Official policy would not have stood to gain by any alteration of the *status quo*.

8 Territorial Claims:
Saudi Arabia and Iran

The strategic location and vast petroleum resources of the Gulf states are the principal reasons for their present overwhelming importance in international affairs. A brief glance at a map of the region, however, reveals the consequences of this prominence: a complex of neutral zones, undefined and disputed boundaries, and territorial claims and counter-claims. The rapidity with which the Gulf states have had to come to terms with the Western concepts of territorial and even offshore limits has only added to the confusion, for nothing is more alien to Arab society (bedouin and other) than the permanent delineation of boundaries. The first time it occurred in eastern Arabia was at the 1922 Conference of 'Uqayr between Percy Cox and Ibn Sa'ud; it was then that Cox formulated the concept of neutral zones as a solution to the problem of disputed areas the exact ownership of which could not conveniently be settled by negotiation.

It was during the interwar period that the Trucial Coast began to experience the complications of attempting to define boundaries. Oil exploration and the growing claims of Saudi Arabia and Iran in the area were the principal factors behind these difficulties, as manifested by the Buraimi dispute and the recent Iranian seizure of the islands of Tunb and Abu Musa. The British authorities did not adequately foresee and tackle these problems.

Furthermore, the arrival of geologists in search of petroleum quickened the rulers' own interest in their shaykhdoms' inland boundaries, and caused them to re-examine their relationships with their inland tribal allies. The result today is that the external boundaries of the United Arab Emirates are still in question, and its internal divisions and subdivisions remain confusing.

The entire question of territorial claims on the Coast is inextricably linked with the various extensions of British policy. The demands of both Iran and Saudi Arabia had to be handled, according to the terms of the 1892 agreement, by the British Government; and the delineation of the borders of the shaykhdoms with each other was also directed to a large extent by the British administrators in the Gulf. However, the role played by Britain in the disputes with Iran and Saudi Arabia was much more significant, since the issues at stake had greater implications. During the 1930s there were a series of Anglo-Iranian and Anglo-Saudi discussions aimed at solving at the diplomatic level those countries' territorial disputes with the smaller Gulf states. Both series bore little fruit. But both had another factor in common: in each case, the British Government seriously contemplated disposing of the conflict by inducing the shaykh whose land was disputed to lease or sell it to Iran or Saudi Arabia, whichever claimed it.

When, in 1928, the Persian authorities seized a dhow from Dubai and mistreated its passengers, the British Government decided not to take a strong stand until the ownership of the Tunbs and Abu Musa had been resolved. Efforts were also under way at the time for the conclusion of a new Anglo-Persian agreement, and in a draft of the treaty in 1929 it was decided that the island of Sirri would be recognised as Iranian, and Tunb and Abu Musa as Arab.[1] In 1930, however, negotiations between the Iranian and British governments were broken off, because of the refusal of the British to accept an Iranian claim to Tunb.[2] Taimurtash, the Iranian Minister of Court, had intimated in August 1929 that the Iranian claim to Abu Musa would be dropped if the British Government were to recognise Iranian ownership of Tunb. The Foreign Office in London was anxious to settle the dispute and was not averse to the idea that Shaykh Sultan of Ras al-Khaimah should grant a lease to Iran. But the Political Resident (Barrett) did not think this would be easy:

> I do not think he will accept any sum of money which Persia is likely to offer for Tanb. He is a man of obstinate and suspicious temper and will suspect the motive of any offer he may receive. The lighthouse which the British Government built on the island gives it a considerable importance to us; and the Shaikh has recently been persuaded by some busybody that he can obtain large revenues from it.[3]

The predictions of the Resident proved accurate. In May 1930 he interviewed Sultan and attempted to persuade him to grant a lease. He had asked Shaykh Saqr bin Sultan of Sharjah to attend the meeting, in order to influence his reluctant cousin; but it turned out that both rulers were opposed to leasing the island and decided that no amount of money would be compensation enough.[4]

The Resident regarded this as a final decision, knowing how weakened the ruler's hold on his people would be if he ceded any part of his acknowledged territory. In October 1930, however, Taimurtash offered to rent Tunb and Abu Musa for fifty years. Both the Foreign Office and the India Office saw this as a suitable compromise, making a formal recognition of the rights of Ras al-Khaimah unnecessary: the implicit recognition underlying the acceptance by Iran of rental agreement with Shaykh Sultan would be sufficient admission of the ruler's sovereignty. In April 1931, therefore, the Residency Agent placed this proposal before Sultan, who now seemed more willing to accept the idea of a lease, but insisted that, under any such agreement, his flag should continue to fly over Tunb, the inhabitants should not be controlled by the Iranian Government, and the Iranian Customs should have no authority in the island.[5] In the meantime, however, negotiations between Britain and Iran had been suspended, primarily because of disagreement over Tunb, and the question of a lease from Sultan was left in abeyance.

It was revived in September 1933, when the Senior Naval Officer reported that in a meeting he had had with Shaykh Sultan the ruler had intimated that he had received a letter from Tehran requesting him to lease Tunb to the Iranian Government.[6] Although the Senior Naval Officer had reminded Sultan of his treaty obligations, which forbade him to cede, sell, or mortgage any territory without permission of the British Government, the Resident in Bushire was alarmed. He uneasily noted the steady growth of Iranian interests on the Trucial Coast during the past two years, and was worried that this might indicate an undue interest in the area. In November his fears were somewhat assuaged when the Residency Agent assured him that Sultan had invented the story of the letter from Tehran in order to induce the British Government to lease Tunb from him.[7]

But Iranian advances to Sultan had been reported before. In September 1933 the Senior Naval Officer informed the Resident that an Iranian merchant had approached Sultan in order to persuade him to switch his allegiance from Great Britain to Iran, 'stating that as Persia will be predominant naval power in Gulf would be to his advantage'.[8] Although there was no proof that the merchant had been an Iranian Government agent in disguise, the visit was regarded with suspicion, especially as it was generally believed that he had made similar visits to other rulers on the Coast.

In 1934, official Iranian interest in Tunb was renewed, once more arousing British fears. In April, the governor, collector of customs and chief of police at Bandar Abbas had visited the island, where they had inquired about the lighthouse and generally been friendly and courteous.[9] Despite the wishes of the India Office, the Foreign Office did not want to make a formal protest to the Iranian Government about the visit: 'The present policy of His Majesty's Government involves the avoidance of anything in the nature of a needless challenge to Persia . . . .'[10] In August of the same year, an Iranian sloop, the *Palang*, searched a dhow belonging to the agent of the British India Steam Navigation Company who lived in Dubai. A few days later an Iranian vessel landed a party at Tunb and anchored off the island.[11]

London viewed these naval activities, coming so soon after the visit of Iranian officials to Tunb, with great alarm. The Foreign Office at first instructed the British Minister in Tehran to warn the Iranian Government that orders had been given to British naval officers to regard as aggression any persistent action connoting a claim to sovereignty; later, following an approach by the Iranian Foreign Minister for the reopening of general treaty negotiations, the Minister was told to tone down the warning. Caught between the two governments' political strategies, and unwilling to wait for the outcome, Shaykh Sultan decided to keep independently in contact with Iran. He incurred the great wrath of the Resident when, on 29 December 1934, he removed his flag and flagstaff from Tunb.[12] A sloop was sent to Sharjah immediately afterwards to inquire into the meaning of this 'extraordinary action'. The Residency Agent reported that the removal of the flagstaff was to call attention to the fact that the British Government did not pay rent for the lighthouse, while the ruler of Sharjah received money for the airport in his shaykhdom;[13] another reason given was that Sultan hoped that Britain would lease the island from him.[14] Despite assurances that Sultan had acted with a view to increasing his personal income and not because of Iranian influence, rumours reached Bushire that steps were being taken to hoist the Iranian flag on Tunb and for Iranian officials to begin collecting customs duties there. The Resident gave Sultan ten days in which to rehoist his flag on Tunb, and was sternly warned that if he did not comply he would lose the island to his Qasimi cousin the ruler of Sharjah, who was anxious to reclaim the island for his own shaykhdom.[15] The ultimatum proved successful, for on 3 April Sultan replaced his flag and flagstaff, after which the matter remained dormant. Britain, however, continued to regard Abu Musa and Tunb as unquestionably Arab, which they remained until December 1971, when Iran occupied them by force of arms.

In the case of Abu Musa, the Iranian claim was not put forward as adamantly, for Iran was willing to forego it in exchange for Tunb. Abu Musa had deposits of red oxide, and a concession to mine it was first granted in 1898 by the ruler of Sharjah, to three Arabs. In 1906 two of these transferred their rights to the German firm of Wönckhaus, without the ruler's permission. The following year, at the instigation of the British, the ruler cancelled the concession and this became a subject of dispute between the British and German governments, especially after a British warship forcibly removed the Wönckhaus workers.[16] After the war the British Government decided that Wönckhaus had no claim to a new concession, and in January 1923 an Englishman by the name of Strick was granted a five-year concession by the ruler of Sharjah. This prompted the Iranian authorities in 1925 to send a man from Lingah to bring back some bags of oxide, after which the Iranian Government reasserted its claim to Abu Musa. In June 1934, the Strick concession having expired, Shaykh Sultan bin Saqr asked the Political Resident for permission to grant a concession to Iranians from Dubai.[17] Since the answer was not immediately forthcoming, a British firm, Golden Valley Ochre and Oxide Company Ltd, stepped in and obtained a six-month option,[18] which was converted into a commercial concession late in January 1935. The Iranian Government saw the concession as a breach of the status quo pending a final decision on who owned sovereignty over Abu Musa, and in a formal protest to London asked for the concession to be cancelled. The Foreign Office ignored the protest, and the matter was dropped.

Britain's failure to resolve the question of the disputed islands—militarily, diplomatically or otherwise—was strongly indicative of the nature of its policy in the Gulf area. Unlike in other parts of the world, it did not, in applying its policy, have to pay much regard to public opinion, whether British or Arab: because of the strong control it exercised over the area, news of events there was unlikely to reach any further than the desks of officials in Delhi or London; the military weakness of the shaykhs made them irrelevant in terms of power politics; and there was still no sign of oil on the Coast, and, thus, of the area's acquiring economic importance.

Had British interest in the islands been strong enough, action to establish Arab ownership of them would have been forthcoming. In the case of the seizure of the Arab dhow, the Treasury, in refusing to sanction the payment of compensation (see above, Chapter 5), stated that the British taxpayer should not have to pay for the actions of the Iranian customs service. When it seemed that an Anglo-Persian agreement was about to be concluded, Shaykh Sultan of Ras al-Khaimah was induced by the British (who hoped that it would speed up negotiations) to consider leasing Tunb to Iran; but when, a short time later, he acted on his own to reach some sort of agreement with the Iranians, he was severely reprimanded, particularly since British interests would have suffered had he been successful. At no point did the recommendations of the local British officials that the rulers, of whose problems they were aware, be given more positive help make enough of an impression on London to change the course of events.

When it was favourable to British interests to uphold territorial claims, or to resist them, British officials expended every effort to ensure the desired end. In the case of Bahrain, another group of islands to which Riza Shah laid claim, the Iranian interest was made particularly ominous by the large Persian and Shi'ah communities residing there. These communities could be, and often were, mobilised to weaken the rule of the Al-Khalifah. But Bahrain was central to British interests in the Gulf: even before oil was struck there, it had been considered as the most likely place to succeed Bushire as the British headquarters in the Gulf. Therefore the British Government continually sought to ensure Bahrain's independence, and in 1970 Iran formally renounced its claim. The contrast with the claim to the Tunbs and Abu Musa is strong, for in 1971 all three islands passed under Iranian rule.

Relations between Iran and the Trucial Coast remained unfriendly, despite the large number of Persians residing on the Coast. Iranian hostility was expressed not only through interference with Arab dhows, in attempts forcibly to halt smuggling, and through constant claims to sovereignty over Abu Musa and Tunb, but also in a refusal to accept British passport arrangements. After 1927, as a result of the Iranian claim to Bahrain, the Iranian Government declined to affix to British passports bearing endorsements for Bahrain and Kuwait, or to passports carrying British visas for travel to these places, visas for travel to Iran. In 1934 the British authorities met the difficulty by allowing a second passport, valid only for journeys to Bahrain and Kuwait, to be issued to people who wished to visit these shaykhdoms and Iran as well. In the middle of 1937 this provision was extended to cover Muscat and the Trucial Coast, straining relations with Iran even further. There was obviously little love lost on either side, the Iranians and the Arabs of the Coast being mutually antagonistic.

The extension of Saudi interests on the Trucial Coast raised far more complex problems than any of the Iranian claims, for it involved wide stretches of land, ownership of which was always difficult to determine. The main areas of Saudi interest after the turbulence of 1925 were the Dafrah and Buraimi regions, although the Saudis made no formal claims to possession in the Western sense. They did, however, during the period when Abu Dhabi, which claimed both regions, was undergoing its greatest turmoil, seek to exact *zakat* from the tribes in these areas—thereby claiming control of them. Both regions were remote from the watchful eyes of the British. Following the accession of Shakhbut as Shaykh of Abu Dhabi, however, the Bani Yas began to re-establish their power, and the Saudi position became less easy to maintain. Furthermore, as the possibility that oil would be found on the Coast became stronger, Ibn Sa'ud became more concerned to make his presence felt in the coastal areas.

When the first indications of a possible Anglo-Saudi controversy over boundaries became apparent, the British authorities, realising that they knew little about the inland regions of the Coast, instructed the Residency Agent to conduct secret investigations into the payments of *zakat* in Buraimi, Dafrah and the surrounding areas.[19] The oasis of Buraimi was occupied by two opposing tribes, the Na'im and the Dawahir: the latter, under the leadership of Ahmad bin Hilal of Jimi, were the more numerous and allied to Abu Dhabi; the former were a Ghafiri tribe previously dominated by the power of Zayid bin Khalifah, but after his death and the consequent deterioration in the power of Abu Dhabi inclined to assert their independence.[20] From 1923 on, the Na'im openly opposed Sultan bin Zayid, and in November 1925, when the forces of 'Isa bin Salih began to move into the Dahirah, Muhammad bin Sultan al-Hammud, who with his brother Saqr had inherited their father's position as head of the Na'im, announced to the Residency Agent that he planned to resist any encroachments on his district by the forces of the imam.[21] The Residency Agent heard at the time that Muhammad bin Sultan had hoped to rally the rulers of Dubai, Sharjah, Ajman, Umm al-Qaiwain and Ras al-Khaimah around him, but that they had not responded to his approach; instead, it was only the bedouin sections of the Bani Ka'b and Bani Qitab that agreed to come to his help if 'Isa reached Buraimi.[22] So Muhammad went to Dhank and tendered his submission to the sultan of Muscat; afterwards, he moved on to 'Ibri with Hamad bin Ahmad al-Yahyayi of Dhank, in order to help Sultan bin Rashid in his struggles against 'Isa. When they returned to Buraimi after the collapse of 'Isa's forces, Muhammad bin Sultan sent Muhammad bin Rahmah of the Al-bu-Shamis to invite Ibn Sa'ud to Buraimi.[23]

The pro-Saudi sentiments of the Na'im were affirmed a few months later when Bertram Thomas conducted an expedition to inland Oman in order to select a landing ground for use by the Royal Air Force. Starting from Sohar in Muscat, he was to reconnoitre to Buraimi and then to Abu Dhabi. His party found themselves unable to enter Buraimi, despite the letters they carried from the Political Resident to the ruler of Abu Dhabi and to the headmen of the Bani Ka'b and the Na'im. The brothers Muhammad and Saqr bin Sultan al-Hammudah of the Na'im[24] obstructed the expedition's progress, and Saqr wrote to Thomas explaining that the area belonged to the al-Hammudah and after them to Ibn Sa'ud.[25] Although Thomas put this statement down to a basic fear of the Wahhabis, rather than to any true admiration for or loyalty to them, he mentioned that Shaykh Rashid bin Hamad of the Al-bu-Shamis had been on a visit to Ibn Sa'ud at the time of the expedition, and that in 1927 the Na'im had reversed their earlier policy of hostility towards the growth of Wahhabi influence in the Buraimi area. They did not, however, ignore the sultan of Muscat, for they obviously were afraid of backing the wrong horse: in 1928 Thomas reported that Muhammad bin Sultan had visited Muscat, where the sultan had made peace between him and Hamad bin Faysal, the *wali* of Sohar (with whom Muhammad had been on bad terms) and had granted him an allowance of 50 rupees per month.[26] In 1929 the Na'im were referred to as being pro-Saudi.[27] In 1930, Thomas, on a visit to Shimayliyyah, reported that Su'ayyid (an agent of Ibn Jaluwi) was collecting *zakat* in Buraimi from the Na'im, 'Awamir, Duru', and part of the Bani Qitab.[28] The Na'im did not seem to have any particular policy other than that of supplanting the power of the Dawahir in Buraimi, in which they were helped immeasurably by the weakness of Abu Dhabi.

The declining power of Abu Dhabi was confirmed in 1934 when 'Isa bin 'Abd al-Latif, as Residency Agent, compiled his report on *zakat* collections by the Saudis in Dafrah and Buraimi. He found that the first payment in Buraimi had been in 1922, while in Dafrah the Manasir and the Bani Yas had been paying *zakat* for nine years, beginning in the year 1343 AH (August 1924–July 1925), when Sultan bin Zayid had been ruler of Abu Dhabi.[29] 'Isa's report also corroborated a statement by the Resident that in March 1926 Su'ayyid, together with Muhammad bin Mansur of the Al-Murrah tribe, had been sent to collect *zakat* from Buraimi and Dafrah.[30]

Later that year, in July 1926, Sultan was murdered and his brother Saqr came to power. Principally because of his overriding fear of the vengeance of Sultan's sons, he tried hard to win the favour of the governor of the Saudi province of Hasa, Ibn Jaluwi, sending him annual presents and helping the *zakat* collectors in Buraimi and Dafrah.[31] In 1927 *zakat* collectors were in Oman when Bertram Thomas made the journey referred to earlier. By the time Saqr had been murdered and Shakhbut had come to power, the prestige of the Al-bu-Falah in Buraimi and Dafrah had dwindled considerably and the Saudis were encountering little opposition to their missions there. The Manasir, especially those living in Dafrah, forgot their past ties with Abu Dhabi and gradually came under the influence of Ibn Jaluwi; in 1934, for example, the Residency Agent reported that the Manasir of Dafrah wished to remain under Saudi protection.

That same year, however, the *zakat* collector in Dafrah, Muhammad al-Sahli al-'Ayf, and his colleagues were treated with total disrespect and beaten up by the Hawamil section of the Bani Yas, who, together with some of the Manasir, refused to give any form of tribute. The Bani Yas complained to Shakhbut about the intrusion of the collectors; Shakhbut in turn complained to Ibn Jaluwi, who backed down, saying that there had been a misunderstanding. After that, no *zakat* was paid in the south of Dafrah, although the collectors continued to ask politely for it. They were, however, able to obtain it from groups of the Manasir: primarily the Al-bu-Mundhir, but also the Al-bu-Sha'r and the Al-bu-Rahmah.[32]

It is clear, then, that during the 1920s there existed some form of Saudi control of the Dafrah and Buraimi regions; it is also clear that the extent of that control was in inverse proportion to the strength and stability of Abu Dhabi. But the ability to enforce *zakat* was variable, as were the boundaries of Saudi Arabia with Abu Dhabi and Muscat: both depended on the political conditions, which were different under different rulers. The Na'im were the gauge by which the strength of the Al-bu-Falah in Abu Dhabi town, and thus their authority in the Buraimi oasis, could be measured: when, after 'Isa bin Salih's expedition, they took a pro-Saudi line, it was a sign of a decline in the power of the Al-bu-Falah. But the accession of Shakhbut radically altered the situation.

In 1931 the animosity that had been building up between the rulers of Abu Dhabi and the Na'im erupted into an armed confrontation that at one point threatened to become a full-scale war. The outcome of the struggle re-established the supremacy of Abu Dhabi in Buraimi, and left no doubt as to Shakhbut's determination to regain the power that had been held by his grandfather.

The confrontation had its origin in a raid by twenty men of the Manasir who came under the overlordship of Abu Dhabi and ten men of the Bani Yas subject to the ruler of Dubai. In April 1931 they attacked and killed a cousin of Muhammad bin Sultan, shaykh of Buraimi. Muhammad protested to both Abu Dhabi and Dubai. Sa'id bin Maktum of Dubai said that he would be willing to compensate for the loss if it could be proved that the ten men of the Bani Yas were his charges, but Shakhbut disclaimed any responsibility for what had happened. Afraid that the Na'imi shaykh would resort to arms, two people tried to mediate: the shaykh of Ras al-Khaimah wrote to all the concerned parties, particularly urging Shakhbut to restrain the Manasir, and the Residency Agent asked Sa'id bin Maktum, who had helped to settle many an inter-tribal dispute in the past, to use his influence to prevent any bloodshed. Furious at Shakhbut's unwillingness to take any action, Muhammad of Buraimi attacked 'Ayn Dawahir, a fort belonging to Abu Dhabi and garrisoned by men from the shaykhdom, early in May 1931. Despite heavy losses on both sides, the Na'im were finally obliged to withdraw, unable to capture the fort. Shakhbut, with a force of 1000 rifles, pursued the retreating men for thirty miles, and then set up camp by a well, sending word to Sa'id bin Maktum to join them. The ruler of Dubai was at first reluctant to enter the fighting; but he changed his mind when two caravans of food sent to Shakhbut's force, one of which had come from Dubai with three men of the Bani Yas sent by Sa'id himself, were captured by the Na'im. On 21 June he left Dubai with a force of 700 men and decided to meet with the Na'imi shaykh at Jimi.[33] At this juncture, Sultan bin Saqr of Sharjah called for a conference to be held at Ras al-Khaimah and attended by him and the rulers of Ras al-Khaimah and Ajman. They decided that, if Sa'id bin Maktum were actively to help Shakhbut, they would band together against them, in a natural alliance of Ghafiriyyah against Hinawiyyah.[34]

Sa'id was able to arrange for a truce from 23 June to 8 July, but even this was violated a number of times, especially by the Manasir.[35] But Shakhbut was clearly not anxious to avert a war; he instead sought revenge for the harm done by the Na'im, reinforced by the Duru' and men from 'Ibri, when they had blocked the springs that watered the date gardens of Abu Dhabi people and had cut down the date trees. The Abu Dhabi force captured Hafit, a village at the foot of Jabal Hafit, immediately south of Buraimi, and on 2 July it destroyed a caravan from Ajman on its way to Buraimi. Sa'id's role as mediator was especially difficult, as Shakhbut wanted compensation for the damage caused by the Na'im, who refused to pay it. Sa'id was, however, able to obtain an extension of the truce,[36] but a peaceful solution to the dispute could not be found and on 17 July war was declared. It did not amount to very much, for the raids and counter-raids that took place were minor, and on 9 August Sa'id finally succeeded in persuading the shaykh of Buraimi to have the blocked springs cleared, so allowing peace to be restored.[37]

The authority of Abu Dhabi in Buraimi was thus re-established. Had Shakhbut backed down in any way, his position would never

have been restored. His insistence, despite the danger of a Ghafiri
alliance against him, that the Na'im restore the property they
had harmed, did much to strengthen his prestige. Throughout the
following decade, his authority grew and became recognised throughout the region.

The inland districts were far removed from the attention of the
British authorities, whose policy of non-interference called for a
mere recording of events. It was only when Ibn Sa'ud officially
approached the British Government about his coastal boundaries
with the Gulf states that the incidents in Buraimi and Dafrah
assumed any kind of importance. After Ibn Sa'ud had granted,
in 1933, a concession to Socal, the United States Government
officially inquired of the British Government where the eastern
frontiers of Saudi Arabia lay. These were defined by the Foreign
Office in April 1934 as being consistent with the Blue Line (running
due south from the head of the bay opposite Zaknuniyyah island
to the line of demarcation between Turkish Arabia and Aden)
agreed under the Anglo-Turkish Conventions of 1913–14.[38] The
Saudi Government protested, saying that much had changed since
1913, but the British Government remained firm. The Foreign Office
statement on the Blue Line was the result not only of the inquiry
by the United States, but also of consideration, at almost the
same time, of a number of points related to the granting of an
oil concession by the ruler of Qatar. He had asked that the British
grant him protection should he dispose of the concession as they
wished, and there was the question of Qatar's boundary with Saudi
Arabia. The Anglo-Persian Oil Company had a licence to explore
in Qatar that was due to expire in August 1934. In the months
preceding this date, Shaykh 'Abdallah showed signs of favouring
Socal, and Fowle attributed this to the influence of Ibn Sa'ud.[39]
The ruler of Kuwait confirmed the Resident's suspicions with a
report that the king had warned 'Abdallah not to grant the APOC
a concession.[40] An earlier rumour, never properly substantiated,
had it that in December 1933 'Abdallah had travelled to Riyadh
and signed an agreement with Ibn Sa'ud to the effect that the
hinterland of Qatar, and consequently any oil therein, belonged
to Saudi Arabia.[41] In March 1934, Fowle met with 'Abdallah
and made it clear to him that the APOC was the only company
he could deal with. The ruler of Qatar was greatly perturbed,
hinting that he had an agreement binding him otherwise.[42] He
admitted that the agreement was with Ibn Sa'ud, but added that
it was private and only to keep him out of danger.[43] It was
after this confession that considerable pressure was placed on 'Abdallah to grant a concession to the APOC. He was severely reprimanded
for making an agreement with Ibn Sa'ud, and taken to task for

thereby contravening the conditions of his treaty with Britain. 'Abdallah was impressed with the interest shown by the APOC and realised that it was a favourable time to strike a bargain: he informed Fowle that he would grant a concession to the APOC if the British Government would in turn undertake to protect him against attack by land, support him in internal matters and recognise his son Hamad as his heir. His terms were accepted, in the face of Ibn Sa'ud's and Socal's interest in Qatar, and in May 1935 an agreement to that effect was signed.[44] On 17 May 1935, therefore, 'Abdallah formally granted a concession to the APOC,[45] which then transferred its rights, according to the Red Line Agreement, to the Iraq Petroleum Company. Shortly afterwards, Ibn Sa'ud, who obviously did not know that an agreement had been concluded, wrote to 'Abdallah warning him not to grant a concession until the boundary issue between them had been settled.

The letter, actually an unsealed *mulhaq* (supplement) attached to a formal sealed leter, is a revealing document, confirming the existence of a private agreement between 'Abdallah and the king, and disclosing the Saudi standpoint on the boundary issue.[46] In it, the king made two oblique references to private arrangements obviously already in force between him and Shaykh 'Abdallah, thus substantiating the latter's declaration in 1930 that he had guaranteed his own protection by payment to the Wahhabi. Furthermore, Ibn Sa'ud explained that, although he considered the people of Oman and Qatar his rightful subjects, he had deferred to the wishes of the British by leaving the towns of those areas alone. He stressed, however, that this could not be the case for the hinterland, which had to be governed by desert law, and at any rate was obviously not controlled by any of the coastal rulers. With specific reference to Saudi boundaries with Qatar, the king repudiated the validity of the Blue Line, on three grounds: that the Ottomans, during their occupation of Hasa, had never exercised extensive authority in the region; that the Anglo-Turkish Convention of 1913 had been signed after his occupation of Hasa; and that the Convention was never ratified. Finally, he warned 'Abdallah in no uncertain terms about the consequences of granting an oil concession before the boundary issue had been settled.

In the meantime, on 3 April 1935, Fu'ad Hamzah, Acting Foreign Minister of Saudi Arabia, put forward proposals for the course of the Saudi frontier with Qatar, the Trucial Coast, the sultanate of Muscat and the Protectorate of Aden; this proposed frontier became known as the Red Line or Fu'ad Line. Under these proposals, Saudi Arabia claimed Jabal Nakhsh and Khawr al-Udayd from Qatar.[48] On 9 April, Sir Andrew Ryan, British Minister in Jeddah, replied by proposing what became known as the Green Line; but this was found unacceptable by the Saudi Government. In June 1935, therefore, Anglo-Saudi conversations on the frontiers took place in London; but these resulted in a deadlock. The Saudi Government claimed most of the Rub' al-Khali, Khawr al-Udayd and a large part of Dhufar. In November 1935, Sir Andrew Ryan presented a modified version of the Green Line, known as Ryan's Line or the Riyadh Line; by this the British Government allowed to Saudi Arabia much of the Rub' al-Khali, but would not recognise its claim to either Jabal Nakhsh, at the western base of the Qatar peninsula, or Khawr al-'Udayd, which it regarded as belonging to Abu Dhabi.[49] In March 1937 a Foreign Office delegation led by George Rendel, head of the Eastern Department, went to Jeddah to discuss Khawr al-'Udayd and Jabal Nakhsh with the Saudi Foreign Minister, Yusuf Yasin.[50] Little came of the talks, but upon Rendel's return to London the Foreign Office and the India Office took the matter up between them, and realised that their respective positions were totally divergent.

The Foreign Office was anxious to arrive at a compromise, since it was eager to retain the goodwill of Ibn Sa'ud, as a prominent Arab leader. On 29 June 1937, at a meeting of the Middle East Sub-Committee, Sir Reader Bullard, Minister to Saudi Arabia, suggested that the king be allowed to share in any oil profits attained from Jabal Nakhsh. The India Office was against this form of compromise, especially after reports had reached London of a recent survey by the Political Agent in Bahrain, Tom Hickinbotham, on the inland boundaries of the Trucial States, where the growing influence of Saudi Arabia was markedly obvious: 'It now transpires that all the Trucial Shaikhs have an agreement, probably unwritten regarding the apprehension and punishment of offenders from Saudi Arabia and that they have all at one time or another corresponded officially with the Saudi Arabian authorities.'[51] The report was based on information supplied by the Residency Agent, who stated, 'As the Trucial Shaikhs were weak and could not prevent outside raids, they were compelled by circumstances to complain to the Saudi Arabian authorities against their subjects and in all cases the punishment was satisfactory and much more than what they would have inflicted against the offenders.'[52] The Residency Agent went on to say that the shaykhs never risked the anger of the Saudi authorities by punishing Saudi offenders caught on the Coast, but instead sent them to Hasa for punishment; offenders on the Coast, by contrast, rarely ran to Saudi Arabia, for they knew they would be punished and never be allowed to return.[53]

Hickinbotham urged a settlement of the boundary question with Saudi Arabia, especially as he found strong evidence that Ibn Sa'ud was extending his influence as far eastwards as Buraimi.

This was particularly alarming in that both Petroleum Concessions and Socal had made it clear that the most likely country for oil was the area from Abu Dhabi to 'Ibri to Buraimi. 'I have little doubt that the Saudi Arabian authorities have come to the same conclusion and if they have not will soon be encouraged to do so, by the California Arabian Standard Oil Company.'[54] The Foreign Office was equally apprehensive at the possibility of further Saudi penetration, and asked whether the tribes in Jabal Hafit, a small area immediately south of Buraimi, owed allegiance to the ruler of Abu Dhabi.

At any rate, we hope so, for if they owe allegiance to no one in particular we may find King Ibn Saud inducing them without very much difficulty to admit that they owe allegiance to him. In that case, despite the fact that Baraimi lies north and east of the line we have offered to King Ibn Saud, we should be likely to find it difficult to keep him out of Baraimi for, as we have suggested before, we cannot hold him, or indeed anyone else, back behind a vacuum.[55]

It was only when Petroleum Concessions Limited sent a party of exploration to Buraimi in the winter of 1938 that it became possible to make a full assessment of the tribal situation there. Before the party started out, investigations had to be made as to who had to be consulted for permission to enter the area. Hugh Weightman, Officiating Political Resident at the time, reported,

Abu Dhabi holds by far the greater part [of the Buraimi oasis] through the Dhawahir tribe with a total of over a hundred houses. . . . It is noteworthy that even the Sultan of Muscat has admitted to Watts [Assistant Political Agent Bahrain] that Abu Dhabi owns the principal villages of Jimi, Muraijib, Mas'udi and Hili in the Oasis.[56]

The importance of having Shakhbut's permission became only too obvious when he refused to give it. The company then turned to the sultan of Muscat for help to enter Buraimi and Jabal Hafit from the Muscat, rather than the Trucial Coast, side. When Sa'id bin Taymur agreed to co-operate, Fowle made it clear that Britain would not commit itself to the sultan regarding the ownership of Buraimi. 'On the other hand, since the Sultan actually claims Baraimi, if he succeeds in getting the Company in that place, his rights to it will be much strengthened.'[57] Before the expedition set out, in the winter of 1938, Weightman was convinced that, even if they were to rely on help from the Na'im, as allies of

the sultan, they would be unsuccessful; Weightman knew the importance of Shakhbut's co-operation, especially in view of the ruler's
excellent relations with the Al-bu-Shamis.[58] After negotiations, Shakhbut promised to make arrangements for another party of exploration
to proceed to Buraimi from Abu Dhabi,[59] but he was resentful
that a party was to approach the oasis from another route and
under the auspices of the sultan of Muscat. Largely owing to
his anger, the expedition he had sanctioned was a failure, for
the movements of the party once it had reached Buraimi were
so restricted that it had to leave after only a short stay.

Howes, Assistant Political Agent at Bahrain, accompanied the
Petroleum Concessions geologists who took part in this expedition,
which was the first by Europeans to Buraimi since Cox had visited it
in 1905.[60] His findings there were summarised as follows: 'The
influence of Ibn Saud is practically nil, though he remains in
the back of people's minds as a possible offset to Muscat, and
I have heard his name used for this purpose.'[61] After receiving
the report of his assistant, the Political Agent in Bahrain commented,

Placing together information from various different sources[62] I
think the hinterland outlook can be estimated briefly as follows:

(i) Abu Dhabi is the big power at the threshold. Shaikh Shakhbut
has a strong and apparently loyal Wali in his part of the Baraimi
Oasis, namely Ibrahim bin Uthman, for whom the Na'im and
Al-bu-Shamis Shaikhs seem to have considerable respect. Abu
Dhabi therefore wields the strongest influence in Baraimi and
much of Dhahira.
(ii) The Sultan of Muscat is recognized as quite an important
ruler—in his own place. Annual visits and fair words to him
are profitable, and serve as an insurance against the possible
closing of the Batineh Coast (not probable but possible only).
Otherwise the Sultan has no very great influence and any suggestion
of his suzerainty over the hinterland would be vigorously rejected.
(iii) Bin Saud is recognised as the really great man, and considerable care is exercised by the Shaikhs to keep on his right side.
Nevertheless he is a long way off, he is getting older every
day, and I doubt if he is regarded as a serious menace to
their independence.[63]

But other considerations prompted the Foreign Office to press for
a compromise with Ibn Sa'ud. These were the realisation of the
general decline of British interests in the Near East, in line with
the degenerating situation in Palestine, and the need, as war threatened in Europe, for a powerful Arab ally. In 1937 the Cabinet

in London agreed on the matter, and in the following year it discussed the following recommendations of a meeting of the Committee of Imperial Defence:

> That, with a view to the settlement of the South Eastern Frontiers of Saudi Arabia on lines acceptable to Ibn Saud, the Foreign Office and India Office should be authorized to take up the question of the cession by the Sheikh of Abu Dhabi of a strip of territory in the Persian Gulf known as the Khor-el-Odeid: and that, should compensation in the form of a cash payment prove necessary, the expenditure of a sum tentatively estimated at £25,000 for this purpose should be provisionally authorized, subject to the usual arrangements for obtaining Treasury sanction.[64]

Thus, in order to ensure the goodwill of Saudi Arabia, the CID suggested that Shakhbut sell a portion of his territory that the British Government had for years regarded as an intrinsic part of Abu Dhabi. It also suggested that the British Government pay for the sale. It must be remembered here that only ten years earlier, and despite treaty regulations that explicitly promised the shaykhdoms protection from attack by sea, the Treasury had refused to sanction the sum of merely 5000 rupees (around £250) as compensation to the victims of the Iranian seizure of an Arab vessel near Tunb. Viewed within this context, the CID proposal demonstrates that British policy towards the Trucial States was governed by the changing requirements of British interests in the area.

The CID suggestion was strongly opposed by both the Government of India and the India Office. No conclusions were reached, and the matter was left in abeyance during the Second World War. It was not until 1949, when Saudi Arabia first put forward its claim to Liwa and Buraimi, that it was taken up again.

9 Boundary Disputes: Chaos in Order

Shortly after Britain's announcement in 1968 that its withdrawal from the Gulf was imminent, the rulers of Dubai and Abu Dhabi declared their forthcoming federation and at the same time announced the settlement of a longstanding dispute between their two shaykhdoms over offshore rights (with, as is only too well known today, implications for the ownership of any oil or other mineral wealth beneath the seabed). A ruler of Abu Dhabi, Shakhbut bin Sultan, had been the first of the Trucial shaykhs to grasp the significance of territorial limits. Before granting an option to the D'Arcy Exploration Company in 1936, he declared his anxiety to have his boundary with Dubai firmly defined. He wrote to Shaykh Sa'id asking him what territories had been included in his option to D'Arcy, and urged that the frontier between them be settled before geologists set out on their work.[1] Sa'id agreed, and in November 1937 the two men met to discuss the matter. The main arbitrators were Ahmad bin Hilal and Ahmad bin Khalaf bin 'Utaybah, a leading merchant of Abu Dhabi who had a strong influence on Shakhbut. After negotiations, the rulers reached a verbal agreement that the area to the west of a line running south from Bandar Hisyan was Abu Dhabi territory, and the land to the east of that Dubai's.[2]

Although this settlement did not prove lasting, it is to Shakhbut's credit that he was able to foresee the entanglements that oil companies would cause through the prospects of wealth they held out. His fellow rulers lacked his insight, and the result today is that the map of the United Arab Emirates is a confusing patchwork of subdivisions which make up the seven shaykhdoms.

Of course, much of this complexity is owing to the shifting pattern of tribal alliances, which have always determined the extent of a ruler's territory. In the early days of oil exploration, the rulers had little appreciation of the need for fixed limits to their territory or of the significance that these would have; and, while the British authorities, pressed by the oil companies, were attempting to evolve some form of policy, no attempt was made to enlighten them. Moreover, the process of policy-forming worked extremely slowly and never achieved any finality. An examination of the means chosen to deal with the problem will reveal not only the bewilderment of the British political authorities, who were often clearly at a loss, but also their deliberate failure to take into account the difficulties that some of the decisions taken might cause. This is best illustrated by the outcome of the interdepartmental meeting that was held in London in February 1936 to examine the problem, after Petroleum Concessions had been given the official go-ahead to negotiate for concessions. The decision then taken was that, in defining the extent of the individual shaykhdoms, such commercial agreements as were concluded should simply carry the vague formula 'the territories of the Sheikh'. There was, of course no precedent to which the India Office could refer, for Britain's interest in the shaykhdoms of the Gulf had previously been almost wholly confined to their coastal regions, and there had never before been any need for precision about the ownership of the hinterland.

But the formula 'the territories of the Sheikh' was not clear enough for Petroleum Concessions. It wanted to know precisely, in order to be able accurately to assess the value of the commercial agreements to be negotiated, the extent of each shaykhdom and the amount of the hinterland that its ruler effectively controlled. The company wished to explore the hinterland and needed access there, either through the rulers who claimed control of it or by direct approach to the local tribes. Fowle considered the company's needs and put forward a plan to give it what it desired. The Political Agent in Bahrain would work out, by consultation with the rulers and the sultan of Muscat, who claimed what territory; then a plan would be devised to test the standing of the claims in the light of effective control. Fowle admitted that an effective plan would be difficult to work out, and suggested the setting up of a test case. The company would ask the accepted ruler of an inland area to address the local shaykh there; if the local shaykh proved to be difficult, it would be up to the ruler to use 'force, bribery, or diplomacy, or all combined' to influence his subordinate.[3] Not thoroughly convinced of the practicability of Fowle's plan, the India Office temporarily shelved the issue by instructing Petroleum Concessions not to explore the hinterland until more was known of the *de facto* position there, and that the *de facto* tribal authorities in the hinterland had to be approached through the *de jure* rulers from whom the company already held concessions.[4]

When Fowle was in London in October 1937, he discussed his plan with the Under-Secretary of State at the India Office, Sir Findlater Stewart. Stewart did not think it advisable to insist on the *de jure* position, as this might, in the view of the League of Nations, be committing the British Government to a number of international obligations with regard to the interior (such as to suppress slavery there). Instead he suggested that, where the company required information about a particular tribe or shaykh, the Government should advise it who was 'the most likely person to help'—that is, the reputed overlord. If the petty shaykh should raise the question of his own rights relative to the possibility of oil in the area, he should, Fowle thought, be sidetracked with the answer that the first thing to be established was whether there were indeed any oil there. The company's representatives would be allowed inland only if the reputed overlord gave suitable guarantees of safety, and any party would have to be accompanied by a political officer. If oil were discovered in the hinterland, the problem of boundaries would have to be dealt with later; if not, the relationship between the minor shaykh and the overlord would no longer be of importance to Britain.[5]

It is clear from this rather tentative formulation of policy that Fowle had little confidence in the Trucial shaykhs' control of the hinterland. He was not alone in this assessment. Clauson, Principal of the Political Department of the India Office, reported, 'Mr Longrigg has expressed the view to me that we are wrong in regarding the Trucial Sheikhs as being only seven in number, and that eventually we shall have to get into direct relations with more petty rulers in the hinterland.'[6] Although they regarded such an eventuality as most undesirable, the British political authorities were willing to help the company as much as possible; and the evolution of policy on inland boundaries proceeded along a very nebulous path. The investigation by the Political Agent in Bahrain of the *de jure* rights of the Trucial shaykhs was dropped. Instead, each boundary problem and each question of the extent of tribal control was treated individually and weighed according to the concerns of the company. Thus no precise policy was attained. Fowle expressed best the basic British attitudes in the matter of seeking exploration rights: 'Briefly that our dealings with a particular Shaikh in order to secure exploration of a particular area by the Company do not imply a recognition by us that this area belongs to the Shaikh.'[7]

The most outstanding example of this principle in action occurred after Petroleum Concessions had expressed a desire to explore the Jabal Fa'iyah district, a hilly area south of Dhayd, situated in territory claimed by Sharjah. The Bani Qitab, whose alliance with the Qawasim had been the main bulwark of Sharjah's power in its heyday, controlled Fa'iyah, but had long since ceased to owe any strong loyalty to the ruler of Sharjah, whose power was thus greatly reduced. The deterioration of relations between the Qawasim and Bani Qitab can be traced back to the rule of Saqr bin Khalid, who was too weak to maintain an effective hold on the Bani Qitab, who then gradually attached themselves to his contemporary and rival, Zayid bin Khalifah of Abu Dhabi. After Zayid's death, the tribe began to assume greater independence, although at first it seemed likely that the succession in 1924 of Sultan bin Saqr would serve to re-establish the old ties with Sharjah: in that year, for instance, one of the signatories of the covenant accepting Sultan as the new ruler of the shaykhdoms was 'Abdallah bin 'Ali bin Huwayydin, paramount leader of the Bani Qitab. In 1927, however, two incidents occurred that caused the tribe to lose all respect for Sultan.

Some of the settled elements of the Bani Qitab lived in the Dhayd oasis, the northern fringes of which were within the *dirah* of the bedouin division of the tribe. Other inhabitants of the oasis were the Khawatir, a branch of the Na'im tribe, who early in 1927 seized the forts of the town from the Bani Qitab. Sultan should then have intervened to defend his allies, especially as Dhayd was part of Sharjah, but he remained inactive even after fierce fighting broke out between the Bani Qitab and the Khawatir. Hostilities were ended by the visit to Dhayd, late in April 1927, of the brothers Muhammad and Saqr bin Sultan of the Na'im, together with Salim bin Duyayn of the Bani Ka'b.[8] The three men intervened for peace and decided that Dhayd had to be restored to the Qawasim, but that, in view of Sharjah's weakness, it should be given to Ras al-Khaimah, which should rule it on behalf of Khalid bin Ahmad, former ruler of Sharjah.[9] Sultan bin Salim went to Dhayd and was given possession of the village; he then appointed a *wali*, Rashid bin Muhammad, and wrote to Sultan bin Saqr informing him of the change.[10]

Disgusted with Sultan's failure to act in support of their alliance, the Bani Qitab obviously regarded the transfer of Dhayd to Ras al-Khaimah as the starting point for the degeneration of that alliance. Shortly after, four bedouin of the tribe tried to kill some of Sultan's relatives and openly flouted their disrespect in other ways. In June 1927 the Bani Qitab joined a force gathered by Khalid bin Ahmad to attack Sharjah and including the ruler of Umm al-Qaiwain, the shaykh of Hamriyyah,[11] and representatives of the Bani Ka'b and Khawatir tribes; the reason for the attack was Sultan's refusal to abide by the terms of his 1924 covenant with Khalid. The Senior Naval Officer actively intervened to avert the impending hostilities, and called for a meeting of rulers. Khalid and his brother 'Abdallah, Hamad bin Ibrahim of Umm al-Qaiwain, 'Abd al-Rahman bin Sayf of Hamriyyah, Sa'id bin Maktum of Dubai and Sultan bin Saqr all attended. The first meeting solved nothing, but at the second, three days later, which Humayd bin 'Abd al-'Aziz also attended, an agreement was reached. Sultan promised to pay Khalid an allowance in return for having confiscated his property, and to appoint him as *wali* of Dhayd.[12]

After having openly sided with Khalid bin Ahmad against Sultan, the Bani Qitab refused to show any signs of friendship, and in July 1931 Muhammad bin 'Ali bin Huwayydin, who had become paramount shaykh of the Bani Qitab when his brother 'Abdallah died in December 1925, declared war on Sultan; he was angry at Sultan's weakness and could not ignore the fact that members of the ruling family, especially Sultan's brother Muhammad, were plundering certain areas around Sharjah. Sultan did not rise to the challenge, and before long he had lost all hold on the Bani Qitab. In 1931, for example, some bedouin of the Bani Qitab carried off a negress belonging to a merchant of Sharjah, and Sultan could do no more than plead with the Residency Agent to intervene.[13] During the war with Ajman in 1933, the Bani Qitab, together with the Manasir, fought on the side of Sharjah, but it must be noted that they had been called in by 'Abd al-Rahman of Hirah.[14] So much did the importance of the Bani Qitab increase during the 1930s that they acquired *de facto* control of the interior of the Trucial Coast from Dhayd in the north to Jabal Fa'iyah in the south, an area under the *de jure* control of Sharjah.

Thus when, in the winter of 1936, a geological party from Petroleum Concessions tried to enter Jabal Fa'iyah with a permit from Shaykh Sultan of Sharjah, it was turned back by the Bani Qitab.[15] The next year, Sultan promised the Resident to try to help the geologists again,[16] but the second party to set out met with no more success than the first had. Fowle could think of only one way to overcome the opposition of the Bani Qitab. The ruler of Ajman, eager to demonstrate his tribal connections, had told the Political Agent in Bahrain that he could arrange for a visit to Fa'iyah, and Fowle suggested in February 1938 that Sultan should be bypassed and the new offer accepted. He realised that, under the terms of its concession from Sharjah, Petroleum Concessions specifically undertook not to visit Fa'iyah without the written permission of the ruler; but the obligation was qualified by the words 'for the present'. Fowle, pointing out that five months had already passed since the signing of the concession, argued, 'I think it may reasonably be assumed that this period is longer than is covered by these words.'[17]

Petroleum Concessions was not eager to antagonise Sultan, especially as it could be argued that five months was only a short period.[18] In May 1938, Fowle reiterated his plan as the only means by which the company could enter Fa'iyah. He suggested that Petroleum Concessions inform Sultan that, in view of his inability to arrange for the visit, it would invoke the political agreement and apply to the Political Resident for help. Fowle would then tell the shaykh that the period covered by 'for the present' had expired, and the company would have to make its own arrangements.[19] The Resident stressed that the company should make no reference to the ownership of the Jabal:

> not withstanding the fact that they eventually explored this area through some agency than that of the Shaikh, it might suit the Company later to develop it . . . under the Sharjah concession. It is impossible to foretell how things will turn out on the Trucial Coast, and both the Company and ourselves should try and keep our hands as free as possible.[20]

A. C. B. Symon, Assistant Principal at the India Office, expressed doubts as to the ethics of Fowle's methods. He did not agree that the political agreement was intended to override specific undertakings by the company, especially as there was no proof that Sultan had failed to take such steps as were reasonably possible to make the area available to geologists.[21] Fowle was asked for more information to support his plan, but the Resident stood firm. 'My opinion is as expressed previously.'[22] He could not see any of the nuances of the situation. The ruler of Sharjah had been unable to arrange for the company to visit Fa'iyah; if the company wished to go, his was the only feasible plan. 'If we are not to pursue this course of action, as far as I can see the Company must remain out of Jabal Faiyah.'[23] Symon still had misgivings about the possible illegalities of the situation and was annoyed at the Resident: 'it looks as though Sir T. Fowle has burked the main issue'.[24]

Luckily for all concerned, however, Petroleum Concessions changed its plans for dispatching a party direct to Jabal Fa'iyah, and decided instead to include the area in a wider scheme of exploration in Oman. This involved sending out simultaneously, in the winter of 1938, two parties: one to proceed from Muscat to 'Ibri and then north to Jabal Hafit, and the other to meet it there after proceeding from Abu Dhabi direct to Buraimi. From Buraimi a party was to go on to Jabal Fa'iyah; but when it came to it the problems of dealing with the Bani Qitab proved, once again, insoluble. In September 1938, Weightman, officiating as Resident, had reported that the Bani Qitab were so strong in the area north of Buraimi that the company would need their help to get there, though he thought that this could be bought if the right price were offered.

In the meantime, Petroleum Concessions had become very interested in the rise to prominence of Khalid bin Ahmad, who, from being deposed as ruler of Sharjah, had become regent of Kalba in 1937. His qualities as a leader had even impressed the towns of Fujairah and Dibba, which now swore allegiance to him, and it was generally believed that he intended to reunite all the Qasimi territories and place them under his control. He had already started to receive taxes from Wadi al-Qawr and Wadi Hilu, areas usually considered part of the shaykhdom of Ras al-Khaimah.[25] Sultan was clearly aware of his predecessor's strength, for Weightman reported having heard, in July 1938, that the ruler of Sharjah had offered Khalid 1500 rupees to arrange a peace with the Bani Qitab on his behalf. Khalid was expected to meet Muhammad bin 'Ali bin Huwayydin of the Bani Qitab at Kalba, and then would try on behalf of Sultan to arrange for the company to visit Fa'iyah. If this proved unsuccessful, Weightman suggested, Khalid should be authorised to make the arrangement with the Bani Qitab independently, acting directly on behalf of Petroleum Concessions.[26] Once this was accomplished, Sultan could be told that the party would go to Fa'iyah with or without his permission, 'and that he had better save his face (and such future prospects he may have) by signing his name'.[27]

Weightman's suggestions were accepted as plausible, although the question of how to approach Sultan was left open for further consideration. At an India Office meeting on 23 September at which Fowle and representatives of Petroleum Concessions were present, it was decided to ask Shaykh Khalid to negotiate directly on behalf of the company if in attempting to negotiate on behalf of the ruler of Sharjah he were to meet with failure.[28] Shaykh Khalid, however, was unable to exert much influence on Muhammad bin 'Ali, and the Bani Qitab country remained inaccessible to the geologists who explored Oman that year. Preparations for another expedition, to set out in 1939, made it essential to conclude a separate agreement with Muhammad bin 'Ali. Although he did not wish to antagonise the ruler of Sharjah, Longrigg weighed the disadvantages of doing so and concluded, 'it is doubtful whether his ill will will be any more effective than his goodwill'.[29] The outbreak of World War II put an end, for the time being, to any further thought of exploring Jabal Fa'iyah, and all plans for negotiations were suspended.

The arrival of the oil company thus underlined the difficulty of attempting to define inter-state boundaries on the Coast and reach firm conclusions about which tribes controlled the areas to the east and south-east of the shaykhdoms. Naturally enough, Petroleum Concessions Limited wanted to know exactly how much land it was buying in the concessions; also naturally, each ruler wanted to claim as much territory as possible, in case oil were discovered.

Previously, none of the Trucial Coast shaykhs had ever attempted to establish accurately the extent of his shaykhdom; only the bedouin tribes and the few, scattered people actually living on the edge of the shaykhdoms knew exactly what the borders were. Furthermore, there were large areas of desert land that, for obvious reasons, no ruler had ever been particularly anxious to claim as his own, but that suddenly became important in terms of potential oil. The first attempt to define the rulers' territorial claims was made in the summer of 1937, when the Residency Agent was sent around the Coast to gather the necessary information from them.

In his report, the Agent said that the rulers had admitted that they had no fixed frontiers with their neighbours, but that they had given him instead the details of what they considered their *ihram* (sacred possession, and therefore inviolable). The only ruler who was absolutely sure of the extent of his territory was Sa'id of Dubai. Sultan of Sharjah, by contrast, was the only one who refused to state which territory he claimed. Obviously aware of his weak position, he proudly declared that his father's realm was well known to everyone and needed no elaboration. He did add, however, that only when he had finally settled his boundaries with his neighbours would he be able to commit himself about them.[30] It is clear from the report that, with the exception of Umm al-Qaiwain and Dubai, both small in area, the shaykhdoms were all of uncertain extent; the coastal rulers had gradually lost command of inland areas that had once been an integral part of their territories but had since come under the largely independent rule of bedouin tribes. The most extreme case of this was, of course, Sharjah, and in 1937 the Political Agent at Bahrain remarked of Sultan, 'he knows that his de facto control *at the moment* only extends a few miles inland from Sharjah. He has not been to Dhayd for seventeen years. He remains on the coast in the summer not because he likes it but because he dares not go inland.'[31]

Most of Sultan's territory was by then controlled by the Bani Qitab, who proved their independence and authority when Petroleum Concessions wanted to explore Jabal Fa'iyah. The other inland areas that the company wished to explore and for which it had to determine who was in control were Buraimi and, immediately to the south, Jabal Hafit. In the case of Buraimi, we have already seen that Shakhbut of Abu Dhabi wielded the greatest power there, through his *wali* at Al-Ain, Ibrahim bin 'Uthman, who succeeded after the death of Ahmad bin Hilal. The same was believed to apply to Hafit, although it was never put to the test.

In 1937, when the geologists of Petroleum Concessions wanted to explore the area around Jabal Hafit, Fowle decided that the best course was to write directly to Rashid bin Hamad of Hamasah in Buraimi and Muhammad bin Rahmah of Sunaynah, a few miles south of Jabal Hafit—both of them leaders of the Al-bu-Shamis —and to Muhammad and Saqr bin Sultan of the Na'im.[32] He obviously considered that the Al-bu-Shamis and the Na'im owed allegiance to no one, and had to be treated independently; but, in reply to his requests for permission, the four leaders sent him polite refusals and made it clear that they were unwilling to discuss the question further.[33] The next year, after the inconclusive visit of Petroleum Concessions geologists to Buraimi, the Assistant Political Agent at Bahrain concluded that the ruler of Abu Dhabi was the real master of the oasis and therefore of the surrounding area.[34] This conclusion was strengthened by the fact that the party under the auspices of the sultan of Muscat failed to achieve any substantial results. So, when Petroleum Concessions planned a similar expedition for 1939, there could be no question as to the procedure: Shakhbut would be approached and asked to make arrangements with the Na'im and Al-bu-Shamis for the success of the expedition.[35]

Because of the outbreak of the war, however, all preparations for the expedition had to be delayed until peace was declared; after that, the situation had altered so radically that the problem of boundaries had acquired a totally new dimension. Had it been solved once and for all with the help of the British authorities during the inter-war period, the present map of the United Arab Emirates would not be such a puzzle.

10 The Reform Movement of Dubai: The Beginnings of Democracy

Dubai is today known as one of the most thriving commercial centres of the world. Well before offshore oil was struck, in 1966, it was a bustling city-state whose citizens were amongst the most sophisticated and enterprising businessmen of the Arab world. In making their imprint on the world of trade and commerce, they did not wait for the discovery of petroleum, but proceeded to make full use of the fact that Dubai had a fine natural harbour to serve as the basis of communication with the outside world. 'Indeed, if any state in the Middle East has lifted itself up into economic prosperity by its own boot straps, it is Dubai.'[1]

Besides being oft referred to as the gold-smuggling centre of the world, as a flourishing entrepot, and as the sparkling Venice of the Arab world, Dubai is well known for having rapidly developed, before it began to benefit from oil receipts, an advanced urban infrastructure. Before it joined the United Arab Emirates, in 1971, it could boast a public administration system comprising a central secretariat and departments with responsibility for education, health, customs, petroleum, passports, the police force, land and property, and postal services. Dubai town had a municipal council, which was founded in March 1957 and became responsible for such varied public utilities as slaughterhouses, markets, baths, fire-brigades and hospitals. Town planning was practised. Among the shaykhdom's achievements were the founding in 1965 of the first Chamber of Commerce on the Trucial Coast, a vast increase of water and electricity supplies, the building of an international airport, the evolution of a modern banking system, and the construction of the largest dry-dock in the world.

Most contemporary observers tend to regard Dubai as a phenomenon isolated from the rest of the Gulf in time and achievement; few realise that the boom it has been experiencing during the past two decades is part of a process that started in the 1930s and today is merely being continued. Stemming from the character of the seafaring merchants that make up the bulk of the Dubai population, the events that occurred then mark the turning-point in the modern history of the shaykhdom. A number of elements were brought into play the action and interaction of which led to the evolution of a strong progressive movement that temporarily thrust Dubai out of the confines of its local framework.

The components of the movement were many. First, the natural setting of Dubai town, divided by a creek, came to symbolise the town's division into two opposing factions, the stronghold of one being on one side, the other's on the other. Second, the dissension that had existed within the ruling family ever since its establishment, a century earlier, came to the fore and became a central feature of the events taking place. Third, the growth of Dubai early in the twentieth century as the main port for the southern regions of the Gulf, and its consequent evolution as the trading centre of the area were reflected in the drive of the movement's leaders not only to create better commercial conditions for themselves, but also to give expression to the political and social consciousness they had acquired through their experiences and dealings with foreign merchants. Fourth, and perhaps most important, the impetus for the movement sprang from a rejection of the poverty from which most of Arabia suffered during the economic depression of the 1930s, coupled with a desire to search out and create alternative sources of income.

The first major attempt to dislodge Sa'id bin Maktum took place in 1929, when the opposition, led by his cousin Mani' bin Rashid, forced him to resign. Mani' informed the British authorities that he had become the new ruler of Dubai, but they refused to accept the fact, and Sa'id was reinstated. He continued, however, to show himself unable to keep command of the members of his family, as is shown by an incident that occurred two years after the abortive deposal. On 5 May 1931 a boat belonging to the Hindu agent of the British India Steam Navigation Company accidentally collided with the boat of the sons of Sa'id bin Butti and slightly damaged it. The crew of the damaged boat, with the approval of the owners, severely handled the agent's men and forced them to pay a fine of 20 rupees. The sons of Sa'id bin Butti then threatened to beat the agent himself, but did not carry out the threat. When the Senior Naval Officer of the Persian Gulf Division arrived in Dubai four days later, he was informed of the incident. He approached Sa'id bin Maktum, who admitted his inability to deal with the matter; proof of this came when his cousins refused his request to meet with the Naval Officer.[2] The case was not settled until 29 August, when Sa'id finally was able to prevail upon his cousins to call on the agent, apologise, and make reparations.[3]

This capitulation did little to restore Sa'id's authority, and three years later, on 23 September 1934, his cousins tried, unsuccessfully, to kill him. In desperation, Sa'id turned to the British authorities for help. On 21 October he saw the Senior Naval Officer and told him that an attempt to depose him was shortly to be made. He said he was torn between his duty as ruler and his obligations to Britain; he knew he could rely on the help of the bedouin to put down his opponents, but he was afraid of the trouble it would cause, especially to the Indian merchants living in Dubai, for whose safety he was responsible.[4]

The Senior Naval Officer recommended that some form of help be given to Sa'id. The recommendation was based on humane considerations, for he was convinced that the ruler was indeed torn between two forces and needed support. But Fowle, as Political Resident, vigorously objected. He saw no reason to interfere in the internal affairs of Dubai, but asked for a sloop to take the Residency Agent to Dubai with a message: Shaykh Sa'id was to do as he saw fit with regard to the movement against him, but any lapse in the protection of British lives and property would be severely reprimanded.[5] The message was delivered on 27 October by K. S. Husayn bin Hasan 'Imad, Assistant Residency Agent, 'Isa bin 'Abd al-Latif being ill at the time. It had a powerful effect on the population, who assumed it meant that the British Government was openly supporting Sa'id.[6] The same day, Sa'id held a *majlis*, to which the sons of Rashid and Butti were not invited. He reaffirmed his position, and demanded obedience. The Al-bu-Falasah admitted his rights, but asked that the sons of Rashid and Butti be interviewed. Long discussions followed, till on 30 October it was reported that Sa'id was going to exile his cousins—a decision about which he later changed his mind.

On 31 October, Colonel Loch, the Political Agent in Bahrain, arrived in Dubai and had an interview with Shaykh Sa'id. The next day, a number of Manasir bedouin entered Dubai at the invitation of the ruler. They received money from Sa'id, and then returned to their camp outside the town. Feeling strengthened by this open display of his allies, Sa'id met with his rebellious cousins in order to obtain their oath of loyalty. On 2 November, Hashar bin Rashid visited Sa'id and took the oath on behalf of his three brothers. On 3 November, Sa'id asked the Al-bu-Falasah for a representative of the Butti faction (three of the sons of Butti were involved in the dispute). Sa'id bin Butti went, no doubt impressed by reports of the arrival of about 800 bedouin outside the town.

The ruler's cousins continued to display contempt for law and order once the earlier incident had been forgotten. They knew that their unruly behaviour would be unopposed, for Shaykh Sa'id dreaded showdowns.[7] Hussah bint Murr, wife of Sa'id, who had considerable commercial interests in Dayrah, was also a source of resentment. Sa'id bin Butti complained of mismanagement in Dayrah, and said that the quarter had become dirty and unsafe. In January 1936, therefore, Sa'id bin Maktum wisely authorised Sa'id bin Butti to become the *wali* of Dayrah,[8] and immediately the new *wali* began a series of reforms. He had the streets cleaned; every householder became responsible for seeing that the frontage of his house was clean; people were employed to clear away rubbish dumps; prostitutes were ordered to get married or leave Dayrah; and anyone caught loitering there after 4 p.m. was to be punished. The effectiveness of these reforms was marked, especially as they led to stolen goods being discovered, but Mani' and Hashar resented the appointment and showed their anger by criticising the new *wali*, exposing his faults, and openly defying his authority.

They instructed their servants to go out at night and to beat Sa'id bin Butti's men if they tried to stop them. On the night of 3 October 1936, Hashar bin Rashid ordered his son Butti to go out and wait for Sa'id bin Butti; if the *wali* interfered, he was to be attacked. The *wali* reported the incident to Shaykh Sa'id, who mildly told him to ignore it. The trouble continued until the notables of the Bani Yas called on Sa'id bin Maktum to intervene. At a meeting on 14 October, Sa'id asked the *majlis* to choose another *wali* if serious complaints about Sa'id bin Butti could be found. No decision was reached until the next day, when the *majlis* decided that it could see no good reason to dismiss the *wali*, but asked that his cousins and brothers be exempted from the regulations he laid down.[9]

This did not appease Sa'id bin Butti's relatives.[10] Rashid's sons resented the fact that one of their former allies was now working alongside the shaykh. Rumour had it that they were purposely goading Sa'id bin Maktum in order to frighten him into giving them one-third of the income of Dubai.[11] The decline of the pearl trade had affected their economic standing, and their unruliness could be traced back to the diminution in their fortunes. Sa'id bin Maktum continued to rule over Dubai, but he had repeatedly to defer to the wishes of his cousins, and at all times to consult the *majlis* before taking any major decision. Above all, he had to contend with British policy.

The aspect of British policy that caused him most difficulty was the pressure on him to act against the slave trade and traffic in arms. The measures he was forced to take against them did much to precipitate the rebelliousness of the ruling elite in 1938. Although Dubai's treaty with Britain did not expressly forbid the sale of slaves, their importation was forbidden and domestic slaves were entitled to manumission if they applied to the Agency at Sharjah or at Bahrain. Between 1932 and 1936, the number of slaves manumitted was very slight, but in 1937 and the early part of 1938 rate of manumission grew to such an extent[12] that slave-owners in Dubai became highly concerned and directed their anger at the Agency in Sharjah, which they threatened to attack. In the case of the traffic in arms, Fowle had become alarmed at its growth in Dubai during the 1930s. Investigations showed that the two people most involved were a Kuwaiti, Khalaf 'Ali al-Zamani, and an Iranian, Rais Muhammad Rasul. The Resident approached Shaykh Sa'id on the matter when he visited him in Dubai on 27 February 1938, and the ruler promised to have the two men deported.[13]

The proposed deportations, coming as they did when the fear of wholesale manumission was haunting slave-owners, caused serious agitation. The Al-bu-Falasah, who held Sa'id personally responsible for both situations, angrily incited demonstrations against him on 14 March 1938. The outbreak was serious, so the sloop HMS *Bideford*, which was on its way to Bombay, was diverted to Dubai, where it lay offshore for three days. It carried a letter from Hugh Weightman, Political Agent in Bahrain, that announced his plans to visit Dubai the following week; the Agent also informed Sa'id that, although the sloop was there to give him enough time to assert his own authority, there would be no interference.[14] The shaykh was reminded of his responsibility for British lives and property.

Owing to the presence of the sloop, the situation improved, and on 18 March the sloop was able to leave. Fowle then sent a message to Dubai warning the inhabitants about the danger of loss of lives or property of British subjects. He also sent a message to all the Trucial Coast rulers: British policy regarding slavery had not changed, and only those slaves who asked for manumission would be entitled to it.[15] The *majlis* met at Dubai and passed two resolutions: first, Shaykh Sa'id was to ask the Resident to have manumitted slaves returned to their owners; second, he was to ask the Resident to pardon the gun-runners, since he had agreed to their deportation without consulting his people. If the requests were not granted, the shaykh would not be allowed to grant facilities for air travel or renew the civil air agreement without first consulting his *majlis*. The Resident refused both petitions, and sent his answer with Weightman when the latter flew to Dubai on 24 March.

Sa'id asked Weightman to attend a *majlis* on 25 March and explain British policy to its members. In his account of the meeting,[16] the Agent said that the spokesmen, Muhammad bin Ahmad bin Dalmuk and Hashar bin Rashid, did not argue with him after he had stated his case clearly and firmly, especially when they realised that they had no alternative but to accept. But they were able to dominate Shaykh Sa'id, for, as soon as the agreement to deport the gun-runners was reached, the shaykh and his *majlis* went out of the room for a few minutes. When they returned, Sa'id asked that the gun-runners be allowed to stay in Dubai, confessing that he would encounter trouble if his request were not granted, and that that would be detrimental to his treaty relations with Britain. Weightman remained firm, so Sa'id finally promised to have the two men deported.[17] But the members of the *majlis* were more anxious to discuss with Weightman the subject of the slaves; it was of greater concern to them because it had a direct bearing on the pearl industry and their own incomes, especially as they had been troubled since 1936 by the threat of a general manumission. Muhammad bin Ahmad bin Dalmuk took the floor, supported by Shaykh Jum'ah, brother of Sa'id.

Sa'id wisely refrained from joining in the debate with Weightman. He had abstained on previous occasions from defying the British by using the few available weapons at his disposal or by trying to enforce the existing regulations. One chance he had had to put effective pressure on the British was, as he recognised, during the period when the preliminary oil concessions were being negotiated. In April 1937, when Petroleum Concessions was trying to complete negotiations for a concession from Dubai, the Political Resident called Shaykh Sa'id and Major Frank Holmes to Bahrain, where the discussions were brought to a close. Shaykh Sa'id insisted, however, that he should sign the resulting agreement in Dubai, 'in the presence of his notables'.[18] When he returned home, the rulers of Sharjah and Ras al-Khaimah attempted to prevent him from signing, and used the opposition of his cousins as a form of pressure;[19] they also suggested that all three of them should join in protest against the manumission of slaves.[20] Sa'id did not agree with the latter suggestion, although it must have occurred to him that, in view of its extreme eagerness for the Trucial shaykh-doms to grant concessions to its chosen company, the British Government might well be prepared to relax certain regulations.

Weightman planned to leave Dubai, quiet once again, on 27 March. Sa'id asked to see him before he left, and then told him that on 26 March the *majlis* had decided that the air agreement was not to be renewed. Weightman assumed that it was a face-saving device on the part of the *majlis*, and thought that negotiations for the renewal might be successful after a delay of two months.[21] Just three months later, however, a recrudescence of trouble, much more serious than any of the previous outbreaks, resulted in a considerable weakening of the position of Shaykh Sa'id.

Once again, the trouble was based on the conflict between the two opposing branches of the ruling family. It is significant that the conflict revolved around yet another matter that affected the financial position of the Al-bu-Falasah. Rashid bin Sa'id, son of the ruler, had, in effect, a monopoly of the taxi service in Dubai, but Maktum bin Rashid ran a taxi service between Dubai and Sharjah. Rashid, incensed at what he saw as open rivalry, collected thirty armed men and on 26 May attacked Maktum's car on its way to Sharjah. Rashid wounded Maktum's driver and put some of Maktum's men in stocks, where they remained until they were released by members of Maktum's party.[22] Maktum was furious, and threatened to stop all cars belonging to Rashid. The dispute soon began to assume serious proportions. The ruler, a mild man by temperament, but dominated by his wife and son, ineffectually tried to reach some form of settlement with his cousins, who by that time had local opinion on their side.[23] The Al-bu-Falasah banded together and presented a unified front in opposition to Sa'id. Strengthened by the support of the people of Dubai, who welcomed the opportunity to weaken the position of the ruler, the Al-bu-Falasah formulated their demands and presented them to Sa'id in a letter. These included: a budget and civil list; proper arrangements for health care and sanitation in the town of Dubai; a police service; reorganisation of the Customs Department; fixed allowances for members of the ruling family; and abolition of the monopolies held by the ruler, his wife and son (of ferry services, motor services, the unloading of ships' cargoes, and so on).[24]

To enforce their demands, the Al-bu-Falasah occupied certain towers of the town with armed men. A truce was later arranged when a conciliation committee, presided over by the Residency Agent, K. S. 'Abd al-Razzaq Al-Mahmud, forced Sa'id to agree to some of the demands. However, outside interference upset the truce. Shaykh Sultan bin Saqr of Sharjah sent a message to Sa'id promising to send him 200 men to help him against the insurgents. The men did not appear, and the Political Agent in Bahrain sent Sultan a message advising him to tend to his own affairs. Then Sultan bin Salim of Ras al-Khaimah, described by the Political Agent in Bahrain as 'having an incurable habit of interfering in matters which do not concern him',[25] arrived in Dubai. He blamed both parties for allowing an outsider like the Residency Agent to bring about a reconciliation, and suggested that the arrangements reached should be cancelled and a fresh start made under his patronage.[26] Weightman restored order when he arrived in Dubai shortly afterwards; he sent word to Sultan bin Salim to go home at once, reminding him of his recent disgrace when he had interfered in the affairs of Kalba,[27] and threatened to have him sent home on a RAF vehicle if he did not obey. He left the next day, and for a time Dubai was comparatively calm.

But Sa'id did little to keep his side of the bargain with his cousins, his only concession being the abolition of the monopolies held by his immediate family. The Al-bu-Falasah began to show signs of restlessness, so on 24 September Sa'id sent his brother Jum'ah to meet Weightman and Fowle in Bahrain and ask for their support. Fowle made it clear to Jum'ah that the matter was internal, and that Britain could in no way interfere.[28] He advised that Sa'id give in to the demand for reform, and reiterated that the shaykh would be considered personally responsible for any damage to British life and property.[29] Sa'id denied that he had promised to introduce reforms, and desperately warned the Resident that he would not be responsible for the safety of British lives if fighting were to break out. In the meantime, he also appealed to the rulers of Abu Dhabi and Qatar for arms and ammunition, but they declined to respond.

The town of Dubai then gradually divided into two armed camps: Shaykh Sa'id and his followers on the Dubai side, and the Al-bu-Falasah on the Dayrah side. By 8 October, the latter were able to occupy the Dayrah customs house,[30] and showed signs of gaining more. The same day a sloop arrived in Dubai to protect British property, for Weightman had already written to both sides giving the usual warning about British interests.[31] The dispute caused great interest and concern throughout the area, as shown by the attempts of the rulers of Sharjah and Ras al-Khaimah to become involved; the concern was prompted by fear of the obstruction that would be caused to trade if Dubai were to become a battlefield. A further attempt to restore order in Dubai was made, this time with positive results, by neighbouring leaders. On 9 October, Shaykh Shakhbut of Abu Dhabi, Shaykh Muhammad bin 'Ali bin Huwayydin of the Bani Qitab and a third, unidentified shaykh arrived in Dubai in order to try to arrange some form of peace. They arranged for a five-day truce, starting on the day of their arrival, and then attempted to reach a settlement between the two parties; this ended in deadlock, for the Al-bu-Falasah insisted on the formation of a representative council like that recently established in Kuwait, with executive and administrative powers.[32] By the time Weightman arrived in Dubai, on 15 October, the position of the ruler had weakened considerably. Shaykh Saʻid, who realised that there was a movement to depose him, told Weightman that he was willing to accept any terms the opposition laid down. Weightman and ʻAbd al-Razzaq negotiated at length with both parties, and an agreement finally was signed on 20 October.

The agreement provided for the existence of a *majlis* presided over by Shaykh Saʻid and with fifteen members, selected by the 'principal people' of Dubai. The financial affairs of the state had to be managed in the name of the state, and any decisions to be taken regarding them had to be taken by the *majlis*, on a majority vote. An allowance of one-eighth of the total revenue of Dubai was to be allocated to the ruler. Weightman made it clear to Maniʻ bin Rashid, who signed the agreement on behalf of the Al-bu-Falasah, that the British Government would continue to deal directly with Shaykh Saʻid, as the legitimate ruler, and would not allow the *majlis* to stop him from fulfilling his treaty obligations.[33] Weightman was warned by Fowle not to guarantee the agreement, which was an internal matter and did not concern the British Government. Thus the movement was given no official British sanction or encouragement; it was left to its own devices and warned that it had to function within the political framework of Shaykh Saʻid's existing treaty obligations.

Once the agreement had been accepted and the fighting was over, the *majlis* began to set up an administration and concern itself with reforms of a commercial, political and social nature. First of all it concentrated its attention on the commercial life of Dubai and factors that could enhance its growth; political and social improvements were dealt with later. People to regulate the customs service were elected, and a proper list of all employees, with their respective salaries, was formulated. The income of the porters of Dubai and Dayrah was fixed, and a list was drawn up naming the only men who were allowed to be porters. A tax on imported goods was decided on, and a council of merchants was set up to operate it; it was further decided that the money should be used to finance municipal and educational projects.[34] A municipal council was set up. Maniʻ bin Rashid was elected Director of Education, and three schools were subsequently opened, the first on the Trucial Coast after the depression. In order to maintain the internal security of Dubai, the *majlis* appointed men to patrol the desert and others to guard the market-places.

This administrative organisation in fact represented only a small part of what the *majlis* wished to do. Even the British authorities, who in 1929 and 1934 referred to the Al-bu-Falasah as the 'wicked cousins', described them as the 'popular party' in 1938 and 1939. The members of the *majlis* were ambitious in their plans for total political reform of Dubai, and were very serious about their purpose. That this was so is plain from copies of the correspondence between the movement's leaders, Shaykh Saʿid and the Residency Agent, and the minutes of meetings of the *majlis*, which documents were carefully conserved and finally, after the collapse of the reform movement, deposited with the Political Agent in Bahrain. The term *wajibat wataniyyah* (national duty) that Maniʿ, as the chief spokesman of the *majlis*, used in his correspondence with Saʿid[36] is indicative of the approach taken by the *majlis* during its brief tenure of power. The members of the *majlis* also expressed the sentiment that their first duty was towards their country (*biladina*) and that their personal wishes had to be put aside in favour of the common good.[37] They specifically referred to themselves as a reform movement (*thawrat al-islah*).[38] Shaykh Saʿid at first forcefully complained about the measures taken by the *majlis*. He protested that changes in Dubai should be brought about with the guidance of the *shariʿah* (the canon law of Islam), which he regarded as the only true basis for law and progress. It is evident that he did not consider the *majlis* a tool of his own power, but regarded it as an alien, usurping body. He rarely attended its meetings, but nevertheless was indignant when decisions were taken without his knowledge and without taking cognisance of his opinion. Maniʿ continued, however, to inform Saʿid when meetings of the *majlis* would take place and what would be the agenda; he remarked to Saʿid on his failure to attend, and stressed that a number of the reforms that the *majlis* was contemplating had been suggested to the ruler many years before.[39]

To enlarge the port of Dubai and to beautify the town were two of the more ambitious projects on which the *majlis* worked. Since the income of the state was not sufficient to cover the costs of enlarging the port, it was decided that they would have to be subsidised from the revenues provided by the oil concession and the air agreement.[40] The streets of Dubai needed to be laid out properly, and the *majlis* considered improving the general appearance of the town.[41] In line with this, improvements to the main roads and the seafront of the town were started, but on 12 February 1939 Shaykh Saʿid issued an order forbidding the work on the roads, saying that he did not wish to have them widened. Annoyed at such disregard of their plans, the members of the *majlis* complained to the Residency Agent, accusing Saʿid of having had personal, probably financial, reasons for putting an end to the road-works.[42]

There is little doubt that Saʿid wished to maintain the growth of his personal investments regardless of the new regulations. The members of the *majlis*, on the other hand, weakened their case considerably, in their programme of reform, by their inability to distinguish between themselves as part of a governing body and themselves as members of the Al-bu-Falasah; they referred to themselves as '*a'ilat al-hukumah* (the governing family). One incident in particular may be used to illustrate thus. Jum'ah bin Maktum wished to have buildings constructed in the Suq al-Jarid of Dubai. The *majlis* disapproved of the venture, but condemned it for two different reasons. One objection stemmed from a family tradition, which had originated during the reign of Butti bin Suhayl, that the income from a building that was constructed on a previously empty lot in the Suq al-Jarid could not be used by the ruler without the permission of his family, who usually allocated the money to its needy members. In the present case, the *majlis* accused Sa'id of ignoring the tradition by selling empty lots and having shops built on them, to his own pecuniary advantage.[43] It also claimed that the late Residency Agent, 'Isa bin 'Abd al-Latif, had been bribed to help Sa'id in his acquisitions.[44] It was not until some time later that the *majlis* referred to its second ground for objection, public welfare, decrying Jum'ah's disobedience of the government.[45]

The weaknesses of the *majlis* gradually became more obvious, for, in the final analysis, the lofty ideals and worthy aims of the reform movement were dissipated by self-interest. Besides allocating a salary of 100 rupees per month to each of its members, the *majlis* provided pensions to the old men and women of the ruling family; these were only two of the state subsidies that the Al-bu-Falasah received. Furthermore, patronage of the newly-created government departments seemed to be monopolised by the same elite. Gradually, the people of Dubai began to manifest their resentment, and, according to the Political Resident, 'a feeling spread that for one despot there had merely been substituted a board of despotism'.[46]

On 3 March 1939 the *majlis* decided that the ruler was to have a fixed annual income of 10,000 rupees,[47] and that the income from the oil concession and the air agreement was to revert to the national treasury.[48] This was extremely trying for Sa'id, for he then realised how dependent he was on the *majlis*, despite the fact that he had virtually ignored it. He wrote a pathetic letter to Hashar, pleading for a reply to his request for more money.[49] He was by then totally alienated from the *majlis*, and had to find a way to rid himself of it. The opportunity presented itself on the occasion of the wedding, on 29 March 1939, of Rashid bin Sa'id to Shaykhah Latifah, daughter of Hamdan bin Zayid of Abu Dhabi, whose family, following his murder in 1922, had lived in exile in Dubai.[50] The bedouin of the hinterland,[51] always Sa'id's allies, had previously promised to help him; they crowded into Dayrah to attend the marriage ceremony, and were soon able to occupy the town. There was little fighting, but Hashar bin Rashid and his son were killed. The members of the *majlis* did not resist for long, half of them surrendering almost immediately. Mani' alone continued to fight. He was besieged in his house, alone except for the help of his young daughter San'a, who later married Shaykh Khalifah bin Sa'id bin Maktum.[52] Finally, however, together with the remaining half of the *majlis*, Mani' fled to Sharjah.

A sloop was sent to Dubai on 1 April, and Weightman arrived the next day, to 'clear up the situation'.[53] He advised Sa'id not to abandon the trend towards a new form of government, and helped him set up an advisory council of fifteen members, five of whom had belonged to the old *majlis*. Shortly after, the situation in Dubai reverted to normal.

Mani' and his party remained in Sharjah, which they used as a centre of intrigue against Sa'id. Weightman hoped that another ruler on the coast might accept the refugees, since their presence in Sharjah, a mere seven miles away, was causing Sa'id to contemplate an attack. After skilful interventions and machinations, Weightman was able to have Mani' and his entourage moved to Ras al-Khaimah, thus averting an outbreak of violence between Dubai and Sharjah.[54] But news of Mani''s continued designs on Dubai persisted, and in October 1939 Sa'id was so agitated by an uncorroborated report of a plot against him that he had five men arrested, summarily tried, and found guilty; their eyes were put out with hot irons as a punishment.[55] This act gave rise to a general feeling of disgust against Sa'id and caused a considerable exodus of Dubai residents; but there could be no doubt that he was at last in full control of Dubai, his traditional opponents having been all but eliminated from the field.[56]

Sa'id continued to rule until his death in 1958, when his son Rashid, the present ruler, came to power. Although the rebellious faction of the Al-bu-Falasah was dispersed after 1939 and all its power was dissipated by the events that followed the breakdown of the reform movement, the reforms advocated by the short-lived *majlis* left their imprint on Dubai. Of the seven shaykhdoms on the Trucial Coast, Dubai was the first, in the years following World War II, to become conscious of the need to alter its social and economic structure. Long before oil wealth made these alterations relatively easy, Dubai was in the vanguard of the movement to modernise the Coast.

11 The Exercise of Power: British Representatives

'Here we have a coast line some 2,500 miles in length from Kuwait to Dhofar consisting of some dozen independent Arab Shaikhdoms, in some of which very primitive conditions prevail. In these Shaikhdoms we have important strategical interests, the Air Route, oil fields and Naval Base, and between these Shaikhdoms and their neighbouring states—Saudi Arabia, Iraq and Persia—are various questions which affect us and the negotiations for which in fact we conduct. We are moreover interested in the trade on the Arab side, and much of this trade is in the hands of British Indian Merchants. In most Shaikhdoms are colonies of British Indian subjects, who even in the more primitive ones enjoy a high standard of security for their lives and security. In addition to our strategical and political interests, under our Orders in Council we actually administer the law in the larger Shaikhdoms both to our own subjects, and generally speaking to foreigners. Yet in spite of all these combined interests . . . we pay no subsidies to any Shaikhs. . . . We raise no tribal levies. . . . We do not maintain a single soldier or policeman on the whole of the Arab side. . . . Our expenses and commitments are in fact limited to one Resident, three Political Agents and their office staffs![1]

In 1938 Fowle could thus point out with pride the extent of British achievements in the Gulf and the minimal cost, in terms both of human effort and of financial expenditure, at which they had been secured. There can be little doubt of the accuracy of the statement, but, in his enthusiasm to praise the system that had established such a firm and profitable position for Britain, the Resident overlooked certain factors. Most outstanding, of course, was the reliance of the British on sea power: the six sloops of war that made up the Persian Gulf Division served as a constant reminder of the unassailable might of Britain and kept the Gulf at its mercy. This fact is of unquestionable importance, and central to any consideration of British policy in the area; the mere threat of the arrival of the Persian Gulf Division was always enough to subdue even the most stubborn resistance to the will of the British authorities.

Despite the changed climate of world opinion after the end of World War I, gunboat diplomacy was employed to a surprisingly large extent on the Trucial Coast in the decade after 1918;[2] it usually took the form of bombarding a ruler's forts or seizing a shaykhdom's pearling fleet. Bombardment was unique to the Trucial Coast and to those parts of Muscat that the sultan was totally unable to subdue; Qatar, Bahrain and Kuwait were spared this means of pressure and punishment. One reason for this was the close control exercised in Bahrain and Kuwait by the Political Agents, and the fact that Qatar was only slowly drawn into the British orbit. Moreover, the Coast was generally viewed as a wild and savage area that would respond effectively only to violent forms of punishment.

It has been mentioned earlier how in 1921 the towers of Ajman were bombarded, after its ruler, Humayd bin 'Abd al-'Aziz, had refused to pay a fine imposed by the Resident. This fine had been imposed because of Humayd's destruction of a certificate of manumission, his refusal to visit the ship of the Political Resident when the standard was hoisted, and his failure to respond to the efforts made by the Senior Naval Officer to mediate for peace in Humayd's fight against 'Abd al-Rahman bin Muhammad of the Al-bu-Shamis. The next year the guns fired on Hamriyyah, a coastal village between Ajman and Umm al-Qaiwain but within the shaykhdom of Sharjah, from which it had made many attempts to secede.

In 1917, its headman, 'Abd al-Rahman bin Sayf of the Al-bu-Shamis, made yet another attempt to assert his independence. Khalid bin Ahmad was determined to deal firmly with the insurgents and sent an armed force to Hamriyyah. This force, however, proved inadequate to subdue 'Abd al-Rahman, and it was only with British intervention that Khalid was able to re-establish his position; the prolonged fighting had hindered the pearl trade enormously and there was a danger that the Indian merchants would not be able to collect their debts, so a sloop was sent to Sharjah to put an end to the hostilities. The captain negotiated an agreement whereby 'Abd al-Rahman recognised the suzerainty of Khalid, and peace was restored.

'Abd al-Rahman adhered to the terms of the agreement, but his son Humayd tried, and very nearly managed, to free himself of them. When he was left in charge during the visit of his father to Sharjah town in December 1921, he seized control of the fort and village and declared his independence, refusing to grant his father permission to return home. Trevor, the Political Resident, happened to visit Sharjah in RIMS *Lawrence* the day after this, so he took Khalid and 'Abd al-Rahman on board with him and sailed to Hamriyyah in order to re-establish 'Abd al-Rahman as headman subject to Sharjah. Humayd resisted this show of force, and refused to go on board. Unable to remain for long, Trevor left Sharjah, leaving the Residency Agent to pursue the matter. 'Isa found it difficult to accomplish much in the face of Humayd's determined stand, and finally the Senior Naval Officer diverted to Hamriyyah at the request of the Resident. He arrived in HMS *Cyclamen* on 31 January 1922, but Humayd refused to visit him, despite promises of a safe conduct. Finally the Naval Officer gave Humayd fourteen days in which to submit and give the town back to his father; at the same time, he asked the Resident for the reinforcement of a political officer to arrive in Hamriyyah at the end of the fortnight. Trevor decided to go himself. He took 'Isa bin 'Abd al-Latif and Khalid bin Ahmad on board RIMS *Lawrence,* arriving in Hamriyyah on 17 February. Preliminary attempts to induce Humayd to meet with Trevor failed completely, and finally Trevor issued an ultimatum: if Humayd did not appear within twenty-four hours, a sloop would arrive at Hamriyyah. Apparently Khalid and 'Abd al-Rahman convinced Trevor that a few shots at the fort would be enough to frighten the rebel, so, when Humayd did not comply, the *Cyclamen,* which had been waiting at Sharjah, arrived and started to bombard Hamriyyah. Khalid and 'Abd al-Rahman obviously had miscalculated the extent of Humayd's determination, for, although the left side of one tower, then the flag tower and a tower at the other end of the village were knocked down, no capitulation was forthcoming.

Trevor, who later admitted that the incident 'caused me more anxiety and worry than any I can remember',[3] allowed Khalid to go to Sharjah in order to collect an armed force. By this time Humayd must have realised what was happening, and after much scurrying back and forth with deputations he surrendered, leaving Hamriyyah on the night of 19 February. The next day, Khalid reinstalled 'Abd al-Rahman bin Sayf as headman of the village. Before he sailed, Trevor warned Khalid that he should supply 'Abd al-Rahman with a strong enough force to maintain his position, since the Residency would not come to his aid in the event of a further challenge from Humayd.[4]

Khalid did not take the warning seriously, and a few weeks later Humayd managed to return. Afraid, his father escaped to Umm al-Qaiwain. The Senior Naval Officer, Captain Brandon, at first tried to settle the matter peacefully, going in HMS *Cyclamen* to Umm al-Qaiwain, where he hoped to obtain the co-operation of its ruler. But the *shamal* winds started, and the *Cyclamen* was forced to leave, since its anchorage had become dangerous. The Residency Agent, however, was successful in negotiating a tentative agreement with Humayd, who promised to leave Hamriyyah and live in Sharjah provided he were given an annuity; the final clauses of the agreement awaited the return of the *Cyclamen*, which was urgently diverted to Abadan at the last moment, and instead appeared at Dubai on 10 April. Brandon found that Humayd was in Dubai trying to persuade Sa'id bin Maktum to help him. Sa'id told Brandon that he would be willing to go to Hamriyyah to mediate provided he could have the support of *Cyclamen*. Sa'id's negotiations bore little fruit, so on 12 April, after he had obtained the requisite permission, Brandon bombed Hamriyyah. Humayd, intimidated by the second attack in a few weeks, surrendered, and his father was again reinstated.[5] The double bombardment provides a striking example of the disregard that could be shown for the official policy of non-interference; aside from its threat to the economic welfare of the Indian merchants, Humayd's behaviour had little relevance to British interests. Of course, he had openly disregarded the orders of British officers, and for that he had to be punished.

Another case of gunboat diplomacy occurred in 1925, when Hamad bin 'Abdallah of Fujairah, by buying the daughter of a Baluchi woman living in Muscat, flouted British regulations about participation in the slave trade. The Political Agent in Muscat, in keeping with British recognition of Fujairah as part of Sharjah, asked the ruler of Sharjah for the release of the slave girl. Shaykh Sultan bin Saqr called on Hamad bin 'Abdallah to release the slave, and this brought two replies from Hamad: in the first, he denied any knowledge of the existence of the girl, and added that the only superior he recognised was God; in the second, after he could no longer deny that the slave was with him, he announced that the girl had died. Prideaux, the Political Resident, would not allow the matter to rest there. He was not concerned with Hamad's insubordination to the ruler of Sharjah, but rather with the fact that the regulations about the slave trade had been disregarded.

Accordingly, Prideaux arranged to visit Fujairah in April 1925. He travelled in RIMS *Lawrence*, which anchored off Gharayfah; the Resident's flag was then hoisted, and 'Isa bin 'Abd-al-Latif, together with K. B. 'Abd al-Razzaq (who was later to succeed him as Residency Agent), went ashore to summon Hamad to the ship. At first, Hamad sent word to Prideaux to meet him on shore, refusing to go on board the *Lawrence*. Later, he changed his mind and asked for a letter of safe conduct before he boarded the vessel. When this was issued, he changed his mind yet again, categorically refusing to board the ship and declaring himself willing to pay a fine for the abduction of the slave. Prideaux was greatly concerned at these insults to British prestige: Hamad had deliberately ignored the signal (the raising of the Resident's flag) to go on board; and he had flouted the regulations about the slave trade. Prideaux was convinced that, if Hamad's disregard of the treaties with Britain should go unpunished, the Political Resident would gradually lose control of the villages of the Shimayliyyah.[6] The least of Prideaux's concerns was Fujairah's wish to secede from Sharjah.

The Resident consulted the Senior Naval Officer, who was at Muscat on HMS *Triad*; HMS *Cyclamen* was also not far away. Together the two men decided, after obtaining the requisite permission from the Naval Commander-in-Chief, on a suitable form of punishment: Hamad's fort would be bombarded and, if necessary, his property would be seized. The headman of Fujairah was given three hours notice to obey Prideaux, failing which his fort would be fired on. Hamad refused to acknowledge the ultimatum, and accordingly the seaward faces of three of his towers were destroyed by shell-fire on 20 April. Although Prideaux claimed 'there was no loss of life directly caused by the bombardment', he admitted that a report reached him that a slave in the fort had been severely wounded, and that Hamad's daughter-in-law, ill to begin with, had died while being transported out of the fort.[7] But Hamad suffered further chastisement. One of his dhows, said to be worth 10,000 rupees, was seized by the *Cyclamen* and the *Triad* in Khawr Fakkan and released only when he agreed to pay a fine of 1200 rupees for having enslaved the Baluchi girl,[8] plus 300 rupees because his men in Gharayfah had refused to help launch a boat of the *Lawrence* that had turned broadside on 19 April.

The next and last time this violent form of punishment was meted out was in 1930, when Shaykh Sultan bin Salim of Ras al-Khaimah refused to give the RAF permission to base a petrol barge in his shaykhdom; the pearling fleet of Ras al-Khaimah was then seized, after which Sultan capitulated. Although the next decade saw the establishment by Britain of the imperial air-route and its securing of oil concessions for Petroleum Concessions Ltd, bombardment was never used again to enforce its authority in the area. British commitments and involvements in the Arab world had by then become so embroiled, especially as regards Palestine, that no interdepartmental meeting in London on Gulf affairs would readily sanction such overt use of force, which would only serve to incite greater anti-British sentiment.

Other, less obvious and dramatic, but nonetheless potent, factors contributed to the British success in the Gulf. The most outstanding of these was the power exerted by its officers in the area, particularly 'Isa bin 'Abd al-Latif, Residency Agent in Sharjah from 1919 to 1935, and T. C. W. Fowle, Political Resident in Bushire from 1932 to 1939.

K. B. 'ISA BIN 'ABD AL-LATIF OBE, RESIDENCY AGENT 1919-35

The enormous personal influence of K. B. 'Isa bin 'Abd al-Latif cannot be overestimated; his functions as British representative on the Coast extended well beyond any official statements of policy. Until 1932, when his authority was curbed by an increase in the authority of the Political Agent in Bahrain, 'Isa was in virtual control of the entire area; this was largely owing to the remoteness of the Coast from the Residency in Bushire, in terms of both distance and communications, and to 'Isa's awareness of his own powers.

He was the third member of his family, known on the Coast as the 'Bayt Sarkali', to have held the position of Residency Agent, his father and grandfather having done so before him. The special power and influence of the family had been built up over the years, and aroused considerable jealousy in the area; members of the family were even reputed to have tried to steal the wives of the rulers, 'sometimes with unfortunate results'.[9] 'Isa succeeded his father in 1919, by which time he was already well acquainted with the intricate procedures of the job. His exact lineage is unclear: some reports identified him as a Perso-Arab from Kuwait, others as a native of Bahrain. His appearance has been more specifically described: 'a big man and a wall-eye adds a somewhat crafty expression to his face, and though genial in manner the impression he creates is that his service and loyalty are dependent on the manner in which he is reimbursed'.[10] He had a large personal fortune, which had been amassed through use (and abuse) of the prestige of his office. He lived in Sharjah, where he owned a valuable part of the *suq* (market place), and in summer he moved to Ras al-Khaimah, where he had rich date gardens.

Until 1929 his salary was a mere 150 rupees a month. With that he had to employ a clerk for the Agency, entertain all official British visitors (political officers and officers of the Navy and RAF) with 'the class of food and cooking to which they are accustomed',[11] and support himself and his large family, a motor launch and a car. But that year he complained that his salary was woefully inadequate, and the Resident recommended a rise of 350 rupees. 'I consider that the salary a man receives should bear some relation to nature of his responsibilities. These in the case of the Residency Agent, approximate to those of a Political Agent.'[12] The increase was sanctioned.

The duties of the Agent were manifold. The Political Resident relied on him to report on all events of major importance and significance and to assess any situation that related to British interests, for many of the decisions taken at Bushire were based on information provided by him. Wherever possible, he intervened in local disputes, whether internal to one shaykhdom or between the rulers. He was responsible for the protection of the interests of the Indian traders and as such played a significant role in enforcing the payment of debts. He was also authorised to issue manumission certificates to any slave who asked for freedom. During the period of negotiations for the setting up of the air-route and for the granting of oil concessions, he laid the groundwork by contacting the various rulers, translating for British officials, and generally acting as go-between for the parties involved.

It is not surprising, therefore, that his omnipotence on the Coast was not questioned or challenged. The successive Residents at Bushire were always aware of the dislike and fear engendered by 'Isa on the Coast, but consistently turned a blind eye and deaf ear to the countless reports of his cupidity, thereby strengthening his position further and giving the people of the Coast little chance to challenge him. In 1929, for example, 'Isa admitted to the Political Resident that the headman of Hamriyyah, 'Abd al-Rahman bin Sayf, considered himself independent because of a declaration signed by Khalid bin Ahmad of Sharjah on 9 August 1923. The Agent had been present at the time the document was signed, but had kept it secret from Bushire.[13] The Resident was furious at 'Isa's conduct, but, beyond disputing the validity of the declaration of independence, on the grounds that the Residency Agent had had no authority to be a witness, little was done to reprimand him.

Since there was no ready replacement for him, and he did his work for the Residency efficiently, little thought was given to dismissing him for misconduct; occasional mild reproof was the only censure he received. The stories of his corruption were widespread, for he used his special position to obtain great financial advantages. There is little doubt that the rulers subsidised him for their protection (the figure of 10,000 rupees is usually cited as his annual income from this source[14]); it was also said that for every case in which he assisted in the collection of debts, he received 10 per cent,[15] and that he made vast profits from slavery and kidnapping.[16] The places where he was most active and where his personal influence was most greatly felt were Dubai, Sharjah and Ras al-Khaimah—a further indication of his desire to extend his private fortunes: Dubai was the commercial centre of the Coast and as such had great financial potential, and in the other two shaykhdoms he had vested interests in commercial property.

'Isa's role in the affairs of Dubai is difficult to assess accurately. That he was on close terms with Shaykh Sa'id is clear, for he often acted as the shaykh's adviser. Unsubstantiated rumour had it that he had engineered the troubles of 1929 in Dubai, in order to secure his own ends. His particular interest in Dubai was founded on its commercial prominence, and, although the extent of his involvement in the numerous attempts to undermine the authority of Shaykh Sa'id is unknown, there can be little doubt that he was so involved. The Indian merchants of Dubai were afraid of him and complained that he encouraged Sa'id to restrict their movements—refusing, for example, to allow boatmen to row the Indians out to warships in the harbour.[17] Despite the fact that Colonel Dickson, whose task it had been to complete the negotiations for the airport at Sharjah, suspected 'Isa of having convinced Sa'id not to allow air facilities in Dubai, little was done to curb the Residency Agent's great predeliction for such intrigue.[18]

Of all the rulers on the Coast, it was Sultan bin Salim of Ras al-Khaimah with whom 'Isa's personal relations were stormiest. This was to a large extent owing to Sultan's animosity towards the British; Sultan concentrated his resentment on the nearest and most available British representative, and 'Isa encouraged this hatred in order to strengthen his own position. The first serious confrontation between the two men occurred in 1926, when 'Abd al-Rahman bin Muhammad of the Al-bu-Shamis, the suspected murderer of 'Isa's cousin, was deported from Sharjah to Ras al-Khaimah. He was placed in the custody of Sultan, who later refused to give him up to the Senior Naval Officer for deportation to Aden. The agitation that followed once Sultan had surrendered 'Abd al-Rahman was so acute that 'Isa was afraid for his life, and he reported that it had all been instigated by Sultan. The die was cast. Sultan received a strongly-worded admonishment and a warning that if any harm befell 'Isa he would be the first suspect; thereafter, the enmity between the two began to manifest itself at almost regular intervals.

In 1929 'Isa deliberately misconstrued events, using Sultan's marked animosity to the air-route as a cover for his own son's misbehaviour. He had a house in Bayt Mu'ayridh, on the eastern side of the creek of Ras al-Khaimah, where he usually spent the summer months. A woman went there for refuge in November 1929, and the same night four armed men tried to take her; a scuffle ensued during which an attempt was made on the life of 'Isa's eldest son, 'Abd al-Rahman. The next day, the Residency Agent reported the incident to Sultan and asked him to arrest the men responsible. Sultan refused, but he agreed to stop any further attempt to have the woman abducted.

This was the story that 'Isa reported to the Senior Naval Officer, who then diverted the HMS *Crocus* to Ras al-Khaimah. The Naval Officer did not regard the incident as very important, but wanted to impress on Sultan that the Residency Agent and his household should be treated with nothing but respect; 'Isa was a British official, and, until it could be proved that he was in the wrong, had to be upheld—especially as Sultan had made no attempt to deny any part of the Agent's report. Impressed by the arrival of the *Crocus*, whose commander reprimanded him and reminded him of his responsibility to maintain order, Sultan ordered the arrest of the men who had stormed 'Isa's house, and had them flogged.[19] It was not until later that the Senior Naval Officer heard from two different sources that the woman in question had been abducted by 'Isa's eldest son, and that, to defend the family honour, her brother had followed her to 'Abd al-Rahman's house— not that of his father. The Senior Naval Officer privately agreed that 'Abd al-Rahman, whose mother was a slave, had a bad reputation. "'Isa himself would gladly put political colour on the matter and obtain our support for his family.'[20] Aware of the truth of the situation and angry that he had been forced to punish men who had acted as honour demanded, Sultan bin Salim ordered 'Abd al-Rahman and his brother out of Ras al-Khaimah. This expulsion served to placate the people of Ras al-Khaimah, who, unhappy that innocent men had been flogged, had been ready to vent their anger on the Residency Agent and his sons. Sultan, for his part, was only too aware that he had been humiliated by the incident, and this deepened his resentment of 'Isa. This showed when he assumed an entrenched position regarding the placement of a petrol barge in his harbour; when it was forced on him, he threatened the life of the Residency Agent and cut off the water supply to his house, so that 'Isa was forced to leave Ras al-Khaimah for a while.

In Sharjah, where he lived throughout the winter, little of importance occurred in which he did not become involved in some way. In 1920 he was called in to mediate when 'Abd al-Rahman bin Muhammad of the Al-bu-Shamis laid claim to Ajman, and he was successful in persuading him to drop his claim. Three years later, however, Khalid bin Ahmad of Sharjah, about to launch an attack on 'Abd al-Rahman in Hirah, asked 'Isa to intervene again; a short-lived peace ensued, but in November 1924 Khalid was deposed by his nephew. He appealed to the Political Resident and claimed that 'Isa's cupidity had been responsible for his downfall. Khalid saw his wish to have telegraphic facilities installed at Sharjah as the root cause of the trouble:[21] the fear that the suggestion might be taken up by the Resident, probably resulting in the stationing of British officers there, had led 'Isa to collude with 'Abd al-Rahman for the ruler's downfall.[22]

This was not the first time that 'Isa had been accused of collusion with 'Abd al-Rahman. In 1920, when he mediated between 'Abd al-Rahman and his opponents, Shaykh Humayd bin 'Abd al-'Aziz of Ajman angrily denounced the Agent's deceit; he claimed that 'Abd al-Rahman, when about to be defeated, had asked for help, and that 'Isa had spirited him away to the safety of the Agency instead of fulfilling his promise to have the usurper tried according to Islamic law.[23] The Political Resident, however, refused to believe any story of connivance on the part of the Residency Agent, despite a letter from Ibn Sa'ud to C. K. Daly, the Political Agent in Bahrain, in which the king clearly stated that his support had been solicited by 'Abd al-Rahman, and that 'Abd al-Rahman had been helped all along by 'Isa bin 'Abd al-Latif.[24]

The relationship between 'Isa and 'Abd al-Rahman is interesting. Both men were masters of intrigue, but their attitude towards each other fluctuated between great friendship and bitter enmity—both of them being capable of changing loyalties if that gave greater opportunity. 'Abd al-Rahman was described as follows by a British naval officer in 1934:

Born to intrigue, his abilities have in no way decreased of late. By far the most clever man in the swindle, he sees himself in the role of 'King Maker' strictly on the basis of payment for services rendered. He has experience enough to know that this is much less risky, and may be quite as profitable as seeking power on his own account.[25]

This description could well have been made to fit 'Isa, but there was one striking difference between the two men: 'Isa came out of any skirmish undefeated, for he could always rely on being upheld by the Resident in Bushire; but 'Abd al-Rahman all too often succumbed to the intrigues of his adversary. It is not surprising, therefore, that the Residency Agent resented any intrusion on his powers[26] and was alarmed at the prospect of being supplemented

by British officers. He realised that his role would be diminished
by the existence of air stations, which would provide the means
for closer control; and, during the negotiations for an airport in
Sharjah, he did not give all the support expected of him by his
superiors in Bushire. But Dickson, the Political Agent in Kuwait,
who voiced his suspicions about 'Isa, did not regard his obstruction
of the negotiations as serious: 'After all, it is only natural that
he also should suspect our future intentions, living as he does
entirely with narrow-minded and ignorant Shaikhs who genuinely
believe they have every ground to fear us.'[27]

'Isa's generally obstructive attitude towards the air stations did,
however, result in his being taken severely to task—one of the
few occasions on which this happened. The British Government
had entrusted to him the first advance payment of 10,000 rupees
for the building of the rest-house that Shaykh Sultan had formally
agreed to provide at Sharjah; but, when the engineer entrusted
with supervising the construction, Captain K. Mackay, went to
Sharjah in August 1932, he found, to his dismay, that little progress
had been made, one of the reasons being that Sultan had had
no control over the money: 'Isa had been spending from it without
any authority for doing so and without accounting for what he
spent, and was deliberately forcing up the price of labour. Mackay
discovered the existence at Sharjah of a lorry syndicate, of which
Shaykh Sultan had at first been the principal shareholder; the
importance of the syndicate to the construction was central, since
the lorry was the only vehicle by which the stones to be used
for the building of the rest-house were transported. 'Isa, however,
had gradually insinuated himself into the syndicate and acquired
what was virtually a monopoly; this in turn made it impossible
for Mackay to lower the cost of labour, and he described the
monopoly held by the Residency Agent as 'a pistol held at my
head'.[28] Fowle went to Sharjah immediately and reprimanded 'Isa
so severely that the Agent's attitude to the air-route improved
noticeably.

'Isa died in September 1935. Although one of his relatives, K.
S. Husayn bin Hasan 'Imad, was appointed interim Agent, it was
finally decided that 'Isa's permanent successor should be a man
who had been head *munshi* (clerk) at the Agency in Bahrain. So
in 1936, with the appointment of K. S. Sayyid 'Abd al-Razzaq
Al-Mahmud as Residency Agent, 'Isa's family's reign of almost
seventy years came to an end. 'Abd al-Razzaq played a much
less important role than 'Isa had, especially as his powers were
curtailed by the appointment of a Political Officer in 1939. Ten
years later, the post of Residency Agent at Sharjah ceased to
exist.

LIEUTENANT-COLONEL SIR T. C. W. FOWLE KCIE, CBE, POLITICAL RESIDENT 1932–9

Fowle's appointment to the Residency in Bushire in July 1932 following the death in office of Hugh Biscoe was the culmination of many years of hard work and an early desire to exert political authority within the framework of the Indian Service. Born in England in 1884, he was educated at Clifton College, joined the British Army in 1905 and was transferred to the Indian Army two years later. Within a few years he was keen to enter the select Political Service,[29] for which he prepared by learning Pushtu, Urdu, Arabic and Persian. He was particularly interested in Arabic and Persian, and between 1910 and 1913 he travelled to Persia and what are now Syria, Iraq and Lebanon in order to perfect his knowledge.[30] At the onset of World War I he was transferred on probation to the Political Department, and served as a Political Officer in Mesopotamia from 1915 to 1918, with a brief spell as assistant to the Political Agent in Bahrain for five months in 1916. It is clear from his personal file[31] that his work in Mesopotamia was not greatly appreciated by his superiors, especially Percy Cox,[32] and he seemed destined to return to the army after the end of the war. In 1920, however, he was confirmed as an officer of the Political Department, and, after a series of postings in Mashhad, Seistan, Baluchistan and Kerman, became Assistant Resident in Aden from 1925 to 1928. The next year he became secretary to the Resident at Bushire, and he was Political Agent at Muscat from 1930 to 1932, during which time he officiated as Political Resident.

He thus brought with him a deep knowledge not only of Arabic customs, language and culture, but also considerable experience as a British official in the Arabian peninsula. There is little doubt that he would have disagreed with Sir Ronald Wingate that his appointment to the Gulf was regarded 'as a form of punishment, or exile, or the reward of eccentricity'.[33] He was clearly convinced of his mission and its importance, and was obviously pleased with his accomplishments. The unusual length of his tenure, in contrast to the shortness of tenure of so many of his predecessors, strengthened his position and allowed him to acquire a greater knowledge of the area while the fact that the period of his office coincided with a crucial time in the development of the Gulf added to the special quality of his rule. His attitudes and the methods he used to enforce policy are thus of particular importance to the study of Britain in the Gulf.

Fowle's attitude, and indeed that of his predecessors, towards the people of the Gulf, especially those on the Arab side, was based on the strong conviction that the British presence was a civilising element in a semi-barbaric land.[34] He often alluded to the Arabs of the Gulf as living in the distant past—any time from the seventh century to the fifteenth, to judge from the references—and intimated that it was up to him and his successors to bring civilisation to the area.[35] How Fowle expected to do this is not clear, unless merely the presence of a handful of British officers was considered to promote some form of social evolution; certainly no encouragement was given to political, educational or health reform. Furthermore, the fact that the Gulf states were deliberately made inaccessible to any visitors[36] did not make them particularly amenable to the stimuli that inevitably accompany the influx of foreign ideas.

Fowle's personal attitude towards the Arabs of the Trucial Coast was in some ways strongly paternalistic: he treated the rulers much like children, to be given a pat on the back when they behaved and a sharp rap on the knuckles when they misbehaved. The harsh realities of life in the Gulf prevented him from indulging in any romantic identification with the people, such as other Englishmen who had come to the Arabian peninsula had manifested; and the fact that he was already well acquainted with the area when he became Resident, having first travelled there twenty years earlier, served to give him a realistic outlook and to strengthen his awareness of himself as an Englishman. Yet he was not totally devoid of romanticism, as is shown by the fact that a raiding party sighted near Hamriyyah made him think of the world of the Border ballads.[37]

Fowle steadfastly argued against interference in local affairs, always pointing out that the existing methods of control were sufficient for the required results and that further commitments would not justify the added expense. His definition of non-interference was, however, highly personal. In 1934, when Shaykh Sa'id of Dubai was about to be deposed, Fowle sent a sloop to the shaykhdom with a strongly worded message that any damage to British lives and property would be treated very seriously. The warning gave rise to the assumption in Dubai that the Resident was openly supporting Shaykh Sa'id, and the opposition temporarily collapsed. In his interpretation of the events, Fowle seemed convinced that Shaykh Sa'id himself had quelled the uprising, with only 'a measure of support' from Britain; in this he saw a powerful justification for continuing the policy of non-interference that he so strongly advocated. He realised the new importance of the Trucial Coast, especially since an airport had been built at Sharjah, with landing grounds, anchorages and petrol stores elsewhere on the Coast; but he thought that preoccupation with the safety of the air-route had tended to obscure Britain's responsibility for protecting the lives and property of Indian merchants, and for preventing traffic in arms and slaves and hostilities at sea.[38] He was averse to assuming any new responsibilities, 'the most important of which would be the preventing of hostilities between Shaikhs on land, though whenever opportunity occurs we should give our good offices to the Rulers for the composition of their differences'.[39]

The Government of India regarded this ambivalent attitude as satisfactory, but the Air Ministry, which took an increased and active interest in the Coast during the 1930s, was opposed to it. It rejected Fowle's passive policy as inadequate, especially in view of the interest that other countries, such as the United States, Japan, Iran and Saudi Arabia, were taking in the area;[40] it was worried that Fowle's policy would lead to a decline in British prestige, thus endangering the security of the air route.[41] The Government of India was not convinced, and remained firm in its view that the foundation of policy had been laid down by Curzon at Sharjah in November 1903, and reconfirmed at the durbar of 1933; furthermore, it recommended that the Air Ministry should limit its concern to the safety of the air-route.[42]

Unwilling to accept the peripheral role suggested by the Government of India, and anxious to obtain approval for a forward policy, the Air Ministry called for a meeting of the Middle East (Sub-)Committee of the Committee of Imperial Defence. This meeting took place in September 1935, and was attended by Fowle, who was then on leave in London. However, despite general agreement that Britain had to admit ultimate international responsibility for the Trucial Coast and Qatar, the various Departments proved unable to agree on much else. A general view of the different positions taken at the meeting reveals the clash of priorities, as well as Fowle's personal interpretation of what constituted interference.

The Air Ministry asked for a redefinition of non-interference, claiming that Fowle's role in the Dubai uprising had been nothing less than direct involvement. The Foreign Office showed concern for the far-reaching implications of the new interests on the Coast, and would have welcomed a more precisely defined policy. But it was Fowle who remained adamantly opposed to any redefinition, convinced of the adequacy of the existing policy. He maintained that it had already shown itself compatible with the obtaining of concessions, and that there was therefore no reason for change.[43] In a private letter to J. G. Laithwaite, Principal at the India Office, he had already sought to justify his action over Dubai, and in so doing had stressed his viewpoint on policy:

That it was not a case of abstract principles of 'intervention' and 'non-intervention', but of gaining the above ends with the minimum of interference. If we could gain our ends by this minimum there was obviously no point in going beyond it, as presumably HMG did not desire to undertake more commitments on the God-forsaken Trucial Coast than was absolutely necessary. If the minimum of interference did not give us our ends I was always prepared to advocate an amount of interference which *would* achieve our ends.[44]

One of the means whereby Fowle was able to gain his ends was the policy he termed enforcement of tribal responsibility. This was at least as effective as such obvious measures as bombardment, for which he showed disdain. The types of punishment threatened or meted out under this policy were calculated not only to cause the ruler to suffer personal loss and humiliation, but also to damage the prosperity and the freedom of mobility of his people—to the further detriment of his prestige and, thus, of his ability to retain power. The enforcement of tribal responsibility took on two different forms. The first was the stronger of the two and as such never went beyond the stage of threats; the threats were invariably taken seriously, and proved capable of breaking any form of resistance.

What was threatened was the destruction of the shaykhdom's pearling fleet if the ruler did not obey or behave as the Resident wished him to do. Naturally, such a catastrophe would have destroyed the financial mainstay of the shaykhdom, and almost certainly would have brought about the downfall of the ruler. In 1935, when Shaykh Shakhbut of Abu Dhabi was adamantly resisting efforts to have a petrol store built in Sir Bani Yas island, he was made to swallow his pride and give the required permission on pain of the destruction of his pearling fleet. The same threat was issued to Shaykh Ahmad bin Rashid of Umm al-Qaiwain in 1937 when he refused to allow a surveying party for the projected air-route to remain for longer than fifteen days. It is interesting to note that on this occasion Fowle threatened Ahmad with another, more ominous, punishment: that 'certain local pressures would be brought to bear against him and his people'. There is no indication as to what these 'pressures' might have been, but there is little doubt that the policy of enforcing tribal responsibility brought ample rewards.

The second type of sanction employed by Fowle was the milder one of 'stoppage of His Majesty's Government's good offices', which meant that the ruler and his people would until further notice be deprived of travel papers. This measure was greatly inconvenient to the ruler and his more prominent notables and merchants. At various intervals in 1938, the rulers of Abu Dhabi, Ras al-Khaimah and Sharjah received this form of punishment. Fowle did not regard the withdrawal as a severe sanction, since it only caused an awkward internal situation, and he never used it for the smaller shaykhdoms, where few people travelled.

Fowle was firm about his method of rule. He was impatient of any signs of insubordination, as he expressed on more than one occasion. 'Owing to the suppliant attitude which we have had inevitably to adopt during the last few years . . . [the Rulers] have got swollen heads . . . .'[45] He was also pragmatic: he could dismiss simple facts or overlook logic if it suited his purpose as Resident and the upholder of British interests. In February 1935, when Shaykh Shakhbut signed an agreement for the stationing of a petrol tank at Sir Bani Yas and for the establishment of a landing ground on the island and near Abu Dhabi, he refused to allow a petrol store to be built in Abu Dhabi, since this had not been specifically mentioned in the agreement. Sweeping aside the qualms of Colonel Loch, the Political Agent in Bahrain, who was conscious of Shakhbut's rights, Fowle informed the ruler that the store was 'one of the natural adjuncts' of a landing ground and had thus been implicitly included in the agreement. Another occasion on which Fowle showed his ability to overlook basic facts in the face of higher goals occurred in 1938, and again concerned Shakhbut, who was not easily swayed by demonstrations of power. In this case the ruler was adamantly refusing to sign an oil concession agreement, and Fowle was hard put to find a means of inducing him to sign. The opportunity presented itself in a third-hand report on the existence of slave-trading in Abu Dhabi. Almost immediately Fowle began to contemplate issuing Shakhbut a strong ultimatum, which he hoped would have a subduing effect on him and make him more amenable to Petroleum Concessions. Weightman was disturbed by the fact that no concrete evidence of the existence of slave-trading in Dubai had been established, especially as it was rumoured on the Coast that the story was being used as an excuse to censure Shakhbut for his refusal to sign the oil concession. Fowle was angry and snapped back that he did not regard local opinion as of importance, and had no intention of pandering to it by the production of concrete evidence.

Despite the firmness and efficiency of Fowle's rule of the Coast, in 1938 Weightman, as Political Agent in Bahrain, questioned its wisdom. In support of his belief that British prestige in the Gulf was declining at a dangerous speed, he cited various recent examples of disrespect to British officers by the rulers of Sharjah, Ras al-Khaimah and Abu Dhabi. In view of the possibility that oil would be found in the shaykhdoms, he strongly urged a redefinition of policy and the establishment of closer political control, through more frequent naval patrols, greater expenditure on intelligence and information services, and the stationing of a British representative on the Coast.[46] Fowle, however, retained his earlier opinion. He disagreed with Weightman's assessment, and regarded it as unnecessarily pessimistic; besides, he could see no reason for altering official policy before oil had been discovered in the area—if ever it would be. Once again, he made it clear that any alteration in the existing policy would necessitate a 'take-over' of the Coast.[47]

Weightman was not convinced. He had been particularly incensed that, owing to personal obstruction by the ruler of Abu Dhabi, a Petroleum Concessions exploration party sent out to Buraimi during the winter of 1938 (with the official blessing of the Political Resident) failed to obtain necessary geological data. The Political Agent expressed 'regret that we seem reluctant to use the means we possess to deter a crew of feeble but ill-conditioned shaikhs from treating the wishes of His Majesty's Government with quite such persistent disrespect',[48] and advocated,

> let us make it perfectly clear that when we say we want a thing we are going to get it ... and without undue delay; and that obstructive tactics do not pay. ... We certainly do not want to administer their disgusting territories and people, *but* if they happen to be on the air route or there is oil underground they have got to behave.[49]

Fowle objected and refused to accept this manner of thinking, finding the accepted definition of policy adequate. He continued to dominate the Coast, using any means he could justify. In 1939, for example, following the collapse of the reform movement in Dubai, he advised Shaykh Sa'id to set up an advisory council. The India Office questioned the reason for Fowle's action and saw it as a deviation from official policy. Fowle argued that advice could hardly be classified as interference, and admitted that he felt duty-bound, since Britain 'put a ring-fence around the Arab states adorned with a large "Hands Off" notice board', to give advice and guidance when necessary.[50]

The India Office was annoyed that Fowle had given Shaykh Sa'id advice without consultation. Fowle realised that he had side-stepped the normal procedure and admitted, 'I quite understand the desire of the India Office for reference to be made before advice of the kind is given in future cases and have noted this point'; but he could not resist adding, in justification of his behaviour, that he had been following a precedent set by the British Government when it gave its consent to similar advice being given to the ruler of Kuwait.[51] This was not the first time that the India Office had been taken unawares by Fowle. In March 1938, upon hearing of a revival of the slave trade, he had withdrawn 'the good offices of His Majesty's Government' from Abu Dhabi without consulting the India Office, which had asked the Resident for a report on the slave trade in the Trucial Coast. Instead of submitting the required report, Fowle gave certain suggestions on how to halt the trade.

Despite such procedural irregularities, Fowle was respected as a good administrator and judge of Gulf affairs. He retired in September 1939 and returned to England, where his knowledge of the Middle East proved useful to the War Government. After a brief spell at the Ministry of Information, he became an adviser on Middle Eastern affairs at the British Council. His work there was cut short when, in February 1940, he died of lung cancer, which thus brought to a close the career of the last of the absolute rulers of the Gulf.

12 The Trucial States in 1939: The Dawn of a New Age

By a curious coincidence, T. C. W. Fowle retired at almost precisely the moment when the guns of World War II first began to fire, heralding the end of the Raj. No successor of his was ever to wield the same power as he had had, for the outcome of the war radically altered the British position and opened the way to the dismemberment of the British Empire. The most significant element of this process, which began almost immediately after peace had been restored, was, of course, the independence of India, following which the British Government of India ceased to exist and the conduct of British relations with the Gulf states was transferred to the Foreign Office in London. The officers of the Indian Political Service were replaced by diplomats from London, and gradually the entire character of Anglo-Arab relations in the Gulf began to change. The climax was reached in January 1968, when the Labour Government in London announced the end of its East of Suez defence policy and, with it, the total withdrawal of British forces from the Gulf by the end of 1971.

In 1939 the Trucial Coast was already in the process of transformation, though the evolution of the shaykhdoms was to continue at a slow pace until the 1960s, when it was ascertained that the region contained vast petroleum resources. It was during the inter-war years, however, that the shaykhdoms began to acquire their present character and their present enormous significance in world affairs.

The situation was diversified by a number of non-political developments, the most important of which was the decline of the pearl trade as a result of the world depression of the 1930s and the introduction of the Japanese cultured pearl. This decline had a profound effect on the social and economic structure of the area, for, while some shaykhdoms, such as Ajman and Umm al-Qaiwain, became more dependent on fishing, the framework of others, such as Dubai, Abu Dhabi and, to a much smaller extent, Sharjah, was modified by the gradual emergence of a new class of merchants and traders. This new class showed a strong sense of awareness of itself and its powers, relative to the existing power structure. The existence of a lorry syndicate in Sharjah in the 1930s is one example, but by far the most outstanding is the reform movement in Dubai, which challenged the authority and power of the ruler while retaining him as a figurehead. One of the first reforms carried out in Dubai was the creation of schools, in a region where they were rare.

The 1930s brought other changes, too. The firm rule of Shakhbut bin Sultan in Abu Dhabi brought about a resurgence in that shaykhdom's powers. Shakhbut showed himself determined to consolidate his position in Buraimi, and was successful, as is affirmed by the *Military Report and Route Book: The Arabian States of the Persian Gulf* (prepared in 1939 by the General Staff, India):[1] 'The Shaikh of Abu Dhabi is a powerful ruler and holds a dominant position in the Baraimi oasis area.'[2] It also remarked, 'There are indications that the influence of Ibn Saud in the Baraimi oasis ... is on the decline and that the dominant position is now held by the Shaikh of Abu Dhabi.'[3]

One reason for the resurgence of Abu Dhabi's prestige was the corresponding decline of the Na'im. The fact that the Na'im was ruled by a duumvirate contributed to this, for the brothers rarely acted together and this eventually caused their people to rebel. In 1938 Saqr was described as being 'disliked and despised by Abu Dhabi (as by everyone else)'.[4] His brother Muhammad, shaykh of Dhank, hated him as well, and it was reported that Saqr lived in constant fear of being killed by his brother. Saqr was also on bad terms with Ahmad al-Salf, Na'imi shaykh of Hafit, who was related by marriage to Muhammad bin Rahmah (from Sunaynah), of the Al-bu-Shamis, and was dominated by him. The Al-bu-Shamis, especially those living at Hamasah, were on good terms with Abu Dhabi, basically because of the discord between Saqr and Rashid bin Hamad, the Ghafiri chief of Hamasah. The Na'im were further weakened when they became involved in a war with the Al-bu-Shamis in the summer of 1938, after Saqr had been to Muscat to tender his loyalty to the sultan, and had returned with money and ammunition.[5] The fact that Hamasah was the chief slave market of Buraimi was one reason for the hostility between the Al-bu-Shamis and the Na'im, Rashid bin Hamad reputedly receiving 20 rupees on every sale.[6] An uneasy peace was brought about by the visit of both parties to Muscat in the spring of 1939, when the sultan negotiated a truce.[7] His influence on both tribes, although tenuous, was to be significant in 1955, when Buraimi and Hamasah were officially incorporated into Muscat by the British Government.

In addition to consolidating his position in the inland areas of his shaykhdom, Shakhbut wished to strengthen his power on the coast. During his struggles with the Na'im the most he had to face was strong tribal opposition. The task was not so simple in Abu Dhabi town, where he had to contend with the forces of British policy, against which he was all but defenceless. However, unlike some of his fellow rulers on the Coast, who were too often intimidated by threats, he did not bow easily to British power; instead, he steadfastly defied British representatives whenever he was convinced of his own rights. His relationship with Fowle was particularly stormy, for the Resident was nothing short of outraged at Shakhbut's hostility to British plans for the air-route and oil concessions. He regarded the ruler's behaviour as a personal insult, and became determined to impose British authority and power on Abu Dhabi at all costs. But he had underestimated Shakhbut, who, though by no means the victor in his struggles with Fowle, managed to remain firmly in control of his shaykhdom.

Considering his defencelessness in face of the power that Fowle could bring to bear upon him, it is remarkable that he was able to achieve what he did. Shakhbut was a very proud man and refused to be treated in the same way as his fellow rulers on the Trucial Coast, but he had the perception to realise that his uncle Khalifah, who had been instrumental in bringing him to power, had a special position in Abu Dhabi. Khalifah was extremely influential, but content to remain in the background and exert his power unobtrusively; his grandsons, known as the Muhammad Khalifah branch of the Al-Nuhayyan, are important members of the governments of Abu Dhabi and the United Arab Emirates today, and so bear witness to the success of Khalifah's tactics. Shakhbut wisely refrained from attempting to cross his uncle, and instead concentrated on restoring the internal stability of Abu Dhabi. It is perhaps ironic that his resoluteness of purpose and his determination in the face of opposition, both qualities that contributed to the stability and unusual length of his rule, did not stand him in good stead when, in 1958, oil was struck off Abu Dhabi.

His beliefs that development must be taken slowly, that his people should not become a minority in their own country as had happened in Kuwait and his attitude to money were not, however, so entirely ridiculous as the many stories current about his attitude to wealth and spending would suggest. He realized that some countries with new wealth to spend had run into the 20th century, after centuries of stagnation, with unhappy results. ... Shaikh Shakhbut ... wanted to crawl in ....[8]

He could not long withstand the pressures created by the newfound wealth, and in 1966 his brother Zayid peacefully deposed him.

Dubai underwent a major upheaval in 1938 and 1939, and emerged changed in many respects. To begin with, Shaykh Sa'id gave much power and authority to his son Rashid, who hastened to restore the commercial reputation of the shaykhdom. His efforts proved worthwhile, for in 1939 the first dispensary on the Coast was opened in Dubai, under the supervision of an Indian doctor, and in 1941 the first post office on the Coast was established there. The importance of Dubai continued to grow, until it completely overshadowed that of its former great rival, Sharjah; but it was not until the 1960s that it enjoyed a real boom. Between 1968 and 1973, for example, the external trade of Dubai grew by more than 700 per cent. Much of the credit for this must be given to Shaykh Rashid, who became ruler when his father died in 1958. 'Sheikh Rashid is Dubai, it is said, and Dubai is Rashid.'[9]

The ebb of Qasimi fortunes was felt most acutely in Sharjah. Although the seeds of decline had been sown by his two predecessors, Sultan bin Saqr was helpless to stop the process. A young man when he seized control of Sharjah from Khalid bin Ahmad, Sultan immediately fell under the influence of his powerful father-in-law, who dominated him, undermining and compromising the ruler's position. With the growth of 'Abd al-Rahman's power, that of Sultan began to diminish, and it was then that the ruler of Sharjah discovered his own lack of authority. Resentment for the older man gradually replaced the earlier feelings of reliance, especially when 'Abd al-Rahman went so far as to claim Hirah independent of Sharjah, saying he had a document signed by Sultan to that effect.[10] Sultan could do little but protest. His secretary, 'Abdullah bin Faris, became the next dominating influence over him, and on more than one occasion caused trouble for his employer.[11] Another influence was Sultan's *wazir*, Humayd bin 'Ali bin Humayd. Sultan did not forget his grudge against 'Abd al-Rahman, and in 1938 plotted against his life; when the plot failed, he made an unsuccessful attempt to have him ostracised from Trucial Coast affairs. He tried to induce Sa'id bin Maktum to invite his fellow rulers to boycott Hirah, because 'Abd al-Rahman had given refuge to the exiled members of the Al-bu-Falasah of Dubai following their over-throw by Sa'id in 1939; but the ruler of Dubai refused to accept the suggestion.[12]

A weak man who needed powerful figures around him to create an illusion of strength, Sultan was incapable of restoring his declining position. Between 1924 and 1939, the last vestiges of the former Qasimi might crumbled. No fewer than six towns belonging to Sharjah attempted secession,[13] although only one, Kalba, succeeded in obtaining British recognition as an independent shaykhdom. The Bani Qitab lost all respect for their traditional ally, and in 1938 Sultan was obliged to swallow his pride and pay Khalid bin Ahmad 1500 rupees to arrange matters for him with the Bani Qitab.[14] He became so desperate to renew his ties of friendship with Muhammad bin 'Ali that in 1939, together with the ruler of Ras al-Khaimah, he tried to persuade the other rulers of the Trucial Coast to enter into an alliance against those inland tribes that refused to recognise the authority of their traditional overlords.[15] None of the rulers was willing to antagonise the fearless Bani Qitab, and that same year Shaykh Sa'id of Dubai and Shaykh Rashid of Ajman both took the opposite course of action and entered into an alliance with the tribe.[16] There is some indication that Muhammad bin 'Ali tried to strengthen his position even further by appealing to Ibn Sa'ud for support: 'Abdallah bin Faris, Sultan bin Saqr's secretary, intercepted a letter written to Muhammad in August 1939 by Ibn Sa'ud, who in it expressed his reluctance to commit himself in writing.[17] The evasiveness of the message prompted the Residency Agent, to whom 'Abdallah bin Faris gave the letter, to suggest that the shaykh of the Bani Qitab had applied for help against the ruler of Sharjah.[18] Sultan continued to attempt to buy the friendship of his erstwhile allies: one report had it that he offered Muhammad up to 80,000 rupees to visit Sharjah.[19] It was not until 1944, and then largely owing to the efforts of the Residency Agent, that the leader of the Bani Qitab consented to enter Sharjah town once again, after an absence of ten years.[20]

In Ras al-Khaimah, Sultan bin Salim learned the trials of independence the hard way. His relationship with the British officials was by far the stormiest and most turbulent part of his career. There was little love lost on either side, and a glance at the Bushire and Bahrain records will reveal a number of derogatory terms that seem almost to be reserved for him: pusillanimous, obstreperous, arrogant, stubborn, recalcitrant and even mentally deficient. The relations of Shaykh Shakhbut of Abu Dhabi with Britain were also far from cordial, but in the case of Sultan the outrage of the British officers was made particularly bitter by his unpredictable and slightly mercurial behaviour; furthermore, Shakhbut ruled over a larger and more powerful shaykhdom. Sultan was aware of his defencelessness in the face of British power, and as a last measure, when desperate, would flaunt his claim to owe allegiance to Ibn

Sa'ud. In 1930, at the height of the crisis over the placement of an RAF petrol barge at Ras al-Khaimah, Sultan warned 'Isa that

> ... he and his people were Wahabis, that the Head of the Wahabis is Ibn Saud and that if the British Government persisted in forcing their policy upon him, he would place himself under the protection of Ibn Saud who would deal with the matter direct with the British Government. So far as he was concerned there the matter ended, he would appeal to Ibn Saud and end the friendly Treaty with Great Britain.[21]

His animosity to the British authorities was by then well established, and his refusal to pay his respects to visiting British dignitaries was such a common occurrence that it is astonishing to note the surprise with which these rebuffs were reported. He was the only ruler on the Coast who refused to attend the festivities accompanying the durbar of 1933, despite the presence of the Officiating Political Resident, the Senior Naval Officer and nine destroyers.

He also deliberately courted any country that he thought might conceivably join him in an anti-British alliance. In 1934, for example, strong rumours circulated that he was negotiating privately with Iranian officials for the sale of the Tunb islands. The next year, he approached the commander of the French sloop *Bougainville* when it stopped at Ras al-Khaimah on its way to Bahrain; he sought a secret agreement with the French admiral, thinking that France and Britain were enemies, but when he realised the situation he merely asked for arms.[22]

Sultan had to learn the hard way the disadvantages of defying Britain. In early 1938 he was censured for delaying the conclusion of an oil concession agreement; he was rude to the Senior Naval Officer and refused to apologise, so he and his people were denied travelling papers. He procrastinated for so long over the matter of the concession that in the end Petroleum Concessions obtained only a permit of exploration; Sultan thus lost the financial advantages, however small, that his fellow rulers had obtained upon granting concessions. It is doubtful whether he carefully considered the outcome of his attitudes before assuming them. He was an independent ruler, and wished always to be treated like one; the fact that he was powerless to resist the stronger forces with which he was confronted did not seem to count. The only strong influence on him was that of his *qadi*, Muhammad Ghubash, and he was only rarely supported by his fellow rulers, who regarded his unpredictable behaviour with mixed feelings:

They have most of them at one time or another crossed swords
with the Shaikh of Ras al-Khaimah and have come off second
best. They have no love for him and all know him to be a
deceitful individual but at the same time I believe they have
a respect for his quick-wittedness.[23]

Never one to miss an opportunity, Sultan seized on the death,
in April 1937, of the recently recognised ruler of Kalba, Sa'id
bin Hamad, to make a bid for his position. Sa'id's only heir
was Hamad, his seven-year-old son, so Kalba was immediately
exposed to intrigues, and three contenders for the control of power
came forward: Barut, a former slave of Shaykh Sa'id, during whose
rule he had become head slave and general factotum; Sultan bin
Salim of Ras al-Khaimah; and Khalid bin Ahmad, former ruler
of Sharjah, whose wife had been the daughter of Shaykh Sa'id.

The young Hamad was elected ruler almost immediately following
the death of his father. Khalid bin Ahmad wished to participate
in the rule, so he left Dhayd with a large force and tried to
enter Kalba. When he found that he was unacceptable to the
people, he withdrew, and set up camp outside the town, hoping
thereby to isolate it and enforce his election as ruler.[24] The Political
Resident watched the events closely—concerned, of course, for the
safety of the emergency landing ground. He decided not to interfere
in Khalid's bid for Kalba and to propose British recognition if
Khalid were successful. In the meantime, he warned the rulers
of Ras al-Khaimah, Sharjah and Umm al-Qaiwain to keep away.

Sultan of Ras al-Khaimah, seeing that Sharjah's great weakness
afforded him an unrivalled opportunity to take Kalba under his
control, took no heed of Fowle's warning and left for Kalba in
early June. On his way, he passed by Dhayd and made an unsuccessful attempt to enlist the support of Khalid bin Ahmad for his
election as regent of Kalba. When Sultan and his party of twelve
followers entered Kalba, Fowle did not interfere, knowing that
'if he [Sultan] were given enough rope [he] would sooner or later
hang himself'.[25] Before long, Sultan's attempts to secure election
got him into trouble with the people of Kalba and he was forced
to ask Fowle for help. He also angered Shaykh Muhammad bin
'Ali of the Bani Qitab, who was an ally of Khalid bin Ahmad; the
bedouin of the Bani Qitab consequently raided the outskirts of Ras
al-Khaimah and cut communications in order to prevent Sultan from
returning home.[26] HMS *Shoreham* went to Kalba on 21 June and Sultan
boarded it at once. He told the Senior Naval Offi.er that 'he had
done a good service to H.M. Government by sending for a ship, but
was quite unable to say why it was that the trouble had only arisen

since his arrival'.[27] He was retained on the sloop and taken to Bahrain, where the Political Agent at first refused to allow him visitors, but after four days let him return home.

Once Sultan had been removed, peace was restored in Kalba. Barut gained in strength, and by the end of June the Residency Agent had reported that Barut had been elected to serve as regent until the coming of age of Shaykh Hamad.[28] Fowle felt, however, that the election of Barut was unsuitable, in view of his 'servile origin',[29] and decided to ask the notables to select a council of regency, which would then be recognised by the British Government. At the end of August, news reached the Residency of a second attempt by Khalid bin Ahmad to gain control of Kalba; once again, he left Dhayd with fifty followers and started the journey to Kalba. Fowle was in London at the time, and Olaf Caroe, officiating as Political Resident, considered that, 'if Khalid could obtain the acquiescence of the people of Kalba, his election as Regent ... was likely in the circumstances that had arisen to afford the most satisfactory solution';[30] he therefore decided to give Khalid 'reasonable encouragement'.[31] The Residency Agent accordingly visited Kalba in HMS *Deptford* 'in pursuance of Sir Trenchard Fowle's decision to induce the notables to agree to elect a Council'.[32] He arrived on 14 September and found that Khalid was at Khawr Fakkan, north of Kalba town, and that Barut and the notables had already invited him to become regent. Khalid at first refused to enter Kalba without the permission of the British authorities, but the Residency Agent assured him that there would be no objection, so he accepted. He was then elected regent, having signed a written agreement to safeguard the interests of Shaykh Hamad, and to retain Barut as *wali* of Kalba.[33]

Khalid was to prove a strong and able ruler. His alliance with the Bani Qitab consolidated his position relative to Shaykh Sultan of Sharjah, and he allayed the fears of Shaykh Sultan of Ras al-Khaimah that Kalba would revert to Sharjah. Khalid gradually came to command the allegiance of Fujairah and Dibba, and became so strong a power in the Shimayliyyah that it was rumoured that he intended to reunite all the Qasimi territories under his rule. He won over to his side areas that Sultan of Ras al-Khaimah regarded as his, especially Wadi al-Qawr, a valley opening in the hills of Oman, between Wadi Hatta and Wadi Ham, and reaching the sea at the Batinah coast of Muscat.

But Khalid did not continue to live at Kalba. In 1941 he moved to Dhayd, and then Hirah became his home. His nearness to Sharjah town so greatly frightened Sultan of Sharjah that the Residency Agent persuaded Khalid to return to Dhayd. Even then he did not stay for long, moving yet again; with time he became a restless transient, thus gradually weakening his hold on Kalba. Shaykh Hamad bin Sa'id, his nephew, who was still very young, did not have the potential for strong leadership,[34] and a power vacuum was created.

It was therefore inevitable that during the 1940s Fujairah would return to the foreground of political affairs in the Shimayliyyah. Following his death, Hamad bin 'Abdallah was succeeded by his son Sayf, who following his own death, in 1938, was succeeded by his brother Muhammad, who it was that restored the Sharqiyy fortunes in the Shimayliyyah. By 1950 he had proved able to win over most of the villages in the area, including Gharayfah, Dibba, Ghurfah, Bidyah, Sikamkam, Masafi and Qarya. Kalba, following the death of Khalid bin Ahmad, had become almost powerless, and as an independent shaykhdom received its death blow in 1951, when Hamad bin Sa'id was murdered. The fact that the landing ground established there had outlived its usefulness meant that the shaykhdom had lost the prime reason for its existence, and it was therefore reincorporated into Sharjah. The strength of Fujairah, by contrast, had grown to such an extent that in 1952 the British Government recognised Muhammad bin Hamad as ruler of the seventh Trucial State, a position he held until his death in 1975, after which his son Hamad succeeded.

Territorial disputes with Sharjah followed, which, in view of the many political upheavals that the Shimayliyyah had undergone since the turn of the century, was only to be expected. Kalba and Khawr Fakkan, though they might have come under Fujairah influence, had so long been established as Qasimi towns that they became enclaves of Sharjah within Fujairah, as they still are. The enclave formed by Khawr Fakkan and its surrounding areas cuts into the Fujairah coastline and divides it into two; and the Kalba enclave lies further south.

But the town that today both Fujairah and Sharjah claim is Dibba, which lies on the border with the Musandam section of Oman. During the 1930s, the shaykh of the southern part of Dibba was Rashid bin Ahmad al-Qasimi, brother of Khalid bin Ahmad of Kalba. He was totally unable to restrain the Shihuh of the northern part of the town from attacking Qasimi people and property, so, when Sa'id bin Taymur became sultan of Muscat in 1932, Rashid went to Muscat and obtained the new sultan's protection. Sultan bin Saqr protested to Fowle soon afterwards that south Dibba belonged to Sharjah and not to Muscat.[35] Matters were further complicated by the fact that Rashid, not content with the sultan's protection, had written to the shaykh of Sharjah in May 1934 swearing allegiance to him.[36] The Residency at Bushire deliberated at length on the issue, and in November 1934 Fowle expressed his confusion: 'This case is formidable!'[37] The same can be said today, as Sharjah, whose hold on Dibba continued to be only nominal, and Fujairah, whose territory naturally takes in the town, share ownership of the southern part of Dibba town, the northern part being still within the jurisdiction of the sultan of Oman; the town is thus divided into three sections, each one ruled by a different state.

The two remaining shaykhdoms, Ajman and Umm al-Qaiwain, because of their tiny size and corresponding lack of influence in the political arena of the Coast, were comparatively quiet and untroubled. Ahmad bin Rashid, who rules over Umm al-Qaiwain today, led a secluded life but managed all the same to acquire considerable wealth for himself, despite the great economic depression. Shaykh Rashid bin Humayd of Ajman had a good reputation with the bedouin, who respected his rigorous punishment of thieves. In Ajman town he was popular, his rule was just and his taxes low, all factors that contributed to a rise in the town's importance. His manner with the British authorities was generally respectful, hospitable and polite, and, although he was not on very good terms with his neighbours, he showed little concern or anxiety.[38] His rule also continues till the present.

13 Epilogue: The Emergence of the United Arab Emirates

In 1962, in an address given before the Royal Central Asian Society in London, J. E. H. Boustead remarked that life in Abu Dhabi had changed very little during the past two centuries.[1] While this observation might have applied in 1962, it would never hold ground today, sixteen years later. The radical transformation of Abu Dhabi can only be classified as one of the phenomena of the modern era, so rapid and fundamental has it been.

This alteration would not, of course, have been possible without the discovery of vast oil reserves, underground and offshore, which are currently bringing thousands of millions of dollars a year into the shaykhdom. Although oil was struck off Abu Dhabi in 1958, it was not until eight years later that the inevitable diversification of the shaykhdom's economic and social structure took place. Until then, Abu Dhabi and the other Trucial states remained in the background of international affairs, still under the aegis of Britain. Since the end of World War II, their internal development had come under greater scrutiny from the British Government, as oil exploration began to be taken seriously again. With this new policy of participation in local affairs came a reorganisation of British administration. In keeping with the pre-war decision, the Political Residency for the Gulf was moved from Bushire to Bahrain, in 1946. The office of Residency Agent in Sharjah was abolished in 1949, and from 1929 to 1953, when a Political Agency for the Trucial Coast was set up, a permanently resident Political Officer was appointed from the Foreign Office in London. The Political Agent, with headquarters in the burgeoning town of Dubai, assumed much greater responsibility and authority than any former

British representative on the Coast had done, and acceptance of his role became a precondition for British recognition of the rulers. A defence force, under the Foreign Office, was created in 1951; called the Trucial Oman Levies (later, Scouts), it was run by British officers with British equipment, although a few Arabs were recruited into it.

During the two decades following World War II, many seeds that had been sown during the inter-war period grew into issues of indisputable importance. The most outstanding of these was that of frontiers, over the definition of which there was much disputation and uncertainty. Despite the 1937 agreement between Abu Dhabi and Dubai regarding their mutual frontiers, a prolonged war took place between them from 1945 to 1948, both their rulers having become well aware of the importance of every square inch of land. Shaykh Sa'id of Dubai claimed Khawr Ghanadah as the coastal boundary between the two shaykhdoms, while Shaykh Shakhbut of Abu Dhabi claimed Jabal al-Jubayl, about twenty-five miles north of Ghanadah, as his dividing line. Both men belonged to the Bani Yas, but there had never been much of an affinity between them or the states that they ruled over. Abu Dhabi covered a much larger area than Dubai, and its ruler consequently was primarily concerned with the extension of his influence over neighbouring tribes. Dubai was a commercial centre consisting of little more than Dubai town and a few water wells. Shaykh Sa'id was more urbanised than Shakhbut, of whom he was scornful, and in 1937 he confided to the Political Agent in Bahrain his opinion of Shakhbut as 'an obstinate bedu' who, 'if he would not listen to reason [over the territorial dispute] . . . could "go to hell"'.[2]

In 1945, when Dubai sent a large force to claim Ghanadah, both shaykhdoms prepared for a major conflict along the coast; but the Political Resident intervened and reminded both rulers of their commitments to desist from any form of maritime warfare. The conflict was therefore carried inland, where Shakhbut's tribesmen displayed their loyalty, and Sa'id was eventually forced to admit defeat, despite his attempt to buy the loyalty of the Bani Qitab tribe.[3] He finally recognised Shakhbut's sovereignty over Ghanadah, at the same time agreeing to pay blood-money for the men killed by his faction and to return all the weapons seized during the fighting. Although the truce, which the British authorities helped to bring about, was accepted by both sides, and no further outbreaks of violence occurred between them, the innate rivalry of the two shaykhdoms continued to grow, strengthened by the different course each had chosen. Abu Dhabi's leadership over the inland tribes became generally recognised, and was strengthened after 1948, when Shakhbut's brother Zayid became his *wali* in the Buraimi oasis, succeeding Ibrahim ibn 'Uthman. Zayid was respected and trusted by the bedouin, and did much to improve conditions in the oasis. Dubai, by contrast, was totally preoccupied with the development and emergence of its port as the only one on the Trucial Coast, especially as Sultan bin Saqr of Sharjah did nothing to prevent the silting of his. The differences between Dubai and Abu Dhabi continue today, but, in the face of greater threats, they have managed to override them and often present a surprisingly united stand.

The principal boundary dispute after World War II was, of course, that concerning Buraimi. The Anglo-Saudi negotiations of the 1930s having come to nothing, and the suggestion that Shakhbut be 'induced' to lease Khawr al-'Udayd to Saudi Arabia having been discarded, in 1949 all the earlier fears of Saudi encroachment were realised. Early in the year, Aramco exploratory parties began field work in the Sabkhat Matti area of Abu Dhabi and around the 'Udayd peninsula, near Khawr al-'Udayd. The British Government protested, saying that the area belonged to Abu Dhabi. A few months later, the Saudi Government officially laid claim to most of the Dafrah, thus claiming considerably more than it had in 1935, when it had proposed the Fu'ad Line. The British Government rejected the claim, and tried to revert to the old Blue Line of 1913, which, needless to say, Saudi Arabia refused to accept.

Despite a number of diplomatic attempts to solve the crisis, the Saudi Government went forward in its claim, and in August 1952 an armed force arrived in Hamasah in Buraimi. Saudi Arabia claimed that Buraimi was independent of any government, and therefore that Britain had no case for interference. The Trucial Oman Levies were called in, and, helped by the RAF, produced a stalemate; as a result, it was agreed between the contenders that further negotiations should take place and that for the duration of them all military action in the oasis should cease. These negotiations took the following form: in 1955 both sides presented to an international tribunal memorials detailing, as a basis for decision, tribal loyalties, past and present, and their influence on the jurisdiction of Buraimi.[4] But, in the wake of dramatic accusations, the proceedings broke down, when the British representative, Sir Reader Bullard, who had served as British Minister in Jeddah during the Anglo-Saudi conversations of the 1930s, resigned in protest at the behaviour of his Saudi counterpart, Yusuf Yasin.

Once again, negotiations had come to nothing, and force was again employed. In the latter part of 1955, the Trucial Oman Levies dislodged the Saudi force from Hamasah, and the British Government made it clear that it regarded Abu Dhabi's boundaries as consistent with the Ryan Line of 1935. But Abu Dhabi was not given full possession of Buraimi. The sultanate of Muscat and

Oman also had certain claims on it, albeit weakly exercised—as demonstrated by the fact that in 1938 a Petroleum Concessions party of exploration failed, despite authorisation from the sultan, to gain access to the oasis. Britain finally decided to give Buraimi town and Hamasah, controlled by the Na'im and Al-bu-Shamis, respectively, to Muscat, the rest to Abu Dhabi. The most important village granted the latter was Al-Ain; hence the name given to the oasis by Abu Dhabi today. Saudi Arabia never formally acknow-ledged the rights of Abu Dhabi and Muscat in Buraimi, and the boundary was not accepted by the Saudi Government until recently; it was principally owing to their disagreement on this score that Saudi Arabia and the United Arab Emirates had previously had no diplomatic relations with each other.

The core of the Buraimi dispute was the recognition that the eastern coast of the Arabian peninsula possessed one of the largest and richest oilfields in the world. After the discovery of oil in Bahrain in 1932, Saudi Arabia, Kuwait and Qatar were the next in line; the revelations of the quantity of the precious mineral exceeded the companies' wildest dreams, and production there began shortly after World War II. On the Trucial Coast, the process was slower, and the first discoveries were off the shores of Abu Dhabi. In 1950 Shakhbut, in pursuance of his earlier stand with the oil companies, and aware of the post-war concept of the 'continen-tal shelf',[5] granted the Superior Oil Company a concession for working his continental shelf. Petroleum Development Trucial Coast (PDTC) contested the validity of the concession, so the matter was put forward for arbitration: the decision reached was that Shakhbut had had every right to conclude a separate concession for his continental shelf, since there had been no reference to it in the 1939 concession. In 1952, however, Superior relinquished its concession, and D'Arcy Exploration, after acquiring it, formed Abu Dhabi Marine Areas Ltd (ADMA); of this company the Com-pagnie Française des Petroles owned one-third, and British Petroleum (formerly the Anglo-Iranian Oil Company) two-thirds.

1958 was the principal turning-point in the modern history of the Trucial Coast, for it was then that oil was struck off Abu Dhabi by the ADMA.[6] Two years later, the PDTC found oil on the Abu Dhabi mainland, and as a result it changed its name to the Abu Dhabi Petroleum Company (ADPC).[7] Soon after, it abandoned its 1937 concession from Dubai in order to concentrate on production in Abu Dhabi. Oil was discovered off Dubai in 1966, but in nowhere near the same quantity as the oil found off Abu Dhabi; Dubai Marine Areas Ltd, originally formed with the same structure as the ADMA, held the concession there. The remaining shaykhdoms have shown themselves eager for the benefits

already enjoyed by their oil-producing neighbours, but, aside from
the discovery in 1973 of oil for Sharjah, off Abu Musa, and despite
the many oil companies at work, exploration in these shaykhdoms
has so far largely drawn a blank.

The story of Shakhbut's reluctance to allow the vast revenues
that suddenly began to pour in to Abu Dhabi to alter any aspect
of the traditional way of life there is too well known to need
reiteration here. The same goes for his deposal in 1966 by his
brother Zayid of Buraimi, who almost immediately started development projects for the shaykhdom and its less fortunate neighbours.
By 1970, the rate of growth of Abu Dhabi had become three
times faster than that of Kuwait, the oil-rich state whose rise to
affluence and prominence has become almost legendary.[8] At about
the same time as these were unleased the tremendous forces that
suddenly came into play when the extent of the oil reserves of
Abu Dhabi became known, the British Government announced,
in January 1968, that its forces would withdraw entirely from the
Gulf region by the end of 1971. Before the shock of the announcement
had had time to take effect, Abu Dhabi and Dubai settled a
longstanding offshore dispute they had had with each other, and
formed a federation that the other Trucial states, plus Bahrain
and Qatar, were invited to join.

The rulers of various shaykhdoms had since the early part of
1967 been seeking for some way of cooperating for their mutual
security: the enormous wealth, small size and strategic location
of the shaykhdoms made them especially vulnerable to any kind
of threat; and their rulers were particularly concerned about the
strength of the nationalist movements then active in the Federation
of South Arabia, which was due to become independent of Britain
in January 1968.[9] Fear of similar troubles in the Gulf region led
to a move, reportedly initiated by Shaykh Zayid of Abu Dhabi,
to provide for the security of the region by co-operation between
its rulers. This move gained momentum after the British announcement of withdrawal.

When Abu Dhabi and Dubai formed a federation, they invited
neighbouring states to join them. These, after a futile attempt
to persuade Britain to maintain her presence in the Gulf at Arab
expense, announced about ten days later that they would join
with Abu Dhabi and Dubai. For just under two years, from late
in February 1968 until late in October 1969, there seemed a fair
likelihood that a federation of the nine shaykhdoms concerned (the
seven Trucial states, plus Bahrain and Qatar) would indeed be
established. Bahrain, however, was motivated primarily by her desire
to protect herself from the renewed spate of Iranian claims, and
Qatar was anxious to assume a leading role. When the Iranian

claim was finally dropped, in May 1970, Bahrain, whose social structure, system of administration and services were far more advanced than those of its proposed partners, lost all interest in the proposed federation and opted, as was only natural, for complete independence. Qatar, on the other hand, realised that its alliance with Dubai—through the long friendship, bolstered by commercial and marital links, between their ruling families—was not enough to dislodge Zayid of Abu Dhabi from the position of greatest importance in the federation. In May 1970, therefore, Qatar named its first cabinet, and it gradually withdrew from the move towards unity.

That left the seven Trucial states. Of them, Abu Dhabi was undoubtedly the leading power, owing to its great wealth and Shaykh Zayid's energetic role in cementing the relationships between the shaykhdoms' rulers and asserting himself as leader. Abu Dhabi was particularly conscious of the vagueness of its borders, and, as the state with the greatest potential for oil, had the greatest interest in promoting a successful union. Dubai, next in importance, was not as eager: its location and the great aptitude of its townsmen for business had made it a bustling commercial centre of the Gulf, and it jealously wanted to preserve its role; furthermore, it had a large and prosperous Iranian community, which, owing to the generally anti-Iranian sentiments of the other states, could have become a complication. After much deliberation and dispute over such matters as proportional representation in the forthcoming federation, serious plans to set up a constitution and plan constructively for a modern nation were made. A provisional constitution accepted, in July 1971, by all but one of the rulers gave the greatest share of authority to Abu Dhabi and Dubai; it was because of this that Saqr bin Muhammad al-Qasimi of Ras al-Khaimah, who had deposed his uncle Sultan bin Salim in 1948, refused to join the federation, which Ras al-Khaimah stayed out of until February 1972.

On the eve of the British withdrawal, Iran occupied the islands of Abu Musa and the Tunbs, claimed by Sharjah and Ras al-Khaimah, respectively. The ruler of Sharjah, Khalid bin Muhammad al-Qasimi, who had deposed his cousin Saqr bin Sultan in 1965, had made a last-minute agreement with the Iranian Government; in it he had agreed to the establishment of an Iranian military post on Abu Musa, in exchange for aid of $3 million a year from Iran over a period of nine years. A further stipulation was that any revenues from the island should be shared equally by Sharjah and Iran. Shaykh Saqr of Ras al-Khaimah refused to sign a similar agreement, and the Iranian occupation was fierce and dramatic, with a certain amount of bloodshed. Although both

Iraq and Libya reacted strongly to the occupation, the former severing its diplomatic relations with Britain, the latter nationalising the Libyan assets of British Petroleum, Saqr received little real help. The occupation having occurred one day before British withdrawal, he fell between two stools.

On 2 December 1971, the United Arab Emirates came into being. The next day, the UAE signed a Treaty of Friendship with Britain that cancelled and replaced all previous British treaties with the member shaykhdoms. The bitter-sweet remark of one senior British official thus acquired further reality:

> Now all our pomp of yesterday is one with Nineveh and Tyre, and the Lord God of Hosts, with a pardonable sense of realism, appears to be on the side of the big battalions to the east and west of us, as we are reduced again to being an island off the north-west coast of Europe, leaving our memorials scattered around the world and our language as the means of Asian communication.[10]

The UAE, having been removed from British protection, thus became a fully independent state, with membership of the Arab League, the United Nations and all their affiliated bodies.

One of the UAE's first tests came about a month after its birth. In January 1972, Saqr bin Sultan of Sharjah, who had been living in exile in Egypt since his deposal in 1965, attempted to regain power by killing Khalid bin Muhammad, who had signed the traitorous agreement with Iran. But the government of the UAE refused to allow Saqr to succeed in the old manner, and intervened immediately. Although Khalid and a number of others had already died, the government decided to bring in Khalid's brother Sultan, a young graduate in agriculture from Cairo University, as ruler, at the same time sending Saqr back into exile. The next month Saqr bin Muhammad of Ras al-Khaimah, by then fully aware of his weakness in isolation, joined the UAE.

Despite these positive moves, the future course of the new state does not promise to be an easy one. Although it is unusually well-endowed financially, it has to cope with innumerable problems, for it is undergoing the reverse of the usual process of decolonisation: economic independence was achieved before *de facto* political independence. It can easily afford to allocate a large share of its vast financial resources for social investments in order to develop its public administration and its health, educational and other welfare services. But the structure of a state takes longer than four years (1968 to 1971) to come into being, especially as the withdrawal of British forces was a completely unilateral move undertaken as part of a general policy of cutting defence costs and not owing to any nationalistic clamour for independence on the Trucial Coast. Since Britain had only very recently started to play a role in the internal affairs of the Coast, there was little chance for the seeds of change that are usually sown, albeit unwittingly, by a colonial power to take effect. Furthermore, the society on the Coast had not had time to become totally aware of its own limitations, an awareness that would have stimulated the process of development, directing it to attack first the power that had dominated it. As it was, the shaykhdoms expressed unique reluctance at the prospect of British withdrawal, for it was Britain that had preserved them from being absorbed by their larger and more powerful neighbours.

One of the reasons for the formation of the UAE was the strong desire for mutual security: in an increasingly energy-conscious age, a practical and efficient defence system for what is a strategically and financially important area is essential. Until it is able to bridge the gap between its past and its present, the UAE will have to rely on imported models and manpower for the structure of its defence, economy and political life, especially as its population is very small (about 700,000) and spread over a large area (about 30,000 square miles). Most of all, it will have to reconcile all the differences between its member states, for whom the formation of a union was the only logical solution to the vacuum left by Britain.

The former Trucial shaykhdoms have more in common than a history of treaty relations with Britain. Their social structure, their geography, their political characteristics, their maritime past and former dependence on pearl-fishing all combine to link them together. The first time all the rulers of the Coast gathered together was in 1905, when Zayid bin Khalifah called a meeting in Abu Dhabi in order to solve outstanding territorial disputes. The meeting was generally successful, but was not to be repeated for almost fifty years. In the meantime, others had thought of the possibility of uniting the Trucial states. In the 1930s the *qadi* of Ras al-Khaimah lived for a while in Buraimi in order to promote some form of union of the rulers on the Coast; when his plans came to nothing, he left Buraimi and settled in Ras al-Khaimah. Another premature suggestion for the formation of a federation came from an unlikely and rather remote source. In 1938 an anti-British article in a Cairo newspaper reported that the British Government was plotting the formation of a union on the Coast. Since the report was without any foundation in truth, it can only be deduced that the possibility of a federation was being discussed as far away as Egypt; the idea of a union sponsored by Britain was then, however, regarded with suspicion as imperial strategy to curtail the independence of the people of the Coast. The Trucial States Council, set up in 1952 by the British Government, was the first serious attempt to bring some sort of unity to the area. Its main purpose was to bring the rulers together in order to discuss problems of mutual interest. It met at least twice a year under the chairmanship of the Political Agent in Dubai. The meetings gave the rulers a chance to realise what interests and problems they had in common, and served to lay the groundwork for the negotiations that led to the formation of the UAE in 1971.

The later 1970s and early 1980s can be expected to determine the future course of the federation. Two opposing factors must be borne in mind. On the one hand, time will not be on the side of the UAE, which entered the field of international relations at a late and critical moment, and it will have to work hard and fast at laying a sound basis for its internal and external affiars, in order to maintain its sovereignty. On the other hand, the UAE has one distinct advantage in its favour: its characteristics have not been fragmented by the artificial superimpositions of a colonial power—Aden, India, and Nigeria all come to mind as examples. It can structure its future by choosing any mode that best suits it. Much depends on this choice.

Notes

INTRODUCTION

1. In the notes that follow, they are distinguished from reports in English by the inclusion of the Islamic date.
2. Elizabeth Monroe, *Britain's Moment in the Middle East, 1914–1956* (London, 1965) ch. 3 ('The Years of Good Management, 1922–1945') pp. 71–94.
3. Ibid., p. 81.
4. L/P&S/18, B478, 'Oil Concessions in the Arab Sheikhdoms of the Persian Gulf', 13 Mar 1944.
5. *Al-Anwar* (Beirut daily newspaper), 22 Aug 1973. Luckily, no one was seriously injured.

CHAPTER 1

1. L/P&S/10, P619/07(7), P4389/10, Naval Commander-in-Chief to Admiralty, 30 Dec 1910 (telegram).
2. For an account of the European rivalry in the Gulf region during this period, see B. C. Busch, *Britain and the Persian Gulf, 1894–1914* (Berkeley and Los Angeles, Calif., 1967).
3. J. G. Lorimer, *Gazetteer of the Persian Gulf, Oman and Central Arabia*, 2 vols (Calcutta, 1908–1915) vol. II, p. 1437.
4. L/P&S/20, C242, 'Military Report and Route Book: The Arabian States of the Persian Gulf', prepared by the General Staff, India, 1939.
5. Although British treaty relations with the shaykhdoms on the Coast did not technically claim any overall right by the British Government to make laws for peace and order, the Political Resident did exercise a certain jurisdiction. This jurisdiction had no legal basis and had grown up by long usage, relying very much on the paramount influence of the British Government. The same case applied to British jurisdiction over foreigners; legally, the rulers of the Coast had jurisdiction over all individuals in their respective states, but did not seem to be aware

of this fact. Since the only foreign community that seriously concerned the British authorities was that of the Indians, it was with some relief that the Political Resident in 1936 noted that 'I believe that the Shaikhs are under the wholesome impression that they cannot touch British subjects' (R/15/2/1865, Political Resident to Political Agent Bahrain, 5 July 1936). When negotiations for oil concessions were underway two years later, the British authorities brought up the question of extra-territorial jurisdiction before foreign employees of oil companies began to arrive in sizable numbers. The officiating Political Resident urged that the concessions proceed without any legal complications, arguing that the matter could be settled if and when the oil company started drilling and foreign employees arrived. It was not until December 1946 that Orders-in-Council for the Coast were enacted; they provided extra-territorial jurisdiction for British subjects, British-protected persons and non-Muslim foreigners.

6. Sir Rupert Hay, 'The Persian Gulf States and their Boundary Disputes', *Geographical Journal*, cxx (1954) 435.

7. One of the principal obligations of Islam, *zakat* is an alms tax levied on different kinds of property and distributed amongst the needy. Its evolution into the form referred to above has its roots in the initial reluctance of the bedouin to pay it, as a result of which payment had to be enforced.

8. See Sir Charles D. Belgrave, 'Pearl Diving in Bahrain', *Journal of the Royal Central Asian Society*, xxi (1934); Richard le B. Bowen, Jr, 'Pearl Fisheries of the Persian Gulf', *Middle East Journal* v (1951), and 'Marine Industries of Eastern Arabia', *Geographical Review* xli (1951).

9. In 1939, it was estimated that about 20 per cent of the population of Dubai was made up of Persians and Baluchis, excluding the Hindus and Khojahs. In Abu Dhabi foreign merchants made for 4 per cent of the total population, but for Sharjah there are no available figures. (L/P&S/20, C242.)

10. John B. Kelly, *Britain and the Persian Gulf, 1795–1880* (Oxford, 1968) p. 834.

11. L/P&S/18, B407, 'Slavery in the Persian Gulf', Sep 1928.

12. Major-General Sir Percy Cox, 'Some Excursions in Oman', *Geographical Journal*, lxvi (1925) 200.

13. After Nuhayyan, ancestor of the Al-bu-Falah.

14. The Mazari' are sometimes considered a separate tribe. Bertram Thomas regarded them in this light, but qualified the consideration by adding that they were a 'section of the Minasir with whom they are in close touch' (L/P&S/11/294, P6690/28, Thomas to Political Resident, 13 June 1927). In 1934, the Residency Agent counted them as a section of the Bani Yas (R/15/2/544, Residency Agent to Officiating Political Resident, 9 Jumada ii 1353 (19 Sep 1934). Lorimer, in his *Gazetteer*, vol. ii, p. 1933, also placed them within the Bani Yas, but said that the Mazari' outside Abu Dhabi town and Liwa 'may or may not be identical with this section of the Bani Yas'.

15. Lorimer, *Gazetteer*, vol. ii, pp. 1932–4.

16. Ibid., vol. ii, p. 1164.

17. Ibid., vol. ii p. 405.

18. Ibid. It must be noted here, however, that in the historical section of the *Gazetteer*, Lorimer states that Buraimi 'became almost an annexe of the principality of Abu Dhabi' (ibid., vol. I, p. 771).
19. Cox, in *Geographical Journal*, LXVI, 207.
20. S. B. Miles, *The Countries and Tribes of the Persian Gulf*, new edition (London, 1966) p. 539.
21. Lorimer, *Gazetteer*, vol. II, p. 414.
22. W. Thesiger, 'A Further Journey across the Empty Quarter', *Geographical Journal*, CXIII (1949) 39–40. Thesiger was the first European in modern times to visit Liwa; although he was not far from Liwa in 1946 after he crossed the Rub' al-Khali, he did not actually visit Liwa until late 1948.
23. Lorimer, *Gazetteer*, vol. II, p. 405. Lorimer's belief was based on the fact that Shaykh Zayid's influence was predominant in al-Khatam.
24. Ibid., vol. I, pp. 772–4.
25. Hay, in *Geographical Journal*, CXX, 439.
26. See Sir Charles D. Belgrave, *The Pirate Coast* (London, 1966); Kelly, *Britain and the Persian Gulf, 1795–1880*; Lorimer, *Gazetteer*; Miles, *Countries and Tribes of the Persian Gulf*; H. Moyse-Barlett, *The Pirates of Trucial Oman* (London, 1966); Sir Arnold T. Wilson, *The Persian Gulf* (Oxford, 1928).
27. C. U. Aitchison, *A Collection of Treaties, Engagements and Sanads Relating to India and Neighbouring Countries*, fifth edition (Delhi, 1933), vol. XI, pp. 245–8.

CHAPTER 2

1. Sir Percy Zachariah Cox (1864–1937), who was Political Resident in Bushire from 1909 to 1920, after five years as Acting Resident there. His career included service as Chief Political Officer, Indian Expeditionary Force in Mesopotamia, 1914–18; Acting Minister Tehran, 1918–20; and High Commissioner in Iraq, 1920–3. See Philip Graves, *The Life of Sir Percy Cox* (London, 1941).
2. See Busch, *Britain and the Persian Gulf, 1894–1914*; and Ravinder Kumar, *India and the Persian Gulf, 1858–1907. A Study of British Imperial Policy* (New York, 1965).
3. A district within the Ottoman administration, ruled by a *qa'immaqam*.
4. Lorimer, *Gazetteer*, vol. I, pp. 2638–9.
5. *Parliamentary Debates*, fourth ser., vol. CXXI, p. 1348.
6. The adviser was Charles Belgrave, who remained in Bahrain from 1926 to 1957, and exercised the greatest personal influence in the shaykhdom. For an account of his years in Bahrain, see his autobiography, *Personal Column* (London, 1960).
7. L/P&S/10, P595/1927(1), P4575/27, Government of India to India Office, 8 Sep 1927.
8. R/15/1/268, Political Resident to Political Agent Bahrain, 25 Apr 1924.
9. L/P&S/10, P4535/1928(8), Viceroy to Secretary of State for India, 5 Oct 1928 (telegraph), first of five parts.
10. Ibid., second of five parts.
11. Ibid, 16 Oct 1928, fourth of five parts.

12. Ibid.

13. PG22, 31 Oct 1928. Available in L/P&S/10, P4535/1928(8).

14. L/P&S/18, B419, 'Future Policy on the Trucial Coast' (P3840/29, Political Resident to Government of India, 23 Apr 1929).

15. L/P&S/12/3747, PZ1724/39, Political Agent Bahrain to Political Resident, 5 Feb 1939. Enclosed in Political Resident to Government of India, 21 Feb 1939.

16. Busch, *Britain and the Persian Gulf, 1894–1914*, p. 386.

17. The Political Agency in Muscat was initially established in 1800.

18. From 1900 to 1904, an Assistant Political Agent was posted to Bahrain. In 1904 the position became that of Political Agent.

19. The first Political Agent to Kuwait was sent in 1904.

20. For details of the setting up of the Committee, see B. C. Busch, *Britain, India and the Arabs, 1914–1921* (Berkeley and Los Angeles, Calif., 1971) pp. 456–63.

21. CAB 23/24, 7(21)2, 14 Feb 1921.

22. Established in 1902, the CID was until 1939 the principal advisory and consultative body on all matters concerned with home and overseas defence.

23. CID no. 174-D, PG (sub) 18.

24. This recommendation was approved by the Cabinet on 30 July 1930 (CAB 23/24, 46(30)8, 30 July 1930).

25. On these points, the Secretary of State for India reported, 'The appointment is already sufficiently attractive from the aspect of prestige and remuneration . . . and [I doubt] whether it is necessary to associate the Imperial Government, who have already in practice an opportunity of expressing their views before an Officer is posted to Bushire, more closely with the appointments' (ibid.).

26. CAB 23/76, 48(33)6, 26 July 1933.

27. Texts available in Aitchison, *A Collection of Treaties*, vol. xi, pp. 256–7.

28. Ibid, vol. xi, 238.

29. For details of the events leading to this, see Busch, *Britain and the Persian Gulf, 1894–1914*, pp. 94–113.

30. See Aitchison, *A Collection of Treaties*, vol. xi, p. 262, for text.

31. Ibid., vol. xi, pp. 262–3.

32. Ibid., vol. xi, p. 263.

33. Ibid., vol. xi, pp. 265–6.

34. Ibid., vol. xi, 258–61.

35. Ibid., vol. xi, p. 257.

36. Ibid., vol. xi p. 263.

37. Ibid., vol. xi, pp. 264–5.

38. Ibid., vol. xi, p. 239.

39. 'Let it not be hidden from you that we agree, if oil is expected to be found in our territory, not to grant any concession in this connection to any one except to the person appointed by the High British Government' (Undertaking by the ruler of Dubai, signed on 2 May 1922, ibid., vol. xi, 261).

40. For a description of the varied duties of the Political Resident, see the account given by a former Resident, Sir Rupert Hay, *The Persian Gulf States* (Washington DC, 1959) pp. 19–27.

41. L/P&S/12/3747, P6406/29, Political Resident to Government of India, 1 Sep 1929.
42. Ibid., P2870/30, Political Resident to Government of India, 9 Apr 1930.
43. Ibid., PZ2870/30, Political Resident to Government of India, 14 Mar 1930.
44. It is interesting to note that in 1926 the Government of India proposed that the post be reduced from a first-class to a second-class appointment. However, in view of the responsibilities of the office, the difficulty of the duties, and the unhealthy climate of the Gulf, it also recommended that the Resident be given a special payment. (L/P&S/10, P5184/1913, Viceroy to Secretary of State for India, 20 Sep 1926 (telegram).) These proposals were dropped, and the Resident continued to hold a first-class appointment; in 1927 the appointment of a personal assistant to the Resident was sanctioned by India.
45. L/P&S/12/3747, minute by Laithwaite (India Office), 11 Nov 1929.
46. Quoted ibid.
47. L/P&S/18, B419, 'Future Policy on the Trucial Coast' (P3840/29, Political Resident to Government of India, 23 Apr 1929).
48. Ibid. (P6406/29, Political Resident to Government of India, 5 Sep 1929).
49. L/P&S/12/3747, P2870/30, Political Resident to Government of India, 14 Mar 1930.
50. L/P&S/12/1965, Political Resident to Residency Agent, 11 Dec 1932.
51. Except in Kuwait, where the expenses were shared equally with the Foreign Office.
52. L/P&S/12/3645, PZ7531/33, Political Resident to Government of India, 30 Oct 1933.
53. For an account of the life and work of one of these missionaries, see the autobiography of Paul W. Harrison, *Doctor in Arabia* (London, 1943).
54. This fact particularly shocked Ameen Rihani when he visited the Coast. See Ameen Rihani, *Around the Coasts of Arabia* (London, 1930) p. 262.
55. Olaf Caroe, *Wells of Power* (London, 1951) p. 110. Sir Olaf Caroe was an Officer of the Indian Political Service and in 1937 he was Officiating Political Resident in Bushire. He later became Secretary of the External Affairs Department and Governor of the North-West Frontier Province in India.
56. L/P&S/12/3867, PZ833/36, Political Agent Bahrain to Political Resident, 21 Feb 1935.
57. Donald Hawley, *The Trucial States* (London, 1970) p. 226.
58. See J. F. Standish, 'British Maritime Policy in the Persian Gulf', *Middle East Studies*, III, no. 4 (1967).
59. Captain R. St P. Parry, 'The Navy in the Persian Gulf', *Journal of the Royal United Service Institution*, LXXV (May, 1930).

CHAPTER 3
1. Lorimer, *Gazetteer*, vol. II, p. 1933.
2. Ibid., vol. II, p. 1547.

3. Ibid., vol. II, p. 1932.

4. A large Ghafiri tribe whose *dirah* stretched from each of Ras al-Khaimah town into the Dahirah. A settled branch of the Bani Qitab lived in Dhayd, an oasis about fifty miles east of Sharjah town. In the nineteenth century the Bani Qitab formed the basis of the land power of their allies the Qawasim, but by 1891 they had attached themselves to Zayid bin Khalifah of Abu Dhabi. (Ibid., vol. I, p. 771.) Later, however, as the standing of the ruler of Abu Dhabi declined, the Bani Qitab ceased to be influenced by that shaykhdom.

5. R/15/1/265, Residency Agent to Political Resident, 1 Sep 1922 (translation).

6. Ibid., Residency Agent to Political Resident, 9 Nov 1922 (translation).

7. Ibid., Sa'id bin Ahmad to Political Resident, 23 Oct 1922 (translation).

8. Ibid., Residency Agent to Political Resident, 3 Aug 1923 (translation).

9. Ibid., Residency Agent to Political Resident, 29 Sep 1923 (translation).

10. Ibid., Residency Agent to Political Resident, 27 Oct 1923 (translation).

11. Ibid., Residency Agent to Political Resident, 11 Nov 1923 (translation).

12. Ibid., Political Resident to Government of India, 19 Mar 1924.

13. Ibid., Political Resident to Government of India, 20 Feb 1929.

14. Ibid.

15. Ibid., Political Resident to Government of India, 17 Mar 1929.

16. Compare this entire account with Hawley, *The Trucial States*, p. 348, where he states that Ahmad bin Rashid succeeded his father, Rashid bin Ahmad, in 1929.

17. R/15/1/265, Political Resident to Government of India, 17 Mar 1929.

18. R/15/1/275, extract from Senior Naval Officer's memo. no. 31/619, 27 July 1935.

19. R/15/2/916, 'Dubai Ruling Family', n.d.

20. R/15/1/265, Residency Agent to Political Resident, 29 Dhu'l Hijjah 1340 (23 Aug 1922). These grievances were described to the Residency Agent by Saqr bin Zayid.

21. L/P&S/11/22, P1719/23, Political Resident to Government of India, 18 Mar 1922.

22. R/15/1/265, Residency Agent to Political Resident, 13 Aug 1926 (translation).

23. Ibid., Residency Agent to Political Resident, 17 Nov 1926 (extract).

24. Ibid., 3 Ramadan 1345(7 Mar 1927). Also on 4 Ramadan 1345(8 Mar 1927), in which his brother 'Abd al-Rahman referred to the boys as the sons of *Shaytan* (Satan), a play on the name 'Sultan'.

25. L/P&S/11/195, P1345/21, Political Resident to Government of India, 13 Dec 1927.

26. This is recorded in R/15/1/265, Shakhbut and Hazza' to Ahmad bin Khalifah, n.d.

27. According to a messenger of the Residency Agent, this consisted of 400 armed men, twelve boats and two *bums* (cargo vessels used in Gulf waters) which had four guns (ibid., Residency Agent to Political Resident, 9 Mar 1927). The Resident at Bushire reacted strongly to the force, and he warned Saqr that he would not 'tolerate any breach of the maritime peace' (ibid., Political Resident to Saqr bin Zayid, 23 July 1927).

28. Principally Bani Yas from Dafrah, who migrated to the island in winter.
29. R/15/1/265, Shakbut and Hazza' to Ahmad bin Khalifah, n. d.
30. Clarence C. Mann, *Abu Dhabi* (Beirut, 1969) p. 71.
31. R/15/1/265, Residency Agent to Political Resident, 25 Jan 1928.
32. Ibid., Residency Agent to Political Resident, 27 Aug 1928.
33. L/P&S/11/222, P3935/22, Political Resident to Government of India, 20 Apr 1928 (enclosed in P2561/28).
34. R/15/1/236, 'Arab States News Summary', no. 9 of 1930 (Sep 1930).
35. The claim was based on the right of 'Abd al-Rahman, as a member of the Al-bu-Shamis, to a Na'im position.
36. The agreement is available in R/15/1/267. It was signed by Khalid, 'Abd al-Rahman, the Residency Agent, and Captain Pearson on 8 January 1921.
37. L/P&S/11/195, P1343/21: Political Resident to Government of India, 13 May 1921. Humayd brought on the anger of the British authorities by appealing to Ibn Sa'ud for help against 'Abd al-Rahman.
38. R/15/1/268, 'Abd al-Rahman bin Muhammad to Residency Agent, 16 Dhu'l Hijjah 1341 (30 July 1923).
39. Available ibid., 18 Dhu'l Hijjah 1341 (1 Aug 1923).
40. Available in R/15/1/268, 22 Jumada 1 1343 (31 Dec 1923).
41. Ibid., same date.
42. R/15/1/268, Residency Agent to Political Resident, 10 Jumada II 1342 (18 Jan 1924).
43. Sultan had obviously hired non-residents of Sharjah to join his forces, for in 1939 an Omani resident of Dubai appealed to the imam to help him retrieve from Sultan bin Saqr the fee he had been promised for fighting against Khalid in 1924. The imam wrote to Sultan, who ignored the letter. The British authorities decided not to press Sultan for payment, since by 1939 Khalid had become regent of Kalba and was necessary for help with the oil concessions; knowledge of the claim might have antagonised him. (R/15/2/617.)
44. Available in R/15/1/276, 14 Rabi' II 1343 (12 Nov 1924). HMS *Cyclamen* had arrived off the coast of Sharjah on 10 November, in case British subjects needed protection and in case she was needed to transmit information of the events to Bahrain and Bushire.
45. R/15/2/617, Residency Agent to Political Resident, 8 Dhu'l Hijjah 1345 (9 June 1927).
46. The name Ras al-Khaimah, literally 'the point of the tent', refers to a tent, erected on a low hill in the place formerly called Julfar, above which a torch was lit as a guide for sailors passing through the Straits of Hormuz.
47. Sultan bin Saqr became shaykh of the Qawasim in 1803, but in 1809 the Wahhabis, who had arrived in Buraimi nine years before and had begun to assume great authority on the Coast, deposed him and exiled him to Dar'iyyah. In 1812 Sultan escaped, but in 1814 agreed with Sa'id bin Sultan of Muscat to relinquish all claims to Ras al-Khaimah, which was governed by Hasan bin Rahmah, and to confine himself to Sharjah and the Persian port of Lingah. In 1820, after a British naval force had bombarded Ras al-Khaimah

town, Hasan bin Rahmah was deposed by W. G. Keir, the commander of the British expedition, and Ras al-Khaimah was restored to Sultan. See Kelly, *Britain and the Persian Gulf, 1795–1880*, ch. 4; Miles, *Countries and Tribes of the Persian Gulf*, ch. 5; and Wilson, *The Persian Gulf*, ch. 13.

48. Lorimer, *Gazetteer*, vol. I, p. 756.
49. Ibid., vol. I, pp. 756–63.
50. L/P&S/11/31, P3412/1912, Political Resident to Government of India, 4 Aug 1912. See Ch. 8 below.
51. R/15/1/244, Residency Agent to Political Resident, 14 Shawwal 1337 (13 July 1919).
52. L/P&S/11/31, P1147/21, Political Resident to Government of India, 22 Dec 1920.
53. Ibid.
54. Ibid.
55. Ibid., P4552/21, Political Resident to Government of India, 30 Aug 1921.
56. Cox, in *Geographical Journal*, LXVI, 205.
57. R/15/1/244, Residency Agent to Political Resident, 11 Rajab 1345 (15 Jan 1927).
58. R/15/2/916, 'Dubai Ruling Family', n. d.
59. For a study on the position of women in the Trucial Coast, and a consideration of the role played by Hussah bint Murr, see P. A. Lienhardt, 'Some Social Aspects of the Trucial States', in *The Arabian Peninsula: Society and Politics*, ed. D. Hopwood (London, 1972) pp. 219–30.
60. See below, Ch. 6.
61. L/P&S/12/3827 P5783/29, Commanding Officer HMS *Lupin* to Senior Naval Officer, 21 Apr 1929.
62. Ibid., P2921/29, Political Resident to India Office, 17 Apr 1929 (telegram).
63. Ibid., P2964/29, HMS *Lupin* to Admiralty, 18 Apr 1929 (telegram).

CHAPTER 4

1. Calculated as follows: $MT 3 = 4 rupees; and 15 rupees = £1 sterling.
2. Lorimer, *Gazetteer*, vol. II, p. 409.
3. In 1907 the shaykhdom had only seventy boats, as compared with 410, 360 and 335 in Abu Dhabi, Sharjah and Dubai respectively (ibid., vol. I, p. 2256).
4. Ibid., vol. I, p. 2285.
5. Ibid., vol. I, pp. 2284–7.
6. R/15/1/239, Residency Agent to Deputy Political Resident, 27 Safar 1338(20 Nov 1919).
7. Ibid., Residency Agent to Political Resident, 1 Rabi' I 1338(14 Dec 1919).
8. Ibid., Political Resident to Rashid bin Ahmad, 11 Dec 1919.
9. Ibid., Political Resident to Sultan bin Salim, 13 Sep 1923 (translation).

10. Ibid., Political Resident to Sultan bin Salim, 8 Dec 1923 (translation).
11. Today, however, claim to it is contested by Sharjah and Fujairah.
12. Here it should be noted that in the winter of 1971–2 an expedition sent out by the Royal Geographical Society in London explored the Musandam peninsula for the first time in history. See N. L. Falcon, 'The Musandam (Northern Oman) Expedition 1971–1972', *Geographical Journal*, CXXXIX (1973).
13. Bertram Thomas, 'The Musandam Peninsula and its People the Shihuh', *Journal of the Central Asian Society*, XVI (1929) p. 79. See also Walter Dostal, 'The Shihuh of Northern Oman: A Contribution to Cultural Ecology', *Geographical Journal*, CXXXVIII (1972).
14. Thomas, in *JCAS*, XVI, p. 75.
15. A Ghafiri tribe whose settled population was in Rams, and whose bedouin section roamed the area around the Dhayd oasis in Sharjah.
16. These included 209 divers from Dubai, 213 from Sharjah, and about 100 from Umm al-Qaiwain, Ajman and Lingah (L/P&S/11/213, P1600/22, Political Resident to Government of India, 25 Feb 1922).
17. Sultan bin Salim apparently was suspected of having instigated the murder, but, apart from a note to that effect in the files of the Bushire Residency, no further information is available (R/15/1/275, n. d.).
18. L/P&S/11/213, P1600/22, Political Resident to Government of India, 25 Feb 1922.
19. Ibid.
20. A translation of the agreements is enclosed ibid., P1777/22, Political Resident to Government of India, 14 Mar 1922.
21. Relations between the ruler and the village of Rams remained good until 1933, when Rams suffered great losses from an epidemic and a stagnant trade situation, and could not therefore afford to send the annual tribute agreed on in 1922. In 1934, 130 rupees was all that the village could spare. This was unacceptable to Sultan bin Salim, who insisted on the full amount. The *wali* of Rams consequently appealed to the Senior Naval Officer for help. The latter gave it as his opinion to the Political Resident that the *wali* of Rams was capable of launching a successful attack on Ras al-Khaimah, since he could depend on the help of the Shilhuh, but that he was obviously anxious to reach a solution (R/15/1/275, Senior Naval Officer to Political Resident, 23 Oct 1934). The Naval Officer told the *wali* that if Sultan bin Salim pressed him again for the tribute, he was to say that the matter had been referred to the Political Resident. That there is no further mention of the case indicates the success of the Senior Naval Officer's plan.
22. R/15/1/267, Senior Naval Officer to Political Resident, 13 Jan 1921.
23. L/P&S/11/195, P1343/21 (P3031/21), Political Resident to Government of India, 13 May 1921.
24. Ibid.
25. Ibid.
26. R/15/1/279, Residency Agent to Political Resident, 4 Rabi' II 1344(22 Oct 1925).
27. Ibid., Political Resident to Government of India, 13 Feb 1926.

28. A leading merchant of Bahrain who was a banker, an agent for steamer lines, and agent for the Anglo-Persian Oil Co., Yusuf Kanu was a figure of considerable importance in the Gulf region and in Saudi Arabia. He had a great interest in political affairs, to which he devoted much of his time.

29. Available in R/15/1/279, 9 Jumada II 1344(25 Dec 1925).

30. Ibid., 28 Sha'ban 1344 (13 Mar 1926).

31. Ibid., Political Resident to Government of India, 13 Feb 1926.

32. L/P&S/11/195, P1343/21 (P2494/26), Political Resident to Government of India, 26 June 1926.

33. Ibid.

34. R/15/1/236, 'Arab States News Summary', no. 9 of 1929, Sep 1929.

35. Ibid., no. 2 of 1931, Feb 1931.

36. R/15/1/268, Saqr bin Sultan to Residency Agent, 28 July 1933 (translation).

37. Ibid., Residency Agent to Political Resident, 29 July 1933 (telegram).

38. L/P&S/12/3710, Senior Naval Officer to Commander-in-Chief East Indies Station, 14 Oct 1933 (extract).

39. R/15/1/268, Political Agent Bahrain to Political Resident, 27 Jan 1934 (telegram).

40. L/P&S/10, P595/1927(1), P3996/27, Political Resident to Government of India, 30 Apr and 7 May 1927. Enclosed in P4575/27, 8 Sep 1927. It is interesting to note that, two years later, in a lecture given to the Central Asian Society in London, Haworth upheld the policy of non-interference, specifically citing the case of Abu Dhabi, and argued that interference 'would entail control on the mainland which we have no desire to assume, it would mean an extension of the British Empire' (*Journal of the Central Asian Society*, XVI (1929) 501).

41. Lorimer, *Gazetteer*, vol. I, pp. 777–84.

42. Ibid., vol. I, p. 2639.

43. R/15/6/239, Thomas to Political Resident, 24 June 1926, from which this account has been drawn. A copy of the peace agreement is available in R/15/1/278, 21 May 1926. The other signatories were Salih bin Muhammad, Shihhi the Shaykh of Dibba; Muhammad and Saqr bin Sultan of the Na'im; and Salim bin Duyayn of the Bani Ka'b.

44. R/15/1/278, Residency Agent to Political Resident, 16 Rabi' I 1345 (24 Sep 1926).

45. Ibid., Political Resident to Political Agent Muscat, 5 Nov 1926 (telegram).

46. Ibid., Thomas to Political Agent Muscat, 12 Feb 1927.

47. Ibid., Residency Agent to Political Resident, 24 Dhu'l Hijjah 1346 (20 Nov 1927). The agreement is available ibid.

CHAPTER 5
1. See Fu'ad Hamzah, *Al-Bilad al-'Arabiyyah al Sa'udiyyah* (Mecca, 1937, and Riyadh, 1968); Kelly, *Britain and the Persian Gulf, 1795–1880*; H. St J. B. Philby, *Saudi Arabia* (London, 1955); Ameen Rihani, *Tarikh Najd wa Mulhaqatihi*, new edition (Beirut, 1972); Hafiz Wahbah, *Jazirat al-'Arab fi'l-Qarn al 'Ishrin* (Cairo, 1967).

2. See A. Cunningham, 'The Wrong Horse: A Study of Anglo-Turkish Relations before the First World War', (*St Antony's Papers*, no. 17), *Middle Eastern Affairs*, no. 4 (1965).

3. Aitchison, *A Collection of Treaties*, vol. XI, pp. 206–8. For an account of early Anglo-Saudi relations, see Gary Troeller, *The Birth of Saudi Arabia* (London, 1976).

4. L/P&S/10, P5027/22, P2749/26, Secretary of State for India to Viceroy, 21 Aug 1926 (telegram).

5. Cmd 2951 of 1927, in Aitchison, *A Collection of Treaties*, vol. XI, pp. 227–9.

6. For an account of the fall of the *Ikhwan*, see H. R. P. Dickson, *Kuwait and her Neighbours* (London, 1968); J. B. Glubb, *War in the Desert* (London, 1960).

7. Philby, *Saudi Arabia*, p. 337.

8. The Conference held between Cox and Ibn Sa'ud to delineate the borders of Nejd with Iraq, Transjordan and Kuwait. This followed the Treaty of Muhammarah early in 1922, which had been drawn up by Cox and contested by Ibn Sa'ud. See H. St J. B. Philby, 'A Survey of Wahhabi Arabia, 1929', *Journal of the Central Asian Society*, XVI (1929), and *Arabian Jubilee* (London, 1952); Ameen Rihani, *Ibn Sa'oud of Arabia* (London, 1928); and 'The Iraq–Najd Frontier', *Journal of the Central Asian Society*, XVII (1930)

9. Rihani, *Ibn Sa'oud*, p. 67.

10. L/P&S/11/294, P6690/1928, Thomas to Political Resident, 13 June 1927.

11. Note in R/15/2/474 3 Mar 1933. It is interesting to note that a strikingly similar tale is told of the Wahhabis in the nineteenth century, an indication of the influence and power of historical precedent, by which tradition could be confused with reality.

12. L/P&S/11/222, P5027/22, Political Resident to Government of India, 13 May 1921.

13. Ibid., Political Resident to Government of India, 10 Nov 1922.

14. In an interesting minute G. A. Simpson of the Political Department of the India Office remarked uneasily, 'it would have been a better sign if Ibn Saud had argued the point bitterly and fiercely' (ibid., P731/23, 2 Mar 1923).

15. L/P&S/11/222, P5875/30, Political Agent Bahrain to Political Resident, 2 Aug 1930. Enclosed in Political Resident to Government of India, 18 Aug 1930.

16. R. M. Burrell, 'Britain, Iran and the Persian Gulf: Some Aspects of the Situation in the 1920s and 1930s', in *The Arabian Peninsula: Society and Politics*, ed. Derek Hopwood (London, 1972).

17. Tunb lies about seventeen miles south of the south-west corner of Qishm, and Little Tunb (Nabiyu Tunb) is an uninhabited island about one mile long and lying eight miles west of Tunb. Sparsely inhabited and almost waterless, Tunb had deposits of red oxide. Generally speaking, Little Tunb was not explicitly referred to in the dispute, but it was included with Tunb.

18. Larger and more populous than Tunb, Abu Musa lies closer to Sharjah than to Lingah. It had good supplies of water and valuable deposits of red oxide. The population of Tunb and Abu Musa varied with

the season. In winter, Tunb had about twenty-five Arabs to every four Iranians, exclusive of their families; in the summer, the Arabs would go to the pearl fisheries and only the Iranians remained. The Iranian population consisted of the shaykh of Ras al-Khaimah's servant, and two men employed as water-carriers for the staff of the lighthouse. The population of Abu Musa was estimated in 1929 to be made up of fifty Arabs, two Iranians and three Baluchis. (L/P&S/10, P4535/28(2), P6794/29, Political Resident to Government of India, 25 Sep 1929.)

19. Forty miles south by west of Bustaneh, the nearest point on the Iranian coast, Sirri was more prosperous and fertile than Tunb.

20. It is outside the scope of this study to discuss the claim that Iran made to Bahrain in 1927, various studies of which are listed below. The claim was based on the fact that Persia occupied Bahrain early in the seventeenth century and remained until 1783, when ancestors of the present ruling family, the Khalifah, conquered it. Persia, however, never accepted the sovereignty of the Khalifah, and it was not until 1970 that the Iranian Government finally renounced its claim. See Fereydoun Adamiyat, *Bahrain Islands, A Legal and Diplomatic Study of the British–Iranian Controversy* (New York, 1955); Husain M. Al-Baharna, *The Legal Status of the Arabian Gulf States* (Manchester, 1968); Malek Esmail, *Le Golfe persique et les îles de Bahrein* (Paris, 1938); Abbas Faroughy, *The Bahrain Islands (750–1951)* (New York, 1951). J. B. Kelly, 'The Persian Claim to Bahrain', *International Affairs*, 1957; Majid Khadduri, 'Iran's Claim to Sovereignty of Bahrain', *American Journal of International Law*, 1951; Arnold Toynbee, 'The Dispute between Persia and Great Britain over Bahrain (1927–1934)', *Survey of International Affairs*, 1934.

21. Lorimer, *Gazetteer*, vol. I, pp. 746 and 2138.

22. L/P&S/10, P4949/12(1), P2664/23, British Minister Tehran to Foreign Office, 18 May 1923 (copy).

23. Ibid., P1625/23, British Minister Tehran to Foreign Office, 27 Apr 1923 (copy of telegram).

24. L/P&S/11/262, P2243/26, British Minister Tehran to Foreign Office, 31 May 1926 (copy).

25. It was the money from this tax that went to finance the Trans-Iranian Railway, work on which was started in 1927.

26. L/P&S/10, P4535/1928(11), P4783/28, Viceroy to Secretary of State for India, 4 Sep 1928 (telegram).

27. L/P&S/11/222, P5027/22, Political Resident to Government of India, 18 Aug 1930.

28. A branch of the Khariji sect of Islam, predominant in Oman. See Roberto Rubinacci, 'The Ibadis', in *Religion in the Middle East*, ed. A. J. Arberry, vol. II (Cambridge, 1969). In the eighteenth century the founder of the present Al-bu-Sa'id dynasty changed his title from imam to sultan, and at the beginning of the present century a separate movement under an imam was formed inland, with headquarters at Nizwa. It challenged the authority of the sultan, who, with British support, could control only the coastal areas of Muscat and Oman.

29. A Ghafiri tribe whose range extended through the Rub' al-Khali and north to Buraimi. Described by Bertram Thomas as follows: 'Treacherous, poor and a universal terror. They speak intelligible Arabic, not grunts mentioned in books; roam everywhere but bazaar Ibri and Buraimi ... a loose confederacy, every section a law unto itself' (L/P&S/11/294, P6690/28, Thomas to Political Resident, 13 June 1927).

30. A Ghafiri tribe who had been previously at war with the 'Awamir. Their main centre was at Tun'um in Dahirah, although their range extended from Dahirat al-Sir to Buraimi.

31. A Ghafiri tribe that had been a branch of the Na'im but that in the twentieth century assumed an entity of their own, the Al-bu-Shamis were led by Shaykh Rashid bin Hamad, who lived in Hamasah, a village in the Buraimi oasis. There seems to be conflicting evidence on the participation of the Al-bu-Shamis in this dispute. The Residency Agent, who sent an agent to collect information on Dafrah and Buraimi about ten years later, did not include them in his account of events. (R/15/2/544, Residency Agent to Officiating Political Resident, 9 Jumada II 1353 (19 Sep 1934).) J. B. Kelly, *Eastern Arabian Frontiers* (London, 1964), p. 115, referred to them in this context.

32. Some of the Manasir, the Al-bu-Mundhir section under Shaykh Qiran bin Mani', as well as certain members of the Mazari', decided to remain in Hasa, and Qiran was still there in 1934. (R/15/2/544, Residency Agent to Officiating Political Resident, 9 Jumada II 1353 (19 Sep 1934).) On the Mazari', see above, Ch. 1, note 14.

33. R/15/1/250, note from Political Agent Bahrain to Political Resident, 12 Feb 1925.

34. Although the report from which this entire account has been drawn refers specifically to al-Falayah more than once, the 140 miles separating this village from al-Mu'tarid make it an unlikely place for attack and counter-attack from Buraimi. The number of spelling errors that exist in the report suggest, however, a possible mistake, and that Aflaj Bani Qitab, a cluster of tiny settlements located in the Dahirah, north-west of 'Ibri and south of Dhank, and inhabited by the Bani Qitab, was the scene of the fighting. (R/15/1/250, Residency Agent to Political Resident, 25 Safar 1343 (25 Sep 1924).)

35. Whose home was in Mahadah in the Dahirah. Captain G. J. Eccles, who accompanied a D'Arcy Exploration Company survey to Oman in 1925 described him as 'altogether more polished, more intelligent and broad-minded, though no less virile, than his Bedouin brother' ('Sultanate of Muscat and 'Oman', *Journal of the Central Asian Society*, XIV (1927) 36). His brother Mu'adad lived in Sharm and murdered Salim in 1930, when he became Shaykh of Bani Ka'b. He was later removed from power by Salim's sons.

36. The shaykh of 'Ibri, a large settlement in the Omani section of the Dahirah, was an Ibadi of the Bani Ya'aqib tribe. In 1925 he was replaced by 'Abdallah bin Rashid, who was under the influence of 'Isa bin Salih and the imam.

37. At the time, the shaykh was 'Abdallah bin 'Ali bin Huwayydin, but, as he was ill, and died on 16 December 1925, the man referred

to in the report by the Residency Agent from which this account has been drawn was probably his brother and successor, Muhammad.

38. R/15/1/250, Residency Agent to Political Resident, 2 Ramadan 1343 (27 Mar 1925).

39. One of the oldest tribes in Arabia, the Al-Murrah had a range extending from Hasa to Riyadh, and were thus well within the confines of Ibn Sa'ud's authority.

40. There seems to be some confusion as to his complete name. He has been referred to as Su'ayyid bin Faysal and as Su'ayyid bin 'Arafah. For the sake of simplicity, he is referred to here as Su'ayyid, the same name given to him by the Residency Agent in Sharjah. (R/15/2/544, Residency Agent to Officiating Political Resident, 9 Jumada II 1353 (19 Sep 1934).)

41. L/P&S/11/222, P2433/26, Political Resident to Colonial Office, 9 June 1926.

42. R/15/2/544, Residency Agent to Officiating Political Resident, 9 Jumada II 1353 (19 Sep 1934).

43. L/P&S/11/222, P2433/26, Political Resident to Colonial Office, 9 June 1926.

44. L/P&S/11/294, P6690/28, Thomas to Political Resident, 13 June 1927. See also Bertram Thomas, *Alarms and Excursions in Arabia* (London, 1931).

45. R/15/6/39, Shaykh Rashid bin 'Uzayz (Minister for Religious Affairs, Muscat Council of Ministers) to Political Agent Muscat, n. d. (translation).

46. Ibid., Clerk of the *wali* of Sohar to Council of Ministers, Muscat and Oman, 11 Dhu'l Hijjah 1343 (4 July 1925).

47. He claimed that the purpose of their visit was to inspect their date gardens in the Batinah, and he told the Residency Agent that he was not in the least afraid of Ibn Jaluwi (ibid., Residency Agent to Political Resident, 7 Oct 1925).

48. *Al-Shura*, edited by Muhammad 'Ali Tahir, who previously had lived in the Hijaz under Hashimi rule, was in print only from 1924 to 1931.

49. Originally from Tripoli, Libya, al-Nafusi went to Muscat in 1924. Two years later he became Finance Minister to the imam of Oman. A powerful man who was regarded with great suspicion by the British authorities in Muscat and Bushire, al-Nafusi was also a friend of King Faisal of Iraq, and in 1929 he left Oman to live in Basrah and Baghdad. At first refused re-entry into Muscat, he returned in 1938, this time to work for the sultan.

50. R/15/6/39, note by Soofi (*Munshi*, or scribe, at the Political Agency in Muscat) to Political Agent Muscat, 29 Nov 1925. Soofi also mentioned that Sa'id had been so nervous about the possibility of Wahhabi aggression that he had an Arab from Zubayr who was visiting Dubai deported merely because he 'spoke an ill-word' about Ibn Sa'ud.

51. 10 Jumada I 1344 (27 Nov 1925). Translation enclosed in L/P&S/11/222, P2433/26, Political Resident to Colonial Office, 9 June 1926.

52. Details available in R/15/6/39. See also Eccles, in *Journal of the Central Asian Society*, XIV; J. B. Kelly, 'A Prevalence of Furies: Tribes, Politics,

and Religion in Oman and Trucial Oman', in *The Arabian Peninsula*: *Society and Politics* ed. Derek Hopwood (London, 1972).

53. Before the outcome of 'Isa's expedition had become known, the rulers on the Coast were naturally apprehensive of the possibility of a Wahhabi counter-move, which inevitably would have had violent repercussions in the different shaykhdoms. It obviously was the wrong time for the perpetuation of a feud between Abu Dhabi and the Bani Qitab, so Hamad bin Ibrahim of Umm al-Qaiwain successfully arranged for the conclusion of peace between Sultan bin Zayd and Muhammad bin 'Ali bin Huwayydin early in December 1925. (R/15/1/250, Residency Agent to Political Resident, 17 Jumada I 1344 (4 Dec 1925) and 2 Jumada II 1344 (18 Dec 1925).) Sultan had little choice but to agree to the terms of the peace agreement, his tribal control in the area that his father had commanded with ease being severely challenged by the presence of the Wahhabi *zakat* collectors.

54. L/P&S/11/294, P6690/28, Thomas to Political Resident, 13 June 1927.

55. L/P&S/11/222, P2433/1926, Political Resident to Colonial Office, 9 June 1926.

56. L/P&S/11/195, P1343/21 (P2494/26), Political Resident to Government of India, 26 June 1926.

57. Ameen Rihani, the Lebanese writer, was present when Hazza' bin Sultan arrived in Riyadh, and he gave his impressions of the scene: 'a boy of fifteen, who came with a retinue of sheikhs and slaves and a gift of ten beautiful Oman dromedaries;—came riding across the many deserts from Dubai on the Gulf to al-Riyadh ... bringing the salaam of his father, the biggest of the sheikhs of Oman.... And this son of Ibn Zaied carried a big jewelled sword, walked barefoot, and wore, as another mark of distinction, an embroidered head-kerchief of Cashmere weave' (*Ibn Sa'oud*, p. 230). In return, Hazza' was given 8000 rupees (£70) twenty rifles and two mares; each of his twenty men was given a suit of clothes and a sum of money (ibid., p. 231).

58. R/15/2/544. Residency Agent to Officiating Political Resident, 9 Jumada II 1353 (19 Sep 1934).

59. L/P&S/10, P595/1927(1), P4575/27 (P3996/27), Political Resident to Government of India, 30 Apr and 7 May 1927.

60. L/P&S/11/277, P1958/27, P3945/27, Report from Senior Naval Officer to India Office, 1 May 1927.

61. Ibid., P1958/27, P2367/27, Secretary of Political Resident to British Minister Tehran, 14 Apr 1927 (telegram).

62. L/P&S/10, P4011/1923(2), P3077/28, Political Resident to Government of India, 12 June 1928 (telegram).

63. Ibid., P5125/28, Political Resident to Government of India, 20 Sep 1928.

64. L/P&S/10, P4535/1928(2), P4017/28, Senior Naval Officer to Admiralty, 30 July 1928 (telegram).

65. In the treaty of 1820 Britain undertook to protect the Trucial Coast from attack by sea, and in that of 1892 the rulers of the Trucial Coast were forbidden to enter into any agreement or correspondence with any country other than Great Britain. In 1903 Curzon promised

that, while the treaties were binding on the rulers, 'they are also binding in their reciprocal effect upon the British Government, and so long as they are faithfully observed by the Chiefs, there is no fear that anyone else will be allowed to tamper with your rights and liberties' (Lorimer, *Gazetteer*, vol. I, p. 2638).

66. L/P&S/10, P4535/1928(2), P4078/28, Political Resident to India Office, 2 Aug 1928 (telegram).
67. Ibid., P4157/28, Viceroy to Secretary of State for India, 7 Aug 1928.
68. Ibid., P4219/28, British Chargé d'Affaires in Tehran to Foreign Office, 8 Aug 1928 (telegram).
69. Ibid., P5470/28, Political Resident to Government of India, 8 Oct 1928 (telegram).
70. Ibid., P6119/28, enclosure no. 2, letter of proceedings from Senior Naval Officer to Commander-in-Chief East Indies 17 Aug 1928.
71. Ibid., minute, 12 Dec 1928.
72. A claim had been put to the Iranian Government on 7 February 1929 for a compensation fee of 5000 rupees.
73. 'Surely the answer is fairly obvious. It was owing to diplomatic action by His Majesty's representatives that the release of the dhow and passengers was secured. . . . . Considering what might have happened to the women and children passengers, that surely is a substantial achievement to which we can point. (I can hardly believe that the Arabs would have obtained as good results by a cutting-out expedition; rather I should imagine that by saving them from such a rash act we have done them another good service)' (L/P&S/10, P4535/1928(2), P3034/1929, Treasury to Foreign Office, 3 Apr 1929 (copy)).
74. Burrell, in *The Arabian Peninsula*, ed. Hopwood, pp. 172–3.
75. L/P&S/10, P4535/1928(2): Quoted in Political Resident to Government of India, 20 June 1929 (telegram).
76. Ibid., P5769, Rendel (Foreign Office) to Walton (India Office), 2 Sep 1929.
77. Ibid., P8086/29, Government of India to Political Resident, 7 Nov 1929 (telegram).

CHAPTER 6

1. G. W. Bentley, 'The Development of the Air Route in the Persian Gulf', *Journal of the Royal Central Asian Society*, xx (Apr 1933).
2. L/P&S/10, P595/1927(1), P7451/29, Political Resident to Government of India, 23 Aug 1929.
3. Ibid.
4. In 1913 the Government of India, with the concurrence of the ruler of Sharjah, had erected a lighthouse on Tunb island. This became a symbol of its Qasimi ownership.
5. L/P&S/10, P595/1927(1), P3083/29, Political Resident to Government of India, 4 Nov 1929.
6. L/P&S/12/3747, P3165/30, Political Resident to Government of India, 9 Apr 1930.
7. Ibid.
8. L/P&S/12/1966, Biscoe to Walton (India Office), 30 Mar 1932.
9. L/P&S/18, B419, 'Future Policy on the Trucial Coast', 1929.

10. L/P&S/10, P595/1927(3), P3999/30, Political Resident to Government of India, 29 May 1930 (telegram).
11. Ibid., P3516/30, Political Resident to Government of India, 4 June 1930.
12. Ibid., minute by Laithwaite (India Office) at P3516/30, 4 June 1930.
13. It is interesting to note here that Bentley, in *Journal of the Royal Central Asian Society*, xx, omits to mention the seizure of the Ras al-Khaimah pearling fleet: 'Lengthy negotiations followed, and at last the Shaikh, acting on the advice of his relative the Shaikh of Sharjah, agreed to allow aircraft to use the lagoon unmolested and to guard the fuel' (p. 183).
14. L/P&S/10, P595/1927(3), P4195/30, Political Resident to Government of India, 23 June 1930.
15. Biscoe described the negotiations as follows: 'The Shaikh of Sharjah would come on board in the morning with some ridiculous proposal and when that was refused return to the shore for another 24 hours and so it went on' (ibid.).
16. Ibid., P3742/30, Political Resident to India Office, 15 June 1930 (telegram).
17. R/15/1/226, 'Arab States News Summary', no. 6 of 1930, June 1930. The question of who would pay for the guard was not settled. Sultan asked that the British Government should cover the costs, and suggested a salary of 100 rupees per month; but the matter was left standing when the Resident left Ras al-Khaimah in June, and in October the same year the Residency Agent reported that Sultan was adamant that he could not be made responsible for the costs. 'Isa accordingly offered Sultan some money on account, but Sultan refused to accept it, saying that if he did it would preclude further discussion with the Resident on the subject of the barge, which he now wanted to have removed. Sultan confided to 'Isa that he was afraid that, having made one concession, he would be obliged to give more and thus gradually lose his sovereignty.
18. Which in 1940 became the British Overseas Airways Corporation.
19. CAB 23/67, 40(31)5, 30 July 1931.
20. L/P&S/12/1955, PZ7920/31, Political Resident to Government of India, 20 Dec 1931 (telegram).
21. Ibid., PZ1429/32, Political Resident to Government of India, 3 Mar 1932 (telegram).
22. L/P&S/12/1966, PZ6085/32, Appendix no. 1 to Senior Naval Officer, Communication no. 126/587, 10 June 1932.
23. Ibid., PZ2736/32, Political Resident to Government of India, 5 May 1932 (telegram). Before presenting Sultan with this ultimatum, the Resident had ascertained the extent of the opposition to the signing of an air agreement. He admitted that Muhammad bin Saqr, who lived in the same house as his brother, thus making Sultan particularly vulnerable to attack, was supported in his opposition by the rulers of Ajman, Dubai and Ras al-Khaimah; also, that the ruler of Ras al-Khaimah had threatened to kill Sultan bin Saqr if he signed. Furthermore, Sultan had asked for an additional sum of 5000 rupees per annum for the facilities, so that he could subsidise his younger brothers.

24. Ibid., PZ6085/32, Appendix no. 1 to Senior Naval Officer, Communication no. 126/587, 10 June 1932.
25. Ibid.
26. Ibid.
27. Ibid., PZ3859/32, Political Resident to Government of India, 21 June 1932.
28. Ibid.
29. Dickson belonged to a British family that for two generations before him had had ties in the Near East. His grandfather had been a physician at the British Embassy in Constantinople, and his father was British Consul-General in Damascus when his son Harold was born in Beirut in 1881. After an education at Oxford, H. R. P. Dickson joined the Indian Army and during World War I served in Mesopotamia, at which time he was transferred to the Political Department. After service as Political Agent in Bahrain and Secretary to the Political Resident at Bushire, he became Political Agent in Kuwait from 1929 to 1936. He spent the remainder of his life, until 1959, in Kuwait, as chief local representative of the Kuwait Oil Company. Dickson published two books that are invaluable to any study of Arabia: *Kuwait and her Neighbours* (London, 1968), and *The Arabs of the Desert* (London, 1967). His wife and daughter also recorded their reminiscences of life in Kuwait: Violet Dickson, *Forty Years in Kuwait* (London, 1970); and Zahra Freeth, *Kuwait was my Home* (London, 1956).
30. For an account of Biscoe's death and funeral, see Dickson, *Kuwait and her Neighbours*, pp. 346–7.
31. Enclosed in L/P&S/12/1966, PZ4664/32, Political Resident to Government of India, 26 July 1932.
32. Ibid., PZ5015/32, Political Agent Kuwait to Government of India, 4 Aug 1932.
33. Ibid.
34. L/P&S/12/1963, Political Resident to Sa'id bin Hamad, 5 Mar 1933. Enclosed in PZ2239/33, Political Resident to India Office, 24 Mar 1933.
35. Ibid., PZ1815/33, extract from report of proceedings of the Commander-in-Chief East Indies, n.d.
36. Ibid., Officiating Political Agent Bahrain to Political Resident, 23 May 1936 (extract). Enclosed in PZ3881/36, Political Resident to India Office, 29 May 1936.
37. Ibid., PZ3902/36, Political Resident to India Office, 6 June 1936 (telegram).
38. L/P&S/12/1966, Political Agent Kuwait to Sultan bin Saqr, 22 July 1932. Enclosed in PZ4664/32, Political Resident to Government of India, 26 July 1932.
39. The question then was whether Kalba belonged to Sharjah or to Muscat; the Government of India decided in favour of Sharjah (Lorimer, *Gazetteer* vol. 1, p. 783).
40. L/P&S/12/1963, minute by S. Hood (India Office) at PZ3902/36, 9 June 1936. The Shaykh of Sharjah, however, had been present at the 1903 durbar.

41. Ibid.
42. Ibid., PZ3902/36, India Office to Political Resident (draft telegram, sent on 19 June 1936).
43. Ibid., PZ4385/36, Political Resident to India Office, 22 June 1936 (telegram), first of two parts.
44. Ibid., second of two parts.
45. Ibid. Signed by Hickinbotham and Sa'id bin Hamad. Enclosed in PZ7109/36, Officiating Political Resident to India Office, 21 Sep 1936. The agreement was to last twelve years.
46. Enclosed ibid., PZ7109/36.
47. Fowle could see 'no reason we should do something for nothing for the Shaikh of Abu Dhabi' (L/P&S/12/3835, PZ5260/34, Political Resident to Political Agent Bahrain, 9 Aug 1934).
48. L/P&S/12/1963, PZ7109/36, Officiating Political Resident to India Office, 21 Sep 1936.
49. Copy available in L/P&S/12/1990, PZ1471/35. Enclosed in Political Agent Bahrain to Political Resident, 17 Feb 1935.
50. L/P&S/12/3767, PZ3612/35, 'Bahrain Intelligence Summary', no. 9 of 1935, 1–15 May 1935.
51. Ibid.
52. L/P&S/12/1990, PZ3525/35, Political Resident to India Office, 15 May 1935.
53. Ibid., PZ4076/35, Political Resident to India Office, 12 June 1935 (telegram), first of two parts.
54. Ibid., second of two parts.
55. Ibid., PZ4405/35, Political Resident to India Office, 26 June 1935 (telegram).
56. L/P&S/12/1978, PZ5866/36, Political Resident to India Office, 13 Aug 1936 (telegram).
57. Ibid., PZ3181/37, Political Resident to India Office, 2 May 1937.
58. Ibid., PZ3752/37, Political Resident to India Office, 8 June 1937 (telegram).
59. Ibid., PZ5576/36, enclosed in Political Resident to India Office, 5 Aug 1937.
60. See below, Ch. 10.
61. L/P&S/12/1978, PZ4168/38, Political Resident to India Office, 10 June 1938. The agreement was to take effect on 22 July 1938.
62. L/P&S/12/3747, PZ410/39, Political Resident to Political Agent Bahrain, 5 Jan 1939.

CHAPTER 7

1. 'We are not going to throw this century of costly and triumphant enterprise; we shall not wipe out the most unselfish page in history' (extract from Lord Curzon's speech at the 1903 Sharjah durbar).
2. A comprehensive account of the early history of oil in Saudi Arabia, from the early, abortive efforts to secure concessions (in the 1920s) to the signing of the concession with the Standard Oil Company of California in 1933, is given in H. St J. B. Philby, *Arabian Oil Ventures* (Washington DC, 1964). The 1933 concession not only renewed interest in the hinterland of the Trucial shaykhdoms (as discussed

later in this chapter), but also, in response to fears of the expansion of American interests, tightened British control of the development of oil on the Coast.

3. L/P&S/12/3835, PZ3432/35, Political Resident to India Office, 27 Apr 1935.

4. Ibid., PZ5593/35, Political Resident to India Office, 13 Aug 1935 (telegram).

5. For an account of his unusual life, see W. E. Stanton-Hope, *Arabian Adventurer: The Story of Hajji Williamson* (London, 1951).

6. L/P&S/12/3835, PZ7001/35, Political Resident to India Office, 1 Oct 1935 (telegram).

7. Here it must be noted that the Iraq Petroleum Company was operated as a thoroughly British company, despite shares held by Dutch, American and French interests, and the 5 per cent owned by Gulbenkian. The APOC owned 23·75 per cent of the shares. For the history of the companies, see David H. Finnie, *Desert Enterprise* (Cambridge, Mass., 1958); and Stephen H. Longrigg, *Oil in the Middle East* (London, 1968). Other useful studies are George Lenczowski, *Oil and State in the Middle East* (Ithaca, NY, 1960); B. Schwadran, *The Middle East, Oil and the Great Powers* (New York, 1959).

8. L/P&S/12/3835, PZ271/35, note by Laithwaite of discussion at India Office with the APOC, 10 Jan 1935.

9. Following the granting of a new concession in Iraq in 1925, the old Turkish Petroleum Company was absorbed into the IPC. The Red Line Agreement was a pledge by the participants in the new company not to operate within the area of the former Ottoman Empire except through the IPC. See Longrigg, *Oil in the Middle East*, pp. 67–70.

10. Regarding the events leading up to the conclusion of the Saudi oil concession, Philby explained that 'Ibn Saud, strangely enough, like a bird mesmerized by a snake, was known to be personally desirous of giving this very Hasa concession to a British company, if only he could get something solid in return' (*Arabian Oil Ventures*, p. 126). Longrigg, who negotiated on behalf of the IPC, realised why the American company won through despite the king's desire to grant the concession to the British: 'the IPC Directors were slow and cautious in their offers and would speak only of rupees when gold was demanded. Their negotiator, so handicapped, could do little' (*Oil in the Middle East*, p. 107).

11. These culminated in a decision in April 1932 to adhere to an 'open-door policy' regarding American oil interests. Previously, the United States Government had protested against the Colonial Office's insistence on the inclusion of a British nationality clause in any transfer of the option obtained by Frank Holmes for Eastern and General Syndicate, and urged that American interests be allowed equal opportunities in a commercial concession with Kuwait. The Foreign Office was averse to the adoption of a 'dog-in-the-manger' attitude regarding the entry of American interests, but suggested that Sir John Cadman, Chairman of the APOC, be consulted first. (CAB 23/71, 20(32)6, 6 Apr 1932.) On 9 April, however, the Foreign Secretary officially informed the

US Minister in London that the British Government would not insist on a British nationality clause in the Kuwait concession. Cadman did not object when told of the policy, and on 13 April 1932 the Cabinet formally approved it. (CAB 23/71, 21(32)2, 13 Apr 1932.)

12. Known as *Abu-Naft* (The Father of Oil) in Arabia. No account of the history of oil concessions is complete without reference to the mining engineer from New Zealand who, with almost supernatural insight, foresaw the great potential of Arabia long before anyone else. It was mainly owing to his personal efforts that the large oil companies began to show an interest in the area. In 1920 he registered in London the Eastern and General Syndicate—a company that would buy oil concessions from Arabia and sell them to the larger companies. In 1922 he attended the 'Uqayr Conference between the British Government and Ibn Sa'ud (its aim was to define the borders of Iraq and Jordan with Nejd) and personally impressed Ibn Sa'ud, who granted him a concession in 1923 despite Percy Cox's obvious dislike of him. Holmes was a controversial figure: the British authorities always viewed him with distaste and suspicion, probably one of the main reasons that the great wealth of Arabian oil eluded him. He was popular primarily with the Arabs. 'His intimate relationships with the shaikhs and rulers were the envy of the few Englishmen in the area, who could find no explanation for the success of a man who refused to bother with learning the simplest Arabic phrases' (Wayne Mineau, *The Go-Devils* (London, 1958) p. 182). An account of his relationship with Ibn Sa'ud is included in Philby, *Arabian Oil Ventures*, which notes, interestingly (p. 70), that Holmes and his 1923 concession from Ibn Sa'ud is entirely ignored in Olaf Caroe's account (*Wells of Power*) of the history of oil in south-west Asia. It was Holmes who, through the Eastern and General, first obtained an option to explore the Neutral Zone of Kuwait in 1924, and Bahrain in 1925. Holmes also acted as representative in Kuwait of the Gulf Oil Corporation, which finally shared the concession for the shaykhdom.

13. L/P&S/12/3835, Holmes to Political Resident, 28 May 1935. Enclosed in PZ4126/35, Political Resident to India Office, 5 June 1935.

14. Ibid., PZ7762/35, Holmes to India Office, 24 Oct 1935.

15. Ibid., PZ6577/35, proceedings of Senior Naval Officer, 1–31 July 1935 (extract).

16. Ibid., PZ7948/35, Political Resident to India Office, 4 Nov 1935.

17. Recorded ibid., Political Resident to India Office, 3 Oct 1935.

18. Contained ibid., draft letter to Skliros, 12 Dec 1935.

19. The problem is succinctly put forward in Sir Rupert Hay, 'The Persian Gulf States and their Boundary Problems', *Geographical Journal*, cxx (1954).

20. L/P&S/12/3835, PZ1254/36, notes of conclusions of meeting, 21 Feb 1936.

21. Sir George W. Rendel, Head of Eastern Department of the Foreign Office, 1930–3.

22. L/P&S/12/3835, PZ4606/36, Political Resident to India Office, 2 June 1936.

23. Ibid., PZ946/36, Skliros to India Office, 6 Feb 1936.

24. Copies of letters addressed to the rulers available ibid., PZ2051/36, 9 Mar 1936.
25. Copies of letters addressed to the rulers available ibid., PZ2723/36, 14 Apr 1936.
26. Quoted in L/P&S/12/3836, PZ6366/36, Longrigg to India Office, 2 Sep 1936.
27. This was agreed at a meeting at the India Office on 8 October; Fowle, on leave in London, was present (ibid., PZ7265/36, minute, n.d.).
28. Ibid., PZ739/37, Political Resident to India Office, 15 Jan 1937.
29. Ibid., PZ1445/37, Political Resident to India Office, 15 Jan 1937.
30. The meeting was recorded by Clauson of the India Office (ibid., PZ7421/36, 16 Oct 1936.
31. Ibid., PZ8679/36, India Office to Ballantyne, 16 Dec 1936.
32. In 1944, Casoc became the Arabian American Oil Company (Aramco), and two years later the Standard Oil Company of New Jersey and the Socony-Vacuum Oil Company (now the Mobil Oil Corporation) became participants.
33. L/P&S/12/3836, PZ8906/36, Political Resident to India Office, 14 Dec 1936 (telegram), part i.
34. Ibid., part ii.
35. Ibid., PZ9080/36, Political Resident to India Office, 21 Dec 1936 (telegram).
36. Ibid., PZ1964/36, Political Resident to Government of India, 1 Mar 1937.
37. Ibid., PZ1761/37, Political Agent Bahrain to Political Resident, 12 Feb 1937.
38. Ibid., PZ7112/36, Political Resident to India Office, 23 Sep 1936.
39. L/P&S/12/3886, PZ3448/37, Political Resident to India Office, 25 May 1937.
40. L/P&S/12/3836, PZ7613/37, B. H. Lermitte (who replaced Holmes as representative of Petroleum Concessions Ltd) to Political Agent Bahrain, 14 Oct 1937 (copy).
41. Ibid., Political Agent Bahrain to Political Resident, 23 Oct 1937.
42. David Finnie, *Desert Enterprise*, p. 45.
43. L/P&S/12/3836, PZ3759/37, Political Resident to India Office, 8 June 1937 (telegram).
44. Ibid., PZ3833/37, Political Resident to India Office, 12 June 1937 (telegram).
45. Ibid., PZ3759/37, Political Resident to India Office, 8 June 1937 (telegram).
46. L/P&S/12/3837, PZ4230/39, Political Resident to India Office, 3 July 1939.
47. L/P&S/12/3836, PZ3759/37, Political Resident to India Office, 8 June 1937.
48. Ibid., PZ3833/37, India Office to Political Resident, 17 June 1937 (telegram).
49. Ibid., PZ5753/37, Political Resident to India Office, 12 Aug 1937. Sultan did exactly so. He contacted Socal in secret, but the company was obliged to turn him down. (Ibid., PZ6608/37, record of meeting

with Ballantyne at the India Office, 6 Oct 1937.)

50. Roughly translated, 'hot air'. (Ibid., PZ1624/38, Political Resident to India Office, 3 Mar 1938).

51. The demands included a 20 per cent interest in the company, 1000 rifles, the establishment of a school, the appointment of his representative at a salary of £500 in gold, and the right to try all foreigners in local courts (ibid., PZ6722/37, Political Agent Bahrain to Political Resident, 10 Sep 1937 (extract)).

52. L/P&S/12/3886, PZ4370/37, Political Resident to India Office, 4 July 1937 (telegram).

53. Ibid., PZ4578/37, Political Resident to India Office, 12 July 1937 (telegram).

54. Ibid., PZ1241/38, Political Resident to India Office, 16 Feb 1938.

55. Ibid., PZ2253/38, Officiating Political Resident to India Office, 27 Mar 1938. See also L/P&S/18, B467, 'Sharjah Oil Concession'.

56. L/P&S/12/3836, PZ2689/38, Officiating Political Resident to India Office, 11 Apr 1938.

57. Ibid., PZ2420/38, Longrigg to India Office, 5 Apr 1938.

58. Ibid., PZ4942/38, Fowle to Peel (India Office), 6 July 1938.

59. The question of inland exploration is discussed separately later.

60. L/P&S/12/3836, PZ217/39, Political Agent Bahrain to Political Resident, 13 Dec 1938.

61. Ibid., PZ8362/38, enclosed in Lewisohn (Petroleum Concessions) to India Office, 19 Dec 1938.

62. Ibid., Ext. 4844/46, enclosed in Longrigg to India Office, 16 July 1945.

63. L/P&S/12/3901, PZ6232/38, India Office to Longrigg, 28 Sep 1938 (draft).

64. Reported by Ballantyne to Gibson on a visit to the India Office. L/P&S/12/3836, PZ3881/38, note by Gibson, 1 June 1938.

65. Ibid., PZ1009/38, meeting recorded in a note by A. Simon, India Office, 1 Feb 1938.

66. Ibid., PZ1237/38, Political Resident to India Office, 15 Feb 1938.

67. Ibid.

68. For a reference to Basil Lermitte as a 'sort of Lawrence of Arabia of the Trucial Coast', see Richard H. Sanger, *The Arabian Peninsula* (Ithaca, NY, 1954) pp. 148–50.

69. 'Abd al-Razzaq was in many ways different from his predecessor, who had been the third member of his family to be the Residency Agent at Sharjah. 'Abd al-Razzaq was educated in India, where he took a degree in law. He then entered the Indian Civil Service, and in 1922 he was *munshi* of the Political Resident in Bushire. He was a rich man, and 'invariably took the side of the poor man and fought strenuously against the tyranny of the shaikhs and the attempts of the rich merchants to victimise the peasantry' (Raymond O'Shea, *Sand Kings of Oman* (London, 1947, p. 71).

70. L/P&S/12/4099, PZ2456/38, Political Resident to Political Agent Bahrain, 4 Mar 1938.

71. L/P&S/12/3767, PZ3545/38, 'Bahrain Intelligence Summary', no. 8 of 1938, 16–30 Apr 1938.

72. Ibid., PZ4679/38, 'Bahrain Intelligence Summary', no. 10 of 1938, 16 May–15 June 1938.
73. Ibid.
74. R/15/1/228, Political Agent Bahrain to Political Resident, 2 June 1938.
75. An agreement had been reached whereby Saudi Arabia would enforce regulations to stop the importation of slaves into the kingdom. The regulations were promulgated under Article 1(2) issued on 2 October 1936 by the Government of Saudi Arabia.
76. L/P&S/12/4099, PZ3270/38, India Office to Political Resident, 28 May 1938 (draft).
77. Ibid., PZ4402/38, Political Resident to India Office, 19 June 1938.
78. Ibid.
79. Ibid., minute, 29 June 1938.
80. Ibid., PZ5038/38, minute, 25 July 1938.
81. L/P&S/12/3836, PZ6290/38, Officiating Political Resident to India Office, 3 Sep 1938.
82. L/P&S/12/3837, PZ36/39, Political Agent Bahrain to Political Resident, 3 Jan 1939 (telegram).
83. Copy available in L/P&S/12/3910. Enclosed in PZ508/39, Lewisohn to India Office, 23 Jan 1939. The political agreement was signed on 11 April 1940. At ibid., PZ1938/40.
84. Ibid., PZ776/39, Longrigg to Petroleum Concessions, 13 Jan 1939. Enclosed in Longrigg to Political Agent Bahrain, 12 Jan 1939.
85. Ibid., PZ776/39, Political Resident to India Office, 26 Jan 1939.
86. Note inscribed in margin, ibid., at the India Office. In the meantime, Fowle had changed his mind about the proposed action against Shakhbut. After investigations and consideration of the evidence (including that of an unnamed secret agent engaged for the purpose), Weightman was satisfied that Shakhbut was quite innocent of the charges against him of complicity in the slave trade. Furthermore, Fowle acknowledged that it would be wise to cultivate better relations with the ruler of Abu Dhabi, especially in view of the strong anti-British sentiments in Palestine at the time. Anglo-Arab relations could only be further exacerbated if the fort of an Arab ruler were bombarded by British guns. Fowle also felt that Shakhbut had suffered sufficient inconvenience from the withdrawal of his travel papers and that they should therefore be restored to him. (L/P&S/12/4099, PZ2114/39, Political Resident to India Office, 18 Mar 1939.)
87. Longrigg, *Oil in the Middle East*, p. 116.

CHAPTER 8
1. Burrell, in *The Arabian Peninsula*, ed. Hopwood, pp. 172–3.
2. Ibid.
3. L/P&S/10, P4535/1928(2), P6794/29, Political Resident to Government of India, 5 Sep 1929.
4. Ibid., P2958/30, Political Resident to India Office, 11 May 1930 (telegram).
5. L/P&S/12/3709, list of conditions enclosed in PZ3254/31, Political Resident to Government of India, 11 May 1931.

6. Ibid., PZ6130/33, Political Resident to Government of India, 25 Sep 1933 (telegram).
7. Ibid., PZ7757/33, Political Resident to British Minister Tehran, 16 Nov 1933 (telegram).
8. Ibid., PZ5820/33, Senior Naval Officer to Political Resident, 4 Sep 1933 (telegram). This had been communicated to the SNO by the Residency Agent.
9. Ibid., PZ3360/34, Senior Naval Officer to Commander-in-Chief East Indies, 17 May 1934 (telegram).
10. Ibid., PZ4383/34, Foreign Office to India Office, 2 July 1934.
11. Ibid., PZ5735/34, Political Resident to British Minister Tehran, 1 Sep 1934 (telegram).
12. Ibid., PZ46/35, Political Resident to India Office, 2 Jan 1935 (telegram).
13. Ibid., PZ121/35, Political Resident to Government of India, 5 Jan 1935 (telegram).
14. Ibid., PZ504/35, Political Resident to Government of India, 22 Jan 1935 (telegram).
15. Ibid., PZ122/35, Political Resident to India Office, 5 Jan 1935.
16. Eugene Staley, 'Business and Politics in the Persian Gulf: The Story of the Wönckhaus Firm', *Political Science Quarterly*, Sep 1933. See also Busch, *Britain and the Persian Gulf 1894–1914*, pp. 369–72.
17. L/P&S/12/3798, PZ4313/34, Political Resident to India Office, 28 June 1934 (telegram).
18. Ibid., PZ6269/34, translation of agreement signed by Shaykh of Sharjah, 27 Jumada 1 1353 (7 Sep 1934). The option cost 500 rupees.
19. R/15/2/589, Political Agent Bahrain to Residency Agent, 3 July 1934.
20. J. B. Kelly, 'A Prevalence of Furies: Tribes, Politics, and Religion in Oman and Trucial Oman', in *The Arabian Peninsula*, ed. Hopwood.
21. R/15/6/39, Muhammad bin Sultan to Residency Agent, 14 Nov 1925 (translation). Enclosed in Residency Agent to Political Resident, 17 Nov 1925.
22. Ibid., Residency Agent to Political Resident, 17 Nov 1925.
23. This greatly annoyed Salim bin Dayayn of the Bani Ka'b, who strongly disliked the Wahhabis, but, as an ally of the Na'im, was presented with a *fait accompli* (Eccles, in *Journal of the Central Asian Society*, XIV, p. 36). It also angered Hamad bin Ahmad al-Yahyayyi, the chief of Dhank, who expressed this in a letter to the Muscat Council on 1 January 1926 (available in R/15/6/39).
24. After the death of Sultan bin Muhammad al-Hammudah, paramount shaykh of the Na'im and shaykh of Buraimi town, his sons Saqr and Muhammad succeeded him. At first they were influenced by Abu Sanda, their *wali*, who had originally been a slave. When Thomas made his journey in 1927, he regarded Muhammad as the shaykh of Buraimi, since he was living in the fort of the town. The brothers seem at first to have acted together, but over the years Saqr became the stronger. In 1936 the Na'im were so annoyed with the duumvirate that they revolted against the brothers; they claimed that the disparity between Saqr and Muhammad divided the Na'im territory into two parts, each one ruled without concern for the other (R/15/2/1865,

'Sharjah News Report', no. 8 of 1936 (Apr 1936)). The Na'im asked Rashid bin Humayd of Ajman to intervene, but he was unsuccessful. It was only the Bani Qitab and Al-bu-Shamis who lived around Buraimi who were able to settle the dispute. In 1939, when Muhammad died, he was ruling in Dhank, and Saqr was in Buraimi. The latter then assumed complete control of the Na'im.

25. L/P&S/11/294, copy of letter available in P6690/1928, Thomas to Political Resident, 13 June 1927, Appendix D (translation).
26. R/15/6/39, Thomas to Political Agent Muscat, 9 Mar 1928.
27. R/15/1/236, 'Arab States Monthly Summary', no. 2 of 1929.
28. R/15/6/39, Thomas to Political Agent Muscat, 10 Sep 1930.
29. R/15/2/544, Residency Agent to Officiating Political Resident, 9 Jumada II 1353 (19 Sept 1934).
30. An interesting note on the *zakat* paid by the Manasir and the 'Awamir was made by the Senior Naval Officer in 1931. He stated that it was no secret that the tribute paid to Ibn Sa'ud by these tribes 'came originally from the loot captured from the Trucial Coast principalities'. (L/P&S/12/1955, extract from Senior Naval Officer's letter of proceedings, 12 Oct 1931.)
31. L/P&S/11/222, P2433/26, Political Resident to Colonial Office, 9 June 1926.
32. R/15/2/544, Residency Agent to Officiating Political Resident, 9 Jumada II 1353 (19 Sep 1934).
33. R/15/1/250, enclosure in Commanding Officer HMS *Penzance* to Senior Naval Officer, 26 June 1931.
34. Abu Dhabi were Hinawi, the others all Ghafiri.
35. Although news of the truce was reported by the Residency Agent to the Commander of HMS *Hastings*, Hazza' bin Sultan denied that it had taken place; he did admit, however, that Sa'id bin Maktum was trying to reach a peaceful solution.
36. R/15/1/250, HMS *Hastings* to Senior Naval Officer, 11 July 1931 (telegram).
37. L/P&S/12/3731, PZ6573/31, 'Arab States News Summary', Aug 1931.
38. See J. C. Hurewitz, *Diplomacy in the Near and Middle East* (Princeton, NJ, 1956) vol. 1, pp. 269–72.
39. L/P&S/12/3800, PZ431/34, Political Resident to India Office, 17 Jan 1934 (telegram).
40. Ibid., PZ712/34, Political Resident to Government of India, 29 Jan 1934 (telegram).
41. This rumour originated from the Air Officer Commanding in Iraq (ibid., PZ1703/34, Political Resident to India Office, 22 Dec 1933).
42. Ibid., PZ1788/34, Political Resident to India Office, 11 Mar 1934 (telegram).
43. Ibid., PZ2300/34, Political Resident to India Office, 5 Apr 1934 (telegram).
44. Ibid., PZ2854/34, Political Resident to India Office, 22 Apr 1934 (telegram).
45. Copy available at L/P&S/18, B444.
46. A copy of the *mulhaq* is available at L/P&S/12/3848, PZ6396/35, 6

Jumada 1 1354 (6 Aug 1935). Enclosed in Political Resident to India Office, 29 Aug 1935.

47. The disclosure of the existence of direct correspondence between Ibn Sa'ud and 'Abdallah, in defiance of the treaty relations of the latter with Britain, caused the British Minister in Jeddah to protest to the king.

48. *Arbitration for the Settlement of the Territorial Dispute between Muscat and Abu Dhabi on One Side and Saudi Arabia on the Other*, Memorial of the Government of Saudi Arabia, 3 vols (Cairo, 1955).

49. For a complete account of the conversations, see ibid. See also *Arbitration Concerning Buraimi and the Common Frontier between Abu Dhabi and Saudi Arabia*, Memorial submitted by the Government of the United Kingdom of Great Britain and Northern Ireland, 2 vols (London, 1955); and J. B. Kelly, *Eastern Arabian Frontiers*.

50. For an account by Rendel of this visit, see George W. Rendel, *The Sword and the Olive* (London, 1957).

51. L/P&S/12/3837, PZ7019/37, Political Agent Bahrain to Political Resident, 27 Aug 1937.

52. Ibid., PZ7019/37, memorandum from Residency Agent to Political Agent Bahrain, 22 Aug 1937. Copy enclosed in Political Agent Bahrain to Political Resident, 27 Aug 1937.

53. Ibid.

54. Ibid., PZ7019/37, Political Agent Bahrain to Political Resident, 27 Aug 1937.

55. Ibid., PZ473/38, Foreign Office to India Office, 22 Jan 1938.

56. Ibid., PZ6291/38, Officiating Political Resident to India Office, 3 Sep 1938.

57. Ibid.

58. Ibid., PZ6291/38, Officiating Political Resident to India Office, 3 Sep 1938.

59. Ibid., PZ8037/38, Political Resident to India Office, 23 Nov 1938.

60. He was not strictly correct, for Petroleum Concessions geologists had paid a short visit to Buraimi in May 1937. For an account of Cox's visit, see Cox, in *Geographical Journal*, LXVI.

61. L/P&S/12/3837, PZ470/39, Assistant Political Agent Bahrain to Officiating Political Resident, 21 Dec 1938. Enclosed in Political Resident to India Office, 9 Jan 1939.

62. These included the above-mentioned report, plus information supplied by an unnamed agent sent to the area.

63. Quoted by Fowle in a letter to Peel (India Office): L/P&S/12/3837, PZ1191/39, 16 Feb 1939.

64. CAB 23/94, 35(38)10, 27 July 1938.

CHAPTER 9

1. L/P&S/12/3836, PZ7112/36, Officiating Political Resident to India Office, 23 Sep 1936.

2. L/P&S/12/3767, PZ8357/37, 'Bahrain Intelligence Summary', no. 20 of 1937 (1–15 Nov 1937).

3. L/P&S/12/3837, PZ5407/37, Political Resident to Political Agent Bahrain, 25 July 1935.
4. Ibid., PZ6341/37, Walton to Longrigg, 12 Oct 1937 (draft).
5. Ibid., note to Walton written at India Office by Fowle, 25 Oct 1937.
6. Ibid., PZ6341/37, note from Clauson to Symon (Assistant Principal), 25 Sep 1937.
7. Ibid., PZ3227/39, Political Resident to India Office, 4 May 1939.
8. The visit had been planned for an earlier date, but was delayed because of the death of the wife of the shaykh of Buraimi (R/15/1/276, Residency Agent to Political Resident, 25 Shawwal 1346 (17 Apr 1928)).
9. Ibid., Residency Agent to Political Resident, 25 Dhu'l Qa'dah 1346 (16 May 1928).
10. Ibid., Sultan bin Salim to Sultan bin Saqr, Dhu'l Qa'dah 1346 (May 1928) (copy). Although he did not contest the transfer of Dhayd to Ras al-Khaimah, Sultan never recognised it, and today Dhayd is still within the shaykhdom of Sharjah.
11. Muhammad bin Saqr, brother of Sultan, had raided Hamriyyah and Umm al-Qaiwain with considerable plunder of the latter; it was so serious that no one was crossing from Umm al-Qaiwain to Sharjah (R/15/1/276, Residency Agent to Political Resident, 8 Dhu'l Hijjah 1345 (9 June 1927)).
12. Ibid., Residency Agent to Political Resident, 29 Dhu'l Hijjah 1345 (30 June 1927), in which the Residency Agent enclosed copies of the agreement.
13. R/15/1/236, 'Arab States Monthly Summary', no. 7 of 1931 (Aug 1931).
14. R/15/1/268, 'Diary of Trucial Oman', no. 23 (extract), 15–31 Dec 1933.
15. L/P&S/12/3837, PZ5803/37, Longrigg to India Office, 1 Sep 1937.
16. Ibid., PZ8241/37, Political Resident to Longrigg, 10 Dec 1937.
17. Ibid., PZ1243/38, Political Resident to India Office, 16 Feb 1938.
18. Ibid., PZ1626/38, Political Resident to India Office, 4 Mar 1938.
19. Ibid., PZ3549/38, Political Resident to India Office, 13 May 1938.
20. Ibid.
21. Ibid., PZ3549/38, note to Legal Adviser of the India Office, 3 June 1938.
22. Ibid., PZ5551/38, Political Resident to India Office, 21 July 1938.
23. Ibid.
24. Ibid., PZ5551/38, minute, 3 Sep 1938.
25. L/P&S/12/3901, PZ5251/38, Longrigg to India Office, 25 July 1938.
26. L/P&S/12/3837, PZ6291/38, Officiating Political Resident to India Office, 3 Sep 1938.
27. Ibid.
28. Ibid., PZ6291/38, note by Symon (India Office) regarding discussion, 23 Sep 1938.
29. Ibid., PZ2347/39, Longrigg to India Office, 20 Apr 1939.
30. R/15/2/589, Residency Agent to Political Agent Bahrain, 4 Aug 1937, with enclosures on the territory claimed by each ruler.

31. R/15/1/294, Political Agent Bahrain to Assistant Political Agent Bahrain, 18 Sep 1937.
32. L/P&S/12/3837, PZ8241/37, Political Resident to Longrigg, 10 Dec 1937.
33. Ibid., PZ3549/38, Political Resident to India Office, 13 May 1938.
34. Ibid., PZ470/39, Assistant Political Agent Bahrain to Officiating Political Resident, 21 Dec 1938. Enclosed in Political Resident to India Office, 9 Jan 1939.
35. Ibid., PZ2945/39, minutes of meeting held with representatives of Petroleum Concessions and Political Agent Bahrain, 27–9 Apr 1939. Enclosed in Longrigg to India Office, 10 May 1939.

CHAPTER 10

1. K. G. Fenelon, *The United Arab Emirates*, (London, 1973) p. 61.
2. L/P&S/12/3827, PZ5710/31, Political Resident to Government of India, 31 July 1931.
3. Ibid., PZ6337/31, Political Resident to Government of India, 3 Sep 1931.
4. Ibid., PZ6637/34, Political Resident to Government of India, 24 Oct 1934 (telegram), first part.
5. Ibid., second part.
6. Ibid., PZ694/33, memorandum from HMS *Lupin*, 4 Nov 1934.
7. For example, a report from Dubai had it that in November 1935 Rashid bin Butti was crossing the creek of Dubai with a number of people; he was talking with someone from Sharjah, whom he suddenly threw into the sea and beat severely. Rashid's victim reported the incident to Shaykh Sa'id, but never received a reply. (R/15/2/1865, 'News Report' (Sharjah), no. 22 of 1935.)
8. Ibid., 'News Report' (Sharjah), no. 2 of 1936.
9. Ibid., 'News Report' (Sharjah), no. 19 of 1936.
10. Five days later, on 19 October, Maktum bin Rashid hit one of Sa'id bin Butti's men who was on duty as a night guard. Sa'id bin Maktum was not in Dubai at the time, so the *wali* complained to Sa'id's son Rashid, who decided to put off the matter till his father's return. (Ibid., 'News Report' (Sharjah), no. 20 of 1936.)
11. Ibid., 'News Report' (Sharjah), no. 13 of 1936.
12. Between March 1937 and March 1938, forty-seven slaves, mostly from Dubai, were set free (R/15/1/227, Political Agent Bahrain to Political Resident, 17 Mar 1938 (telegram)).
13. L/P&S/12/2198, PZ2145/38, Political Resident to India Office, 21 Mar 1938.
14. R/15/1/227, Political Agent Bahrain to Political Resident, 15 Mar 1938 (telegram).
15. L/P&S/12/2198, PZ2145/38, Political Resident to India Office, 21 Mar 1938.
16. Available in R/15/1/227, 25 Mar 1938.
17. Rais Muhammad Rasul finally· left on 26 March, and Khalaf 'Ali Zamani left on 8 April (L/P&S/12/2198, PZ2855/38, Political Agent

Bahrain to India Office, 19 Apr 1938). The leading men of the Al-bu-Falasah did not refer to the matter again, although it was reported that Umm Rashid was very much annoyed that the two men had been made to leave Dubai.

18. R/15/1/675, Political Resident to India Office, 12 Apr 1937 (telegram).

19. Ibid., Political Agent Bahrain to Political Resident, 15 May 1937 (telegram).

20. R/15/1/227, Residency Agent to Political Agent Bahrain, 19 Mar 1938.

21. L/P&S/12/2198, PZ2252/28, Political Agent Bahrain to Political Resident, 27 Mar 1938. The agreement was renewed on 22 July 1938, for five years.

22. L/P&S/12/3767, PZ4679/38, 'Bahrain Intelligence Summary', 16 May–15 June 1938.

23. Ibid., 'Bahrain Intelligence Summary', 16–30 June 1938.

24. L/P&S/12/3827, PZ5010/38, Political Resident to India Office, 8 July 1938.

25. R/15/1/916, 'Dubai Ruling Family', n. d.

26. L/P&S/12/3827, PZ5010/38, Political Resident to India Office, 8 July 1938.

27. In June 1937, during the period of indecision following the death of the ruler of Kalba, whose son was only seven years old, Sultan bin Salim ignored the Political Resident's warning to the Trucial shaykhs that they should not interfere, and went to Kalba. There he got into difficulties with the people, and had to be taken away by sloop to Bahrain, where he was suitably housed but not allowed to receive visitors. A few days later he was given permission to go home. See below, Ch. 12.

28. L/P&S/12/3827, PZ7832/38, Political Resident to Sa'id bin Maktum, 1 Oct 1938. Enclosure in letter of 8 Nov from Political Resident to India Office.

29. Ibid.

30. Ibid., PZ6911/38, Political Agent Bahrain to India Office, 9 Oct 1938 (telegram).

31. Ibid., PZ532/39, 'Persian Gulf Intelligence Report', Oct 1938.

32. Ibid., PZ6973/38, Political Agent Bahrain to India Office, 11 Oct 1938 (telegram). A movement calling for reform in Kuwait was established in July 1938, when the ruler signed a document giving power to an elected council.

33. Ibid., PZ7612/38, Political Agent Bahrain to Political Resident, 18 Oct 1938 (telegram).

34. The Indian merchants strongly opposed this form of taxation, and it was only with the help of the Residency Agent that the matter was resolved.

35. The correspondence is available in R/15/2/1882. For a transcription and annotation of the entire correspondence, see Rosemarie J. Said, 'The 1938 Reform Movement in Dubai', *Al-Abhath*, XXIII (1970) 264–318.

36. R/15/2/1882, Mani' bin Rashid to Sa'id bin Maktum, 27 Ramadan 1357 (20 Nov 1938).

37. Ibid., Hashar bin Rashid to Sa'id bin Maktum, 7 Muharram 1358 (27 Feb 1939).
38. Ibid., Mani' bin Rashid to Residency Agent, 27 Shawwal 1357 (20 Dec 1938).
39. Ibid., Mani' bin Rashid to Sa'id bin Maktum, 24 Ramadan 1357 (17 Nov 1938).
40. Ibid., Mani' bin Rashid to Sa'id bin Maktum, 11 Dhu'l Qa'dah 1357 (2 Jan 1939).
41. Ibid., Hashar bin Rashid to Sa'id bin Maktum, 7 Muharram 1358 (27 Feb 1939).
42. Ibid., Hashar bin Rashid to Residency Agent, 23 Dhu'l Hijjah 1357 (13 Feb 1939). The role of the Residency Agent during the few months for which the *majlis* survived reflected the official British policy of non-interference in internal affairs. Although the *majlis* kept the Agent informed of developments in Dubai, he did little to help either it or the ruler. When trouble broke out between the two in March 1939, he wrote to Mani', who had appealed to him for help, that he could in no way interfere with internal affairs (ibid., Residency Agent to Mani' bin Rashid, 5 Safar 1358 (26 Mar 1939)).
43. Ibid., Hashar bin Rashid to Sa'id bin Maktum, 26 Dhu'l Hijjah 1357 (16 Feb 1939).
44. Ibid.
45. Ibid., Hashar bin Rashid to Sa'id bin Maktum, 9 Muharram 1358 (1 Mar 1939).
46. L/P&S/12/3827, PZ2705/39, Political Resident to India Office, 20 Apr 1939.
47. This sum was expected to cover not only his personal, but also his official, expenses, such as the subsidies paid to visiting bedouin.
48. R/15/2/1882, Hashar bin Rashid to Sa'id bin Maktum, 11 Muharram 1358 (3 Mar 1939).
49. Ibid., Sa'id bin Maktum to Hashar bin Rashid, 17 Muharram 1358 (9 Mar 1939).
50. I am grateful to Mr Ali Tajir of Dubai for this information on Shaykhah Latifah.
51. Although Mani' complained to Sa'id about their unruly behaviour, he did not mention to which tribe they belonged, referring to them simply as bedouin (R/15/2/1882, Mani' bin Rashid to Sa'id bin Maktum, 8 Safar 1358 (30 Mar 1939). Mr Ali Tajir has informed me that the desert bedouin did not take part in the actual fighting; the only ones involved in the conflict were, on Shaykh Sa'id's side, his own men and those of his son Rashid.
52. I am grateful to Mr Ali Tajir for this information.
53. L/P&S/12/3827, PZ2705/39, Political Resident to India Office, 20 Apr 1939.
54. Fighting did finally break out in 1930, but it 'was a gentlemanly affair, and both sides used to go out at night to recover the solid cannonballs which they had fired from their ancient cannons in the previous day' (Hawley. *The Trucial States*, p. 340). The war resulted in a stalemate and the desire by Sultan bin Saqr of Sharjah to help

Mani' leave the area entirely; Mani' went to Bombay on 24 April, leaving his family behind in Buraimi.

55. L/P&S/12/3827, PZ6973/39, Political Resident to India Office, 6 Nov 1939 (telegram).

56. An interesting postscript to the career of Mani' bin Rashid is disclosed by the existence of a detailed map in Arabic of the pearl banks from Ru'us al-Jibal to Qatar; this was published in Bombay in July 1940 and is by Mani' himself. A note on the map makes reference to his own career in pearl fisheries and his need then for a good map. (Available in R/15/1/616.)

CHAPTER 11

1. L/P&S/12/3747, PZ4113/38, Political Resident to Government of India, 23 May 1938.
2. Here it must be noted that the deliberate isolation of the Coast from any outside influence made it simpler to take such drastic action; it could be reasonably assumed that no word of the bombardments would reach beyond official circles in London and Delhi.
3. L/P&S/11/195, P1343/21 (P1599/22), Political Resident to Government of India, 25 Feb 1922.
4. Ibid.
5. Ibid., P1343/21 (P2867/22), Political Resident to Government of India, 11 May 1922.
6. R/15/6/239, Political Resident to Government of India, 2 May 1925.
7. Ibid.
8. This amount Prideaux promised to return if Hamad freed the slave (ibid.).
9. L/P&S/18, B419, 'Future Policy on the Trucial Coast' (P6406/29, Political Resident to Government of India, 5 Sep 1929).
10. L/P&S/12/1966, PZ1815/33, proceedings of Commander-in-Chief East Indies, 15–16 Dec 1932 (extract).
11. L/P&S/12/3626, P6741/29, Political Resident to Government of India, 4 Aug 1929.
12. Ibid., P8047/29, Political Resident to Government of India, 24 Aug 1929.
13. A copy of the declaration of independence is available in R/15/1/276.
14. This was the figure quoted by Khalid bin Ahmad in 1924 (ibid., Khalid bin Ahmad to Political Resident (Prideaux), 25 Rabi' 11 1343 (24 Nov 1924)). It was also the figure reported to Barrett in 1929 (L/P&S/18, B419: see above, note 9).
15. Ibid.
16. R/15/1/279, Political Resident to Senior Naval Officer, 17 July 1926.
17. L/P&S/18, B419: see above, note 9.
18. L/P&S/12/3626, PZ5015/32, Political Agent Kuwait to Government of India, 4 Aug 1932 (extract).
19. R/15/1/277, Commander of HMS *Crocus* to Senior Naval Officer, 29 Nov 1929.
20. Ibid., Senior Naval Officer to Political Resident, 18 Dec 1929.
21. The nearest telegraphic facilities were at Bahrain.

22. R/15/1/276, Khalid bin Ahmad to Political Resident, Rabi' II 1343 (Nov 1924).

23. R/15/1/267, Humayd bin 'Abd al-Aziz to Political Resident, Shawwal 1338 (June, 1920).

24. Ibid., Ibn Sa'ud to Political Agent Bahrain, 1 Mar 1921 (translation). Enclosed in Political Agent Bahrain to Political Resident, 29 Mar 1921.

25. R/15/1/275, Commanding Officer HMS *Fowey* to Senior Naval Officer July 1934.

26. 'Isa's relationship with the Indian merchants who lived on the Coast is an excellent example of this. Their special position as British subjects was a constant challenge to the Agent's omnipotence. Furthermore, his own commercial interests overlapped with his duties as Agent, and one of the most common causes of strife between him and the Indians was the matter of enforcing the payment of debts.

27. L/P&S/12/1966, PZ5015/32, Political Agent Kuwait to Government of India, 4 Aug 1932.

28. L/P&S/12/1965, PZ6975/32, memorandum by Captain K. Mackay (Royal Engineers), 18 Oct 1932. Enclosed in Air Ministry to India Office, 17 Nov 1932.

29. Of the men who belonged to the Political Service Philip Woodruff remarked, 'They were picked men, picked from picked men. The service presented the possibility of a career, which, as Lord Curzon had said, might be as fascinating as any the history of the world could offer' *The Men Who Ruled India: The Guardians* (London, 1954) p. 270).

30. He later published an account of these visits: *Travels in the Middle East* (London, 1916).

31. R/1/4/143, Crown Representative Records.

32. Although Cox's appreciation of Fowle is not available in R/1/4/143, the references made to it there are not particularly laudatory. Further light on Fowle's early career in Mesopotamia is shed by H. St J. B. Philby, his colleague in those days. Trying to understand why Cox was obviously pleased with his work, Philby ruminated, 'Perhaps we shone by contrast with the lesser luminaries of the Political mess, of whom I would single out for special mention Leachman . . . and T. C. Fowle. . . . The latter was an intelligent but uninspired person who always said the commonplace thing in a commonplace way and scorned every enthusiasm for any cause or thing. I twitted him one day . . . with always talking like a leading article in the *Daily Telegraph* and I think he took it as a compliment' (*Arabian Days* (London, 1948) p. 135).

33. Sir Ronald Wingate, *Not in the Limelight* (London, 1959) p. 73. Wingate served as Political Agent in Muscat from 1919 to 1921.

34. One of the most eloquent expressions of this was written by Lieutenant-Colonel Sir A. T. Wilson, himself Officiating Political Resident from 1918 to 1920: 'We have maintained order and thereby promoted trade; we have raised the standard of living and thereby encouraged the spread of education; we have thus fostered the growth of individual

freedom and of aspiration to succeed in life. This is what we understand as civilisation and what we call progress lies in the changes of structure in the social organism which entail such consequences' (*The Persian Gulf*, p. 272).

35. A former Political Agent at Bahrain gave his views thus: 'Conditions there [on the Trucial Coast] are not unlike those on our own border in the fifteenth century—indeed, I have found a study of early Scottish history invaluable in helping me to understand their somewhat mediaeval ways' (Lieutenant-Colonel G. Dalyell of the Binns (formerly Lt-Col. Loch), 'The Persian Gulf', *Journal of the Royal Central Asian Society*, xxv (1938)).

36. 'As a jealous sheikh veils his favourite wife, so the British authorities shroud conditions in the Arab states [of the Gulf] in such thick mystery that ill-disposed propagandists might almost be excused for thinking that something dreadful is going on there' (A. R. Lindt, 'Politics in the Persian Gulf', *Journal of the Royal Central Asian Society* xxvi (1939) p. 622).

37. 'The whole affair reminds one of the old Scotch, or North Country, ballads. . . . Incidentally, it shows that in spite of an air route, air facilities, and the general opening up of the Trucial Coast, the folk there are still quite "primitive"' (L/P&S/12/3710, PZ1970/35, Political Resident to India Office, 28 Feb 1935).

38. L/P&S/12/3747, PZ7199/34, Political Resident to Government of India, 16 Nov 1934.

39. Ibid.

40. With the granting of oil concessions to American companies by Bahrain in 1932 and Saudi Arabia in 1933, American commercial interests in the Gulf became a force regarded with continual fear and suspicion by the British authorities. Japanese trade interests in Bahrain and Kuwait were particularly strong; and by 1938, when Bahrain was the only oil-producing state in the Gulf, Japanese trade held the predominant share of the Bahrain market. (L/P&S/12/3797, PZ5638/38, Political Agent Bahrain to Government of India, 6 Apr 1938).

41. L/P&S/12/3747, PZ1365/35, Air Ministry to India Office, 26 Feb 1935.

42. Ibid., PZ2853/35, Government of India to India Office, 22 Apr 1935 (telegram in three parts).

43. Ibid., minutes of Forty-Second Meeting of Middle-East (Official) Sub-Committee of CID, 24 Sep 1935 (copy).

44. Ibid., PZ2853/35, Political Resident to India Office, 21 Feb 1935 (extract).

45. L/P&S/12/1990, PZ4115/35, Political Resident to India Office, 14 June 1935 (telegram).

46. L/P&S/12/3747, PZ2367/38, Political Agent Bahrain to Political Resident, 22 Mar 1938. For information on secret-service funds and how they were allocated for the Gulf Shaykhdoms, see R/15/2/922.

47. Ibid., PZ4111/38, Political Resident to India Office, 19 May 1938.

48. Ibid., PZ1724/39, Political Agent Bahrain to Political Resident, 5 Feb 1939. Enclosed in Political Resident to Government of India, 21 Feb 1939.

49. Ibid.

50. Ibid., PZ4544/39, Political Resident to India Office, 12 July 1939.
51. Ibid.

CHAPTER 12
 1. L/P&S/20, C252.
 2. Ibid., p. 124.
 3. Ibid., p. 122.
 4. L/P&S/12/3837, Assistant Political Agent Bahrain to Political Agent Bahrain, 21 Dec 1938. Enclosed in PZ470/39, Political Resident to India Office, 9 Jan 1939.
 5. Ibid., PZ6291/38, Officiating Political Resident to India Office, 3 Sep 1938.
 6. Ibid., Assistant Political Agent Bahrain to Political Agent Bahrain, 21 Dec 1938. Enclosed in PZ470/39, Political Resident to India Office, 9 Jan 1939.
 7. Ibid., PZ3616/39, Political Resident to India Office, 9 June 1939 (telegram).
 8. K. G. Fenelon, *The Trucial States* (Beirut, 1969) p. 76.
 9. 'Rashid—Merchant Prince of the Persian Gulf', *Christian Science Monitor*, 9 Aug 1973.
10. R/15/2/1690, Residency Agent to Political Agent Bahrain, 23 Rabi' I 1355 (13 June 1936). The document itself was said to be in the safekeeping of 'Abd al-Rahman (R/15/294, Political Agent Bahrain to Assistant Political Resident, 18 Sept 1937).
11. In 1940, following the uneasy truce between Sharjah and Dubai, 'Abdallah bin Faris was sent to Dubai to discuss the terms for peace. On his returning, he was found to be trying to smuggle in ammunition concealed at the bottom of a tin of nails (L/P&S/12/3767, PZ2443/40, 'Bahrain Intelligence Summary', no. 7 of 1940 (1–15 Apr 1940).
12. L/P&S/12/3767, PZ4830/40, 'Bahrain Intelligence Summary', no. 13 of 1940 (1–15 July 1940).
13. These were Kalba, Hirah, Dibba, Fujairah, Dhayd and Hamriyyah. Hamriyyah, for example, was so strong that in 1937 the Political Agent in Bahrain, Hickinbotham, suggested that Britain enter into treaty relations with its headman, Humayd bin 'Abd al-Rahman, who had succeeded in 1931 when his father was murdered by his nephew (R/15/1/277, Political Agent Bahrain to Political Resident, 5 July 1937).
14. L/P&S/12/3767, PZ4679/38, 'Bahrain Intelligence Summary', no. 10 of 1938, 16 May –15 June 1938.
15. Ibid., PZ1115/39, 'Bahrain Intelligence Summary', no. 3 of 1939 (1–15 Feb 1939).
16. Ibid., PZ7567/39, 'Bahrain Intelligence Summary', no. 21 of 1939 (1–15 Nov 1939).
17. Copy of letter available in R/15/4/1.
18. Ibid., Residency Agent to Political Agent Bahrain, 5 Oct 1939.
19. L/P&S/12/3838, Ext. 2236/43, Political Agent Bahrain to Political Resident, 14 May 1944.
20. Ibid.

21. L/P&S/10, P595/1927(3), PZ1160/31, Senior Naval Officer to Commander-in-Chief East Indies, 18 Nov 1930 (extract).
22. L/P&S/12/3767, PZ1562, 'Bahrain Intelligence Summary', no. 6 of 1935 (15–31 Mar 1935).
23. R/15/1/677, Political Agent Bahrain to Political Resident, 31 July 1937.
24. L/P&S/12/3882, PZ3286/37, Political Resident to Government of India, 19 May 1937 (telegram).
25. Ibid., PZ4140/37, Political Resident to Government of India, 24 June 1937 (telegram).
26. Ibid.
27. Ibid., PZ5958/37, 'Persian Gulf Intelligence Report', June 1937 (extracts).
28. Ibid., PZ7615/37, Officiating Political Resident to India Office, 13 Nov 1937.
29. Ibid.
30. Ibid.
31. Ibid.
32. Ibid.
33. A translation of the undertaking, signed on 11 Rajab 1356 (17 Sep 1937), is enclosed ibid.
34. 'Handsome in a negro fashion, he was a sulky-looking youth and, I was confidentially informed, was already a past-master in the traditional desert intrigues (O'Shea, *The Sand Kings of Oman*, p. 24).
35. R/15/1/284, Sultan bin Saqr to Political Resident, 27 Safar 1353 (11 June 1934).
36. Ibid., 29 Muharram 1353 (14 May 1934).
37. Ibid., minute, 6 Nov 1934.
38. R/15/2/916, 'Dubai Ruling Family', n. d.

CHAPTER 13
1. J. E. H. Boustead, 'Abu Dhabi, 1761–1963', *Journal of the Royal Central Asian Society*, L (1963) 273.
2. L/P&S/12/3837, PZ6237/37, Political Agent Bahrain to Political Resident, 12 Aug 1937. Enclosed in Officiating Political Resident to India Office, 27 Aug 1937.
3. L/P&S/12/3828, Political Resident to India Office, 28 Oct 1945 (telegram).
4. *Arbitration Concerning Buraimi* ... (UK memorial); and *Arbitration for the Settlement of the Territorial Dispute* ... (Saudi memorial).
5. The USA was the first country to claim ownership of its continental shelf, defined as the area of the seabed running from the coast down to a depth of 100 fathoms (i.e. regardless of whether or not it was covered by the pre-war definition of the extent of territorial waters). By being able to claim ownership of its continental shelf, the riparian state acquired ownership of such oil deposits as lay beneath it.
6. The ADMA was later to give up a portion of its concession to the Abu Dhabi Oil (Japan) Company.
7. In 1965 the ADPC gave up part of its concession, and this was taken over by Philips Petroleum.

8. Ragei El Mallakh, 'The Challenge of Affluence: Abu Dhabi', *Middle East Journal*, XXIV (1970).

9. The political situation in Aden during the last two years of British rule was dominated by the emergence of two nationalist organisations: the Front for the Liberation of Occupied South Yemen (FLOSY), and the National Liberation Front (NLF). It was the latter that claimed the creation of the People's Republic of South Yemen (known today as the People's Democratic Republic of Yemen) when the British forces hurriedly evacuated in November 1967.

10. Trevelyan, in *Journal of the Royal Central Asian Society*, LX, 254.

Appendix 1: Genealogy of the Ruling Families of the Trucial States

Qawāsim: Ruling Family of Sharjah, Ras al-Khaimah and Kalba

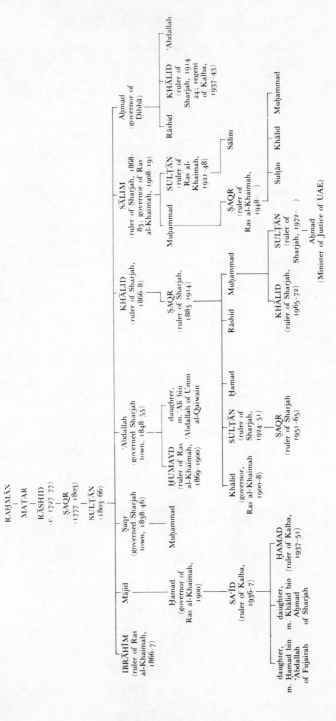

Āl-bū-Khuraybān (Naʿīm): Ruling Family of Ajman

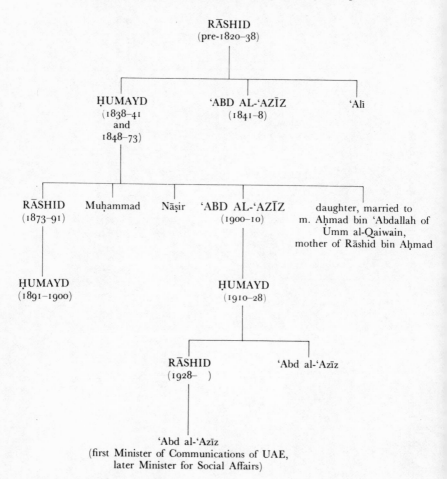

RĀSHID
(pre-1820–38)

HUMAYD
(1838–41
and
1848–73)

ʿABD AL-ʿAZĪZ
(1841–8)

ʿAlī

RĀSHID
(1873–91)

Muḥammad

Nāṣir

ʿABD AL-ʿAZĪZ
(1900–10)

daughter, married to
m. Aḥmad bin ʿAbdallah of
Umm al-Qaiwain,
mother of Rāshid bin Aḥmad

HUMAYD
(1891–1900)

HUMAYD
(1910–28)

RĀSHID
(1928–)

ʿAbd al-ʿAzīz

ʿAbd al-ʿAzīz
(first Minister of Communications of UAE,
later Minister for Social Affairs)

Sharqiyyin: Ruling Family of Fujairah

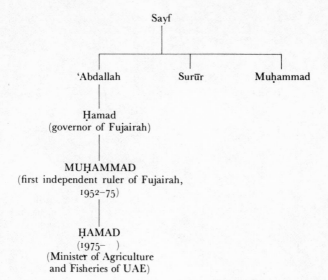

Sayf

'Abdallah   Surūr   Muḥammad

Ḥamad
(governor of Fujairah)

MUḤAMMAD
(first independent ruler of Fujairah,
1952–75)

ḤAMAD
(1975–   )
(Minister of Agriculture
and Fisheries of UAE)

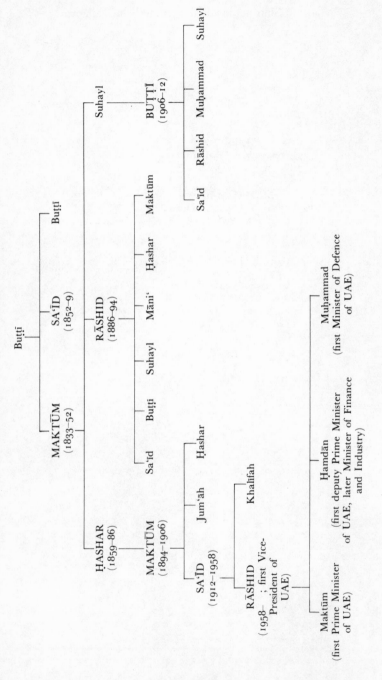

Āl-bu-Falāsah (Banī Yās): Ruling Family of Dubai

Āl-bū-Falaḥ (Banī Yās): Ruling Family of Abu Dhabi

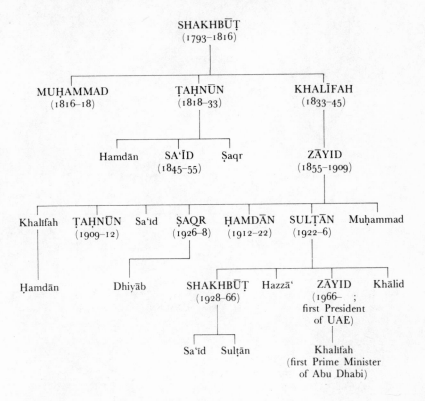

Āl-'Alī: Ruling Family of Umm al-Qaiwain

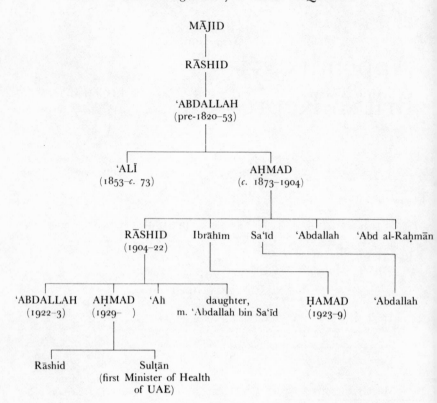

MĀJID

RĀSHID

'ABDALLAH
(pre-1820–53)

'ALĪ
(1853–c. 73)

AḤMAD
(c. 1873–1904)

RĀSHID
(1904–22)

Ibrāhīm

Sa'īd

'Abdallah

'Abd al-Raḥmān

'ABDALLAH
(1922–3)

AḤMAD
(1929–)

'Alī

daughter,
m. 'Abdallah bin Sa'īd

ḤAMAD
(1923–9)

'Abdallah

Rāshid

Sulṭān
(first Minister of Health
of UAE)

Appendix 2:
British Representatives[1]

BUSHIRE:

1. Political Resident

April 1904: Major P. Z. Cox to act as Political Resident.
October 1905: Cox appointed P.R. protem.
Jan. 1909: Cox confirmed as Political Resident.
August 1909–March 1910: Major A. P. Trevor in charge during Cox's leave.
March 1910–December 1913: Major P. Z. Cox.
December 1913–February 1914: J. G. Lorimer in charge during Cox's leave, and died in office.
February 1914: Captain L. Birdwood in charge.
March 1914: Major S. G. Knox in charge during Cox's absence.
November 1914–January 1915: Sir Percy Cox resumed charge.
January to April 1915: Major S. G. Knox on special duty.
April 1915–November 1917: Major A. P. Trevor designated as Deputy Political Resident.
November 1917–September 1919: J. H. Bill, Deputy Political Resident.

[1] Compiled from a list prepared by the staff of the India Office Records, Foreign and Commonwealth Office, London. The dates shown here are those of the appointment of the individual officers. However, an officer may have at times assumed his duties before the official confirmation of his appointment, hence the occasional discrepancy between the date of the performance of his duties and that of his actual appointment. Other discrepancies arise from the complexity of the records.

March 1918: Lt. Col. Sir A. T. Wilson officiating.

September 1919: Major C. H. Gabriel in charge.

October 1920: Lt. Col. Wilson P.R. protem (replacing Cox).

November 1920: Lt. Col. A. P. Trevor officiating. Title of Deputy Political Resident abolished.

April 1923: Col. S. G. Knox acted during Colonel Trevor's leave.

October 1923: Colonel Trevor resumed charge.

April 1924: Lt. Col. F. B. Prideaux assumed charge.

June 1925: Lt. Col. C. G. Crosthwaite assumed charge during Prideaux's leave.

October 1925: Col. Prideaux resumed charge.

January 1927: Lt. Col. Lionel Haworth became Resident.

November 1928: Sir Frederick W. Johnston became Resident.

April 1929: Lt. Col. C. C. J. Barrett.

November 1929: Lt. Col. H. V. Biscoe.

May 1931: Major T. C. Fowle acted during Biscoe's leave.

October 1931: Biscoe resumed charge.

19 July 1932: Biscoe died in office.

28 July 1932: Lt. Col. T. C. Fowle took charge.

September 1932: Fowle confirmed as Political Resident.

July–October 1933: Loch in charge during Fowle's leave.

July–October 1934: Loch in charge during Fowle's leave.

July–October 1935: Loch in charge during Fowle's leave.

July–October 1936: Loch in charge during Fowle's leave.

August–November 1937: Olaf K. Caroe acted during Fowle's leave.

August–September 1938: H. Weightman acted during Sir T. C. Fowle's absence.

September 1939: Lt. Col. C. G. Prior became Resident.

October 1941: Lt. Col. W. R. Hay officiated as Resident.

September 1942: Lt. Col. Prior resumed charge.

October 1944: Major T. Hickinbotham.

November 1944: Sir Geoffrey Prior.

May–November 1945: Lt. Col. A. C. Galloway in charge during Prior's leave.

November 1945–May 1946: Lt. Col. Sir G. Prior.

May 1946–June 1947: Lt. Col. W. R. Hay.

August 1946: Residency moved to Bahrain.

November 1946: Lt. Col. Hay resumed charge.

June–October 1947: Galloway officiating.

October 1947–July 1948: Hay resumed charge.

July–October 1948: Galloway in charge.

October 1948: Sir Rupert Hay resumed charge.

2. Assistant to The Political Resident

August 1904: Captain A. P. Trevor.

July 1906: J. H. H. Bill temp. From November 1907 he was on special duty under orders of Political Resident.

July 1909: Major A. P. Trevor was in charge as Political Resident from August 1909 to early 1910.

April 1910: Lt. R. L. Birdwood.

February 1914: Lt. P. G. Loch.

March–August 1915: Lt. Col. R. E. A. Hamilton.

August 1915: Major M. E. Rae.

January–November 1919: Major C. H. Gabriel.

November 1919: Captain D. de M. S. Fraser.

March–August 1921: C. H. Gidney. Now called Secretary to Political Resident instead of 1st Assistant.

August–October 1921: Major M. E. Rae.

October 1921: Major G. F. W. Anson.

November 1922: H. D. G. Law.

May–November 1924: Captain G. L. Mallam.

November 1924: Captain B. Stuart-Horner.

April–December 1927: Captain C. G. Prior.

December 1927: Captain R. P. Watts.

December 1928: Major H. R. P. Dickson.

May–November 1929: Captain A. A. Russell.

November 1929: Major T. C. Fowle.

June 1930: Captain A. A. Russell.

December 1931: Captain E. H. Gastrell.

June–October 1934: Captain A. C. Galloway.

October 1934: Major R. P. Watts.

June to November 1935: G. Bazalgette.

November 1935: Major C. C. L. Ryan.

April–November 1937: Captain A. C. Galloway.

November 1937: Captain T. Hickinbotham.

March–November 1939: Captain D. H. Rushton.

November 1939: Captain A. C. Stewart.

December 1942: Captain J. B. Howes.

May 1943: P. J. Keen.

June 1943: R. G. Daubney.

July–November 1945: T. E. Rogers.

November 1945: C. J. Pelly.

March–May 1947: Major G. I. Pettigrew.

May–June 1947: G. N. Jackson.

June–December 1947: Major Pettigrew.

December 1947: Major A. L. A. Dredge.

BAHRAIN:

1. Political Agent

1904: The appointment of a Graded Officer, Political Department approved. In August, Captain F. B. Prideaux took charge as Assistant Political Agent.

September 1905: Personal and local rank of Political Agent conferred.

May 1909: Captain C. F. Mackenzie.

November 1910: Major S. G. Knox.

April 1911: Captain D. L. R. Lorimer.

November 1912: Major A. P. Trevor.

May 1914: Captain T. H. Keyes.

March–July 1916: Major H. Stewart.

July–November 1916: Captain T. C. Fowle (acting).

November 1916–March 1918: Captain P. G. Loch.

March–December 1918: G. A. Mungavin.

December 1918–June 1919: Captain N. N. E. Bray.

June–November 1919: Syed Siddiq Hasan (acting).

November 1919: Major H. R. P. Dickson.

November 1920: Syed Siddiq Hasan (acting).

January 1921: Captain C. K. Daly.

May 1925: Captain G. L. Mallam (acting).

November 1925: Lieutenant-Colonel C. K. Daly resumed charge.

September 1926: Colonel C. C. J. Barrett.

April–November 1927: Major R. G. E. W. Alban.

November 1927: Colonel Barrett.

April 1929: Captain C. G. Prior.

November 1932: Colonel P. G. Loch.

July–November 1933: Colonel E. H. Gastrell (acting).

November 1933: Colonel P. G. Loch.

July–October 1934: M. Worth (acting).

October 1934: Colonel Loch resumed charge.

March–October 1935: Captain G. A. Cole (acting).

October 1935: Colonel Loch resumed charge.

May–October 1936: Captain T. Hickinbotham (acting).

October 1936: Colonel Loch resumed charge.

April–August 1937: Captain T. Hickinbotham (acting).

August–September 1937: Lieutenant B. L. M. Tomlinson (acting).

September–October 1937: Captain T. Hickinbotham (acting).

October 1937: Hugh Weightman.

August–September 1938: Captain J. B. Howes (acting).

September 1938: H. Weightman resumed charge.

October 1940: Major R. G. E. W. Alban.

January 1942: B. B. Wakefield.
August–October 1943: Captain M. G. Dixon (acting).
One day in October 1943: Mr. Wakefield resumed charge.
7 October 1943: Major T. Hickinbotham.
July–August 1944: T. E. Rogers (acting).
August 1944: Major Hickinbotham resumed charge.
March–November 1945: C. J. Pelly.
November 1945: Lieutenant Colonel A. C. Galloway.
July–September 1946: Major H. D. H. Rance.
September–October 1946: Colonel A. C. Galloway.
October–November 1946: Major Rance.
November 1946: Colonel A. C. Galloway.
March–July 1947: C. J. Pelly.
One week in July 1947: G. N. Jackson.
July–August 1947: Major H. D. H. Rance.
August–November 1947: G. N. Jackson.
November 1947: C. J. Pelly.
10 days in June 1949: P. D. Stobart.
June–October 1949: H. G. Jakins.
October–November 1949: J. A. F. Gethin.
November 1949: C. J. Pelly.

2. *Assistant Political Agent*

February 1900: J. C. Gaskin appointed temporarily.
June 1901: J. C. Gaskin appointed.
October 1904: Captain F. B. Prideaux.
January 1905: Captain Prideaux appointed Assistant Political Agent.
May 1924: Sanction given to temporary appointment for six months of military probationer for Political Department of Government of India as Assistant to Political Agent Bahrain. Captain D. R. Smith appointed.
In October 1924, Captain Smith was transferred and Government of India said another officer could not be spared.
March 1934: Government of India agreed to temporary post as ex-cadre appointment to be filled by junior officer of Political Department for six months at first, but it was prolonged from time to time and was still temporary for one year from March 1947.
May 1934: M. Morth assumed duties.
March–April 1935: Captain G. A. Cole.
April–October 1935: Lt. R. D. Metcalfe.
October, 1935: Captain G. A. Cole.
April–May 1936: Captain T. Hickinbotham.

May–December 1936: Lt. J. B. Howes.
December 1936: Captain A. C. Stewart.
April–November 1937: Lt. B. L. M. Tomlinson.
November 1937: Captain A. C. Galloway.
February–September 1938: Lt. R. E. R. Bird.
September 1938: Captain J. B. Howes.
May 1939: R. I. Hallows.
March–July 1940: C. R. Latimer (acting).
July 1940: Captain R. D. Metcalfe (acting).
January 1941: G. N. Jackson took charge from R. I. Hallows.
June 1942: Captain M. G. Dixon.
December 1942: R. M. Hadow.
August–October 1943: Captain M. P. O'C. Tandy (acting).
October–December 1943: Captain M. G. Dixon.
December 1943: R. M. Hadow.
June–July 1944: T. E. Rogers.
July–August 1944: R. M. Hadow in addition to Political Officer, Trucial Coast.
August–October 1944: T. E. Rogers.
October–November 1944: R. M. Hadow.
November 1944: Captain M. P. O'C. Tandy.
February–March 1945: Captain R. E. R. Bird.
March–April 1945: Captain Tandy.
April 1945: Captain Bird.
February–July 1946: Captain H. D. H. Rance.
July–September 1946: Captain J. E. H. Hudson.
September–October 1946: Captain Rance.
October–November 1946: Captain Hudson.
November 1946: Captain Rance.
June–July 1947: C. J. Pelly (in addition to Political Agent).
July–August 1947: G. N. Jackson.
August–November 1947: G. N. Jackson (in addition to Political Agent).
One week in November 1947: G. N. Jackson.
November 1947: C. J. Pelly (in addition to Political Agent).
January–August 1948: Major J. E. H. Hudson.
August–September 1948: P. D. Stobart.
September 1948: Major Hudson.

RESIDENCY AGENTS IN SHARJAH

1890–1909: K. B. 'Abd al-Latif
1909–1935: K. B. 'Isa bin 'Abd al-Latif

1935: K. S. Husayn 'Imad (interim)
1936: K. B. 'Abd al-Razzaq Razzuqi al-Mahmud
1945: Jasim bin Muhammad Kadmar.[1]
(Appointment abolished in 1949)

MUSCAT

Political Agent

January 1904: Captain W. G. Grey.
July–November 1906: Captain W. H. I. Shakespear.
November 1906: Major W. G. Grey.
April–July 1908: Captain N. Scott.
July–November 1908: Captain F. McConaghey.
November 1908: Mr. R. E. Holland.
April 1910: Major A. P. Trevor.
April 1911: Major S. G. Knox.
March 1914: Lt. Col. R. A. E. Benn.
October 1915: Major H. Stewart.
January–February 1916: Lt. Col. C. T. Ducat.
February–March 1916: Major H. Stewart.
March–June 1916: Lt. Col. C. T. Ducat.
8 days in June 1916: Major A. R. Burton (acting).
June–October 1916: Major E. B. Howell.
October–November 1916: Major A. R. L. King-Mason (acting).
November 1916: Major L. B. H. Haworth.
November–December 1917: Captain J. M. Brickman (acting).
December 1917: Major L. B. H. Haworth.
October 1919: R. E. L. Wingate.
October 1921: Major R. E. Rae.
March–September 1923: R. E. L. Wingate.
18 days in September 1923: M. J. Gadzar.
September 1923: Major R. G. Hinde.
October 1924: Lt. Col. C. G. Crosthwaite.
April–October 1925: Captain R. G. E. W. Alban (acting).
October 1925: Lt. Col. C. G. Crosthwaite.
February–September 1926: Major C. C. J. Barrett.
13 days in September 1926: G. A. Richardson (acting).
September 1926: Major G. P. Murphy.
June 1930: Major T. C. Fowle.
April–November 1931: Captain R. G. Alban (acting).

---

[1] Donald Hawley, *op. cit.*, p. 328.

November 1931: Major T. C. Fowle.
July–November 1932: Captain R. G. Alban (acting).
November 1932: Major C. E. U. Bremmer.
March–June 1933: Captain R. G. Alban.
June 1933: Major C. E. U. Bremmer.
June 1935: Major R. P. Watts.
April 1939: Capt. T. Hickinbotham.
April–June 1940: Captain J. B. Howes (acting).
July 1940: Captain T. Hickinbotham.
August 1941: Captain J. B. Howes.
January–May 1942: Major R. G. E. W. Alban.
May 1942: C. J. Pelly.
September–November 1943: Captain R. E. R. Bird.
November 1943: Captain R. D. Metcalfe.
October 1944: Lt. Col. A. C. Galloway.
April 1945: R. I. Hallows.
9 days in November 1946: Major J. E. H. Hudson.
November 1946: Major A. C. Stewart.
June–August 1947: Captain J. E. H. Hudson.
August 1947: Major A. C. Stewart.
April–August 1948: P. D. Stobart.
August 1948: R. E. Ellison.
July–September 1949: R. McC. Andrew.
September 1949: Major F. C. L. Chauncy.

Bibliography

INDIA OFFICE RECORDS (FOREIGN AND COMMONWEALTH OFFICE, LONDON)*

R/15 Persian Gulf Territories, Residency Records

R/15/1 Bushire, Political Residency

The records of the Persian Gulf Residency at Bushire cover the period 1763–1948. They were deposited with the India Office Library and Records in 1957–65 and include correspondence between the Resident and the Political Agents in the Gulf; the Government of India; various Departments of the British Government; the Air Officer Commanding, Iraq; the Senior Naval Officer Persian Gulf Division; the British Minister in Tehran; the High Commission in Baghdad; local rulers and notables; the Residency Agent at Sharjah; and various oil companies.

For the period covered in this study these records were organised into subject files. General subjects have a number, and a second number indicates the specific topic within that general subject. The files also include internal minutes, which can be found at the end of each volume.

---

* For a complete guide to these records with relevance to the Gulf, see Penelope Tuson, *The Records of the British Residency and Agencies in the Persian Gulf* (London: HM Stationery Office, forthcoming).

The following files were the most useful for this study:

Slave Trade: vols 199–234
Arab Coast and Islands: vols 239–94
Arab Coast Miscellaneous
Judicial: vols 295–312
Bahrain: vols 314–77
Muscat: vols 408–47
Kuwait: vols 478–85, 513–49

R/15/2   Bahrain Political Agency

The Agency at Bahrain had three separate offices: the Confidential Office, the English Office and the Vernacular Office. The files of the Confidential Office were based on a subject-file system: each subject was given a number and each file on the subject a part number. The files are organised at the India Office Records according to the three different methods of classification used, at different times, at the Agency. The groups are as follows: 1899–1921, files R/15/2/1–72; 1921–32, files R/15/2/73–138; and 1932–50, files R/15/2/139–916. The English Office files (R/15/2/946–1823) run from 1907 to 1950 and are organised on the same basic principles as the Confidential Office files (i.e. by subject). The Vernacular Office files (R/15/2/1824–1980) contain two different kinds of correspondence: first, consular and judicial; and, second, translations of documents sent and received by the Agency.

For the present study, the most valuable files from the different offices were those in the following subject groups:

Confidential
Political Administration
Bahrain State
Saudi Relations
Shipping
Diaries
Trucial Coast
Qatar
Arab Coast
Slavery
Royal Air Force
Saudi Arabia
Treaties
Visits

English
Bahrain State
Trade and Commerce
Shipping
Qatar
Consular
Slave Trade

Vernacular
Slavery
Miscellaneous Claims
Miscellaneous Correspondence

R/15/4   Political Agency, Trucial Oman

When, in 1939, a Political Officer for the Trucial Coast was appointed, his headquarters were in Sharjah. Only ten files survive, the remainder probably having been destroyed. Of these the following are at present open to readers:

R/15/4/1   Sharjah affairs, 1937–48
R/15/4/2   Fujairah affairs, 1941–8
R/15/4/3   Boundaries, 1935–49
R/15/4/4   Copies of agreements, concessions, etc., 1930–48

R/15/5   Political Agency, Kuwait

The Political Agency in Kuwait was established in 1904, and the Agency files preserved in the India Office Records cover the period 1904–49. They are basically all classified by subject.

R/15/6   Political Agency, Muscat

Although the Political Agency in Muscat was founded in 1800, little has been preserved from before 1865. Classification is by subject. For the purposes of the present study, reference was made to files in the following subject groups:

Arms Traffic
Aviation
Books and Publications
Establishment
Foreign Interests
Judicial
Muscat State Affairs

Naval and Shipping
Political
Trade and Commerce
Visitors, Suspects and Undesirables
Travels in Oman
Internal Politics and Relations with Oman

L/P&S/10   Departmental Papers: Political and Secret Subject Files, 1902–31

L/P&S/11   Departmental Papers: Political and Secret Annual Files, 1912–30 (vols. 30–308)

L/P&S/12   Departmental Records: Political (External) Files and Collections, c. 1931–50

Until 1930, the Political Department of the India Office, with just one secretary, was concerned with both the affairs of the Indian states and the foreign policy of the Government of India. L/P&S/10 and L/P&S/11 contain political and secret (P&S) subject and annual files, respectively; the individual papers of the Political Department at this time all had the prefix P.

After 1930, the work of the Political Department was divided between two new sections, each with its own secretary: the Political (Internal) Department, concerned with all work related to the Indian states; and the Political (External) Department, which dealt with foreign affairs. It is in the records of the latter, L/P&S/12, that post-1930 Political Department records relating to the Gulf are to be found.

In the L/P&S/12 records, the individual papers all have a prefix of PZ, to distinguish them from those of the Political (Internal) Department, PY. In 1941, when the Political (External) Department became the External Department, the prefix was changed to Ext.

Of the fifty-nine subject divisions, or collections, in L/P&S/12, the following were used for the present study:

Aircraft and Aviation: vols 1947–66
Arabia: vols 2064–158
Arms and Ammunition and Arms Traffic: vols 2186–212
Establishment and Secretariat Procedure: vols 2773, 2782–4, 2790–1, 2800
Muscat: vols 2951–95
Orders-in-Council: vols 3304, 3306, 3312, 3314–19, 3321–38
Passports: vols 3369–84
Persia, Persian Gulf (HM Consuls and Consulates in): vols 3551–698

Persian Gulf: vols 3709–967
Slavery and Slave Trade: vols 4088–99
Telegraphs, Postal, Wireless: vols 4125–37, 4143–8
Travellers: vols 4252, 4256, 4338–40
War (Defence, Protective and Other Measures): vols 4487–500

L/P&S/18 Political and Secret Memoranda, Section B (includes
          Persian Gulf)

B367 Foreign Office Memorandum on Arabian Policy.
      Major H. W. Young, c. Jan 1921. 18 pp., confidential

B368 Eastern (Arabia). Memorandum by Col. Kinahan Cornwallis
      on the Future Policy of His Majesty's Government with
      Regard to Subsidies to the Chiefs of the Arabian Peninsula.
      Foreign Office, 16 Dec 1920. 7 pp.

B376 Arabia. Subsidies to Rulers.
      Oct 1923. 2 pp.

B381 Anglo-Turkish Agreement. Collection of Documents Signed
      on July 29, 1913.
      Foreign Office (Asiatic Turkey and Arabia), 29 Jul 1913.
      Section 5. 14 pp., map; confidential

B385 The Kuwait Order in Council, 1925.
      Buckingham Palace, 17 Mar 1925

B386 Arabia. Agreements with the Sultan of Nejd Regarding Cer-
      tain Questions Relating to the Nejd—Transjordan and
      Nejd—Iraq frontier.
      Parliamentary Papers (House of Commons), 1924–5, vol. xxx,
      Cmd 2566.

B387 Memorandum by the Political Department, India Office,
      on Treaties and Agreements between the British Government
      and the Various Rulers and Chiefs in Arabia and the Persian
      Gulf.
      D. T. Monteath, July 1927. 6 pp., confidential

B389 Treaty between His Majesty and His Majesty the King
      of Hejaz and of Nejd and its Dependencies, May 20th 1927,
      together with Notes Exchanged, May 19th–21st 1927.
      Parliamentary Papers (House of Commons), 1927, vol. xxvi,
      Cmd 2951. 8 pp.

B390 Memorandum: (a) the Sultanate of Muscat and Oman, (b) His Highness The Sultan Saiyid Taimur bin Faisal bin Turki. Bertram Thomas, Wazir, 1928. 5 pp.

B391 British Political Relations with Koweit.
J. W. Field, Foreign Office, 29 Mar 1922, 3 pp., confidential

B392 Wireless Telegraph Stations in the Persian Gulf.
Aug 1928. 3 pp., confidential

B393 Political Control in the Persian Gulf.
J. G. Laithwaite, 5 Oct 1928. 3 pp., confidential

B394 Quarantine control in the Persian Gulf.
J. G. Laithwaite, 19 Aug 1928. 6 pp., confidential

B395 Koweit, 1908–1928.
J. G. Laithwaite, 1 Oct 1928. 14 pp., confidential

B396 Bahrein, 1908–1928.
J. G. Laithwaite, 8 Oct 1928. 12 pp., confidential

B397 Status of the Islands of Tamb, Little Tamb, Abu Musa, and Sirri.
J. G. Laithwaite, 24 Aug 1928. 8 pp., confidential

B398 The Rebellion against the Sultan of Muscat, May 1913–July 1916.
Gertrude Bell. 11 pp. (Received from the Chief Political Officer, Basra, under cover of Sir Percy Cox's letter of 18 Aug 1916)

B399 Status of Certain Groups of Islands in the Persian Gulf.
J. G. Laithwaite, 27 Aug 1928. 4 pp., confidential

B400 Muscat, 1900–28.
J. G. Laithwaite, 25 Aug 1928. 17 pp., confidential

B401 Lighting and Buoying of the Persian Gulf, 1908–1928.
M. J. Clauson, 29 Aug 1928. 6 pp., confidential

B402 El Katr, 1908–1916.
J. G. Laithwaite, 5 Sep 1928. 2 pp., confidential

B403 The Trucial Chiefs, 1908–1928.
J. G. Laithwaite, 4 Oct 1928. 8 pp., confidential

B404 Position and Rights of His Majesty's Government in Basidu.
J. G. Laithwaite, 1 Oct 1928. 6 pp., confidential

B405 Henjam. Position and Rights of His Majesty's Government in the Island of Henjam. The Sheikh of Henjam and His Affairs.
J. G. Laithwaite, 26 Sep 1928. 8 pp., confidential

B406 Question of British Consular representation in El Hasa and Qatif.
J. G. Laithwaite, 24 Sep 1928. 2 pp., confidential

B407 Slavery in the Persian Gulf.
J. G. Laithwaite, 29 Sep 1928. 4 pp., confidential

B408 Persian Complaints of Smuggling in the Persian Gulf.
J. G. Laithwaite, 1 Oct 1928. 2 pp., confidential

B409 Précis of Treaties and Engagements between the British Government and the Chiefs of the Arabian Coast of the Persian Gulf.
29 Sep 1928. 6 pp., confidential

B410 Arms Traffic in the Persian Gulf, 1908–1928.
J. G. Laithwaite, 8 Oct 1923. 4 pp., confidential

B411 Note on Trade in the Persian Gulf (Communicated by the Board of Trade).
Oct 1928. 4 pp., confidential

B412 Persian Coasting Trade (Communicated by the Board of Trade, 20 Aug 1928).
Oct 1928. 2 pp., confidential

B413 Oil Interests in the Persian Gulf. Communicated by the Board of Trade and Revised to 28 June 1928.
Oct 1928. 1 p., confidential

B414 Air Communication in the Persian Gulf (Communicated by the Air Ministry, 23 August 1928).
Sep 1928. 5 pp., confidential

B415 Question of Issue of Persian Passports or Travelling Passes (Ilm-o-khabar) to subjects of Bahrein, 1910–1922.
J. G. Laithwaite, 14 Aug 1928. 8 pp.

B416   Report on Sur. Major G. P. Murphy IA, Indian Political
       Department, Political Agent Muscat. (Corrected up to 10th
       October 1928.)
       Jan 1928. 20 pp., confidential

B417   Grant by Certain Political Officers in the Persian Gulf of
       Licences to Ply the Coasting Trade and Fly the British
       Flag. Question of the Extension of this Practice to Cover
       the Subjects of the Arab Protectorates.
       J. G. Laithwaite, 15 Feb 1929. 5 pp.

B419   Future Policy on the Trucial Coast. Correspondence between
       the Secretary of State for India, the Government of India
       and the Political Resident in the Persian Gulf (1929).
       J. G. Laithwaite, 23 Oct 1929. 10 pp., confidential

B420   Question of British Interference in the Administration of
       Bahrein. Despatch no. 385S from the Hon. Lt.-Col. C. C.
       J. Barrett CSI, CIE, Political Resident in the Persian Gulf,
       to the Foreign Secretary to the Government of India, Simla
       (28 August 1929).
       Oct 1929. 8 pp., secret

B421   Situation of Persian Gulf Residency. Arguments for and
       against Koweit and Bahrein as alternatives to Bushire. Lt.-Col.
       C. C. J. Barrett, Jul–Aug 1929.
       10 Jan 1930. 5 pp., secret

B422   Exercise of Jurisdiction in Cases Affecting Foreign Subjects
       in Bahrein by the British Political Authorities.
       J. G. Laithwaite, 3 Mar 1930. 4 pp., confidential

B425   Translation of Lease by Sheikh Mubarak of Koweit of the
       Bunder Shweikh lands and of the Acceptance of that Lease
       by the Political Agent, Koweit, both dated 15 October 1907.
       17 pp.

B426   Oil Concessions Signed by the Sheikh of Bahrein in Favour
       of the Eastern and General Syndicate on the 2nd December
       1925.
       Aug 1933. 7 pp.

B427   Final Record of a Meeting Held at the Foreign Office on
       Thursday, 5 Oct [1933] to Discuss Relations between His

Majesty's Government in the United Kingdom and the Sheikh of Koweit.
17 pp.

Including note by Sir A. Ryan on 'Ibn Saud's attitude towards Koweit', *with* provisional note by J. G. Laithwaite on 'Obligations of His Majesty's Government towards the Sheikh of Koweit'.
11 Oct 1933. 8 pp., confidential

B429 Text of Treaty, Dated November 3, 1916 and Ratified on March 23, 1918, between His Majesty's Government and Sheikh Abdullah-bin-Jasim-bin-Thani of al-Katar.
Dec 1933. 3 pp.

B430 The Southern Boundary of Qatar and the Connected Problems.
J. G. Laithwaite, 26 Jan 1934. 9 pp., secret

With Note on Discussion with Sir Percy Cox on 24th February on Question of Boundaries of Qatar.
J. G. Laithwaite, 27 Feb 1934. 2 pp.

B431 Relations between His Majesty's Government in the United Kingdom and the Sheikh of Koweit.
Foreign Office, 1934. 20 pp., secret

B432 Koweit Oil. 1. Political Agreement of 5th March 1934 between His Majesty's Government in the United Kingdom and the Kuwait Oil Company. 2. Commercial Agreement of 23rd December 1934 between His Excellency the Sheikh of Koweit and the Kuwait Oil Company.
Mar 1935. 11 pp., confidential

B433 Red Oxide on Abu Musa, 1898–1934.
J. G. Laithwaite, May 1934. 6 pp.

B434 Koweit Civil Air Agreement (23 May 1934).
July 1934. 6 pp., confidential

With typescript copy amended to July 1940.
7 pp., confidential

B435 Bahrein Civil Air Agreement (6 June 1934).
July 1934, 5 pp., confidential

With typescript copy amended to July 1940.
7 pp., confidential

B436   Historical Memorandum on Bahrein.
        J. G. Laithwaite, 14 July 1934. 46 pp., confidential

B437   Historical Memorandum on the Relations of the Wahabi
        Amirs and Ibn Saud with Eastern Arabia and the British
        Government, 1800–1934.
        J. G. Laithwaite, 1 Sep 1934. Revised version: 26 Sep 1934.
        55 pp., map; confidential

B438   Muscat. Question of Whether a Naval Station Could be
        Established for Use by His Majesty's Ships at Khor Quwai
        or Elsewhere in Muscat Territory Compatibly with the Exist-
        ing International Agreements of His Majesty's Government.
        J. G. Laithwaite, 2 Nov 1934. 12 pp., confidential

B440   Air Navigation Regulations for Civil Aircraft for the Territory
        of Bahrein, and Conditions Governing the Use of the Aero-
        drome at Muharraq Approved by His Excellency Sheikh
        Hamad bin 'Isa Al Khalifah csi, Ruler of Bahrein.
        Aug 1934. 3 pp.

        With duplicate of B435

B441   Air Navigation Regulations for Civil Aircraft for the Territory
        of Koweit, and the Conditions Governing the Use of the
        Aerodrome at Koweit, Approved by His Excellency Sheikh
        Sir Ahmad Al-Jabir As-Sabah kcie, csi, Ruler of Koweit.
        Aug 1934. 3 pp.

B442   Territory of Muscat and Oman. 1. Air Navigation Regulations
        for Civil Aircraft Made by His Highness the Sultan of Muscat
        and Oman. 2. Gwadur Aerodrome. Conditions Laid Down
        with the Approval of the Sultan to Govern the Use of
        the Aerodrome.
        May 1935. 4 pp.

B443   Muscat Civil Air Agreement.
        June 1935. 8 pp., confidential

B444   Oil Concession Granted by Shaikh of Qatar to the Anglo-Per-
        sian Oil Co. Ltd., Dated 17th May 1935.
        Feb 1936. 7 pp., confidential

With typescript copy of 'Agreement Relating to the Transfer of the Qatar Oil Concession' (to the Anglo-Iranian Oil Co. Ltd, 5 Feb 1937). 1 p.

B445 Political Agreement of 5th June 1935 between His Majesty's Government in the United Kingdom and the Anglo-Persian Oil Company Ltd.
1935. 7 pp., confidential

B446 The Seven Independent Arabian States (Yemen, Asir, Hejaz, Nejd, Koweit, Jebel Shammar and Jauf).
W. J. Childs, Foreign Office, May 1935. 19 pp., confidential

B450 The Persian Gulf.
25 June 1935. 4 pp., secret

B452 His Excellency Sheikh Hamad bin Sheikh Issa Al Khalifah Sheikh of Bahrein and the Bahrein Petroleum Company Limited. Lease.
29 Dec 1934. 15 pp., map

B453 His Excellency Shaikh Sir Hamad bin Shaikh 'Isa Al Khalifah KCIE, CSI, Shaikh of Bahrein and the Bahrein Petroleum Co. Ltd. Deed of Modification of Lease, dated 29 December 1934.
3 June 1936. 4 pp.

B454 Note on Bahrein Islands.
N.d. 5 pp.

B456 Agreement between His Majesty's Government in the United Kingdom and Petroleum Concessions Limited relating to the Debai Oil Concession.
5 Feb 1937. 4 pp.

B467 Sharjah Oil Concession, 1938.

B478 Oil Concessions in the Arab Sheikhdoms of the Persian Gulf, 13 March 1944.

L/P&S/20

C252 Military Report and Route Book: The Arabian States of the Persian Gulf.
Prepared by General Staff, India, 1939

R/1/4/143   Crown Representative Records

PUBLIC RECORD OFFICE

FO371   Eastern Affairs
CAB   Cabinet Conclusions

OFFICIAL PUBLICATIONS

Admiralty (Naval Intelligence Division), *Iraq and the Persian Gulf* (London, 1944).

Aitchison, C. U., *A Collection of Treaties, Engagements and Sanads Relating to India and Neighbouring Countries*, fifth edition (Delhi, 1933), vol. XI.

Arbitration Concerning Buraimi and the Common Frontier between Abu Dhabi and Saudi Arabia, Memorial submitted by the Government of the United Kingdom of Great Britain and Northern Ireland, 2 vols (London, 1955).

Arbitration for the Settlement of the Territorial Dispute between Muscat and Abu Dhabi on One Side and Saudi Arabia on the Other, Memorial of the Government of Saudi Arabia, 3 vols (Cairo, 1955).

J. G. Lorimer, *Gazetteer of the Persian Gulf, 'Oman and Central Arabia*, 5 vols (Calcutta, 1908–15).

The Persian Gulf Pilot, seventh edition (London: HM Stationery Office, 1924).

ARABIC PUBLICATIONS

al-'Aqqād, Ṣalāḥ, *Al-Istʿimār fī'l-Khalīj al-Fārisī* (Cairo, 1956).

al-'Aqqād, Ṣalāḥ, *Al-Tayyārāt al-Siyāsiyyah fī'l-Khalīj al-ʿArabī* (Cairo, 1965).

al-Buraynī, Aḥmad Qāsim, *Al-Imārāt al-Sabʿa ʿala'l-Sāḥil al-Akhḍar* (Beirut, 1957).

al-Dāwūd, Maḥmūd 'Alī, *Al-Khalīj al-ʿArabī wa'l-ʿAlaqāt al-Duwaliyyah 1890–1914* (Cairo, 1963).

Ḥamzah, Fu'ād, *Al-Bilād al-ʿArabiyyah al-Saʿūdiyyah* (Mecca, 1937, and Riyadh, 1968).

Ḥamzah, Fu'ād, *Qalb Jazīrat al-ʿArab* (Cairo, 1933).

Nawfal, al-Sayyid Muḥammad 'Alī, *Al-Awḍāʿ al-Siyasiyyah li Imārāt al-Khalīj al-ʿArabī* (Cairo, 1960).

Qāsim, Jamāl Zakariyya, *Al-Khalīj al-ʿArabī, 1914–19* (Cairo, 1973).

Rayyis, Riyāḍ Najīb, *Sirāʿ al-Wāḥāt w'al-Nafṭ* (Beirut, 1973).

Riḍa, 'Ādil, *'Umān wa'l Khalīj* (Cairo, 1969).

Rihani, Ameen, *Mulūk al-'Arab* (Beirut, 1925).

Rihani, Ameen, *Tarīkh Najd wa Mulḥaqātihi*, new edition (Beirut, 1972).

al-Sālimī, Muḥammad, bin 'Abdallah and Nājī 'Assāf, *Tarīkh . . . Yatakallam* (Damascus, 1963).

al-Shaybānī, Muhammad Sharīf, *Imārat Qaṭar al-'Arabiyyah bayn al-Māḍī wa'l-Ḥāḍir* (Beirut, 1962).

Sinān, Maḥmūd Bahjat, *Tarīkh Qaṭar al-'Ām* (Baghdad, 1966).

al-Siyābī, Sālim bin Ḥamūd, *Is'āf al-'Ayān fī Ansāb Ahl 'Umān* (Beirut, 1965).

al-Takrītī, SālimṬāhā, *al-Ṣirā' 'ala al-Khalīj al-'Arabī* (Baghdad, 1966).

Wahbah, Ḥāfiz, *Jazīrat al-'Arāb fī'l-Qarn al-'Ishrīn* (Cairo, 1967).

Zallūm, 'Abd al-Qādir, *'Umān wa'l Imārāt al-Sab'a* (Beirut, 1963).

EUROPEAN PUBLICATIONS

Books

Place of publication London, unless otherwise stated.

Abir, Mordechai, *Oil, Power and Politics: Conflict in Arabia, the Red Sea and the Gulf* (1974).

Adamiyat, Fereydoun, *Bahrain Islands, A Legal and Diplomatic Study of the British–Iranian Controversy* (New York, 1955).

Alfree, P. S., *Warlords of Oman* (1967).

Anthony, John Duke, *Arab States of the Lower Gulf: People, Politics, Petroleum* (Washington DC, 1975).

Aramco, *Oman and the Southern Shore of the Persian Gulf* (Cairo, 1952).

Arberry, A. J. (ed), *Religion in the Middle East*, vol. II (Cambridge, 1969).

Armstrong, H. C., *Lord of Arabia* (Beirut, 1966).

Avery, Peter, *Modern Iran* (1965).

al-Baharana, Husain M., *The Legal Status of the Arabian Gulf States* (Manchester, 1968).

Belgrave, Sir Charles Dalyrymple, *Personal Column* (1960).

Belgrave, Sir Charles Dalyrymple, *The Pirate Coast* (1966).

Bell, Gertrude, *The Arab War* (1940).

Benoist-Mechin, *Le Roi Saud ou l'Orient à l'heure des relèves* (Paris, 1960).

Benoist-Mechin, *Le Loup et le léopard, Ibn Séoud* (Paris, 1955).

Berreby, J. J., *Le Golfe persique* (Paris, 1959).

Boustead, Colonel Sir Hugh, *The Wind of Morning* (1972).

Bullard, Sir Reader, *Britain and the Middle East* (1951).

Bullard, Sir Reader, *The Camels Must Go: An Autobiography* (1961).

Busch, Briton C., *Britain and the Persian Gulf, 1894–1914* (Berkeley and Los Angeles, Calif., 1967).

Busch, Briton C., *Britain, India and the Arabs, 1914–1921* (Berkeley and Los Angeles, Calif., 1971).

Caroe, Olaf, *Wells of Power* (1951).

Cheesman, R. E., *In Unknown Arabia* (1926).

Chisholm, Archibald H. T., *The First Kuwait Oil Concession Agreement: A Record of the Negotiations, 1911–1934* (1975).

Coen, Terence Greagh, *The Indian Political Service* (1971).

Dickson, H. R. P., *The Arab of the Desert* (1967).

Dickson, H. R. P., *Kuwait and her Neighbours* (1968).

Dickson, Violet, *Forty Years in Kuwait* (1971).

Dodwell, H. H. (ed.), *The Cambridge History of India*, vol. vi (Delhi, 1958).

Esmail, Malek, *Le Golfe persique et les îles de Bahrein* (Paris, 1938).

Faroughy, Abbas, *The Bahrein Islands (750–1951)* (New York, 1951).

Fenelon, K. G., *The Trucial States* (Beirut, 1969).

Fenelon, K. G., *The United Arab Emirates* (1973).

Finnie, David H., *Desert Enterprise* (Cambridge, Mass., 1958).

Fowle, Captain T. C. W., *Travels in the Middle East* (1916).

Fraser, Lovat, *India Under Curzon and After* (1911).

Freeth, Zahra, *Kuwait was my Home* (1958).

Gaury, Lieutenant-Colonel Gerald de, *Arabian Journey and Other Desert Travels* (1950).

Gaury, Lieutenant-Colonel Gerald de, *Arabia Phoenix* (1946).

Gaury, Lieutenant-Colonel Gerald de, *Faisal: King of Saudi Arabia* (1966).

Gaury, Lieutenant-Colonel Gerald de, *Three Kings in Baghdad, 1921–1958* (1961).

Glubb, Sir John Bagot, *War in the Desert: An RAF Frontier Campaign* (1960).

Gooch, G. P. and Temperley, H. W. V., *British Documents on the Origins of the War, 1898–1914* (1938).

Graves, Philip, *The Life of Sir Percy Cox* (1941).

Hanighen, F. C., *The Secret War* (New York, 1934).

Harrison, David, *Footsteps in the Sand* (1959).

Harrison, Paul W., *The Arab at Home* (1924).

Harrison, Paul W., *Doctor in Arabia* (1943).

Hawley, Donald, *The Trucial States* (1970).

Hay, Sir Rupert, *The Persian Gulf States* (Washington DC, 1959).

Hopwood, Derek (ed.), *The Arabian Peninsula: Society and Politics* (1972).

Humaidan, Ali, *Les Princes de l'or noir, evolution politique du Golfe persique* (Paris, 1968).

Hurewitz, J. C., *Diplomacy in the Near and Middle East*, 2 vols (Princeton, NJ, 1956).

Kelly, J. B., *Britain and the Persian Gulf, 1795–1880* (Oxford, 1968).

Kelly, J. B., *Eastern Arabian Frontiers* (1964).

Kumar, Ravinder, *India and the Persian Gulf, 1858–1907, A Study of British Imperial Policy* (New York, 1965).

Landen, Robert Geran, *Oman since 1856: Disruptive Modernization in a Traditional Arab Society* (Princeton, NJ, 1967).

Lenczowski, George, *Oil and State in the Middle East* (Ithaca, NY, 1960).

Longrigg, Stephen H., *Oil in the Middle East* (1968).

Mann, Clarence C., *Abu Dhabi* (Beirut, 1969).

Marlowe, John, *The Persian Gulf in the Twentieth Century* (New York, 1962).

Masani, Sir Rustum Pestonji, *Britain in India: An Account of British Rule in the Indian Subcontinent* (1960).

Medlicott, W. N., *British Foreign Policy Since Versailles, 1919–1963*, (1968).

Miles, S. B., *The Countries and Tribes of the Persian Gulf* (repr. London, 1966).

Mineau, Wayne, *The Go-Devils* (1958).

Monroe, Elizabeth, *Britain's Moment in the Middle East, 1914–1956* (1965).

Monroe, Elizabeth, *The Changing Balance of Power in the Persian Gulf*, American Universities Field Staff (New York, 1972).

Moyse-Bartlett, H., *The Pirates of Trucial Oman* (1966).

Murphy, C. C. R., *Soldiers of the Prophet* (1921).

Nevakivi, Jukka, *Britain, France, and the Arab Middle East, 1914–1920* (1969).

O'Shea, Raymond, *The Sand Kings of Oman* (1947).

Owen, Roderic, *Away to Eden* (1960).

Owen, Roderic, *Golden Bubble* (1957).

Philby, H. St J. B., *Arabian Oil Ventures* (Washington DC, 1964).

Philby, H. St J. B., *Arabian Days* (1948).

Philby, H. St J. B., *Arabian Jubilee* (1952).

Philby, H. St J. B., *The Empty Quarter* (1933).

Phillips, Wendell, *Oman: A History* (1967).

Phillips, Wendell, *Unknown Oman* (Beirut, 1971).

Ramazani, Rouhallah K., *The Persian Gulf: Iran's Role* (Charlottesville Va, 1972).

Raswan, Carl, *The Black Tents of Arabia* (1935).

Raunkiaer, Barclay, *Through Wahhabiland on Camelback*, intro. Gerald de Gaury (1969).

Rendel, Sir George W., *The Sword and the Olive* (1957).

Rihani, Ameen, *Around the Coasts of Arabia* (1930).

Rihani, Ameen, *Ibn Sa'oud of Arabia* (1928).
Roskill, Stephen, *Hankey, Man of Secrets*, vol. 1: 1877–1918 (1970).
Sanger, Richard H., *The Arabian Peninsula* (Ithaca, NY, 1954).
Shwadran, Benjamin, *The Middle East, Oil and the Great Powers* (New York, 1959).
Stanford Research Institute, *Area Handbook for the Peripheral States of the Arabian Peninsula* (Washington DC, 1971).
Stanton-Hope, W. E., *Arabian Adventurer: The Story of Haji Williamson* (1951).
Stanton-Hope, W. E., *The Battle for Oil* (1958).
Sykes, Brigadier-General Sir Percy, *A History of Persia*, 2 vols. (1958).
Thomas, Bertram, *Alarms and Excursions in Arabia* (1931).
Troeller, Gary, *The Birth of Saudi Arabia: Britain and the Rise of the House of Sa'ud* (1976).
Tweedy, Maureen, *Bahrain and the Persian Gulf* (England, 1952).
Twitchell, K. S., *Saudi Arabia* (Princeton, NJ, 1958).
Vadala, R., *Le Golfe persique* (Paris, 1920).
Van der Meulen, D., *The Wells of Ibn Sa'ud* (1957).
Vidal, F. S., *The Oasis of al-Hasa* (New York, 1955).
Villiers, Alan, *Sons of Sindbad* (1940).
Wilson, Lieutenant-Colonel Sir Arnold T., *The Persian Gulf* (Oxford, 1928).
Wilson, Lieutenant-Colonel Sir Arnold T., *South West Persia: A Political Officer's Diary, 1907–1914* (1941).
Winder, R. Bayley, *Saudi Arabia in the Nineteenth Century* (New York, 1965).
Wingate, Ronald, *Not in the Limelight* (1959).
Woodruff, Phillip, *The Men who Ruled India: The Guardians* (1954).
Young, H., *The Independent Arab* (1933).

Articles

Ajjaj, Ali, 'Social Development of the Pirate Coast', *Middle East Forum*, Summer 1962.
Anthony, John Duke, 'The Union of Arab Emirates', *Middle East Journal*, XXVI (1972).
Belgrave, Sir Charles Dalyrymple, 'Pearl Diving in Bahrain', *Journal of the Royal Central Asian Society*, XXI (1934).
Belgrave, Sir Charles Dalyrymple, 'Persian Gulf—Past and Present', *Journal of the Royal Central Asian Society*, LV (1968).
Bentley, G. W., 'The Development of the Air Route in the Persian Gulf' *Journal of the Royal Central Asian Society*, XX (1933).
Berreby, Jean-Jacques, 'Progrès et evolution des principautés arabes du Golfe persique', *Orient*, no. 25 (1963).

Bidwell, Robin, 'A British Official Guide to the Gulf', *Geographical Journal*, CXXXVIII (1972).

Boustead, J. E. H., 'Abu Dhabi, 1761–1963', *Journal of the Royal Central Asian Society*, L (1963).

Bowen, Richard Le B., Jr, 'Marine Industries of Eastern Arabia', *Geographical Review*, XLI (1951).

Bowen, Richard Le B., Jr, 'Pearl Fisheries of the Persian Gulf', *Middle East Journal*, V (1951).

Burchall, Colonel H. D. S. O., 'The Political Aspect of Commercial Air Routes', *Journal of the Royal Central Asian Society*, XX (1933).

Caskel, Werner, 'The Bedouinization of Arabia', in *Studies in Islamic Cultural History*, ed. G. E. von Grunebaum (American Anthropological Association, Apr 1954).

Codrai, Ronald, 'Desert Sheikhdoms of Arabia's Pirate Coast', *National Geographic Magazine*, July 1956.

Cox, Sir Percy Z., 'Some Gulf Memories', *Times of India Annual*, *1928*.

Cox, Sir Percy, Z., 'Some Excursions in Oman', *Geographical Journal*, LXVI (1925).

Cunningham, A., 'The Wrong Horse—A Study of Anglo-Turkish Relations before the First World War' (*St Antony's Papers*, no. 17), *Middle Eastern Affairs*, no. 4 (1965).

Dalyell of the Binns, Lieutenant-Colonel G., 'The Persian Gulf', *Journal of the Royal Central Asian Society*, XXV (1938).

Dame, L. P., 'From Bahrein to Taif: A Missionary Journey Across Arabia', *Muslim World*, XXIII (1933).

Dostal, Walter, 'The Shiḥūḥ of Northern Oman: A Contribution to Cultural Ecology', *Geographical Journal*, CXXXVIII (1972).

Eccles, Captain G. J., 'The Sultanate of Muscat and Oman', *Journal of the Central Asian Society*, XIV (1927).

Falcon, N. L., 'The Musandam (Northern Oman) Expedition 1971–1972', *Geographical Journal*, CXXXIX (1973).

Gaury, Gerald de, 'The End of Arabian Isolation', *Foreign Affairs*, XXV (1946).

Harrison, P. W., 'Economic and Social Conditions in East Arabia', *Muslim World*, XIV (1924).

Harrison, P. W., and Storm, W. H., 'The Arabs of Oman', *Muslim World*, XXIV (1934).

Haworth, Colonel Sir Lionel, 'Persia and the Persian Gulf', *Journal of the Central Asian Society*, XVI (1929).

Hay, Sir Rupert, 'The Impact of the Oil Industry on the Persian Gulf Sheikhdoms', *Middle East Journal*, IX (1955).

Hay, Sir Rupert, 'The Persian Gulf States and their Boundary Problems', *Geographical Journal*, CXX (1954).

Hay, Sir Rupert, 'Great Britain's Relations with Yemen and Oman', *Middle Eastern Affairs*, XI (1960).

Heard-Bey, Frauke, 'The Gulf States and Oman in Transition', *Asian Affairs*, LIX (n.s., III) (1972).

Hogarth, D. G., 'Wahhabism and British Interests', *Journal of the British Institute of International Affairs*, IV (1925).

Hoskins, H. L., 'Background of the British Position in Arabia', *Middle East Journal*, I (1947).

'The Iraq–Najd Frontier', *Journal of the Central Asian Society*, XVII (1930).

Jong, Garett de, 'Slavery in Arabia', *Muslin World*, XXXIII (1934).

Kelly, J. B., 'The Persian Claim to Bahrain', *International Affairs*, XXXIII (1957).

Kelly, J. B., 'Legal and Historic Basis of the British Position in the Persian Gulf', *St Antony's Papers*, no. 4 (1958).

Kelly, J. B., 'The Persian Claim to Bahrain', *International Affairs*, xxxiii (1957).

Khadduri, Majid, 'Iran's Claim to Sovereignty of Bahrain', *American Journal of International Law* (1951).

Kumar, Ravinder, 'The Dismemberment of Oman and British Policy towards the Persian Gulf', *Islamic Culture*, XXXVI (1962).

Lees, G. M., 'The Physical Geography of Southern Arabia', *Geographical Journal*, LXXI (1928).

Liebesny, Herbert J., 'Administration and Legal Development in Arabia: the Persian Gulf Principalities', *Middle East Journal*, X (1956).

Liebesny, Herbert J., 'British Jurisdiction in the States of the Persian Gulf', *Middle East Journal*, III (1949).

Liebesny, Herbert J., 'The International Relations of Arabia: The Dependent Areas', *Middle East Journal*, I (1947).

Lindt, Dr A. R., 'Politics in the Persian Gulf', *Journal of the Royal Central Asian Society*, XXVI (1939).

Lockhart, L., 'Outline of the History of Kuwait', *Journal of the Royal Central Asian Society*, XXXIV (1947).

Mackie, J. B., 'Hasa: An Arabian Oasis', *Geographical Journal*, LXIII (1924).

Mahan, A. T., 'The Persian Gulf and International Relations', *National Review*, XL (1902).

Mallakh, Ragei El, 'The Challenge of Affluence: Abu Dhabi', *Middle East Journal*, XXIV (1970).

MicKitterick, T. E. M., 'Politics and Economics in the Middle East', *Political Quarterly*, XXVI, no. 1 (Jan 1955).

Melamid, Alexander, 'Boundaries and Petroleum Developments in Saudi Arabia', *Geographical Review*, XLVIII (1957).

Melamid, Alexander, 'Oil and the Evolution of Boundaries in Eastern Arabia', *Geographical Review*, XLIV (1954).

Melamid, Alexander, 'Political Boundaries and Nomadic Grazing', *Geographical Review*, LV (1965).

Melamid, Alexander, 'Political Geography of Trucial Oman and Qatar', *Geographical Review*, XLIII (1953).

O'Leary, Patrick, 'The Butterfly Hunter Who Found Arabia's Oil Riches', *The Times*, 16 Dec 1971.

Parry, Captain R. St P., 'The Navy in the Persian Gulf', *Journal of the Royal United Service Institution*, LXXXV (1930).

Philby, H. St J. B., 'A Survey of Wahhabi Arabia, 1929', *Journal of the Central Asian Society*, XVI (1929).

Philby, H. St J. B., 'The New Reign in Saudi Arabia', *Foreign Affairs*, XXXII (1954).

al-Rumaihi, Mohammad, 'The 1938 Reform Movement in Kuwait, Bahrain and Dubai' (in Arabic), *Journal of the Gulf and Arabian Peninsula Studies*, I, no. 4 (1975).

Rutter, Eldon, 'Slavery in Arabia', *Journal of the Royal Central Asian Society*, XX (1933).

Said, Rosemarie J., 'The Conflict over the Arab Islands in the Gulf, 1918–1971' (in Arabic), *Journal of the Gulf and Arabian Peninsula Studies*, II, no. 6 (1976).

Said, Rosemarie J., 'The 1938 Reform Movement in Dubai', *Al-Abhath*, Dec 1970.

Staley, Eugene, 'Business and Politics in the Persian Gulf: The Story of the Wönckhaus Firm', *Political Science Quarterly*, Sep 1933.

Standish, J. F., 'British Maritime Policy in the Persian Gulf', *Middle East Studies*, III, no. 4 (1967).

Thesiger, Wilfred, 'A Further Journey Across the Empty Quarter', *Geographical Journal*, CXIII (1949).

Thesiger, Wilfred, 'Across the Empty Quarter', *Geographical Journal*, CXI (1948).

Thesiger, Wilfred, 'Desert Borderlands of Oman', *Geographical Journal*, CXVI (1950).

Thesiger, Wilfred, 'Travel on the Trucial Coast', *Geographical Magazine*, XXI (1949).

Thomas, Bertram, 'Arab Rule Under the Albusaid Dynasty of Oman 1741–1937', The Raleigh Lecture on History, *Proceedings of the British Academy*, XXIV (1938).

Thomas, Bertram, 'The Kumzari Dialect of the Shihuh Tribe (Musandam), Arabia', *Journal of the Royal Asiatic Society*, XVI (1929).

Thomas, Bertram, 'The Musandam Peninsula and its People the Shihuh', *Journal of the Central Asian Society*, XVI (1929).

Toynbee, Arnold (ed.), 'The Dispute between Persia and Great

Britain over Bahrain (1927–1934)', *Survey of International Affairs*, 1934.

Toynbee, Arnold (ed.), 'The Rise of the Wahhabi Power' and 'The Delimitation of Frontiers'. *Survey of International Affairs*, 1925, I (1927).

Trevelyan, Lord Humphrey, 'Postscript to Asian Empire', *Journal of the Royal Central Asian Society*, LX (1968).

Van Pelt, Mary, 'The Shaikhdom of Kuwait', *Middle East Journal*, IV (1950).

Vesey-Fitzgerald, Desmond, 'From Hasa to Oman by Car', *Geographical Review*, XLI (1951).

Wahba, Hafiz, 'Wahhabism in Arabia', *Journal of Central Asian Society*, XVI (1929).

Wilkinson, J. C., 'The Oman Question: The Background to the Geography of South-East Arabia', *Geographical Journal*, CXXXVII (1971).

Wilson, Sir Arnold Talbot, 'A Periplus of the Persian Gulf', *Geographical Journal*, LXIX (1927).

NEWSPAPERS

Umm al-Qura, Mecca.
Al-Ahrām, Cairo.
Al-Anwār, *Al-Nahār*, Beirut.
Cuttings from the British and French presses available at the Press Archives, Royal Institute of International Affairs, London.
Al-Ittihād, Abu Dhabi.

UNPUBLISHED MATERIAL

Talley, Robert E. L., 'Dubai, Past, Present and Future', 2 vols, master's dissertation, American University of Beirut, 1967.

Index